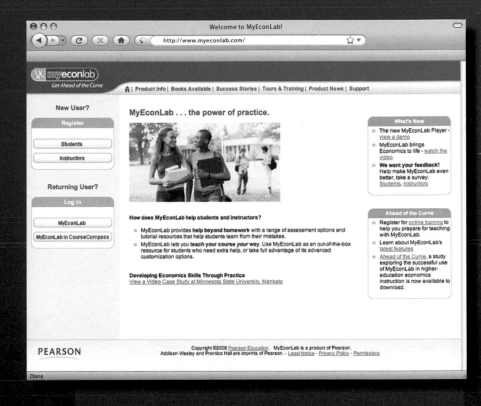

myeconlab

Get Ahead of the Curve

Save Time. Improve Results!

Use *MyEconLab* to prepare for tests and exams and to go to class ready to learn.

When you use *MyEconLab* you don't just learn more about economics—you learn how to learn.

Since 2002, more than 70 000 students have used *MyEconLab* at more than 600 institutions around the world.

We asked some of these students what they thought about *MyEconLab*. Here are some of the things they had to say:

"MyEconLab allowed me to see where I stood on all the topics so I knew what to study more."

"MyEconLab was a good asset to the course. It almost serves as an online tutor when you don't have an answer."

"I was able to study better and teach myself without costly errors. I could see where I went wrong and go back and understand the concept."

"MyEconLab helped me master economic concepts. Using it put the textbook to work before test day."

90% of students surveyed who used the Study Plan practice questions and feedback felt it helped them to prepare for tests.

87% of students who regularly used *MyEconLab* felt it improved their grades.

84% said they would recommend *MyEconLab* to a friend.

Unlimited Practice!

MyEconLab offers a wide variety of problems that let you practise the theories and models being learned.

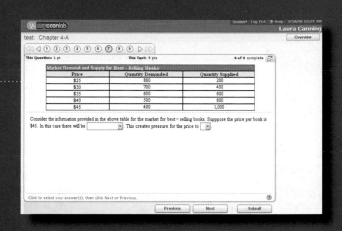

Practice Problems

Many Study Plan and instructor-assigned problems contain algorithmically generated values, ensuring you get as much practice as you need.

Learning Resources

Each problem links to the eText page discussing the very concept being applied. You also have access to guided solutions and a suite of other practice tools.

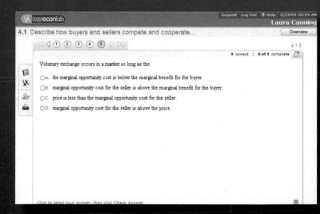

Full eText

Included in your MyEconLab is an online version of your textbook. You can navigate your eText by key concept and post notes online.

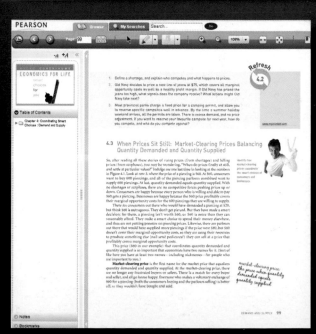

Personalized Learning!

The *MyEconLab* Study Plan is based on your specific learning needs.

Auto-Graded Tests and Assignments

MyEconLab comes with two pre-loaded Sample Tests for each chapter so you can self-assess your understanding of the material.

Personalized Study Plan

A Study Plan is generated based on your results on Sample Tests and instructor assignments. You can clearly see which topics you have mastered and, more importantly, which topics you need to work on!

"I just wanted to let you know how helpful the Study Plan in MyEconLab is. Everything's clicking... so two thumbs up!"
—Student, Ryerson University

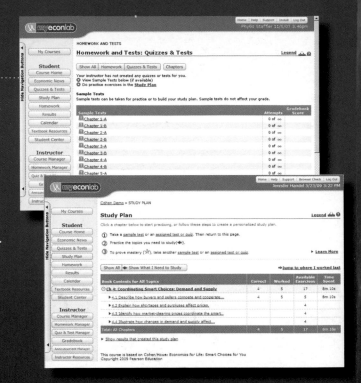

Practice Problems

Use the Study Plan exercises to get practice where you need it. To check how you're doing, click Results to get an overview of all your scores.

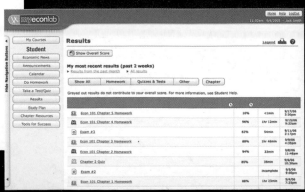

MICRO
ECONOMICS FOR LIFE

smart
choices
for
you

Avi J. Cohen
York University

Ian Howe

BENEFITS

OPPORTUNITY COSTS

EFFICIENCY

Pearson Canada
Toronto

Library and Archives Canada Cataloguing in Publication

Cohen, Avi J.
    Economics for life: smart choices for you / Avi J. Cohen, Ian Howe.

Includes index.
ISBN 978-0-321-36449-4

1. Microeconomics — Textbooks.
I. Howe, Ian, 1981– II. Title.

HB172.C63 2010   338.5   C2009-901277-4

ISBN-13: 978-0-321-36449-4
ISBN-10: 0-321-36449-X

Vice-President, Editorial Director: Gary Bennett
Acquisitions Editor: Don Thompson
Marketing Manager: Leigh-Anne Graham
Project Developer: Joseph Gladstone
Developmental Editor: Toni Chahley
Production Editor: Cheryl Jackson
Copy Editor: Kelli Howey
Proofreaders: Susan Bindernagel and Colleen Ste. Marie
Production Coordinator: Deborah Starks
Compositor: Debbie Kumpf
Photo and Permissions Researcher: Heather L. Jackson
Art Director: Julia Hall
Cover and Interior Designer: Anthony Leung
Cover Image: Jupiter Images

1 2 3 4 5   13 12 11 10 09

Printed and bound in United States of America.

To Susan — for encouraging me to find my voice.

A.J.C.

About the Authors

Given his interest in technology and teaching, Professor Cohen is holding an actual piece of the first transatlantic telegraph cable, laid in 1856 between Cape Breton and Newfoundland, and on to London, England.

Avi J. Cohen

Avi J. Cohen is Professor of Economics and Dean's Advisor on Technology Enhanced Learning at York University. He has a PhD from Stanford University; is a Life Fellow of Clare Hall, University of Cambridge; and is past Co-Chair of the Canadian Economics Association Education Committee.

Professor Cohen is the President of the History of Economics Society, and has research interests in the history of economics, economic history, and economic education. He has published in *Journal of Economic Perspectives*, *Journal of Economic Education*, *History of Political Economy*, *Journal of the History of Economic Thought*, *Journal of Economic History*, and *Explorations in Economic History*, among other journals.

Professor Cohen is co-author of the best-selling *Study Guide* that accompanies Parkin/Bade's *Economics* (seventh edition). He is the winner of numerous teaching awards, including Canada's most prestigious national award for educational leadership, the 3M Teaching Fellowship.

Ian Howe

Ian Howe is a policy analyst with the Strategic Policy and Research Branch at Human Resources and Skills Development Canada.* Ian has an M.A. in Economic Policy from McMaster University and a BCom degree from the University of Toronto.

As the head undergraduate teaching assistant for the Department of Economics and as a workshop facilitator for the Academic Skills Centre at the University of Toronto at Mississauga, Ian provided tutorials and workshops in economics for first and second year undergraduates. Ian was awarded the Mississauga Board of Trade Scholarship for Commerce and Management in 2001 based on his tutoring involvement in the community.

*The views expressed are the author's and do not necessarily represent the views of the Department.

Brief Contents

Table of Contents

Preface to *Students*

Economics for Life is not a typical economics textbook. As you work through the book, you will discover that there are almost no graphs and no math. This book is not designed to teach you how to be an economist.

Instead, my goal is to show you how to use economic ideas to make smart choices in life. I focus on core concepts that you can use regularly, to make smart choices in your life as a consumer, as a businessperson, and as an informed citizen.

You, like most people, are probably not interested in economic concepts for their own sake. It is my responsibility as the author to present important ideas, concepts, and decision-making strategies — based on an economic way of thinking — that will help you to be more successful throughout life. The stories in the book reflect real-life situations. You will, I hope, quickly see how you can make yourself better off by learning the economic lessons they contain.

The Three Keys shown are at the heart of making smart choices and are at the heart of this book. You can always spot them by the key icon in the margin.

You will first learn about the Three Keys to Smart Choices in Chapter 1, and they will reappear many times. The Three Keys are like a map, helping you choose a direction to take at decision points — forks in the road. When you face a decision, they focus your attention on the information that is most useful to making your smart choice.

If you learn to use the three keys well and start making smarter choices in life, then I will have done my job well and you will have gained strong tools in your quest for success. If you do not enjoy reading this book or do not learn to make smarter choices in life, then I will have failed.

The only way for me to know how close I've come to achieving the goal of helping you make smart choices is to hear from you. Let me know what works for you in this book — and, more importantly, what doesn't. You can write to me at **avicohen@yorku.ca**. In future editions I will acknowledge by name all students who help improve *Economics for Life*.

Now start learning how economics will help you make smarter choices in life!

Professor Avi J. Cohen
Department of Economics
York University

Three Keys to Smart Choices

Choose only when additional benefits are greater than additional opportunity costs.

Count only additional benefits and additional opportunity costs.

Be sure to count all additional benefits and costs, including implicit costs and externalities.

P.S. Your first smart choice will be to read the tour of the features in the book to find out how you can get the most out of your textbook.

Features of This Book

Welcome to *Economics for Life: Smart Choices for You.* This tour of your textbook is designed to help you use this book effectively and complete your course successfully.

Chapter Opener

Every chapter begins with a two-page spread. These two pages set the theme for the chapter. Like a trailer for a movie, this opening spread gives you a preview of what is coming and prepares you for the "feature presentation."

Every chapter has a title and a subtitle. The main title summarizes the content of the chapter in plain language. The subtitle for the chapter is in the language economists use when referring to the concepts.

Every chapter is divided into main sections, and each of these sections is accompanied by a learning objective. The learning objective describes what you will have learned after reading each section. Once you have read the chapter, you can review these learning objectives to test your understanding of the chapter material.

Every chapter begins with an overview that introduces you to the main ideas and themes in the chapter. This introduction connects the economic principles discussed in the chapter to the choices and decisions you make in your everyday life.

Learning Objectives

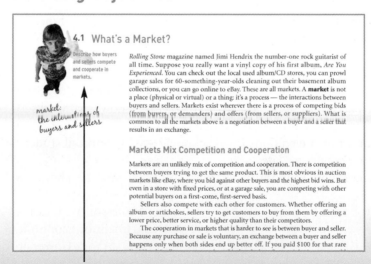

Learning objectives are repeated at the beginning of each main section of the book and provide an important reminder of what you will learn in each section.

Special Features

What if you choose to spend the evening studying, and your friend gets angry and shouts "Is your stupid economics course more important than I am?!" At the margin, the answer is yes. Your choice to study tonight doesn't necessarily mean that, overall, you value the course more than the friend (well, depending on the friend, you might). What your choice means is that tonight, at the margin, you value the next few hours spent studying more than you value spending the next few hours with your friend.

But margins, and circumstances, change. Your choice would be different if you had another week before the test, or if you hadn't seen your friend for months. The value you place on an activity or thing depends on the margin, and *that* additional value is marginal benefit.

Your friend's angry accusation comes from the common mistake (not smart) of looking at choices as all or nothing—friend versus economics. That's not the (smart) choice you made at the margin—the marginal benefit of the time spent studying tonight was greater than the value, or marginal benefit, of the same time spent with your friend.

Making smart choices means living life on the edge.

FOR YOUR INFORMATION

Did your family mark your height on a wall or door jamb every time you had a birthday? Mine did. The highest mark represents your total height, or total growth at that date. But the *difference* between the second highest mark and the highest represents your *marginal*, or *additional*, growth during the past year.

For Your Information

These FYI boxes introduce interesting facts and figures related to the economic principle being explored.

Refresh 4.1

1. What is a market?
2. You are negotiating with a car dealer over the price of a new car. Explain where competition enters the process, and where cooperation enters.
3. The Recording Industry Association of America's (RIAA) mission is "to foster a business and legal climate that supports and promotes our members' . . . intellectual property rights worldwide." Have you ever downloaded music? If so, what arguments do you use to counter RIAA's defence of property rights?

www.myeconlab.com

Refresh

The Refresh feature provides three questions that require you to review and apply the concepts in the preceding section. These questions give you the opportunity to assess your understanding of the principles developed in the section. Answers to these questions are located on the MyEconLab (**www.myeconlab.com**) that accompanies this book.

The Law of Demand

The market for any product or service consists of millions of potential customers, each trying to make a smart choice about what to buy. **Market demand** is the sum of the demands of all individuals willing and able to buy a particular product/service.

Whether it is the market for iPods, water, or anything else, substitutes exist, so that consumers buy a smaller quantity at higher prices, and a larger quantity at lower prices. This inverse relationship (when one goes up, the other goes down) between price and quantity demanded is so universal that economists call it (somewhat grandiosely) the **law of demand**: If the price of a product/service rises, the quantity demanded of the product/service decreases. The law of demand works as long as other factors besides price do not change. The next section will explore what happens when other factors do change. Will the law of demand then fail? Stay tuned.

market demand: sum of demands of all individuals willing and able to buy a particular product/service

law of demand: if the price of a product/service rises, quantity demanded decreases

Key Terms

Key terms are bolded in the text where they first appear, and definitions for key terms are provided in the margin. A complete list of all key terms and definitions are in the glossary at the end of the book.

When Marginal Revenue Equals Price In the market structure of extreme competition, like the wheat market, every business is a price taker. You can't raise your price because thousands of other businesses are selling identical products at the market price. And there is no incentive to lower your price, because you are so small relative to the market you can sell as much as you can produce at the market price. Your decision about what quantity to produce has no effect on the market because as a bit player — one of thousands of suppliers — your increase in supply does not affect market supply or market price.

Because you can sell each additional unit at the market price, your marginal revenue from each additional unit sold is the same as the price. For businesses in extreme competition, *marginal revenue equals price for price takers.* This sounds obvious, but it turns out not to be true for price makers.

When Marginal Revenue Is Less Than Price What about businesses with some price power? Price makers — whether monopolies, oligopolies, or small monopolistic competitors like Paola's Piercing and Fingernail Parlour — can raise prices without losing all their sales to competitors. Barriers to entry, brand loyalty, or advertising all can create pricing power. But

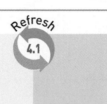

iResentment
Less than three months after introducing the iPhone in 2007 at US$599, Apple cut the price by one-third, to $299. This was an attempt to increase sales to those not willing to pay the original price.

This caused so much resentment among original customers that Apple was forced to back-pedal. Steve Jobs quickly apologized and offered original customers a US$100 credit.

• This is the kind of resentment that enforces the one-price rule among products that can be easily resold (which iPhones can).

Economics Out There

These feature boxes provide real-world examples of the economic principle being discussed. The stories told in Economics Out There help you make connections between the concepts in the chapter and everyday life.

Notes

In the margin, you will see "hand-written" notes. These notes provide a quick explanation of the idea, concept, or principle being discussed in the narrative.

Increased number of consumers causes an increase in demand. Decreased number of consumers causes a decrease in demand.

It is no surprise that with the additional households (last column), at any price (first column) the quantity demanded is greater than it was originally (middle column). The increased number of consumers causes an increase in demand, just as an increase in preferences or an increase in income (for normal goods) causes an increase in demand. A decrease in the number of consumers causes a decrease in demand, just as a decrease in the price of a substitute product/service or a decrease in expected future prices causes a decrease in demand.

Any increase (or decrease) in demand can be described in alternative ways. For the four previous factors, the description for an increase in demand is:

- At any given quantity demanded, consumers are willing and able to pay a higher price.

For the number of consumers, the description for an increase in demand is:

- At any given price, consumers plan to buy a larger quantity.

Three Keys Icon

In keeping with the theme of making smart choices, you will also find an icon in the margin beside text that discusses the Three Keys to Smart Choices. The key (or keys) being discussed is indicated by the number on the tag on the key icon.

two midterms the following week, and your out-of-town boy/girlfriend is coming in next weekend for the only visit you will have in two months. How many hours then are you willing to work?

Of course you will make a smart choice, weighing the additional benefits and costs of working extra hours. The additional, or marginal, benefits are the $10 per hour you earn (plus something for the boss's goodwill). The additional costs are opportunity costs — the alternative uses of the time you have to give up.

You want to attend all your classes, keep time for studying for midterms, and definitely keep the weekend free. You are willing to give up the 10 hours a week you spend playing *World of Warcraft*. When your boss hears you are willing to work only a total of 20 hours, while she is hoping for 60 hours, she instantly replies, "What if I pay you double time for all your hours next week?"

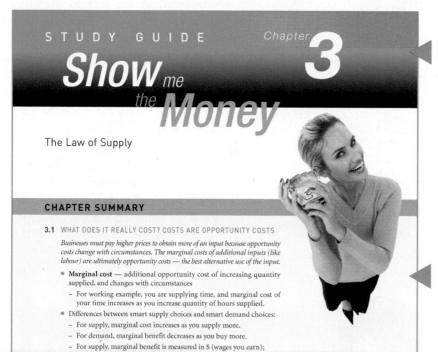

Study Guide

At the end of each chapter you will find a study guide designed to assist you in reviewing and testing your understanding of the material in the chapter. The study guide for each chapter includes:

- Chapter Summary
- True/False Questions
- Multiple Choice Questions
- Short Answer Questions

Chapter Summary

Organized by section, the summary recaps the main ideas in each chapter. The first item (in *italics*) under each section head is the most important point in that section. All key terms are in bold.

True/False Questions

There are 15 true/false questions, organized by learning objective. The heading next to each learning objective number gives you the topic of the questions that follow. Each question is answered at the end of the book, and questions with "false" answers have explanations why.

TRUE/FALSE

Circle the correct answer.

3.1 COSTS ARE OPPORTUNITY COSTS

1. When higher-paying jobs are harder to find for workers, a business will have to pay more to hire labour.   **True**   **False**

2. Any smart business supply decision involves a choice between a business's marginal benefit (or reward) from supplying (or selling) its product/service and the business's marginal opportunity cost of producing the product/service.   **True**   **False**

3. Any smart worker supply decision involves a choice between a worker's marginal benefit (or reward) from supplying (or selling) her work and the worker's marginal opportunity cost of working.   **True**   **False**

Multiple Choice Questions

There are 15 multiple choice questions organized by learning objective. The heading next to each learning objective number gives you the topic of the questions that follow. Each question is answered at the end of the book.

MULTIPLE CHOICE

Circle the correct answer.

3.1 COSTS ARE OPPORTUNITY COSTS

1. Your opportunity cost of watching *American Idol* increases if
   A) it is your favourite TV show.
   B) you have a very expensive television.
   C) you have an exam the next day.
   D) all of the above.

2. The opportunity cost of going to school is highest for someone who
   A) has to give up a job paying $10 an hour.
   B) has to give up a job paying $15 an hour.
   C) loves school.
   D) has to give up a volunteer opportunity.

3. Which statement is *false*?
   A) Marginal costs are opportunity costs.
   B) Opportunity costs are marginal costs.
   C) Sunk costs are marginal costs.
   D) Marginal opportunity costs increase as quantity increases.

Short Answer Questions

There are 10 short answer questions that test your overall understanding of the chapter. These questions help you connect the main ideas in the different sections of the chapter. Answers to these questions are at the end of the book.

SHORT ANSWER

Write a short answer to each question. Your answer may be in point form.

1. Your boss asks you to work 20 additional hours next weekend. If you work those 20 hours, you will not be able to see your significant other. You really value the time you spend with your significant other, and the only time you've gone a weekend without seeing each other was when your friends offered to pay you $300 to spend the weekend with them instead. You agreed because this is the minimum amount you must be compensated for giving up a weekend with your significant other.

   A) Should you agree to work the 20 weekend hours if your boss pays your regular hourly wage rate of $10?
   B) Should you agree to work the 20 weekend hours if your boss pays the overtime rate of $15 per hour for the whole weekend?

Using Your Textbook to Achieve Success in Your Course

This textbook is set up for your success. Each element is designed to help you organize, understand, and learn the material efficiently and easily. Here is a quick guide to being successful in this course.

1: Fully understand the learning objectives

The learning objectives in each chapter are presented in the chapter opener and repeated in the margin at the beginning of each section of the chapter. If you can do what each learning objective asks, you will understand what is most important in each section. These learning objectives are the core of the course. Master these and you have mastered the course. The most important point in each section — a one- to two-sentence summary of what each learning objective asks — appears in italics after each section head in the Study Guide's Chapter Summary.

2: Check your understanding of the learning objectives

At the end of each complete section, there are three questions titled Refresh. When you complete a section, take the 5 to 10 minutes required to answer the Refresh questions. These questions are designed for you to assess how well you have mastered the learning objective. They will help you make sure you understand what is important.

3: Complete the Study Guide material

After finishing the chapter, complete the Study Guide pages — it will save you study time and reinforce what you have mastered. The Study Guide is divided into two main sections, a chapter summary and a set of exam-like questions.

Chapter Summary The Chapter Summary contains the key points you need to know. It is organized using the same major sections as the chapter. The first item in *italics* under each section head is the most important point in that section. The chapter summary is an excellent study aid for the night before a test. It's a final check of the ideas — the learning objectives — you have studied.

Exam-like Questions Do the True/False, Multiple-Choice, and Short Answer questions *without looking at the answers*. This is the single most important tip for profitably using the Study Guide. Struggling for the answers to questions you find challenging is one of the most effective ways to learn. The athletic saying of "No pain, no gain" applies equally to studying. You will learn the most from right answers you have had to struggle for and from your wrong answers and mistakes. Look at the answers only *after* you have attempted all the questions. When you finally do check the answers, be sure to understand where you went wrong and why your right answers are right.

4: Know it before you go on

Master each chapter by taking the above three actions before moving on. Feel confident that you understand the chapter's objectives. By following this plan you will be making a smart choice for learning, and you will do well in the course.

When people ask me what I do, I say, "I teach Economics at York University." While I am a Full Professor, a productive academic with an active research program (currently President of the History of Economics Society) and honourable service commitments to my school, my professional identity is largely tied to my teaching.

As a young assistant professor, the immortality of publishing articles in journals that would forever be in libraries was an important goal. But over time, I came to realize how few people would read those articles, let alone be affected by them. Most of my, and I suspect your, "academic footprint" on this earth will be through our students. Over a career, we teach tens of thousands students.

As economists and teachers, what do we want our lasting "economic footprint" to be? There is a wonderful old *Saturday Night Live* skit by Father Guido Sarducci called "The Five Minute University" (**www.youtube.com/watch?v=kO8x8eoU3L4**). Watch it. His premise is to teach in five minutes what an average college or university graduate remembers five years after graduating. For economics, he states it's the two words "supply and demand." That's it.

The serious question behind the skit, the one that motivates this book, is "What do we really want our students to remember of what we teach them in an introductory economics class?" I posed this question to college and university instructors at the British Columbia Economics Articulation meeting in May 2008.

Specifically, I asked instructors the following questions. Five years after your students have gone, what microeconomic concepts would you

- want students to remember as *essential*?
  (What would you be upset at hearing they didn't remember?)

- want students to remember as *nice to have*?

- allow students to *let go*?
  (It wouldn't bother you if they didn't remember these.)

After half an hour of spirited discussion, the *essential* concepts on their list were **opportunity cost**, **marginal analysis**, and **external and implicit costs**. That list matches the "Three Keys to Smart Choices," which form the core of *Economics for Life*.

Key 1: Choose only when additional benefits are greater than additional *opportunity costs*.

Key 2: Count only *additional* benefits and *additional* opportunity costs.

Key 3: Be sure to count *all* additional benefits and costs, including *implicit costs* and *externalities*.

These three keys were considered *essential* for students to remember five years after graduating. They contain the microeconomic core of what it means to think like an economist. The *nice to have* list that the B.C. economists generated closely matches the chapters of this book. The *let go* list included more intricate economic concepts and tools. These have been excluded from this new textbook.

Concepts not covered in this textbook include the following:

- Tools for understanding utility maximization, including the equalization of MU/P, indifference curve analysis
- Detailed elasticity concepts like cross-elasticity and extreme (zero, infinity) values
- Detailed derivation of firms' cost curves from production functions and a wide range of short-run and long-run cost curves (average variable cost, average fixed cost, long-run average cost) beyond MC and ATC. There are no discussions of nuances of shutdown points, intersections of cost curves, or scalloped $LRAC$ curves.
- Detailed models of perfect competition, monopolistic competition, oligopoly, perfect price discrimination, pure monopoly, or monopsony. (Instead, market structure distinctions are collapsed into a continuum based on elasticity of demand and a firm's pricing power.)
- Graphical demonstrations of efficiency based on areas of consumer and producer surpluses and deadweight loss

I consider these exclusions to be a major strength of this textbook. The excluded topics detract from the student's accepting the value of the basic economic analysis that will enhance her decision-making throughout her life. As one strays beyond the core concepts and stories set out in this book, diminishing returns set in rapidly.

It is far more valuable, I believe, for most students to understand and apply the core economic concepts well (the "Three Keys to Smart Choices") than to be exposed to a wide range of concepts they will not master and therefore will likely soon forget.

The Three Keys are so important that they appear in the Preface to Students, in Chapter 1, and in the concluding Summing Up to Students. The Three Keys also have their own icons, which appear in the margin every time they are applied in the narrative.

Economics for Life is designed to get students interested in economics as a way of thinking that will help them make smarter choices in their lives. This is reflected in the narrative style of the book. The economic concepts are not presented as theories that must be learned but as concepts to enhance the students' decision-making skills. The concepts emerge logically from the narrative as an economic way of choosing the smart direction to take when faced with a choice. For example, in Chapter 3, *Show Me the Money: The Law of Supply,* we begin with a student working part-time, who gets a call from his panicked boss requesting more hours of work. When the student doesn't offer up many additional hours, the boss offers double time. When that elicits more hours, but still not enough, the boss offers triple time. In having the student think through that choice about how many hours to work, we develop the law of supply.

The scenarios form the basis of each chapter and show the students how to use economic concepts to make smart choices. The concepts are not presented as theoretical ideas that must be learned in isolation, or as formulas for a set of problems.

Economics for Life uses no abstract graphs (bar graphs and tables of data are used for visual clarity) and almost no math. Many of my colleagues exclaim, "How can you teach economics without graphs? No math! Where is the rigour of the discipline?"

Economics for Life has the same rigour as *The Economist*, *The Wall Street Journal*, *The New York Times*, and *The Globe and Mail*. None of these publications use abstract graphs or equations, yet they present sophisticated economic analysis. The rigour comes from learning to think about and analyze situations like an economist.

If Stephen Hawking can explain theoretical physics in his book *A Brief History of Time* with only one equation, I believe a similar explanation can be made for economics.

What I find exciting about this book is the possibility of helping far more students "get" the benefit of thinking like an economist. Since working on *Economics for Life*, I have been using the stories in my introductory university course for economics majors. Instead of lecturing on elasticity of demand, for example, I ask why on earth a profit-seeking business would ever cut its prices. There has been a marked improvement in student interest and engagement. Instead of struggling to get them to pay attention to topics most view as irrelevant, I present narratives like those in this book, that come from their everyday experiences to make the concepts both meaningful and useful.

If this book succeeds in doing what it has set out to do — and you and your students will be the judges of that — then your students will be more actively engaged with the material. Students will learn economics in a way that will stay with them — even five years after leaving your classroom.

This brings us back to the question of your "economic footprint." You will cover fewer topics using *Economics for Life* (the 11 chapters can easily be covered in a semester, with room for discussion), but your students will retain more. After five years, they will actually be *ahead* of students who were exposed to the full range of topics. Your economic footprint will be larger. You will have produced more students who have better learned the fundamentals of thinking like an economist, and who are making smarter choices in their lives as consumers, as businesspeople, and as citizens evaluating policies proposed by politicians.

You will have succeeded in helping your students learn how to use economics in life.

Avi Cohen
http://dept.econ.yorku.ca/~avicohen
Toronto
January 2009

Organization of This Book

The table of contents for this book might look unusual and unfamiliar to you. How it developed reveals why this book is different from other textbooks, and how that difference is an advantage to you and your students.

Many authors, including me, have tried for years to write a textbook that would meet the needs of students in introductory, non-transfer economics courses. These students come from different majors and most take the course only to fulfill their diploma requirements — not because they are particularly interested in economics. They all bring special skill sets and special skill-based needs to your classroom.

The challenge was to get these students to recognize that economic literacy enables them to gain personal benefits and become more intelligent consumers and better-informed citizens. There are gains beyond the classroom for learning economics.

At first, we tried stripping down the table of contents for a standard university or college economics text and simplifying the contents of each chapter. We kept hitting brick walls. One day, I had an epiphany — it was the table of contents that was the problem! The standard economics textbook has a table of contents and chapter content that makes sense to economists — elasticity, perfect competition, monopolistic competition, externalities — but to non-economists, the material is meaningless jargon. I realized that the chapter titles and content must make sense to, and have relevance for, your students — most of whom will not be economists. As the book evolved, it also became clear that this book would be useful and important to a wide range of students, beyond just those in non-transfer courses.

In *Economics for Life*, chapter titles are designed for student understanding. The subtitles reflect the economic content and will be familiar to you, the instructor. The section heads within chapters use the same dual convention — titles for students, subtitles for economic content. This juxtaposition of titles adds more meaning to the economic concepts, provides an initial purpose for the student reading, and more closely ties the content to life outside the classroom.

The following is an overview of what each chapter covers. The **Instructor's Manual** contains a more detailed discussion of what's in each chapter, what's not, and why.

Chapter 1
What's in Economics for You?
Scarcity, Opportunity Cost, and Trade
Presents the key concepts for making smart choices — scarcity and opportunity cost. We explain the most basic choice — producing for yourself or specializing, trading in markets and depending on others. There is a simple example — using tables of numbers that are implicit production possibility frontiers — illustrating the gains from trade and comparative advantage. The last two sections use the implicit metaphor of economic theory as a road map, and end with the map of the Three Keys that are the core principles that guide smart choices.

Chapter 2
Making Smart Choices:
The Law of Demand

Develops demand as a response to two questions: "How badly do you want it?" and "How much are you willing and able to give up for it?" Demands are smart choices when expected benefits are greater than costs, and we explain the importance of *marginal* benefit (Key 2). We develop quantity demanded and the law of demand from an example of choice among substitutes, focusing on what happens to buying decisions when prices change. We then provide examples of the five factors that change demand, and discuss substitutes, complements, and normal/inferior goods. The final section on elasticity of demand focuses on the intuition of elasticity as responsiveness, and the relation between elasticity and total revenue. Elasticity is presented as a crucial concept for making smart business pricing decisions.

Chapter 3
Show Me the Money:
The Law of Supply

Motivates the supply decision as a choice among alternative opportunities, comparing expected benefits and costs at the margin. We show that all costs are ultimately opportunity costs. Quantity supplied is developed using examples of willingness to work, and a business example of choosing among alternative products to supply. The example of Paola's Piercing and Fingernail (PPF) Parlour is an implicit production possibilities frontier (without ever using that term) that yields increasing marginal costs (and the law of supply). We emphasize the simple calculation of opportunity cost as *give up/get*. The five factors changing supply are illustrated with examples. The final section illustrates price elasticity of supply, emphasizing how to avoid (not-smart) business decisions to promise more than you can deliver over time.

Chapter 4
Coordinating Smart Choices:
Demand and Supply

Describes markets as a process — the interaction between buyers and sellers. Markets combine competition and cooperation (voluntary exchanges) and require property rights as the rules of the game. We explain the miracle of markets in providing the goods and services we most value. We begin with excess demand (shortages, frustrated buyers) and excess supply (surpluses, frustrated sellers) and focus on the quantity and price adjustments that will be made to smart decisions, driving prices to market-clearing. We explain equilibrium as a balance of forces of competition and cooperation. The final section examines how markets respond to changes in demand or supply. Price signals in markets create incentives so that self-interest, coordinated through Adam Smith's invisible hand of competition, results in the "miracle of markets" — an intuitive shorthand for efficiency.

Chapter 5
What Gives When Prices Don't?
Government Choices, Markets, Efficiency, and Equity

Examines the unintended consequences of government price-fixing policies — quantities adjust instead. We examine problems caused by rent controls, and discuss more effective policies to help the homeless. We discuss minimum wage laws, and explain unemployment as quantity adjustment. We discuss debates about the effectiveness of minimum wage laws and show how the impact on employment depends on the elasticity of demand for labour. The message is that to have an informed political viewpoint about living wage laws you need to understand elasticity of demand. The final sections examine efficiency/equity trade-offs, to show that policies that hamper price adjustments and cause inefficiencies may still be justified on equity grounds. We compare health care in the U.S. and Canada, and discuss the difference between an efficient market outcome (when many cannot afford health care) and an equitable outcome (where there are waiting lists due to lack of price adjustments). We introduce the positive/normative distinction for understanding which policy choices can be decided by empirical evidence, and which require values. The emphasis is on helping students make informed policy choices as citizens.

Chapter 6
Finding the Bottom Line:
Opportunity Costs, Economic Profits and Losses, and the Miracle of Markets

Focuses on economic profits as a measure of business success and as the signal directing markets. The distinction between accounting profits and economic profits is illustrated with a small business example. We then show what the accountants miss — the opportunity costs of your time and money — and develop the economist's conceptions of normal profits and economic profits. This is the importance of Key 3 — count *implicit* costs. The final section illustrates how economic profits direct the invisible hand, using examples of economic loss, breakeven, and economic profits as signals for smart business decisions to exit, continue in, or enter an industry.

Chapter 7
The Power to Price:
Monopoly and Competition

Focuses on how market prices are set somewhere between the maximum consumers are willing to pay and the minimum businesses are willing to accept. Where prices settle depends on competitive conditions and a business's market power (which in turn depend on the availability of substitutes and the elasticity of demand). Market power is presented as a continuum, ranging between the extremes of pure monopoly (price maker) to our intuitive term for perfect competition, extreme competition (price taker). We describe the characteristics of market structure — substitutes, product differentiation, number of businesses, barriers to entry. In describing economies of scale, we define fixed costs, variable costs and total costs, and average total costs. We describe market power as inversely related to elasticity of demand. We characterize competition as an active attempt to increase profits and gain the market power of monopoly, whether through cutting costs, increasing quality, product differentiation, advertising, buying out competitors, or erecting barriers to entry. We end with Schumpeter's concept of creative destruction to explain the inherent change and growth of the market economy, and to explain controversial trends like offshoring, the destruction of manufacturing jobs in Canada, and technological obsolescence of products, which nonetheless improve overall living standards over time.

Chapter 8
Pricing for Profits:
Marginal Revenue and Marginal Cost

Develops, for any market structure, the common "recipe" for setting the profit-maximizing price and quantity: estimate marginal revenues and marginal costs, and then set prices that allow you to sell all quantities for which marginal revenue is greater then marginal cost. Based on the "one-price rule" (when buyers can resell), we explain when marginal revenue equals price (the price taker of extreme competition) and when marginal revenue is less than price (businesses with some pricing power). For marginal cost, we develop examples where marginal cost increases with increasing output and where marginal cost is constant (for most businesses not operating at capacity). We combine this information for the business's quantity decision (choose quantity where marginal cost equals marginal revenue) and the decision to set the highest possible price allowing sale of the target quantity. We tie the recipe back to the Three Keys, and emphasize the importance of Key 2 (*marginal* decisions). Finally, we look at industries where the one-price rule does not apply, and explain how businesses can increase profits through price discrimination.

Chapter 9
Monopoly Rules:
Government Regulation, Competition, and the Law

Focuses on market failures caused by economies of scale or collusion, and government attempts to correct the failures. The policy challenge is gaining efficiencies of economies of scale, but avoiding inefficiencies of restricted output and increased price. We examine public ownership and regulated private monopoly, focusing on simple rate of return policy. To motivate competition law, we describe cycles of gasoline price wars, and explain them as strategic, competitive decisions. We use a simple prisoners' dilemma game to explain the tension between the Nash equilibrium outcome and the fact that players would be better off if they could trust each other. With the complication of trust, there are now *two smart choices* — high prices are a smart choice based on trust, while price wars are a smart choice based on non-trust. We discuss cartels (OPEC), and competition law as government attempts to counter collusion. We contrast public-interest and capture views of government, and focus not on the normative question of "should governments intervene?" but on the positive question, "When will government action improve market failures, and when will it produce a worse outcome?" A citizen must evaluate evidence to decide which is worse — market failure or government failure — and make normative, political decisions about regulation policies that may trade off public safety versus efficiency and lower prices.

Chapter 10
Acid Rain on Others' Parades:
Externalities, Carbon Taxes, Free Riders, and Public Goods

Focuses on how to make smart personal and social choices about pollution. We revisit Chapter 4's invisible hand conclusion, and ask why markets also produce "bads" like pollution and traffic jams. In explaining externalities (Key 3 — count *external costs*) we show that smart personal choices are not the same as smart social choices, for both negative and positive externalities. We explain the policy rule: choose the quantity of output where marginal social cost equals marginal social benefit. We discuss policy options for remedying this market failure (carbon

taxes and cap-and-trade systems), and emphasize the phrase behind all policies (internalize the externality). For positive externalities, we explain free riders and why markets won't produce lighthouses. Using a numerical education example we again show differences between smart private and social choices, pointing out the role for government in providing public goods, and examine subsidies and public provision.

Chapter 11
What Are You Worth?
Demand and Supply in Input Markets, and Income and Wealth Distributions
Explains income as a function of prices and quantities in input markets. Even efficient market outcomes may yield serious inequality and poverty. We present this market "failure" as an efficiency/equity trade-off. Input prices are wages for labour, interest for capital, rent for land, profits for entrepreneurship. We explain wages from derived labour demand, and use the Three Keys, especially Key 2's *marginal* focus, to explain smart business hiring decisions. The rule is: Hire additional labour as long as marginal revenue product is greater than the wage. Returns to capital focuses on *present value* as essential for smart investment choices, when benefits are spread out over the future and cost is in the present. The rule is: Choose if present value of stream of future returns is greater than the price of the investment. Economic rent is a return to any input in relatively inelastic supply, which we illustrate with superstar salaries. The final section presents income and wealth data, and we discuss education/training and progressive taxes/transfers policies to help those who are poor. We discuss the Robin Hood principle — take from the rich and give to the poor — and that the opportunity costs of tax-changed income distributions are incentive effects. For the normative question of *should* we help those who are poor, we outline "yes" and "no" answers that students will hear from politicians and must decide for themselves, depending on whether they are being taken from/given to, on equity conceptions (equal opportunity or equal outcomes), and on values about efficiency/equity trade-offs.

Adapting This Book to Your Course

This detailed overview of the chapters in this book shows how they can be mapped onto your current course. Chapters 1 to 4 cover opportunity costs, gains from trade, demand, supply, elasticity, and market successes in allocating resources. Chapter 5 is similar to other textbooks' "markets in action" chapters and includes topics of efficiency, equity, and the positive/normative distinction. Chapters 6 to 8 cover market structures and firms' decisions about costs, pricing, and profits. And Chapters 9 to 11 examine market failures — monopoly and regulation, externalities, poverty, and inequality — as well as marginal productivity and factor incomes.

    The unique nature of this textbook helps you make the course material more relevant to your students and thus provides a solid basis for a more positive classroom experience. In addition, the style of the textbook, its features, and its learning aids are designed to meet the skill levels, interests, and needs of a wide range of students who are not training to be economists but who — as consumers, as businesspeople, and as citizens — will benefit from learning to think like an economist. All these features enable students to learn economics in a way that will stay with them — even five years after leaving your classroom.

Supplements

This textbook is supported by many materials designed to enhance learning and understanding for students and to make the course exciting and rewarding for instructors. The following support materials are available for instructors.

Instructor's Resource CD-ROM

The Instructor's Resource CD-ROM contains the Instructor's Manual, PowerPoint® Presentations, and Pearson TestGen.

Instructor's Manual: Includes teaching notes and suggestions for classroom discussion.

PowerPoint Presentations: PowerPoint® presentations are available for each chapter of the book. The presentations integrate key concepts and visuals from the text and have been designed to reflect and embody the unique philosophy behind and structure of the textbook.

Pearson TestGen: This computerized test item file enables instructors to view and edit existing test questions, add questions, generate tests, and print tests in a variety of formats. Powerful search and sort functions make it easy to locate questions and arrange them in any order desired. TestGen also enables instructors to administer tests on a local area network, have the tests graded electronically, and have the results prepared in electronic or printed reports. These questions are also available in MyTest, which is available through MyEconLab at www.myeconlab.com.

MyEconLab

Pearson Canada's online resource, MyEconLab, offers instructors and students all of their resources in one place, written and designed to accompany this text. MyEconLab creates a perfect pedagogical loop that provides not only text-specific assessment and practice problems, but also tutorial support to make sure students learn from their mistakes.

MyEconLab is available to instructors by going to www.myeconlab.com and following the instructions. Students access MyEconLab with an access code that is available with the purchase of a new text.

At the core of MyEconLab are the following features:

Auto-Graded Tests and Assignments: MyEconLab comes with two preloaded Sample Tests for each chapter. Students can use these tests for self-assessment and obtain immediate feedback. Instructors can assign the Sample Tests or use them along with Test Bank questions or their own exercises to create tests or quizzes.

Study Plan: A Study Plan is generated from each student's results on Sample Tests and instructor assignments. Students can clearly see which topics they have mastered—and, more importantly, which they need to work on. The Study Plan consists of material from the in-text Review Quizzes and end-of-chapter Problems and Applications. The Study Plan links to additional practice problems and tutorial help on those topics.

Unlimited Practice: Many Study Plan and instructor-assigned exercises contain algorithmically generated values to ensure that students get as much practice as they need. Every problem links students to learning resources that further reinforce concepts they need to master.

Learning Resources: Each practice problem contains a link to the eText page that discusses the concept being applied. Students also have access to guided solutions, animated graphs with audio narrative, flashcards, and live tutoring.

Economics in the News: Each Economics in the News article is accompanied by additional links, discussion questions, and a reference to relevant textbook chapters.

Technology Specialists

Pearson's Technology Specialists work with faculty and campus course designers to ensure that Pearson technology products, assessment tools, and online course materials are tailored to meet your specific needs. This highly qualified team is dedicated to helping schools take full advantage of a wide range of educational resources, by assisting in the integration of a variety of instructional materials and media formats. Your local Pearson Education sales representative can provide you with more details on this service program.

CourseSmart

CourseSmart is a new way for instructors and students to access textbooks online anytime from anywhere. With thousands of titles across hundreds of courses, CourseSmart helps instructors choose the best textbook for their class and give their students a new option for buying the assigned textbook as a lower cost eTextbook. For more information, visit www.coursesmart.com.

Acknowledgments

Joseph Gladstone, Project Developer, had the original vision for this book. While we have developed that vision collaboratively, Joseph has been the guiding force and, in all but title, a co-author. Without his counsel, wisdom, and vast experience in teaching and publishing, this book would not have come to life.

Much of what is good (I think; you judge) in this book comes from my long association with Robin Bade and Michael Parkin. During almost 20 years as an author to the *Study Guide* accompanying their *Economics: Canada In the Global Environment,* I have learned so much from their skills as teachers, writers, and economists. Their commitment to clarity, conciseness, and helping students learn has made them both an inspiration and role models. Although this textbook is intended for a different audience, I can only hope that it will be judged to be in their league.

I also want to acknowledge two books that helped shape this one. The Three Keys to Smart Choices are derived from a similar set of three steps in Bruce Madariaga's *Economics For Life: 101 Lessons You Can Use Every Day!* (Boston: Houghton Mifflin, 2006). This excellent book, written as a companion to more comprehensive textbooks, provides many wonderful, discrete examples of how economic thinking improves everyday decisions. While my textbook is intended to be very different from most other introductory texts, the book that it most resembles in chapter structure is Paul Heyne's *The Economic Way of Thinking, 10th Edition* (Saddle River, NJ: Prentice-Hall, 2003). Although I did not know him, Paul Heyne was obviously a gifted and inspirational teacher. I found his choices in organizing content and many of his examples very helpful in deciding what to focus on and what to omit. If you have taught from his book, you will see his influence.

Many others have contributed to the development of this book. My co-author, Ian Howe, not only has written an excellent Study Guide for the end of each chapter, but also has contributed to the content and improved the presentation of the text. Thanks also to George Archer, Ilia Avroutine, Gord Fairfield, George Fallis, Eric Kam, Harvey King, Peter MacDonald, and John Sloane. Thanks to all who participated in the 2008 B.C. Economics Articulation meetings at Malaspina University College, and especially to Raimo Marttala for the invitation to attend.

The Pearson team — Don Thompson, Cheryl Jackson, Toni Chahley, Leigh-Anne Graham, Kelli Howey — have taught me how much skill and professionalism go into transforming a manuscript into a book. Thank you.

Gary Bennett and Alan Reynolds at Pearson deserve special thanks. Without their faith (often tested) and support, this book would not be before you.

Avi J. Cohen
Toronto
January 2009

The authors and the publisher thank the reviewers and consultants for their time, ideas, and suggestions that have helped make this textbook better. Their input has been extremely positive and their expertise invaluable in making this new economics book more accessible and useful to both professors and students.

Ross Gowan, Fanshawe College
Gordon Holyer, Vancouver Island University
Mark Loken, Malaspina University College
Patricia Margeson, New Brunswick Community College
Brian Murray, Holland College
John O'Laney , New Brunswick Community College
Dustin Quirk, Red Deer College
Patrick Sherlock, Nova Scotia Community College

MICRO

ECONOMICS FOR LIFE

smart choices **for** you

What's in Economics for You?

Scarcity, Opportunity Cost, and Trade

WHAT DO YOU WANT OUT OF LIFE? Riches? Fame?
Love? Adventure? A successful career? To make the world a better place?
To live a life that respects the environment? To express your creativity?
Happiness? Children? A long and healthy life? All of the above?

Economics will help you get what you want out of life. Many
people believe economics is just about money and business. But the
real definition of **economics** is how individuals, businesses, and
governments make the best possible choices to get what they want,
and how those choices interact in markets.

The title of this book comes from a quote by Nobel Prize-winning
author George Bernard Shaw: "Economy is the art of making the
most of life." Economics is partly about getting the most for your
money, but it is also about making smart choices generally. I wrote
this book because I believe that if you learn a little economics, it will
help you make the most of your life, whatever you are after. That
same knowledge will also help you better understand the world
around you and the choices you face as a citizen.

You don't need to be trained as an economist to lead a productive
and satisfying life. But if you can learn *to think like an economist*, you
can get more out of whatever life you choose to lead, and the world
will be better for it.

economics:
how individuals,
businesses, and
governments make the
best possible choices to
get what they want,
and how those choices
interact in markets

1.1 Are You Getting Enough? Scarcity and Choice

Explain scarcity and describe why you must make smart choices among your wants.

Can you afford to buy everything you want? If not, every dollar you spend involves a choice. If you buy the Nintendo Wii, you might not be able to afford your English textbook. If you treat your friends to a movie, you might have to work an extra shift at your job or give up your weekend camping trip.

It would be great to have enough money to buy everything you want, but it would not eliminate the need to make smart choices. Imagine winning the biggest lottery in the world. You can buy whatever you want for yourself, your family, and your friends. But you still have only 80-some years on this planet (if you are lucky and healthy), only 24 hours in a day, and a limited amount of energy. Do you want to spend the week boarding in Whistler or surfing in Australia? Do you want to spend time raising your kids or exploring the world? Will you go to that third party on New Year's Eve or give in to sleep? Do you want to spend money on yourself, or set up a charitable foundation to help others? Bill Gates, one of the richest people on Earth, has chosen to set up the Bill and Melinda Gates Foundation. With billions of dollars in assets, the Foundation still receives more requests for worthy causes than it has dollars. How does it choose which requests to fund?

Economists call this inability to satisfy all of our wants the problem of **scarcity**. Scarcity arises from our limited money, time, and energy. All mortals, even billionaires, face the problem of scarcity. We all have to make choices about what we will get and what we will give up. Businesses with limited capital have to choose between spending more on research or on marketing. Governments have to make similar choices in facing the problem of scarcity. Spending more on colleges and universities leaves less to spend on health care. Or if governments tried to spend more on all social programs, the higher taxes to pay for them would mean less take-home pay for all of us.

Because none of us — individuals, businesses, governments — can ever satisfy all of our wants, smart choices are essential to making the most of our lives.

scarcity: the problem that arises because we all have limited money, time, and energy

Refresh 1.1

1. Define scarcity.

2. What does the definition of economics have to do with scarcity?

3. Social activists argue that materialism is one of the biggest problems with society: If we all wanted less, instead of always wanting more, there would be plenty to go around for everyone. What do you think of this argument?

1.2 Give It Up for Opportunity Cost! Opportunity Cost

Scarcity means you have to choose, and if you want the most out of what limited money and time you have, you need to make smart choices. A choice is like a fork in the road. You have to compare the alternatives and then pick one. You make a smart choice by weighing benefits and costs.

Define and describe opportunity cost.

Choose to Snooze?

What are you going to do with the next hour? Since you are reading this, you must be considering studying as one choice. If you were out far too late last night, sleep might be your alternative choice. If those are your top choices, let's compare benefits of the two paths from the fork. For studying, the benefits are higher marks on your next test, learning something, and (if I have done my job well) perhaps enjoying reading this chapter. For sleep, the benefits are being more alert, more productive, less grumpy, and (if I have done my job poorly) avoiding the pain of reading this chapter.

If you choose the studying path, what is *the cost of your decision*? It is the hour of sleep you give up (with the benefits of rest). And if you choose sleep, the cost is the studying you give up (leading to lower marks).

In weighing the benefits and costs of any decision, we compare what we get from each fork with what we give up from the other. For any choice (what we get), its true cost is what we have to give up to get it. The true cost of any choice is what economists call **opportunity cost**: the cost of the best alternative given up.

opportunity cost: cost of best alternative given up

Opportunity Cost Beats Money Cost

For smart decisions, it turns out that opportunity cost is more important than money cost. Suppose you win a free trip for one to Bermuda that has to be taken the first week in December. What is the money cost of the trip? (This is not a trick question.) Zero — it's free.

But imagine you have a business client in Saskatoon who can meet to sign a million-dollar contract *only* during the first week in December. What is the opportunity cost of your "free" trip to Bermuda? $1 million. A smart decision to take or not take the trip depends on opportunity cost, not money cost.

Or what if you have an out-of-town boyfriend, and the only time you can get together is during the first week in December? What is the opportunity cost of taking your "free" trip for one? Besides losing out on the benefits of time together, you may be kissing that relationship goodbye.

All choices are forks in the road, and the cost of any path taken is the value of the path you must give up. Because of scarcity, every choice involves a trade-off — to get something, you have to give up something else. *To make a smart choice, the value of what you get must be greater than the value of what you give up.* The benefits of a smart choice must outweigh the opportunity cost.

FOR YOUR INFORMATION

If there were an official slogan for the concept of opportunity cost, it would be, "There is no such thing as a free lunch." The usual meaning of the slogan is that there are strings attached to any gift: the giver will expect something in return. The economist's take on the slogan is that every choice involves a trade-off: To get anything, including lunch, you must always give up something else. What you give up may be money or time, but every choice has an opportunity cost.

Scarcity means every choice involves a trade-off.

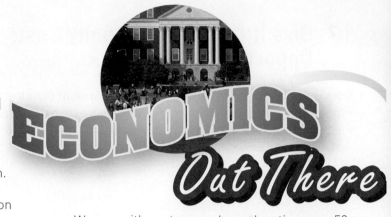

Where Have All the Men Gone?

Women make up 60 percent of the undergraduate college and university population. Why do women so outnumber men? There have been many explanations, from women's liberation to schools' rewarding girls' more obedient behaviour and punishing boys' ADD (attention deficit disorder). There is also a simple economic explanation based on opportunity cost.

- Think of going or not going to college or university as a fork in the road.

- Weigh the costs and benefits of each choice. Everyone pays the same tuition and fees, but the benefits given up with each choice are different for women and men.

- More women than men go to college and university because the cost of *not* going is higher for women — men's alternative is higher-paying blue-collar jobs. Women's alternative tends to be lower-paying clerical or retail jobs.

Women with post-secondary education earn 50 to 80 percent more a year than women with only a high-school diploma. Men with the same post-secondary education earn only 25 to 30 percent more a year than men with only a high-school diploma. The *gap in pay* between high-school and post-secondary women is larger than the same gap for men.

Because of the differences in opportunity cost — women who don't go to college or university *give up* a bigger income gain than men do — the rate of return for a college diploma or university degree is 9 percent for women, and only around 6 percent for men. Incentives matter, and people are responding to the incentives. For women, it pays more to get a post-secondary education.

incentives: rewards and penalties for choices

If you read the preface, you might recognize that this section is about the Three Keys to Smart Choices, which re-appear in Section 1.5

Incentives Work Since smart choices compare costs and benefits, obviously your decision will change with changes in costs or benefits. We all respond to **incentives** — rewards and penalties for choices. You are more likely to choose a fork with a reward, and avoid a fork with a penalty. A change in incentives causes a change in choices. If your Saskatoon business deal was worth only $100 instead of one million dollars, you might take the trip to Bermuda. If you had been out really late last night, you would be more likely to sleep than to study. If you had a test tomorrow instead of next week, you would be more likely to study than to sleep.

To make the most out of life and make smart decisions, you always need to be asking the question, "What is the opportunity cost of my choice, and do the benefits outweigh the opportunity cost?"

Refresh

1.2

1. What is the opportunity cost of any choice?

2. What is the biggest difference between the money cost of attending college and the opportunity cost?

3. This weekend, your top choices are going camping with your friends or working extra hours at your part-time job. What facts (think rewards and penalties), if they changed, would influence your decision?

1.3 Why Don't You Cook Breakfast? Gains from Trade

Define and describe opportunity cost.

What did you have for breakfast today? Did you have cereal and orange juice at home, or did you buy coffee and a bagel at Tim Hortons on the way to school? Either way, you made a choice — to make breakfast for yourself, or to buy it from a business. This is the most basic choice you and everyone else makes in trying to do the best you can: Do you produce yourself the products/services you want, or do you earn money at a job and then buy (or trade money for) products/services made by others?

These days, that basic choice sounds absurd. We all work (or hope to) at jobs, earning money by specializing in a particular profession or occupation. We use that money to buy what we want. Even a "homemade" breakfast uses cereal and juice bought at a supermarket. But if you go back only a few hundred years in Canadian history, most aboriginal peoples and pioneers were largely self-sufficient, making for themselves most of what they needed — hunting and growing their own food, making clothes from animal hides, and building shelters from wood.

Voluntary Trade   What happened to lead us all away from self-sufficiency toward specializing and trading? The historical answer to that question is complex, but the simple economic answer is that specializing and trading makes us better off, so of course people made that basic choice. It's simple self-interest at work.

Our standard of living, in terms of material products/services, is much higher than it was hundreds of years ago in Canada. (What we have done to the environment, which in the past was better than in the present, is another story that I will also explain economically in terms of self-interest in Chapter 10.) The irony is that *as individuals* we are hopeless at supporting ourselves compared to our ancestors. Yet *collectively* our standard of living is vastly superior.

Trade is the key to our prosperity. Trade makes all of us better off. Why? Trade is voluntary. Any time two people make a voluntary trade, each person must feel that what they get is of greater value than what they give up. If there weren't mutual benefits, the trade wouldn't happen.

When you "trade" money for coffee at Tim's, that is a voluntary exchange. If you thought you would be better off keeping the money instead of the coffee, you wouldn't pay. If Tim's weren't better off with your money instead of the coffee, it wouldn't sell.

Bake or Chop?

It turns out that opportunity cost is the key to the mutual benefits from trade. To illustrate, let's take a simple imaginary example of two early Canadians who are each self-sufficient in producing food and shelter.

Jacqueline grows her own wheat to make bread, and chops wood for fire and shelter. If she spends an entire month producing only bread, she can make 50 loaves. Alternatively, if she spends all her time chopping wood, she can produce 100 cords. Her monthly choice of how to spend her time looks like this:

Since Jacqueline is self-sufficient, that means she can consume only what she produces herself, so she must divide her time and produce some bread and some wood. Figure 1.1 shows different combinations of bread and wood she can produce, depending on how she divides up her time during the month. From these production possibilities, Jacqueline chooses to produce 20 loaves of bread and 60 cords of wood.

Figure 1.1 Jacqueline's Production Possibilities (monthly)

Bread (loaves)	Wood (cords)
50	0
40	20
30	40
20	60
10	80
0	100

Samantha, who lives a day's journey away from Jacqueline, also grows her own wheat to make bread, and chops wood for fire and shelter. Samantha is older and weaker than Jacqueline, so if Samantha spends an entire month producing only bread, she can make 40 loaves. Alternatively, if she spends all her time chopping wood, she can produce only 20 cords.

Since Samantha is also self-sufficient, and can consume only what she produces herself, she divides her time and produces some bread and some wood. Figure 1.2 shows different monthly combinations of bread and wood she can produce, depending on how she divides up her time. From these production possibilities, Samantha chooses to produce 20 loaves of bread and 10 cords of wood.

Figure 1.2 Samantha's Production Possibilities (monthly)

Bread (loaves)	Wood (cords)
40	0
30	5
20	10
10	15
0	20

Deal or No Deal? Do the Numbers

absolute advantage: ability to produce a product at lower absolute cost than another producer

How could trade make both Jacqueline and Samantha better off? It doesn't look promising, especially for Jacqueline. She is a better bread maker than Samantha (50 loaves versus 40 loaves) *and* a better wood chopper (100 cords versus 20 cords). An economist would describe Jacqueline as having an **absolute advantage** — the ability to produce a product/service at a *lower absolute cost* than another producer — over Samantha in both bread production and wood production. That is, Jacqueline is more productive as a bread maker and as a wood chopper. If we were to measure dollar costs (which I have left out to keep the example as simple as possible), absolute advantage would mean Jacqueline could produce both bread and wood at lower absolute dollar costs than could Samantha.

If you are not keen on history, then in place of Jacqueline and Samantha, think China and Canada. If China can produce everything at lower cost than Canada, can there be mutually beneficial gains from trade for both countries? What's in it for China? Won't all Canadians end up unemployed?

Comparative Advantage But mutually beneficial gains from trade do not depend on absolute advantage. They depend on what economists call **comparative advantage** — the ability to produce a product/service at a *lower opportunity cost* than another producer. To figure out comparative advantage, we need to calculate *opportunity costs* for Jacqueline and Samantha.

Jacqueline's choice in Figure 1.1 is between producing 50 loaves of bread or 100 cords of wood. If she chooses to bake 50 loaves of bread, the opportunity cost is 100 cords of wood. If she instead chooses to chop 100 cords of wood, the opportunity cost is 50 loaves of bread. Opportunity cost is the value of the fork in the road *not taken*.

To compare opportunity costs, it is easier if we measure them per unit of the product chosen. There is a simple, useful formula for opportunity cost:

$$\text{Opportunity cost} = \frac{\text{Give Up}}{\text{Get}}$$

So Jacqueline's opportunity cost of producing more bread is

$$\text{Opportunity cost of additional bread} = \frac{100 \text{ cords of wood}}{50 \text{ loaves of bread}} = \frac{2 \text{ cords of wood}}{1 \text{ loaf of bread}}$$

To get each additional loaf of bread, Jacqueline must give up 2 cords of wood.

What is Jacqueline's opportunity cost of producing more wood?

$$\text{Opportunity cost of additional wood} = \frac{50 \text{ loaves of bread}}{100 \text{ cords of wood}} = \frac{\frac{1}{2} \text{ loaf of bread}}{1 \text{ cord of wood}}$$

To get each additional cord of wood, Jacqueline must give up $\frac{1}{2}$ loaf of bread.

If you calculate opportunity costs for Samantha you will find that her opportunity cost of getting an additional loaf of bread is giving up $\frac{1}{2}$ cord of wood, and her opportunity cost of getting an additional cord of wood is giving up 2 loaves of bread.

These opportunity cost calculations are summarized in Figure 1.3. Since comparative advantage is defined as lowest opportunity cost (not lowest absolute cost), you can see that Samantha has a comparative advantage in bread-making (give up $\frac{1}{2}$ cord of wood versus 2 cords of wood), while Jacqueline has a comparative advantage in wood-chopping (give up $\frac{1}{2}$ loaf of bread versus 2 loaves of bread).

Figure 1.3	Opportunity Costs for Jacqueline and Samantha	
	Opportunity Cost of 1 Additional	
	Loaf of Bread	**Cord of Wood**
Jacqueline	Gives up 2 cords of wood	Gives up 1/2 loaf of bread
Samantha	Gives up 1/2 cord of wood	Gives up 2 loaves of bread
Comparative Advantage	Samantha has comparative advantage (lower opportunity cost) in bread-making	Jacqueline has comparative advantage (lower opportunity cost) in wood-chopping

Smart Deals

Here's the payoff to these calculations. Instead of each pioneer being self-sufficient, and producing everything she needs, look what happens if the pioneers specialize in producing what each is best at, and then trade.

According to comparative advantage, Jacqueline should specialize in only chopping wood, and Samantha should specialize in only making bread. If so, Jacqueline will produce 100 cords of wood and no bread, and Samantha will produce 40 loaves of bread and no wood. If they then make the day-long journey and trade 20 cords of wood for 20 loaves of bread:

- Jacqueline ends up with 20 loaves of bread (0 produced plus 20 traded for) and 80 cords of wood (100 produced minus 20 traded away);
- Samantha ends up with 20 loaves of bread (40 produced minus 20 traded away) and 20 cords of wood (0 produced plus 20 traded for).

Check it out. *After trading, Jacqueline and Samantha are both better off than when they were each self-sufficient.* Before trade, the best Jacqueline could produce with 20 loaves of bread was 60 cords of wood, for all her strength, while after trade she has the same amount of bread and more wood. Before trade, the best Samantha could produce with 20 loaves of bread was just 10 cords of wood, while after trade she has the same amount of bread and more wood.

What is remarkable is that these *gains from trade,* which improve both Jacqueline's and Samantha's standard of living (with more wood they can stay warmer or build better houses), *happen without anyone working harder, or without any improvement in technology or new resources.* Both are better off because they have made smart decisions to specialize and trade, rather than each trying to produce only what each will consume. Both can have toast for breakfast (bread roasted over a fire), even though each produced only part of what was necessary to make the breakfast.

Voluntary trade is not a zero-sum game, where one person's gain is the other's loss. Both traders gain. Mutually beneficial gains from trade are caused by differences in comparative advantage. Absolute advantage is not important.

Notice also that there are gains for both Jacqueline and Samantha, even though Jacqueline can produce more bread and wood than Samantha can. Despite Jacqueline's absolute advantage in producing everything at lower cost, there are still differences in opportunity costs, or comparative advantage. *Comparative advantage is the key to mutually beneficial gains from trade.* The trade can be between individuals, or between countries. That is why China trades with Canada, even though China can produce most things more cheaply than we can in Canada. There are still differences in comparative advantage based on opportunity costs. Trade allows us all to work smarter.

So the next time you buy breakfast, don't feel guilty about spending the money when you could have cooked it yourself — feel smart about specializing and trading to make yourself better off!

Refresh 1.3

1. Explain the difference between absolute advantage and comparative advantage.
2. If you spend the next hour working at Sears, you will earn $10. If you instead spend the next hour studying economics, your next test score will improve by 5 marks. Calculate the opportunity cost of studying in terms of dollars given up per mark. Calculate the opportunity cost of working in terms of marks given up per dollar.
3. The best auto mechanic in town (who charges $120/hour) is also a better typist than her office manager (who earns $20/hour). Should the mechanic do her own typing? (*Hint:* The best alternative employment for the office manager is another office job that also pays $20/hour.)

www.myeconlab.com

1.4 Choosing Your Way: The Circular Flow of Economic Life

Canada is a very large country, the second largest in the world in terms of geographical area. Have you ever had the urge to follow in the footsteps of our ancestors and explore the land — perhaps a trip to the northernmost tip of the Northwest Territories, or a cross-country trip from Newfoundland to British Columbia? No? Why not think about it?

Explain how markets connect us all using the circular flow of economic life.

Why Maps (and Economists) Are Useful

How do you start planning your trip? The satellite photo of Canada below, while amazing to look at, is not very useful. It contains too much information and too little information. How can that be? The photo captures every aspect of Canada that can be seen from space — lakes, rivers, mountains, and forests. But the photo doesn't reveal smaller details that are important for your trip — most importantly, roads, railways, or ferry services.

A hybrid (combined) map version of the same photo shows you the auto route (on the next page) along the Trans-Canada Highway (you've decided it's too cold to go up north). Why is the hybrid map so much more useful than the satellite photo? Because it focuses your attention on the information that is most relevant for your task, and leaves all other information in the background.

Learning to think like an economist allows you to look at life like the hybrid map. The key "roads" to making smart choices start to stand out, and making difficult decisions and understanding the complex world around you don't seem to be such daunting tasks.

There are an almost infinite number of choices we could look at, so to keep things manageable, let's limit ourselves to the opening definition of economics: Economics is about how individuals, businesses, and governments make the best possible choices to get what they want, and about how those choices interact in markets. (We will look at markets more closely in Chapter 4, but for the moment, think of a market as the interaction of buyers and sellers.)

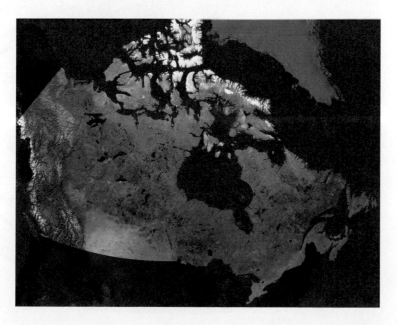

◀ Satellite photo of Canada — not useful for trip planning.

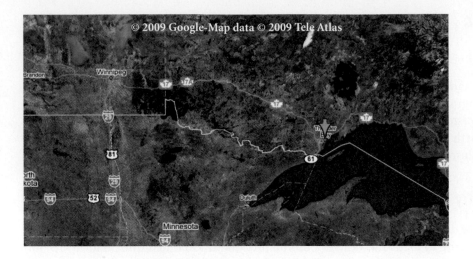

Hybrid map of part of Canada along the Trans-Canada Highway — useful for trip planning.

Another good definition of economics was made in 1890 by Alfred Marshall, the first-ever professor of economics, who created economics as a separate subject at the University of Cambridge. Marshall said: "Economics is the study of mankind in the ordinary business of life."

Going in Circles to Find the Way

Even limiting ourselves to these definitions of economics, the choices are still overwhelming. Imagine 35 million people spread out over 10 million square kilometres, engaged in the "ordinary business of life," earning a living, specializing in producing products/services, selling, and buying. Instead of trying to capture every detail of every action and choice (like the satellite photo), Figure 1.4 shows a hybrid map version of the same economic activity.

> "Economics is the study of mankind in the ordinary business of life."
>
> –Alfred Marshall (1890)

| Figure 1.4 | Circular Flow of Economic Life |

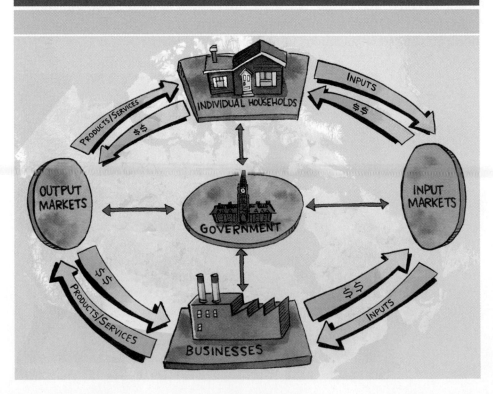

Figure 1.4, which economists call the "circular flow of economic life," shows you the simplest big picture of how an economist thinks about economic choices. All the complexity of the Canadian economy is reduced to three sets of players: households, businesses, and governments. Individuals in households ultimately own all of the inputs of an economy — labour (the ability to work), natural resources, capital equipment, and entrepreneurial ability. Even the assets of the largest corporations, such as Inco, Ford, or Research In Motion, are ultimately owned by individual shareholders. Households and businesses interact in two sets of markets — input markets (where businesses buy the inputs they need to produce products/services), and output markets (where businesses sell their products/services). Governments (in the middle) set the rules of the game and can choose to interact, or not, in almost any aspect of the economy.

Follow the Flow Clockwise Follow the circle, starting at the top. Individuals in households sell or rent to businesses the labour, resources, capital, and entrepreneurial abilities they own. This is the outer blue flow on the right-hand side of the circle, from top to bottom. In exchange, businesses pay wages and other money rewards to households. This is the inner green flow on the right-hand side of the circle, from bottom to top. These exchanges, or trades, happen in input markets, where households are the sellers and businesses are the buyers. When Mr. Sub hires you to work in a Mr. Sub store, that interaction happens in an input market—the job market.

Businesses then use those inputs to produce products/services, which they sell to households. This is the outer blue flow on the left-hand side of the circle, from bottom to top. In exchange, households use the money they have earned in input markets to pay businesses for these purchases. This is the inner green flow on the left-hand side of the circle, from top to bottom. These exchanges, or trades, happen in output markets, where households are the buyers and businesses are the sellers. These are markets where you buy your breakfast from a store or supermarket, your cars from Ford or Toyota, your piercings from a neighbourhood piercing parlour, and so on.

At the end of the trip around the circle, households have the products/services they need to live, and businesses end up with the money. That sets the stage for the next trip around the circle, where businesses again buy inputs from individuals in households, and the flow goes on.

So there you have it—a hybrid map to begin your economics road trip toward understanding and making smart choices.

It's All Greek to Me: Microeconomics or Macroeconomics?

"One size fits all" does *not* apply to maps. The hybrid map of Canada with the highlighted Trans-Canada Highway may be fine for planning the big picture of your trip, but when you are trying to get to a hostel in downtown Winnipeg from the Trans-Canada, a detailed city map is far more useful. Depending on the task, economists also use different kinds of "maps."

The economic way of thinking, while always concerned with smart choices and their interactions in markets, can be applied on different scales to understand *microeconomics* and *macroeconomics*.

Microeconomics

Microeconomics "Micro" comes from the Greek word *mikros,* meaning "little" or "small." A microscope lets us see little details of an object. A micro-manager supervises every tiny detail of an employee's work (ever had a boss like that?). A detailed city map has a micro scale. **Microeconomics** analyzes the choices made by individuals in households, individual businesses, and governments, and how those choices interact in markets.

Microeconomic choices for individuals include whether to go to college or to get a job, whether to be self-sufficient or to specialize and trade, whether to take out a bank loan or to run up a credit card balance, and whether to get married or to stay single. (Yes, there is even a microeconomic analysis comparing the costs and benefits of marriage!)

Microeconomic choices for businesses include what product/service to produce, how much to spend on research and development of new products, which technology to use, which marketing strategy to use, and whether to outsource manufacturing to China versus producing in Canada.

Microeconomic choices for governments focus on *individual industries.* For example, should the government step in and regulate the emerging voice-over-IP phone industry (services such as Skype and Vonage), or let competition determine the winners and losers? How would a carbon tax affect car sales?

Macroeconomics

Macroeconomics When we step back from individual details and look at the big picture, we are taking a "macro" view. Macro comes from the Greek word *makros,* meaning "large." The macrocosm is the cosmos, or the whole of a complex structure. A macrobiotic diet consists of whole, pure foods based on Taoist principles of the overall balance of yin and yang. **Macroeconomics** analyzes the performance of the whole Canadian economy and the global economy, the combined outcomes of all individual microeconomic choices. In the circular flow in Figure 1.4, instead of focusing on the individual exchanges in markets macroeconomics focuses on the *whole* circle, the *combined outcomes* of all of the individual interactions in markets.

Macroeconomics focuses on overall outcomes of market interactions, including Canadian unemployment, inflation rates, government deficits and surpluses, interest rates set by the Bank of Canada, the value of the Canadian dollar, and international trade. Macroeconomics also examines the policy choices governments make that affect the whole economy — for example, whether to play an active economic role by spending and taxing (more likely for New Democrats) or to leave the economy alone (more likely for Progressive Conservatives), whether to raise or lower taxes, whether to raise or lower interest rates, and whether to defend the value of the Canadian dollar or let it be determined by economic forces. Since government macroeconomic policy choices will affect your personal economic fortunes, as a citizen you have a personal incentive to learn some macroeconomics so you can make more informed choices when voting for politicians.

microeconomics: analyzes choices that individuals in households, individual businesses, and governments make, and how those choices interact in markets

macroeconomics: analyzes performance of the whole Canadian economy and global economy, the combined outcomes of all individual micro-economic choices

Looking at the Trees or the Forest? The difference between micro and macro views is reflected in the titles of this book (*Economics for Life: Smart Choices for You*) and its companion book (*Economics for Life: Smart Choices for All*). This book, with the subtitle *Smart Choices for You*, is about microeconomics — individual choices. The companion book, with the subtitle *Smart Choices for All,* is about macroeconomics — the combined market outcomes of all choices. Micro looks at the individual trees, while macro looks at the forest.

Refresh 1.4

1. Who are the three sets of players in the circular flow of economic life?

2. When you find a job through Workopolis.com or Monster.ca, what kind of market are you participating in? Is the answer different for the business that hires you?

3. Find one story in today's news that you think is about microeconomics, and one that is about macroeconomics. What is the difference between microeconomics and macroeconomics in terms of these stories?

www.myeconlab.com

1.5 The Three-Key Map to Smart Choices: Weigh Marginal Benefits and Costs

Good road maps make travel easier. Figure 1.5 shows a second, more detailed hybrid economic "map" to help guide all of your microeconomic choices toward being smart choices. This "map" consists of three keys to consider when standing at any fork in the road, when making any choice. While these three keys don't look like a traditional map (no pictures, colours, roads, or lines), they serve the same function as do maps — focusing your attention on the information that is most useful for making a smart choice, and leaving all other information in the background.

For each key, pay special attention to the red words and italicized words in the explanations on the following page.

Illustrate and explain the Three Keys to Smart Choices.

Figure 1.5 Three Keys to Smart Choices

Choose only when additional benefits are greater than additional opportunity costs.

Count only additional benefits and additional opportunity costs.

Be sure to count all additional benefits and costs, including implicit costs and externalities.

Key 1: Opportunity Costs Rule

To make a smart choice, when you weigh benefits against costs, additional benefits must be greater than additional *opportunity costs*. When counting costs, people who make dumb decisions usually count only money costs, rather than opportunity costs. Remember the "free" trip to Bermuda? The money cost was zero, but the opportunity cost was the $1-million deal you would have given up. Or think about your decision to go to college. For that fork in the road, the additional benefits include the higher lifetime income you will earn from your education. The additional costs are the money spent on tuition and books (these money costs are also opportunity costs, as you could have spent the same money to buy other things), as well as the income you give up by not working full time. The additional benefits must be greater than all additional opportunity costs (and the data show that they are — so congratulations on a smart choice!).

Key 2: Look Forward Only to Additional Benefits and Additional Opportunity Costs

If you are deciding whether or not to study for the next hour, the tuition you paid for this course is irrelevant. You can't get it back, whether you choose to study or not. When standing at a fork in the road, don't look back, only look forward. The previous decisions you made or money you spent are history and can't be undone. The past is the same no matter which fork you choose now, so it shouldn't influence your choice.

Your choices should weigh the *additional* benefit from the next hour of studying against the *additional* cost (giving up sleep, or perhaps working an extra hour at your part-time job). It's not the total benefit of all hours spent studying or the average benefit of an hour of studying that matters, only the *additional* benefit. Economists use the word "marginal" instead of "additional," so you can also read Key 2 as "Count only **marginal benefits** — additional benefits from your next choice — and **marginal opportunity costs** — additional opportunity costs from your next choice." Chapter 2 will explain marginal benefits, and Chapter 3 will explain marginal costs. Thinking like an economist means thinking at the margin.

marginal benefits: additional benefits from the next choice

marginal opportunity costs: additional opportunity costs from the next choice

Key 3: Implicit Costs and Externalities Count, Too

If you invest $1000 in your own business, and expect to get $1100 in a year, is that a smart choice? You don't know until you compare the best alternative use of your money. If the best your bank pays is $1050 in a year, invest in your business. But if the bank is paying 20 percent interest, paying $1200 in a year, your business is not a smart choice. Economists use the term **implicit costs** to describe the opportunity costs of investing your own money or time. These implicit costs will not show up on the books your accountant would prepare, as we will see in Chapter 6. But smart choices must incorporate implicit costs.

implicit costs: opportunity costs of investing your own money or time

Negative Externalities   Driving a car is expensive. Think of the gas bill alone for driving clear across Canada! But your costs also include car payments, insurance, repairs, licence fees, tolls, and parking. What's more, as expensive as those costs are, they don't cover the total cost of driving a car. Your car also emits pollution, but you don't pay for the costs of damage to the environment from acid rain, or for the increased medical costs to treat patients suffering from asthma and other pollution-related illnesses. Economists call these costs that you create, but don't pay directly, **negative externalities**. They are costs that affect others who are external to a choice or trade. But from a social point of view, external costs should be included in making smart decisions.

negative (or positive) externalities: costs (or benefits) that affect others external to a choice or a trade

Positive Externalities   There are also **positive externalities**, benefits that affect others who are external to a choice or trade. If you plant a beautiful garden in your front lawn, you certainly benefit, but so do all of your neighbours who take in the colours and fragrances. Again, from a social point of view, positive externalities should be included in making smart decisions, but they are not.

As we will see in Chapter 10, market economies like ours in Canada tend to produce too many products/services that have negative externalities, and too few products/services that have positive externalities. Government policy can play an important role in adjusting for external costs and benefits to result in smart decisions for society.

Moving On

Now that you have your economic maps to guide you, let's get on with the journey. You will use the Three Keys to make smart decisions time and again over the coming chapters. Don't worry if they seem a bit sketchy for now. Each time we use them, we will fill in some of the pieces that might seem to be missing.

The "maps" in Figures 1.4 and 1.5 will help you learn to think like an economist, which in turn will help you get more out of whatever life you choose to lead, as well as help you make better decisions as a citizen.

Refresh 1.5

1. Can you combine the Three Keys into a single sentence that begins with "Choose only when . . . " and that uses all the economist's terms explained under Steps 2 and 3? That sentence is the key to this entire course.

2. Your employer pays you $1 for every kilometre you drive your own car on company business, or allows you to use a company car at no expense. In deciding whether to drive your own car or use the company car, which of the following costs are relevant to your decision: Purchase price of your car? Yearly licence fee? Insurance premiums? Depreciation? Gasoline costs? Explain your answer.

3. Highway 407 ETR in Toronto is a toll road that uses transponders to keep track of how many kilometres you drive, and then sends a monthly bill. Highway 401 runs parallel to Highway 407 and is free. Why do drivers voluntarily pay the tolls? (Use opportunity cost in your answer.) Suppose the government could estimate the cost per kilometre of the pollution damage from your driving, and send you a similar monthly bill. How would that additional cost affect your decision to drive?

www.myeconlab.com

What's *in Economics* for You?

Scarcity, Opportunity Cost, and Trade

CHAPTER SUMMARY

1.1 ARE YOU GETTING ENOUGH?
SCARCITY AND CHOICE

Because you can never satisfy all of your wants, making the most out of your life requires smart choices about what to go after, and what to give up.

- **Economics** is how individuals, businesses, and governments make the best possible choices to get what they want, and how those choices interact in markets.
- Problem of **scarcity** arises because of limited money, time, and energy.

1.2 GIVE IT UP FOR OPPORTUNITY COST!
OPPORTUNITY COST

Opportunity cost is the single most important concept both in economics and for making smart choices in life.

- Because of scarcity, every choice involves a trade-off — you have to give up something to get something else.
- The true cost of any choice is the **opportunity cost** — cost of best alternative given up.
- For a smart choice, the value of what you get must be greater than value of what you give up.
- **Incentives** — rewards and penalties for choices.
- You are more likely to choose actions with rewards (positive incentives), and avoid actions with penalties (negative incentives).

1.3 WHY DON'T YOU COOK BREAKFAST?
GAINS FROM TRADE

Opportunity cost and comparative advantage are key to understanding why specializing and trading make us all better off.

- With *voluntary* trade, each person feels that what they get is of greater value than what they give up.

- **Absolute advantage** — ability to produce a product/service at a lower absolute cost than another producer.
- **Comparative advantage** — ability to produce a product/service at a lower opportunity cost than another producer.
- Opportunity cost $= \dfrac{\text{Give Up}}{\text{Get}}$
- Comparative advantage is key to mutually beneficial gains from trade. Trade makes individuals better off when each specializes in the product/service where they have a comparative advantage (lower opportunity cost) and then trades for the other product/service.
- Even if one individual has an *absolute* advantage in producing everything at lower cost, as long as there are differences in *comparative* advantage, there are mutually beneficial gains from specializing and trading.

1.4 CHOOSING YOUR WAY: THE CIRCULAR FLOW OF ECONOMIC LIFE

The circular-flow diagram of economic life is a map showing how markets connect us all. It illustrates how smart choices by households, businesses, and governments interact in markets.

- All the complexity of the Canadian economy can be reduced to three sets of players — households, businesses, and governments.
  - In input markets, households are sellers and businesses are buyers.
  - In output markets, households are buyers and businesses are sellers.
  - Governments set rules of the game and can choose to interact in any aspect of the economy.
- **Microeconomics** analyzes choices that individuals in households, individual businesses, and governments make, and how those choices interact in markets.
- **Macroeconomics** analyzes performance of the whole Canadian economy and global economy, the combined outcomes of all individual microeconomic choices.

1.5 THE THREE-KEY MAP TO SMART CHOICES: WEIGH MARGINAL BENEFITS AND COSTS

The three-key plan summarizes the core of microeconomics. It provides the basis for smart choices in all areas of your life.

- Three Keys to Smart Choices:
  1. Choose only when additional benefits are greater than additional *opportunity costs*.
  2. Count only *additional* benefits and *additional* opportunity costs.
  3. Be sure to count *all* additional benefits and costs, including *implicit costs* and *externalities*.
- Marginal = "additional."
- **Marginal benefits** — additional benefits from next choice.
- **Marginal opportunity costs** — additional opportunity costs from next choice.
- **Implicit costs** — opportunity costs of investing your own money or time.
- **Negative** (or **positive**) **externalities** — costs (or benefits) that affect others external to a choice or a trade.

TRUE/FALSE

Circle the correct answer.

1.1 SCARCITY AND CHOICE

1. Economics is about how individuals, businesses, and governments make the best possible choices to get what they want, and how those choices interact in markets. **True**   **False**

2. People who win the lottery don't have to make smart choices. **True**   **False**

1.2 OPPORTUNITY COST

3. Opportunity cost is equal to money cost. **True**   **False**

4. In 2007 the Government of Canada announced a $1000 Apprenticeship Incentive Grant to cover the costs of tuition, travel, and tools for apprentices in the sealing trades. This will eliminate the opportunity cost of being an apprentice for those who receive the cash grant. **True**   **False**

5. According to "Economics Out There" on p. 6, men have a larger incentive to get a post-secondary education because *not* getting a post-secondary education results in a relatively worse outcome compared to women. **True**   **False**

1.3 GAINS FROM TRADE

6. Traditionally, women have specialized in unpaid work at home and men have specialized in paid work outside the house. One possible explanation for this could be that men held a comparative advantage in performing housework (for example, cooking, cleaning, and child care). **True**   **False**

7. The theories of comparative advantage, specialization, and trade in this chapter are consistent with the belief that "opposites attract." **True**   **False**

8. Sheryl and Darrel are trying to decide who should stay at home to take care of their newborn child and who should continue to work full-time outside the house. Sheryl makes $30 an hour and Darrel earns $26 an hour. If both are equally effective (or "productive") at taking care of the child, then based on *opportunity costs* Sheryl should stay at home to take care of their newborn. **True**   **False**

9. The proportion of families with both parents working outside the home and sharing child care responsibilities has risen in recent decades. This indicates that specialization and the traditional division of gender roles are becoming much less common in Canada. **True**   **False**

10. Government programs that make child care more affordable, such as Quebec's $7-a-day child-care program, would likely increase the proportion of parents who work outside the home.

True   **False**

1.4 THE CIRCULAR FLOW OF ECONOMIC LIFE

11. The labour market — where employers demand labour and employees supply labour — is an output market.

True   **False**

12. In input markets, households are sellers and businesses are buyers; in output markets, households are buyers and businesses are sellers.

True   **False**

13. Decisions to go to college or take out a loan are macroeconomic choices.

True   **False**

1.5 WEIGH MARGINAL BENEFITS AND COSTS

14. Implicit costs are the opportunity costs of investing your own money or time.

True   **False**

15. Negative externalities are benefits that affect others external to a choice or a trade.

True   **False**

MULTIPLE CHOICE

Circle the correct answer.

1.1 SCARCITY AND CHOICE

1. You can't get everything you want because you are limited by
   A) time.
   B) money.
   C) energy.
   D) all of the above.

2. Scarcity is
   A) not a challenge for governments.
   B) not a challenge for celebrities.
   C) not a challenge for people who win the lottery.
   D) a challenge for everyone.

3. Economics does not focus on
   A) individuals / households.
   B) animals.
   C) businesses.
   D) government.

4. Opportunity cost includes
   A) time you give up.
   B) energy you spend.
   C) money you spend.
   D) all of the above.

5. In deciding whether to study or sleep for the next hour, your decision should consider all of the following *except*
   A) how much tuition you paid.
   B) how tired you are.
   C) how productive you will be in that hour.
   D) how much value you place on sleeping in that hour.

6. From 1991 to 2001, the proportion of 25- to 29-year-old women with university degrees rose from 21 percent to 34 percent, while the proportion of 25- to 29-year-old men with degrees rose from 16 percent to 21 percent. There is a similar trend for college diplomas. More woman than men are getting post-secondary education because
   A) the gap in pay between post-secondary and high-school graduates is higher for women than it is for men.
   B) the cost of not going to post-secondary education is higher for women.
   C) the opportunity cost of going to post-secondary education is lower for women.
   D) all of the above.

7. According to the table, all of the following statements are true *except*

Median Annual Earnings	Men	Women
College diploma	$51 000	$43 000
High-school diploma	$37 000	$32 000

   A) people with college diplomas earn more than people with high-school diplomas.
   B) men with high-school diplomas earn more than women with high-school diplomas.
   C) men with college diplomas earn more than women with college diplomas.
   D) women with high-school diplomas earn more than men with high-school diplomas.

8. If the resource-rich sector of Alberta's economy starts to slow down,
   A) opportunity costs of upgrading to a college diploma will increase.
   B) opportunity costs of upgrading to a college diploma will decrease.
   C) incentives to drop out of college will increase.
   D) all of the above.

1.3 GAINS FROM TRADE

9. Mutually beneficial gains from trade come from
   A) absolute advantage.
   B) comparative advantage.
   C) self-sufficiency.
   D) China.

10. The easiest way to calculate opportunity cost is
    A) $\dfrac{\text{give up}}{\text{get}}$

    B) $\dfrac{\text{get}}{\text{give up}}$

    C) give up – get
    D) get – give up

1.4 THE CIRCULAR FLOW OF ECONOMIC LIFE

11. Which of the following is *not* a microeconomic choice for businesses?
    A) What interest rates to set
    B) What products/services to supply
    C) What quantity of output to produce
    D) How many workers to hire

12. Which of the following is *not* a microeconomic choice for governments?
    A) Increasing tuition rates
    B) Taxing automobile emissions
    C) Increasing the exchange rate of the Canadian dollar
    D) Increasing the number of taxi licences

13. In the circular-flow diagram,
    A) households ultimately own all the inputs of an economy.
    B) governments set the rules of the game.
    C) businesses are sellers and households are buyers in output markets.
    D) all of the above.

1.5 WEIGH MARGINAL BENEFITS AND COSTS

14. All of the following should be considered when making smart choices, *except*
    A) external costs and benefits.
    B) past costs and benefits.
    C) implicit costs.
    D) additional costs and additional benefits.

15. For any activity, failure to consider
    A) past costs will result in too much of that activity.
    B) past benefits will result in too little of that activity.
    C) external costs will result in too much of that activity.
    D) external benefits will result in too much of that activity.

SHORT ANSWER

Write a short answer to each question. Your answer may be in point form.

1. You're trying to decide whether to go camping with your friends or spend a quiet weekend at home with your significant other. What incentives (think rewards and penalties), if changed, may influence your decision?

2. Olga chooses to live at home rather than move into residence during her first year of college. She often brags about the fact that she saves a lot of money by living at home. Provide some examples of what Olga may have given up by choosing to live at home.

3. Suppose the government was worried about the decline of young men in post-secondary education. What incentives might encourage more men to pursue further education?

4. Your friend has an extra ticket to the Calgary Flames–Ottawa Senators game on a Saturday night. He says he will give you the ticket for free if you pay for all other expenses. You usually work Saturday nights, so if you go you will have to take the night off work. Explain what costs you would include in deciding whether or not to go to the "free" game.

5. Seat belts save lives. Suppose that a city doubles the penalty for being caught driving without a seat belt in attempt to increase seat belt use among drivers.

   A) Explain how this policy will influence driver behaviour.

   B) Now suppose the city evaluates the policy and finds that the number of fatalities actually *increased* after the policy was introduced. Can you think of a reason why this may have occurred?

6. Consider Jacqueline and Samantha from Section 1.3, who specialize and trade to become better off. Suppose that Jack, a new person in town, is deciding between specializing (in either bread or wood) and being self-sufficient. Jack's production possibilities are illustrated below:

Jack's Production Possibilities (monthly)	
Bread (loaves)	**Wood (cords)**
70	0
60	15
50	30
40	45
30	60
20	75
10	90
0	105

If Jack chooses to be self-sufficient, he prefers spending his month making 20 loaves of bread and cutting 75 cords of wood.

Determine who has the comparative advantage between

A) Jack and Jacqueline

B) Jack and Samantha

7. Suppose Jack tells Jacqueline and Samantha that he will form a partnership with the woman who makes him best off after trade. Assuming that 20 cords of wood can be traded for 20 loaves of bread, with whom would Jack prefer to go into a partnership?

8. Back in the old days, professors and students could smoke in the classrooms. Today, smoking indoors in public places is illegal.

A) Provide an example of an "external cost" that indoor smokers fail to consider when deciding to light up inside the classroom.

B) Do you think that those who smoked indoors considered the "external cost" in their decision to smoke? Why or why not?

C) Another way to discourage smoking is to tax the activity. If people respond to incentives, how would we expect smokers to adjust their behaviour in response to an increase in a cigarette tax?

9. Mrs. and Mr. Singh are encouraging both their son and daughter to get a full-time job right after completing high school. According to what you learned from "Economics Out There" on p. 6, which child should they encourage *less* to go to work?

10. From a social point of view, external costs should be included in making smart decisions, but sometimes they are not. In each of the following examples, determine whether the market economy (in the absence of government policy) would result in too few or too many products/services being produced. Then describe one policy or program that the government has in place to force individuals to consider these costs or benefits when they make decisions.

A) Pollution levels

B) Smoking levels

C) Education levels

Chapter 2

Making Smart Choices

The Law of Demand

LEARNING OBJECTIVES

After reading this chapter, you should be able to:

2.1 Describe what determines your willingness to pay for a product/service.

2.2 Identify why smart choices depend on marginal benefit, not total benefit, and explain what changes marginal benefit.

2.3 Describe the relationship between price and quantity demanded, and identify the role of substitutes.

2.4 Explain the difference between a change in quantity demanded and a change in demand, and distinguish five factors that change demand.

2.5 Define elasticity of demand and explain how it determines business pricing strategies.

BELIEVE IT OR NOT, economics is not really about money. It is about how individuals, businesses, and governments make the best possible choices to get what they want. Smart choices help you achieve happiness and success for yourself and others, help businesses make profits, and help governments spend your tax dollars wisely to make Canada a better place.

Of course, not all choices are smart or wise choices, and the Three Keys to Smart Choices from Chapter 1 are the keys to distinguishing smart from not-smart. The three keys are discussed more fully in this chapter.

This chapter focuses on choices you make every day as a consumer, and on the implications of those choices for how businesses price what they sell you. Economists use the term *demand* to summarize all of the influences on consumer choice.

2.1 Put Your Money Where Your Mouth Is: Weighing Benefits, Costs, and Substitutes

Describe what determines your willingness to pay for a product/ service.

You've just finished an intense workout at the gym and desperately want something to drink. You usually bring along your favourite Gatorade (which costs $3 a bottle), but today you forgot it. The snack bar has bottled water and juice, but no Gatorade. Your buddy, who is always trying to make a buck, says, "I have a bottle of what you want — how much will you pay for it?"

Besides wondering if this guy is really a buddy, what do you think about to determine how much you are willing to pay him? Obviously, how thirsty you are and how refreshed you expect to feel from the drink matter a lot. But just because you badly want Gatorade does not mean you will pay, say, $10 for the bottle.

What are your alternatives? You could buy a water or juice for $2, but they don't have the electrolytes for your muscles that Gatorade does. You could drink water from the faucet in the locker room for free. You could head home and drink the bottle you forgot, or head to a store to buy your Gatorade for $3.

You decide you so want the Gatorade *now* that you are willing to make an offer. You know your entrepreneurial buddy won't take less than the $3 he paid for the bottle, so you are willing to pay $4. You make the purchase, quench your thirst — and then ditch the buddy.

We all make hundreds of choices a day that are similar — what to eat, what to wear, what to buy, whether to spend time studying, working, working out, or partying, whom to vote for. . . . All these choices are based (consciously or unconsciously) on a comparison of expected benefits and costs. This is Key 1 of the Three Keys to Smart Choices from Chapter 1: Choose only when additional benefits are greater than additional *opportunity costs*.

▲ Choosing a substitute depends on what you will pay, what substitutes are available, and what they cost. Can you think of anything you use in life that doesn't have a substitute?

How Badly Do You Want It? The first part of the comparison requires you to have a sense of the expected benefits from choosing this product, service, experience, or use of your time. The expected benefit question is, "How badly do you want it?" What satisfaction do you expect to get from this choice? The want and the satisfaction might be quite logical — I want a warm coat so I won't freeze during the winter in Calgary; I want water because I am thirsty. I want to spend the evening studying because I have a test tomorrow. Or your desire for the latest, thinnest cell phone may be based on more emotional reasons — wanting to look cool, or to impress others, or just because, well, you want it. Businesses spend money on advertising, in part, to convince you to want their product. Economists describe all of your wants — and how intense each want is — as your **preferences**.

preferences: your wants and their intensities

What Will You Give Up? For the second part of the comparison, the cost question is, "How much are you willing to give up for it?" I purposely chose the words "give up" when you might have expected me to say, "How much are you willing to pay for it?" There's a reason for this choice, just as there are reasons for all of your choices. Many things we want — Gatorade or cell phones — we have to pay for with money. But with many other things we want, what we have to give up is our time or our effort. Spending the evening studying means not partying with friends or working at your part-time job. Cost always means opportunity cost — what you are willing to give up.

What determines *how much* you are willing to give up? Certainly, how badly you want it plays a role. But just as important is what your alternative choices are. There are substitutes for everything — water for Gatorade, a yoga class for a gym workout, long underwear or a move to Florida for winter coats. Substitutes need not be exactly the same product/service. Substitutes just have to basically satisfy the same want. For any choice you want to make, what you are willing to pay or give up depends on what substitutes are available, and what they cost.

The final factor determining how much you are willing to give up is how much you can afford. Are you able to pay the price of the product/service you want? Can you afford to take the time to party all evening when you have a test tomorrow?

The list of things we want is endless. But the choices we actually make reflect our willingness — and ability — to give up something in exchange. Economists use the term **demand** to describe consumers' willingness and ability to pay for a particular product/service (not just what consumers want). You must put your money (or time) where your mouth is in order to demand a product/service. And those demands, or choices, are smart choices only when expected benefits are greater than opportunity costs.

What you are willing to give up depends on available substitutes and their cost.

What you can "afford" is not just about money, it is also about time. You have limited dollars and limited time.

demand: consumers' willingness and ability to pay for a particular product/service

Refresh
2.1

1. What is the difference between wants and demands?

2. How many songs or albums by your favourite musician or group have you bought? How many have you copied or downloaded? What determined your choice between buying and downloading?

3. You have just started at a college that is a 30-minute drive from home or a 90-minute transit ride. How would you make a smart choice between taking the transit or buying a car? What are the important issues on the benefits comparison? On the cost comparison?

www.myeconlab.com

2.2 Living On the Edge: Smart Choices Are Marginal Choices

Identify why smart choices depend on marginal benefit, not total benefit, and explain what changes marginal benefit.

You make a smart choice only when expected benefits are greater than opportunity costs. But the benefits or satisfaction you expect to get depend on the circumstances.

Marginal Benefits Change with Circumstances

To see how benefits change with circumstances, let's return to the Gatorade example. Suppose you remembered to bring a bottle to the gym, and gulped it all after your workout. If your greedy buddy then asked you how much you were willing to pay for another bottle, chances are it would be much less than the $4 you were willing to pay when you had few convenient Gatorade alternatives. The *additional* benefit you will get from his second bottle is less than the benefit you got from your thirst-quenching first bottle. So your willingness to pay is less for the second bottle.

What if you have a test tomorrow, and you have to choose between spending the evening studying or going to a party with a friend? If you have been studying like mad for days already, the *additional* benefit of a few more hours might not help much, so you choose to party. But if you have been busy working at your job all week and haven't cracked a book, the *additional* benefit of studying will be large, and you give up the party time.

In both cases, the *additional* benefit you expect, and your willingness to pay (either in money or giving up party time you value), depends on the circumstances. The economist's term for *additional* benefit is **marginal benefit**. Marginal means "on or at the edge," just like the margins of these textbook pages are at the edges of the pages.

Key 2 of the Three Keys to Smart Choices says that when you compare expected benefits and costs, count only *additional* benefits and *additional* costs, or marginal benefits and marginal costs. Here we are explaining marginal benefits; in Chapter 3 we will explain marginal costs.

marginal benefit: additional benefit from a choice, and changes with circumstances

A smart decision to study (or not) does not depend on the total value of all hours spent studying, or the average value of an hour spent studying, but only on the *marginal* value of the additional time spent studying (compared with the additional cost of giving up those hours).

What if you choose to spend the evening studying, and your friend gets angry and shouts, "Is your stupid economics course more important than I am?!" At the margin, the answer is yes. Your choice to study tonight doesn't necessarily mean that, overall, you value the course more than the friend (well, depending on the friend, you might). What your choice means is that tonight, at the margin, you value the next few hours spent studying more than you value spending the next few hours with your friend.

The difference between total growth and marginal growth is the difference between "How tall are you?" and "How much have you grown?" Did your family mark your height on every birthday?

But margins, and circumstances, change. Your choice would be different if you had another week before the test, or if you hadn't seen your friend for months. The value you place on an activity or thing depends on the margin, and *that* additional value is marginal benefit.

Your friend's angry accusation comes from the common mistake (not smart) of looking at choices as all or nothing — friend versus economics. That's not the (smart) choice you made at the margin — the marginal benefit of the time spent studying tonight was greater than the value, or marginal benefit, of the same time spent with your friend.

Making smart choices means living life on the edge.

ECONOMICS Out There

Coke's Automatic Price Gouging

In the late 1990s, Coca-Cola Co. was working on technology to automatically raise prices in soft-drink vending machines on hot days. Critics — calling the plan "shameful" and a "cynical ploy" to exploit consumers "when they are most susceptible to price gouging" — suggested Coca-Cola should abandon the plan. The company claimed it was fair that the price should rise with demand, and that the machines simply automate that process. Unconvinced, critics warned that the plan would only alienate customers, with the reminder that "archrival Pepsi is out there, and you can hardly tell the difference."

- The public reaction to these variable-price vending machines was so negative that Coca-Cola never introduced them.

- However, the strategy is based on the correct observation that willingness to pay changes with circumstances — the principle of marginal benefit.

- The strategy failed not because the economics were wrong, but because the idea of paying different prices for the same product seemed so unfair — "price gouging." (However, in Chapter 8 we will look at examples where consumers accept businesses charging different consumers different prices for the same product — cellphone minutes cost providers the same, whether daytime, evening, or weekend. Why are prices different? *Hint:* Consumer willingness to pay.)

- Notice the line about Pepsi — substitutes are always available, which limits willingness to pay for any product, regardless of the marginal benefit.

Source: "Coke's Automatic Price Gouging," *San Francisco Chronicle*, October 29, 1999, p. A22.

The Diamond/Water Paradox

The distinction between looking at choices at the margin (smart) instead of as "all or nothing" or total-value choices helps make sense of the diamond/water paradox you may have heard about. What's more valuable in providing benefit or satisfaction — diamonds or water? One answer is water. Water is essential for survival, while diamonds are an unnecessary frill. But then why do diamonds cost far more than water?

You can solve the paradox by distinguishing marginal value from total value. You would die without any water, so you would be willing to pay everything you can for the first drink. But when water is abundant and cheap, and you are not dying of thirst, what would you be willing to pay, at the margin, for your next drink today? Not much. Marginal benefit is low, even though the total benefit of all water consumed (including the first, life-saving drink) is high.

Diamonds won't keep you alive, but they are relatively scarce, and desirable for that very reason. What would you pay for what is likely your first diamond? A lot. Marginal benefit is high. But because diamonds are scarce, there aren't many out there (compared to drinks of water), so total benefit is low. But willingness to pay depends on marginal benefit, not total benefit, so people are generally willing to pay more for a diamond (high marginal benefit) than for a glass of water (low marginal benefit).

Marginal benefit, as we will see in Chapter 4, is important not only for making smart choices, but also for explaining how prices are determined in the real world.

Willingness to pay, a key part of demand, depends on marginal benefit, not total benefit. If you think about total benefit you will get confused in Section 2.3. Think marginal!

Refresh 2.2

1. What is marginal benefit, and on what does it depend?

2. Why are you willing to pay more for a diamond than a glass of water even though water is essential for survival and diamonds are an unnecessary luxury?

3. You and your entrepreneurial buddy have a concession stand on the beach. It is a hot, sunny, crowded day, and you are selling a few $5 collapsible umbrellas as sun parasols. The skies suddenly darken, rain begins to pour, and your buddy quickly switches the umbrella price sign to $10. Will you sell more or fewer umbrellas? Explain your thinking, including your analysis of the customer's decision.

www.myeconlab.com

2.3 When the Price Isn't Right: The Law of Demand

After weeks of boring bus rides to school and overhearing too many other riders' personal cell phone conversations, you finally decide to buy an iPod. You research the alternatives and decide to buy the low-capacity Nano. You would have loved a bigger hard drive or an iPhone, but decided you couldn't afford those.

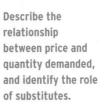

Describe the relationship between price and quantity demanded, and identify the role of substitutes.

Quantity Demanded

Let's presume you made a smart choice, so the additional benefit of this iPod (listening pleasure and blocking out the world) is greater than the additional cost (the $150 price tag). You are willing and able to pay $150. Sold! An economist would say that, at the price of $150, your *quantity demanded* of iPod Nanos is 1.

Quantity demanded, as we will see, is not the same as *demand.* **Quantity demanded** is the amount you actually plan to buy at a given price, taking into account everything that affects your willingness and ability to pay.

We saw in the previous section that when circumstances change the additional benefit, your choice may change. The second bottle of Gatorade wasn't worth as much as the first, and the value of an iPod would change if you were driving to school in a car with a radio instead of riding the bus. But our focus here is not on benefits. Our focus is on *what happens to your buying decision when the additional cost (what you pay) changes.*

quantity demanded: amount you actually plan to buy at a given price

Changing Prices Change Quantity Demanded   What if this iPod model were priced at $175 instead of $150? How might that change your decision to buy? You might want an iPod so badly that you would be willing to pay $175, judging that the additional benefit is still greater than the $175 cost. (That means that at $150, you felt you were getting a bargain!) But since you are a smart shopper and have limited income, you would still be thinking carefully about alternatives. There are substitutes for everything. For music and sound-blocking there are other (cheaper) MP3 players, used iPods, music downloaded to your cell phone, radios, or your older sister's ancient Discman. The extra $25 cost might be enough to change your choice from an iPod Nano to one of these substitutes. And if the price were $225, you, along with many more consumers out there, would definitely change your smart choice away from an iPod Nano to a substitute. At a price of $225, your quantity demanded is zero.

What if Nanos went on sale for $75 instead of $150? Given your willingness and ability to pay, this is such a bargain that you decide to buy two — one for you, and one as a gift for your boy/girlfriend. At a price of $75, your quantity demanded is two.

If we put your combinations of prices (willingness to pay) and quantities demanded into a table, it looks like Figure 2.1.

Figure 2.1   Your Demand for the iPod Nano

Price (willing to pay)	Quantity Demanded
$ 75	2
$150	1
$225	0

As your eye goes down the two columns, notice that as the price rises, the quantity demanded decreases. In general, when prices rise, consumers look for substitutes. When something becomes more expensive, people economize on its use.

Water or Brooms?   Households in the City of Toronto used to pay a flat monthly rate for water that didn't change with the quantity of water used. So the *additional* cost of using more water was zero. With "free" marginal water, many residents would "sweep" their sidewalks and driveways with a hose. But when water became metered, so that users paid for each additional cubic metre, many gave up this practice and started sweeping with a broom. (Only economics teaches you that water and brooms are substitutes!) Other reactions to higher water prices included putting bricks in toilet tanks to save water, placing flow regulators on showers, taking showers instead of baths, and planting groundcover that consumes less water than grass. With a higher price for water, the quantity demanded decreased.

The Law of Demand

The market for any product or service consists of millions of potential customers, each trying to make a smart choice about what to buy. **Market demand** is the sum of the demands of all individuals willing and able to buy a particular product/service.

Whether it is the market for iPods, water, or anything else, substitutes exist, so that consumers buy a smaller quantity at higher prices, and a larger quantity at lower prices. This inverse relationship (when one goes up, the other goes down) between price and quantity demanded is so universal that economists call it (somewhat grandiosely) the **law of demand**: If the price of a product/service rises, the quantity demanded of the product/service decreases. The law of demand works as long as other factors besides price do not change. The next section will explore what happens when other factors do change. Will the law of demand then fail? Stay tuned.

When the price of a product rises, consumers switch to cheaper substitutes. The quantity demanded of the original product, at the now higher price, decreases.

market demand: sum of demands of all individuals willing and able to buy a particular product/service

law of demand: if the price of a product/service rises, quantity demanded decreases

Market Demand for Water   Figure 2.2 illustrates the inverse relationship between price and quantity demanded for the market demand for water.

Figure 2.2	Market Demand for Water
Price (per cubic metre)	**Quantity Demanded** (000's of cubic metres/month)
$1.00	5
$1.50	4
$2.00	3
$2.50	2
$3.00	1

The law of demand is yet another way of saying that when something becomes more expensive, people economize on its use. This law helps explain many decisions beyond shopping decisions. Mother Teresa's charity wanted to open a shelter for the homeless in New York City. When city bureaucrats insisted on expensive but unnecessary renovations to the building, the charity abandoned the project. Mother Teresa didn't abandon her commitment to the poor. When the cost of helping the poor in New York went up, she decided that, at the margin, her efforts would do more good elsewhere. For her charity, a shelter elsewhere was a substitute for a New York shelter.

Because there are substitutes for everything, higher prices create incentives for smart consumers to reduce their purchases of more expensive products/services and look for alternatives.

A change to a new behaviour can often be encouraged by an increase in the cost of an old behaviour. How much would a litre of gas have to cost before you switched to a bicycle?

Refresh
2.3

1. What is the law of demand?

2. You own a car and work at a job that is not accessible by public transit. If the price of gasoline goes up dramatically, does the law of demand apply to you? Explain the choices you might make in response to this increase in price.

3. You have plans to go to a concert tonight, but your mother, who is helping you pay for school, says that it's very important to her that you instead come to Grandma's birthday party. Explain how your decision to celebrate with Grandma illustrates the law of demand in terms of your concert plans.

www.myeconlab.com

2.4 Moving the Margins: What Can Change Demand?

Explain the difference between a change in quantity demanded and a change in demand, and distinguish between five factors that change demand.

The price of gasoline in Halifax rose from $0.99 per litre to $1.36 per litre between 2006 and 2008. But the quantity of gasoline motorists bought actually *increased*. Does that disprove the "law of demand"?

If nothing else changed except the price of gasoline, the answer would be yes — and I'd have to quit this job as an economist and do something more socially useful, like being a trash collector.

But I, and other economists, have enough confidence in the law of demand that if we observe a rise in price leading to an *increase* in purchases, we take it as a signal that something else must have changed at the same time.

Economists use the concept of *demand* to summarize all the influences on consumer choice. Your demand for any product/service reflects your willingness and ability to pay. In the examples of Gatorade, iPods, and water, we have seen that your willingness to pay depends on things like your preferences, what substitutes are available, and marginal benefit. Your ability to pay depends on your income.

As long as all these factors (and a few more) do not change, the law of demand holds true: If the price of a product/service rises, the quantity demanded decreases.

But when change happens, economists distinguish between two kinds of change:

- If the price of a product/service changes, that affects *quantity demanded*.
- If anything else changes, that affects *demand*.

Quantity demanded is a much more limited term than *demand*. Only a change in price changes quantity demanded. A change in any other influence on consumer choice changes demand. This may sound like semantic hair-splitting — quantity demanded versus demand — but it is important for avoiding not-smart thinking.

Why Bother Distinguishing Between Quantity Demanded and Demand?

Suppose you observe a witch placing a curse on some poor young man, who dies a month later. The apparent conclusion is that the curse was fatal. But if the witch had been secretly poisoning his food with arsenic all along, what was the real cause of death? Something else changed that was really behind the observed result.

What if a gasoline supplier decides to raise his prices to increase his sales, based on the observed result that when gasoline prices rose, motorists bought more gasoline. What do you think would happen? Would this be a smart choice?

We live in a complicated world, where everything depends on everything else. There are obvious connections between events like a lottery windfall increasing your spending, or high CD prices increasing music downloads. But non-economic events like the weather can affect coffee prices, and a whiff of a terrorist threat can sink airline stock prices. So when you observe a change in the economy like increased gasoline purchases, how do you decide what caused it when so many interdependent things can change at the same time? (Was the young man's death caused by curse, arsenic, or natural causes?)

In the real world, everything is related to everything else, making it difficult to distinguish an event's actual causes from apparent causes. Scientists use controlled laboratory experiments to keep all interrelated factors unchanged. Economists can't conduct controlled experiments. Instead, we use distinctions like change in quantity demanded versus change in demand to mentally mimic controlled experiments.

Controlled Experiments Scientists deal with this interdependence problem by performing controlled experiments in a laboratory. The law of gravity claims that, all other factors unchanged, objects fall at the same rate regardless of their weight. So if we drop a bowling ball and a feather from a tall building, and find the bowling ball hits the ground first, does that disprove the law of gravity? No, because we are not controlling for air resistance, which changes the path of the feather more than the bowling ball. To accurately test the law of gravity, we must perform the same experiment in a laboratory vacuum, so that we eliminate, or control for, the influence of air resistance as an "other factor." We need to keep all other factors unchanged.

Economists, and citizens like you, have it much tougher than scientists. We can't pause everything in the world except for the factors we are interested in. Instead, we have to use economics to make sense of the changes. The distinction between a change in quantity demanded and a change in demand is the economist's way of trying to mentally mimic a controlled experiment.

The law of demand is the simplest of all the interdependent relationships. *If nothing else changes,* a rise in the price of gasoline will cause a decrease in the quantity demanded of gasoline.

Let's look at the more complicated parts (like air resistance for the law of gravity) — all the important "other things" that can cause a change in demand.

Five Ways to Change Demand

Only a change in the price of a product/service itself changes *quantity demanded* of that product/service. But there are five important other factors that can change market demand — the willingness and ability to pay for a product/service. They are:

- Preferences
- Prices of related products
- Income
- Expected future prices
- Number of consumers

Preferences There are many reasons why businesses advertise, but ultimately they are trying to get you to want their product, to persuade you that you need what they sell. Remember that economists use the term "preferences" to describe your wants and their intensities — so, for an economist, advertising is about increasing your preferences for a product/service.

Most car commercials are not about information but about showing you a fabulous, fun driving experience that the manufacturer wants you to believe will be yours only if you buy its car.

All businesses want to increase your preferences, because if they succeed in increasing the intensity of your want or desire for their product you will be willing to pay more for it. If Apple were to run a successful ad campaign that makes you and many other consumers feel you can't live (and be cool) without an iPod, what would happen to your willingness and ability to pay, according to our earlier example? Look at Figure 2.3 on the next page.

Figure 2.3 Your Demand for iPod Nanos Before and After Advertising

Price (before advertising)	Price (after advertising)	Quantity Demanded
$ 75	$100	2
$150	$200	1
$225	$300	0

Before advertising, you were willing and able to pay $150 for one iPod (row 2), while after you are now willing to pay $200. Before you were willing to buy two iPods at a price of $75 each (row 1), while after you will pay $100 each and buy two.

Your ability to pay has not changed in this example, it's just that you are willing to give up more of your unchanged income because the intensity of your wants has increased. Advertising has succeeded in moving the margin, increasing both the marginal benefit you expect to get from the iPod and your willingness to pay. Economists call any increase in consumers' willingness and ability to pay an **increase in demand**. Consumers will now be willing to pay a higher price for the same quantity of a product.

Changes in preferences can also cause a decrease in demand. What if a Health Canada study shows conclusively that regular listening to an iPod causes serious hearing loss and causes mushrooms to grow out of your ears? If you and other consumers believe the study, consumers' willingness and ability to pay decreases, which results in a **decrease in demand** for iPods. Consumers will now be willing to pay only a lower price for the same quantity of a product.

When the Rolling Stones played their only 2006 Canadian concert in Moncton, New Brunswick, what happened to the demand for hotel rooms in Moncton? The large number of fans attending the concert increased the willingness to pay and *increased the demand* for hotel rooms. On the other hand, think of demand by tourists for hotel rooms in Toronto before and after the 2003 SARS epidemic. The fear of infectious disease decreased tourists' preferences for Toronto hotel bookings. With decreased willingness to pay, there was a decrease in demand for Toronto hotel rooms.

Any change in preferences causes a change in demand. An increase in preferences causes an increase in demand. A decrease in preferences causes a decrease in demand.

Prices of Related Products

Many products/services you choose to buy are related. Changes in price of a different, related product/service will affect your demand for the original product/service. There are two main types of related products: substitutes and complements.

Substitutes are products/services that can be used in place of each other to satisfy the same want. Examples of substitutes are iPods and other MP3 players for listening to music, or water and Gatorade for quenching thirst.

increase in demand: increase in consumers' willingness and ability to pay

decrease in demand: decrease in consumers' willingness and ability to pay

A change in preferences causes a change in demand, not a change in quantity demanded.

substitutes: products/services used in place of each other to satisfy the same want

What happens to your demand for iPods when the price of other MP3 players falls drastically? You are not willing to pay as much for an iPod, as your smart choice now involves a much cheaper alternative. A fall in the price of a substitute causes a decrease in demand for the related product.

If the price of water skyrockets because of a drought, your willingness to pay for Gatorade increases. A rise in the price of a substitute causes an increased demand for the related product.

Complements are products/services that tend to be used together to satisfy the same want. iTunes and iPods are complementary products, as are hot dogs and hot dog buns, or cars and gasoline.

If song prices at the iTunes Store drop from 99 cents to 49 cents, that makes owning an iPod more attractive, and will increase your willingness to pay for an iPod. A fall in the price of a complement causes an increased demand for the related product because the cost of using both products together has decreased.

When gasoline prices rose significantly in 2008, gas-guzzling 8-cylinder SUVs became much more expensive to operate. The rise in gas prices caused a decrease in the demand for 8-cylinder SUVs. A rise in the price of a complement causes a decreased demand for the related product because the cost of using both products together has increased.

complements: products/services used together to satisfy the same want

Income   If you now had a million dollars, that would have a large impact on your demand for products/services. Demand reflects your willingness and ability to pay. With more money, or more income, you are more able (and still willing) to pay for things and not worry about it. But not always.

Take your demand for iPods from Figure 2.3, before any advertising (columns 1 and 3). If your income increased, the impact on your willingness and ability to pay would be similar to the impact of an increase in preferences (column 2). At each quantity, you are still willing and now *able to pay more*, so the increase in income causes an increase in demand. The intensity of your wants doesn't change with a change in income, but what you have to *give up in other products/services* falls. With more income, you can spend more on an iPod and still have lots of extra cash to buy other things. Higher income lowers your real opportunity cost of spending. There is more "get" and less "give up."

If unfortunately your income falls, so does your ability to pay, and your demand for iPods would decrease.

Economists call products like iPods **normal goods** — products/services that you buy more of when your income increases. For a normal good, an increase in income causes an increase in demand, and a decrease in income causes a decrease in demand.

normal goods: products/services you buy more of when your income increases

But not all products are normal goods. Can you think of products/services you buy now as a poor student that you will buy *less of* when your income goes up? If you have been living on Kraft Dinner, you may never want to eat it again once you can afford real food. And what about those endless bus rides? If you could afford a car, what would happen to your demand for public transit?

Economists call these products/services, where an increase in income causes a *decrease* in demand, **inferior goods** — products/services that you buy less of when your income increases. Similarly, a decrease in income causes an increase in demand for inferior goods.

inferior goods: products/services you buy less of when your income increases

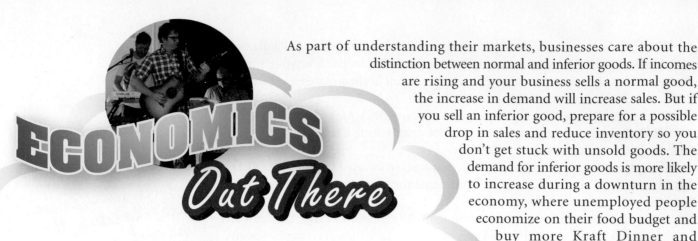

ECONOMICS Out There

As part of understanding their markets, businesses care about the distinction between normal and inferior goods. If incomes are rising and your business sells a normal good, the increase in demand will increase sales. But if you sell an inferior good, prepare for a possible drop in sales and reduce inventory so you don't get stuck with unsold goods. The demand for inferior goods is more likely to increase during a downturn in the economy, where unemployed people economize on their food budget and buy more Kraft Dinner and Hamburger Helper.

Expected Future Prices

Smart choices depend not only on prices and incomes today, but also on our expectation of future prices. Consumers choose between substitutes, and one of many possible substitutions is a purchase tomorrow for a purchase today. We do this all the time with gasoline. If it's the weekend and you decide to wait until mid-week to buy gas because you expect the price to fall, that decreases your demand for gasoline today. Likewise, if you are expecting prices to rise, you fill up now, increasing your demand for gasoline today. Notice that your decision is not determined by the current price (that would be a quantity demanded decision), but only by whether you expect the current price (whatever it may be) to fall or rise in the future.

A fall in expected future price causes a decrease in demand today (bargain in future). A rise in expected future price causes an increase in demand today (bargain today).

An expected future price fall causes a decrease in demand today. An expected future price rise causes an increase in demand today.

Number of Consumers   So far, for all the factors that change demand, the explanations are the same for a single individual as they are for the group of all consumers whose combined willingness and ability to pay make up market demand. For any quantity demanded, we examine how a change in each factor affects the price the consumer is willing and able to pay. Each such change in demand changes marginal benefit and moves the margin. For the fifth factor, the number of consumers, the explanation makes more sense if we reverse the story. Start with any price, and examine how a change in consumer numbers affects quantity demanded. For each price, if the number of consumers increases, we need to add together all the quantities demanded by all consumers at that price.

Let's take our earlier table of the market demand for water, and add a third column showing the quantity demanded after many new households move into the city and start using water. Take a look at Figure 2.4.

Figure 2.4　Market Demand for Water with More Households

Price (cubic metre)	Quantity Demanded (000's of cubic metres/month)	Quantity Demanded with More Households (000's of cubic metres/month)
$1.00	5	10
$1.50	4	8
$2.00	3	6
$2.50	2	4
$3.00	1	2

Not surprisingly with additional households (last column), at any price (first column) the quantity demanded is greater than it was originally (middle column). The increased number of consumers causes an increase in demand, just as an increase in preferences or an increase in income (for normal goods) causes an increase in demand. A decrease in the number of consumers causes a decrease in demand, just as a decrease in the price of a substitute product/service or a decrease in expected future prices causes a decrease in demand.

Increased number of consumers causes an increase in demand. Decreased number of consumers causes a decrease in demand.

Any increase (or decrease) in demand can be described in alternative ways. For the four previous factors, the description for an increase in demand is:

- At any given quantity demanded, consumers are willing and able to pay a higher price.

For the number of consumers, the description for an increase in demand is:

- At any given price, consumers plan to buy a larger quantity.

For an increase in demand, these two alternative descriptions of the connection between price and quantity demanded are summarized in Figure 2.5. Depending on the economic event you are trying to make sense of, sometimes you will use one description, and sometimes the other.

Figure 2.5　Relating Price and Quantity Demanded for an Increase in Demand

Given quantity demanded	⟷	Higher price
Higher quantity demanded	⟷	Given price

Saving the Law of Demand

You have learned to distinguish between a change in quantity demanded (caused by a change in the price of the product) and a change in demand (caused by changes in preferences, prices of related products, income, expected future prices, and/or number of consumers). Can we now explain why, when gasoline prices increased from $0.99 per litre to $1.36 per litre between 2006 and 2008, the quantity of gasoline motorists bought actually increased? Can we save the law of demand?

According to the law of demand, if the price of a product rises, the quantity demanded of the product decreases (as long as other factors besides price do not change). The rise in gas prices alone would have caused a decrease in quantity demanded, *but other things also changed.*

While a complete explanation is more complex (involving supply factors from Chapter 3 as well as demand), a major change was the increased number of drivers and cars on the road. This increase in the number of consumers increased demand for gasoline. The impact of the increase in demand outweighed the impact of the decrease in quantity demanded.

To conclusively explain whether the witch's curse or the arsenic killed the poor young man, you need a controlled experiment. And without the economist's equivalent of a controlled experiment — the mental distinction between quantity demanded and demand — you never would have been able to explain what happened in the gasoline market.

Figure 2.6 is a good study device for reviewing the difference between the law of demand (focused on quantity demanded) and the factors that change demand.

Figure 2.6	Law of Demand and Changes in Demand

The Law of Demand	
The quantity demanded of a product/service	
Decreases if:	*Increases if:*
■ price of the product/service rises	■ price of the product/service falls

Changes in Demand	
The demand for a product/service	
Decreases if:	*Increases if:*
■ preferences decrease	■ preferences increase
■ price of a substitute falls	■ price of a substitute rises
■ price of a complement rises	■ price of a complement falls
■ income decreases (normal good)	■ income increases (normal good)
■ income increases (inferior good)	■ income decreases (inferior good)
■ expected future price falls	■ expected future price rises
■ number of customers decreases	■ number of customers increases

Refresh
2.4

1. Explain the difference between a change in quantity demanded and a change in demand. Distinguish the five factors that can change demand.

2. Roses sell for about $40 a bouquet most of the year, and worldwide sales are 6 million bouquets per month. Every February, the price of roses doubles to $80 a bouquet, but the quantity of roses demanded and sold also increases, to 24 million bouquets per month. The cost of producing roses doesn't change throughout the year. Can you explain what else is going on that saves the law of demand?

3. There are some "status goods," like Rolex watches, that people want to own *because* they are expensive. In contradiction to the law of demand, if Rolex watches were less expensive, few "status seeking" consumers would demand them. Is there any way to reconcile these products/services with the law of demand? You might think about what it is that consumers are buying — watches or status? And how does the existence of cheap "knock-off" imitations of Rolex watches fit with the law of demand?

2.5 Just How Badly Do You Want It?
Price Elasticity of Demand and Total Revenue

Don't you love a good sale — 50 percent off, 70 percent off? Most consumers do. No matter how much you are willing and able to pay for a product/service, it's always a treat to pay less, which leaves you with cash to buy more of anything you want.

But do *businesses* love a good sale? Profit-seeking businesses would rather charge higher prices for what they sell. But to get consumers to buy, businesses must pick price points that match the market's (all consumers') willingness and ability to pay. Higher prices might not always be best for business. Why do businesses have 70-percent-off sales, voluntarily lowering prices and bringing in less per unit?

I'm sure you have heard the answer to this question: "They'll make it up on volume!" Lower prices mean lower profit margins per unit, but a greater quantity sold.

How do businesses decide whether they will be better off selling to consumers at a higher price or a lower price?

We know from the law of demand that (all other things unchanged) a rise in price causes a decrease in quantity demanded, and a fall in price (sale's on!) causes an increase in quantity demanded (more volume). A smart business pricing decision depends on by how much quantity demanded changes when price changes. What changes more, the price or the quantity? This responsiveness of quantity demanded to a change in price is related to just how badly consumers want the product/service.

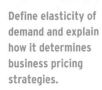

Define elasticity of demand and explain how it determines business pricing strategies.

◄

Sales are good for consumers, but are they always bad for businesses?

The tool that businesses use every day to measure consumer responsiveness and make pricing decisions is what economists call the **price elasticity of demand** (say *that* three times quickly for a tongue twister). This section will help you make sense of that tool, which businesses mercifully abbreviate to elasticity. **Elasticity** measures by how much quantity demanded responds to a change in price.

elasticity (or price elasticity of demand): measures by how much quantity demanded responds to a change in price

Measuring Your Responsiveness

Elasticity is all about responsiveness. When you pull on an elastic, by how much does it stretch or respond? When the price of a product changes, price elasticity of demand measures by how much quantity demanded responds.

If you have diabetes, you have a high willingness to pay for insulin. What happens to the quantity of insulin demanded when the price rises? Not much decrease. If the price rises enough, quantity demanded may decrease slightly as diabetics who are poorest perhaps try to get by with a little less per dose. But for the market demand for insulin, there is very little response of quantity demanded to a rise in price. Economists describe the demand for insulin as **inelastic**: There is a small response (or "give") in the quantity demanded when price rises.

What about the market demand for yellow tennis balls? If the price of yellow tennis balls rises, what happens? Most players consider green or orange tennis balls to be identical substitutes, and aren't willing to pay a premium for yellow. Players switch to non-yellow balls, so the quantity demanded of yellow tennis balls decreases drastically. There is a large response of quantity demanded to a rise in price. The demand for yellow tennis balls is called **elastic**: there is a large response in the quantity demanded when price rises.

Businesses use a simple formula to calculate elasticity.

$$\text{Price elasticity of demand} = \frac{\text{Percentage change in quantity demanded}}{\text{Percentage change in price}}$$

The formula assumes that all of the other five factors that can affect demand are unchanged, so this is a controlled measurement of just the relationship (in the law of demand) between quantity demanded and price.

Let's substitute some numbers into the formula for our examples.

For insulin, if a 10-percent rise in price causes a 2-percent decrease in quantity demanded, the calculation is

$$\begin{array}{l}\text{Price elasticity of demand} \\ \text{for insulin}\end{array} = \frac{2 \text{ percent}}{10 \text{ percent}} = 0.2$$

Because the percentage change in quantity in the numerator (2) is less than the percentage change in price in the denominator (10), the value for elasticity is less than 1. Any elasticity value less than 1 is considered to be inelastic.

(If you are thinking that my math isn't quite right, good for you! Technically, the correct answer would be − 0.2. However, even an economist will ignore the negative sign in calculating price elasticity of demand. You will be pleased to know that economists don't like negative numbers any more than you do.)

For yellow tennis balls, if a 10-percent rise in price causes a 50-percent decrease in quantity demanded, the calculation is

$$\begin{array}{l}\text{Price elasticity of demand} \\ \text{for yellow tennis balls}\end{array} = \frac{50 \text{ percent}}{10 \text{ percent}} = 5$$

Whenever you see the word "elasticity," think "responsiveness."

inelastic:
for inelastic demand, small response in quantity demanded when price rises

elastic:
for elastic demand, large response in quantity demanded when price rises

Demand is inelastic when the calculation of $\frac{(\% \text{ change in quantity})}{(\% \text{ change in price})}$ gives a value less than 1.

Demand is elastic when the calculation of $\frac{(\% \text{ change in quantity})}{(\% \text{ change in price})}$ gives a value greater than 1.

Because the percentage change in quantity in the numerator (50) is greater than the percentage change in price in the denominator (10), the value for elasticity is greater than 1. Any elasticity value greater than 1 is elastic. So when the value for elasticity is less than 1, demand is inelastic. Are you wondering what demand is called when elasticity is exactly equal to 1? No, I didn't think so. But for the sake of completeness, here's your answer: When elasticity equals 1, demand is "unit elastic." The percentage change in quantity equals the percentage change in price.

One other way to think about the different values for elasticity is willingness to shop elsewhere if you don't get a low price.

If the price rises for products/services with:

- *inelastic demands,* consumers have a low willingness to shop elsewhere.
- *elastic demands,* consumers have a high willingness to shop elsewhere.

Why Are You (Un)Responsive? Factors Determining Elasticity

Three main factors influence price elasticity of demand, or "willingness to shop elsewhere if you don't get a low price": the availability of substitutes, time to adjust, and proportion of income spent on a product/service. Let's look at each.

Available Substitutes   The law of demand says that when something becomes more expensive, people economize on its use and look for substitutes. The more substitutes there are, the easier it is to switch away from a product/service whose price rises, and the more elastic is demand. Yellow tennis balls have excellent substitutes, so the demand for tennis balls is elastic. Insulin has almost no substitutes, so the demand for insulin is inelastic.

The more, and better, substitutes available, the greater elasticity of demand.

Time to Adjust to Price Rise   When prices rise, it often takes time to adjust and to find substitutes. If gasoline prices rise and you have to drive to work, you can't do much initially to decrease your quantity of gasoline demanded — you can cut back on pleasure driving and errands. With more time, you could arrange a car pool, and with much more time, you might buy a more fuel-efficient car or move closer to work. Time allows consumers to find substitutes. The longer the time to adjust to a price rise, the more elastic demand becomes.

The longer time to adjust to a price rise, the more elastic demand becomes.

Proportion of Income Spent on a Product/Service   Suppose the price of salt doubles from $1 per kilo to $2 per kilo. By how much will you reduce your quantity demanded of salt? Not much. What if the price of a car doubles from $20 000 to $40 000? The quantity demanded of cars will collapse. The key difference between the examples is in the proportion of income spent on the product. We spend a tiny fraction of our income on salt, so a big price rise doesn't increase our total expenditure much. But buying a car is often the largest purchase you will make, other than buying a house: A big price rise makes it unaffordable. The greater the proportion of income spent on a product, the greater the elasticity of demand.

The greater the proportion of income spent on a product, the greater elasticity of demand.

When Are Price Cuts Smart Business? Elasticity and Total Revenue

If you hold a 70-percent-off sale, consumers will be happy, but will your business be better off? Whether a business will be better off from raising prices or cutting prices depends on the elasticity of demand for its product/service.

"Better off," in this chapter, means the business will have higher total revenue. **Total revenue** is all of the money received from sales, and is equal to the price per unit (P) multiplied by the quantity sold (Q).

$$\text{Total revenue} = P \times Q$$

A wonderfully simple relationship exists between elasticity and total revenue. When a business cuts prices,

- if demand for its product/service is *elastic,* the percentage increase in quantity is greater than the percentage decrease in price, so *total revenue* ($P \times Q$) *increases.*
- if demand for its product/service is *inelastic,* the percentage increase in quantity is less than the percentage decrease in price, so *total revenue* ($P \times Q$) *decreases.*

Figure 2.7 summarizes the relationship between elasticity and total revenue for a price cut.

Figure 2.7	Elasticity and Total Revenue	
When Demand Is:		**Price Cut Causes:**
Elastic (> 1)	% change in Q > % change in P	Increased total revenue
Inelastic (< 1)	% change in Q < % change in P	Decreased total revenue

For the sake of completeness, when demand is unit elastic (= 1), the percentage increase in quantity equals the percentage decrease in price, so total revenue remains the same.

Price Cuts Are Smart When Facing Elastic Demand
So a price cut is a smart decision when your business faces elastic demand. You receive a lower price on each unit sold, but you do make it up on volume! The percentage increase in quantity outweighs the percentage decrease in price, so total revenue increases.

If you are selling yellow tennis balls, consumers' demand for your product is elastic, which means that if they don't get a low price, they are very willing and able to shop elsewhere because good substitutes are available. When you cut the price of yellow tennis balls even a little, you attract all of the bargain-hunters who are currently using green or orange tennis balls. Your total revenue increases because the large increase in quantity outweighs the small cut in price.

total revenue: all money a business receives from sales, equal to price per unit (P) multiplied by quantity sold (Q)

Price cuts are the smart choice facing elastic demand, and, increase total revenue.

Price Rises Are Smart When Facing Inelastic Demand   The smart decision when your business faces inelastic demand is to raise prices. You receive a higher price on each unit sold, and while you lose some sales, the percentage increase in price is greater than the percentage decrease in quantity, so total revenue increases.

If you are selling insulin, consumers' demand is inelastic, which means that they will not easily shop elsewhere because there are no good substitutes. When you raise the price of insulin, you don't lose many customers. Your total revenue increases because the increase in price outweighs the small decrease in quantity.

Smart Pricing Decisions Depend on Elasticity of Demand   Price elasticity of demand is important for any business pricing decision, even the price you get in haggling with a car dealer. Most consumers hate haggling over price because the dealer has better information about costs and knows how low he is willing to go on price. Your best strategy as a buyer is to try to convince the dealer that you will walk out if you don't get a low price, that you don't like this particular car that much and are considering alternative models from other manufacturers, or that you are not very wealthy. In other words, *you want the dealer to believe that your demand is elastic,* that you are willing to shop elsewhere if you don't get a low price because good substitutes are available. If you convince the dealer, then his best pricing decision is to offer you a very low price, because he believes that if he doesn't he will lose the sale entirely.

On the other hand, if the dealer thinks that you are not likely to walk out, that you love this particular car much more than any alternatives, or that you are wealthy and not price conscious, he takes these as signals that your demand is inelastic. His best pricing decision, because he believes this is a pretty sure sale, is to try to convince you to take expensive options that will actually increase the price above the sticker price.

All businesses have to live by the law of demand — a rise in price causes a decrease in quantity demanded. Smart businesses choose their price points depending on how much consumers' quantity demanded responds to a change in price — in other words, on price elasticity of demand.

> *Price rises are the smart choice facing inelastic demand, and increase total revenue.*

Refresh 2.5

1. Explain the relationship between price and quantity demanded for inelastic demand and for elastic demand.

2. If a jewellery store cuts its prices by 20 percent, and finds that its quantity sold increases by 40 percent, calculate its price elasticity of demand. Is it elastic or inelastic?

3. Concession stands at movie theatres charge high prices for popcorn, drinks, and other refreshments. This pricing strategy increases total revenue. What does that imply about the price elasticity of demand for refreshments in movie theatres? What theatre policy helps make this demand elastic or inelastic?

www.myeconlab.com

CHAPTER SUMMARY

2.1 PUT YOUR MONEY WHERE YOUR MOUTH IS: WEIGHING BENEFITS, COSTS, AND SUBSTITUTES

Your willingness to buy a product/service depends on your ability to pay, comparative benefits and costs, and the availability of substitutes.

- **Preferences** — your wants and their intensities.
- **Demand** — consumers' willingness and ability to pay for a particular product/service.
- For any choice, what you are willing to pay or give up depends on the cost and availability of substitutes.

2.2 LIVING ON THE EDGE: SMART CHOICES ARE MARGINAL CHOICES

Key 2 for smart choices states, "Count only additional benefits and additional costs." Additional benefit means marginal benefit — not total benefit — and marginal benefit changes with circumstances.

- **Marginal benefit** — additional benefit from a choice, and changes with circumstances.
- Marginal benefit explains the diamond/water paradox. Why do diamonds cost more than water, when water is far more valuable for survival? Willingness to pay depends on marginal benefit, not total benefit. Because water is abundant, marginal benefit is low. Because diamonds are scarce, marginal benefit is high.

2.3 WHEN THE PRICE ISN'T RIGHT: THE LAW OF DEMAND

If the price of a product/service rises, the quantity demanded decreases. Consumers economize on products/services that become more expensive by switching to substitutes.

- **Quantity demanded** — amount you actually plan to buy at a given price.
- **Market demand** — sum of demands of all individuals willing and able to buy a particular product/service.

- **Law of demand** — if the price of a product/service rises, quantity demanded decreases.

2.4 MOVING THE MARGINS: WHAT CAN CHANGE DEMAND?

Quantity demanded is changed only by a change in price. Demand is changed by all other influences on consumer choice.

- Demand is a catch-all term summarizing all possible influences on consumers' willingness and ability to pay for a particular product/service.
    - **Increase in demand** — increase in consumers' willingness and ability to pay.
    - **Decrease in demand** — decrease in consumers' willingness and ability to pay.
- Demand changes with changes in preferences, prices of related goods, income, expected future price, and number of consumers. For example, demand increases with:
    - increase in preferences.
    - rise in price of a **substitute** — products/services used in place of each other to satisfy the same want.
    - fall in price of a **complement** — products/services used together to satisfy the same want.
    - increase in income for **normal goods** — products/services you buy more of when your income increases.
    - decrease in income for **inferior goods** — products/services you buy less of when your income increases.
    - rise in expected future prices.
    - increase in number of consumers.

2.5 JUST HOW BADLY DO YOU WANT IT? PRICE ELASTICITY OF DEMAND AND TOTAL REVENUE

Elasticity measures how responsive quantity demanded is to a change in price, and determines business pricing strategies to earn maximum total revenue. To earn maximum total revenue, businesses cut prices when demand is elastic and raise prices when demand is inelastic.

- The tool that businesses use to measure consumer responsiveness when making pricing decisions is **elasticity** (or **price elasticity of demand**), which measures by how much quantity demanded responds to a change in price.
- The formula is:

$$\text{Price elasticity of demand} = \frac{\text{Percentage change in quantity demanded}}{\text{Percentage change in price}}$$

- **Inelastic** — For inelastic demand, small response in quantity demanded when price rises.
    - Example: Demand for insulin by a diabetic.
    - Value for formula is less than one.
    - Low willingness to shop elsewhere.

- **Elastic** — For elastic demand, large response in quantity demanded when price rises.
  - Example: Demand for yellow tennis balls.
  - Value for formula is greater than one.
  - High willingness to shop elsewhere.
- The price elasticity of demand of a product/service is influenced by:
  - substitutes — more substitute goods mean more elastic demand.
  - time to adjust — longer time to adjust means more elastic demand.
  - proportion of income spent on a product/service — greater proportion of income spent means more elastic demand.
- **Total revenue** — (all money a business receives from sales) = price per unit *(P)* multiplied by quantity sold *(Q)*.
  - Price rises are the smart choice facing inelastic demand, and increase total revenue.
  - Price cuts are the smart choice facing elastic demand, and increase total revenue.

TRUE/FALSE

Circle the correct answer.

2.1 WEIGHING BENEFITS, COSTS, AND SUBSTITUTES

1. Demand is the same as wants.   **True**   **False**

2. Your willingness to pay for a product depends on what substitutes are available, and what they cost.   **True**   **False**

2.2 SMART CHOICES ARE MARGINAL CHOICES

3. Marginal cost is the same as additional cost.   **True**   **False**

4. The flat fee charged at an all-you-can-eat restaurant should not influence how much food you eat once you are seated.   **True**   **False**

5. Marginal benefit is always equal to average benefit.   **True**   **False**

2.3 THE LAW OF DEMAND

6. Quantity demanded is the same as demand.   **True**   **False**

7. If the price of a product/service changes, that affects quantity demanded.   **True**   **False**

2.4 WHAT CAN CHANGE DEMAND?

8. If your willingness to pay decreases, there will be a decrease in demand.   **True**   **False**

9. If your ability to pay decreases, there will be an increase in demand.   **True**   **False**

10. Throughout the month of December, the quantity of video game consoles purchased often increases even as the price rises. This violates the law of demand.   **True**   **False**

2.5 PRICE ELASTICITY OF DEMAND AND TOTAL REVENUE

11. When customers react quickly to a price change, this product has high elasticity of demand.   **True**   **False**

12. Any elasticity value less than 1 is considered to be inelastic.   **True**   **False**

13. The fewer substitutes available, the greater the elasticity of demand.   **True**   **False**

14. When negotiating a price on an expensive purchase, you want the dealer to believe that your demand is elastic — that is, that you are willing to shop elsewhere if you don't get a low price because good substitutes are available.   **True**   **False**

15. Total revenue ($P \times Q$) decreases when a business lowers the price of an inelastic good.   **True**   **False**

MULTIPLE CHOICE

Circle the correct answer.

2.1 WEIGHING BENEFITS, COSTS, AND SUBSTITUTES

1. Economists describe the list of your wants and their intensities as
   A) demand.
   B) supply.
   C) benefit.
   D) preferences.

2. Costs are
   A) worth money.
   B) whatever we are willing to give up.
   C) the answer to the question "What do we want?"
   D) whatever we are willing to get.

3. All-you-can-eat buffet restaurants charge a fixed fee for eating. With each plate that Anna consumes, she experiences
   A) decreasing marginal costs to eating.
   B) increasing marginal costs to eating.
   C) decreasing marginal benefits to eating.
   D) increasing marginal benefits to eating.

4. Thinking like economists, a dating couple should break up when the
   A) total benefits of dating are greater than the total costs of dating.
   B) total costs of dating are greater than the total benefits of dating.
   C) additional benefits of dating are greater than the additional costs of dating.
   D) additional costs of dating are greater than the additional benefits of dating.

5. Peter would like to have two cars, one for everyday and the other for special occasions. However, he has only $10 000, so he buys only one car. His quantity demanded of cars is
   A) 1.
   B) 2.
   C) 20 000.
   D) 40 000.

2.3 THE LAW OF DEMAND

6. When the price of a product rises,
   A) consumers look for more expensive substitutes.
   B) quantity demanded increases.
   C) consumers look for cheaper substitutes.
   D) consumers use more of the product.

7. If home owners were charged for garbage collection on the basis of the number of garbage bags used, this would result in a(n)
   A) increase in demand.
   B) decrease in demand.
   C) increase in quantity demanded.
   D) decrease in quantity demanded.

8. What of the following is most likely to be an inferior good?

   A) Fast food

   B) Antique furniture

   C) School bags

   D) Textbooks

9. Demand

   A) increases with a rise in price.

   B) is the same as quantity demanded.

   C) changes with income.

   D) decreases with a rise in price.

10. If the price of cars went up, the demand for tires would

   A) increase.

   B) decrease.

   C) stay the same.

   D) depend on the price of tires.

11. Which of the following could cause an increase in demand for a product?

   A) Increase in income

   B) Decrease in income

   C) Increase in the price of a substitute

   D) All of the above

12. If Kraft Dinner is an inferior good, then a rise in the price of Kraft Dinner will cause a(n)

   A) decrease in demand for Kraft Dinner.

   B) increase in demand for Kraft Dinner.

   C) increase in the quantity demanded of Kraft Dinner.

   D) decrease in the quantity demanded of Kraft Dinner.

2.5 PRICE ELASTICITY OF DEMAND AND TOTAL REVENUE

13. If a business lowers prices, total revenue increases if price elasticity of demand is

   A) less than 1.

   B) greater than 1.

   C) equal to 1.

   D) equal to 0.

14. The fact that butter and margarine are close substitutes makes
    A) demand for butter more elastic.
    B) demand for butter more inelastic.
    C) butter an inferior good.
    D) margarine an inferior good.

15. After visiting a number of restaurants in Paris where fee-for-service toilets are commonplace, a Canadian restaurant owner decides to charge customers a fee for bathroom use. How will bathroom use inside the owner's restaurant most likely change?
    A) Quantity demanded will decrease; total revenue will fall.
    B) Quantity demanded will increase; total revenue will rise.
    C) Quantity demanded will decrease; total revenue will rise.
    D) Quantity demanded will increase; total revenue will fall.

SHORT ANSWER

Write a short answer to each question. Your answer may be in point form.

1. What is a smart choice?

2. If you don't have enough money to buy a product, can you still have a demand for it?

3. Consider the diamond/water paradox — diamonds are very expensive but not required for life, but water, a necessity for life, is relatively inexpensive. What if you are Bill Gates walking through the desert alone with pockets full of diamonds? How will this affect your marginal benefits?

4. Advertising is designed to increase your preference for a product/service. Provide an example of a slogan that has changed or shaped your preferences.

5. Suppose your community council is considering the idea of returning to a flat monthly rate payment scheme for water usage. Explain what will happen to the demand for the following products.
    A) Water
    B) Orange juice
    C) Soap
    D) Rubber ducky bath toys

6. Identify which factor (preferences, prices of related products/services, income, expected future prices, or the number of consumers) will cause a *change in demand* in the following circumstances:

   A) The impact of building a new apartment on the demand for groceries at the local store

   B) The impact of downloading music on the demand for CDs

   C) The impact on the demand for cars of delaying buying expensive items in anticipation of a future decrease in the GST

7. Young drivers account for more than 35 percent of all drivers involved in fatal accidents, despite representing only 20 percent of all licensed drivers. Often, alcohol is involved. Explain how each of the following policies would affect the demand for alcohol.

   A) Increasing the minimum age for drinking.

   B) Raising the price (through higher taxes) of alcohol.

   C) Using advertising campaigns to discourage alcohol usage.

8. State whether demand for the following products/services is elastic or inelastic.

   A) Pimple medication

   B) Pencils

   C) Clothes

   D) Parasuco jeans

   E) Newspaper

   F) Toilet paper

9. Evidence suggests that babies are a *normal good* for lower income earners and an *inferior good* for higher income earners. Explain what this means by using the definitions of "normal" and "inferior" goods.

10. In the women's clothing market, which is likely to be more inelastic, demand for the latest fashions or demand for clothing in general? Use your answer to explain why when clothing stores have sales they usually exclude the latest arrivals.

Show Me the Money

The Law of Supply

LEARNING OBJECTIVES

After reading this chapter, you should be able to:

3.1 Explain why marginal costs are ultimately opportunity costs.

3.2 Define sunk costs and explain why they do not influence smart, forward-looking decisions.

3.3 Describe the relationship between price and quantity supplied, and identify the roles of higher profits and marginal opportunity costs of production.

3.4 Explain the difference between a change in quantity supplied and a change in supply, and list five factors that change supply.

3.5 Explain elasticity of supply and how it helps businesses avoid disappointed customers.

MONEY IS THE MARKET'S REWARD to individuals or businesses who give up something of value. Your boss rewards you with an hourly wage for supplying labour services. A business producing a top-selling product is rewarded with profits (as long as revenues are greater than costs).

What goes into decisions to sell, or supply, services or products to the market? What price do you need to get to be willing to work? How much money does it take before a business is willing to supply?

This chapter focuses on choices businesses make every day in producing and selling. Economists use the term *supply* to summarize all the influences on business decisions.

Business decisions seem more "objective" than consumer decisions which seem to be based on "subjective" desires and preferences. After all, there is a bottom line in business with prices, costs, and profits. But business supply decisions are not as straightforward or objective as you might think.

3.1 What Does It Really Cost? Costs Are Opportunity Costs

Explain why marginal costs are ultimately opportunity costs.

Supply, like demand, starts with decision makers choosing among alternative opportunities by comparing expected benefits and costs at the margin.

How Much to Work?

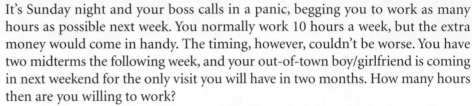

It's Sunday night and your boss calls in a panic, begging you to work as many hours as possible next week. You normally work 10 hours a week, but the extra money would come in handy. The timing, however, couldn't be worse. You have two midterms the following week, and your out-of-town boy/girlfriend is coming in next weekend for the only visit you will have in two months. How many hours then are you willing to work?

Of course you will make a smart choice, weighing the additional benefits and costs of working extra hours. The additional, or marginal, benefits are the $10 per hour you earn (plus something for the boss's goodwill). The additional costs are opportunity costs — the alternative uses of the time you have to give up.

You want to attend all your classes, keep time for studying for midterms, and definitely keep the weekend free. You are willing to give up the 10 hours a week you spend playing *World of Warcraft*. When your boss hears you are willing to work only a total of 20 hours, while she is hoping for 60 hours, she instantly replies, "What if I pay you double time for all your hours next week?"

Well, that changes things. At $20 per hour, you will willingly give up your game time, skip a few classes where you are not having a test, but still keep the weekend free. You are up to 35 hours of work, but your boss is totally desperate and asks again, "What if I pay you triple time?"

At that price, you will also cut back on your sleep, reduce your study time, and try to reschedule your weekend visit. (Is the visit worth giving up $500 for a weekend's work?) Your boss relaxes a bit when you promise 55 hours.

Notice that the quantity of work or time that you are willing to supply to your boss increases as the price she pays you rises. In order to get you to divert more of your time from alternative uses, she has to offer you more money (which increases her costs).

For your supply decision, there are always alternative uses of your time, and each use has a different cost to you. Your game time is worth the least to you, the weekend time the most. As the price offered for your time rises, you work more, first giving up the least valuable alternative use of time, and then giving up increasingly valuable time. Your willingness to work changes with circumstances, depending on the price offered and the opportunity cost — the value you place on alternative uses of your time.

Your willingness to work depends on the price offered and on the opportunity costs of alternative uses of your time.

marginal cost: *additional opportunity cost of increasing quantity supplied, and changes with circumstances*

The economist's term for the additional opportunity cost associated with alternative uses of your time is **marginal cost** — the additional opportunity cost of increasing the quantity of whatever is being supplied. For you, the opportunity cost, or marginal cost, of an hour of game time is less than the opportunity cost, or marginal cost, of an hour of weekend time. As you shift your time away from alternative uses to work, *the marginal cost of your time increases*. You give up the least valuable time first, and continue giving up increasingly valuable time as the price you are offered rises.

Comparing Demand and Supply Decisions   There are similarities between the demand decisions from Chapter 2 and your supply decision. For products or services you are thinking of buying, there are always substitutes available, which is why consumers buy less of a product/service as the price rises — we all switch to cheaper alternatives. Willingness to pay depends on available substitutes and changes with circumstances — the marginal benefit of the first bottle of Gatorade is greater than the marginal benefit of the second bottle. For the hours you are thinking of supplying, there are always alternative uses of your time, with different values to you. Willingness to supply hours depends on those alternatives and changes with circumstances — the opportunity cost of giving up your gaming hours is less than the opportunity cost of giving up your weekend hours. That is one reason why suppliers supply more as the price rises — higher prices are necessary to compensate for the higher opportunity costs of more additional time (or other resources) given up.

There are also two important differences between smart demand choices and smart supply choices. First, for demand, marginal benefit — the maximum you are willing to pay — *decreases as you buy more.* For supply, marginal cost — the minimum you need to be paid — *increases as you supply more.*

Second, the comparison of benefits and costs is reversed. For demand, marginal benefit is your subjective satisfaction, and marginal cost is measured in dollars — the price you must pay. For supply, marginal benefit is measured in dollars — the hourly wage rate you earn — and marginal cost is an opportunity cost, the value of alternative uses of the time that you must give up.

What Do Inputs *Really* Cost?

Any business supply decision involves the same smart choice between marginal benefit and marginal cost as your work decision. The marginal benefit or reward from selling is measured in the dollar price you receive, and all marginal costs are ultimately opportunity costs.

Let's look at a business: Paola's Piercing and Fingernail Parlour (PPF Parlour). To supply her services to the market, Paola, like any businessperson, has to buy inputs (studs, tools, polish), pay rent to her landlord, and pay wages to her employees. What do those hard dollar actual costs have to do with opportunity costs? Which costs are *real* costs?

Take the nickel studs Paola buys today for $1 each from a stud supplier. If the world price of nickel rises because of increasing demand from China for the metal, Paola will have to pay more for her studs. The stud supplier will sell to Paola only as long as she pays as much as the best price he can get from another customer, whether in China or Canada. Paola's stud cost has to cover the opportunity cost of the stud supplier.

The same goes for Paola's rent or the wages she pays to her employees. If Paola's landlord can find another tenant willing to pay more for the shop space, then once Paola's lease is up, she will have to pay that higher amount or the landlord will rent to the other tenant. If Paola's employees, like you, have alternative uses of their time that they value more than what she pays, or if they can get job offers elsewhere at higher wages, Paola will have to match the offers or start advertising for help wanted.

Every buying or selling choice is a fork in the road. Buying — there are substitute products. Selling — there are alternative uses of your time. Opportunity cost of any choice is value of best alternative you give up.

Supply and demand choices reverse the comparison of benefits and costs. Supply — marginal benefit is measured in dollars (wage you earn); marginal cost is opportunity cost of time. Demand — marginal benefit is satisfaction you get; marginal cost is measured in dollars (price you pay).

When businesses purchase an input, marginal cost can be stated in dollars. But marginal costs are ultimately opportunity costs, value of best alternative use of that input.

To hire or purchase inputs, a business must pay a price that matches the best opportunity cost of the input owner. The real cost of any input is determined by the best alternative use of that input. All marginal costs are ultimately opportunity costs. Marginal costs can be stated in dollars, but they are an opportunity cost — the value of the best alternative use of that input.

As we will see in the next section, Paola's smart business supply decision will depend on whether the price she receives for a piercing (marginal benefit) is greater than her marginal opportunity costs.

Refresh

3.1

1. What is the real cost to a business of hiring or purchasing any input?

2. Microsoft released a limited supply of Xbox 360s in 2005 with a list price — or "real" price — of $400. The units immediately started selling on eBay and other online auction websites for far more than $400. What do you think determined the "real" price of an Xbox?

3. If a recession makes it much harder for workers to find better-paying jobs, what might happen to Paola's labour costs?

www.myeconlab.com

3.2 Forget It, It's History: Sunk Costs Don't Matter for Future Choices

Define sunk costs and explain why they do not influence smart, forward-looking decisions.

Past expenses are not part of additional opportunity costs and have no influence on smart choices.

sunk costs: past expenses that cannot be recovered

Paola must base her business supply decisions on her real costs, which are ultimately opportunity costs. But some expenses are not part of opportunity costs. This is another aspect of supply decisions that is not as straightforward as you might think.

Past expenses that cannot be reversed are *not* part of opportunity costs. If Paola has signed a year's lease for her rent that she cannot get out of, then her rent becomes irrelevant for her future decisions. How can that be?

Paola's decisions, or your decisions, are always forward looking. A smart decision about which fork in the road to take compares the expected future benefits and expected future costs of each path. When Paola has to decide whether to supply more piercings or fingernails, or to choose between buying new tools or hiring more employees, the rent expense is the same, so its influence cancels out. The past expense of rent paid (or legally contracted for) is the same no matter which fork Paola chooses, so it doesn't influence her decision.

These irreversible costs are called **sunk costs** — past, already-paid expenses that cannot be recovered. In other words, they are history. And history doesn't matter for forward-looking decisions. Sunk costs are the monies that have already been spent and cannot be recovered.

Suppose you have paid your tuition for this semester, and the refund date has passed. Your boss's request for extra hours comes at a time when you are already finding it hard to juggle work and school, and you are considering dropping out.

Your decision to drop out and work full-time (making your boss very happy), versus staying in school, depends on how you evaluate the expected benefits and costs of each fork in your career road. Dropping out and working more means more income right away, while staying in school means less income now but probably more in the future. (We will look at data connecting education and income in Chapter 11.) The tuition you paid is history. You can't get it back no matter which fork you choose, so it is not part of the opportunity costs of either choice.

Refresh 3.2

1. Why aren't sunk costs part of the opportunity costs of forward-looking decisions?

2. Suppose you have just paid your bus fare. A friend in a car pulls up and offers you a ride. Explain how you would decide between staying on the bus or taking the ride, and the influence of the paid fare.

3. If you bought a $100 textbook for a course, and then dropped out after the tuition refund date, is that $100 a sunk cost? Explain your answer.

www.myeconlab.com

3.3 More for More Money: The Law of Supply

Demand is not just what you want, but your willingness and ability to pay for a product/service — putting your money where your mouth is. Similarly, the economist's idea of supply is not just offering things for sale. **Supply** is the overall willingness of businesses (or individuals) to produce a particular product/service because the price covers all opportunity costs of production.

Let's look at how an economist would describe your supply decision about how many hours to work at your part-time job. Figure 3.1 combines price information — the minimum wage you are willing to accept — and the quantity of work you will supply at each wage.

Describe the relationship between price and quantity supplied, and identify the roles of higher profits and marginal opportunity costs of production.

supply: businesses' willingness to produce a particular product/service because price covers all opportunity costs

Figure 3.1	Your Supply of Hours Worked
Price per Hour (minimum willing to accept)	**Quantity Supplied** (hours of work)
$10	10–20
$20	35
$30	55

At a price of $10 per hour, your quantity supplied of work could be anywhere between 10 and 20 hours. At $20 per hour, your quantity supplied of work is 35 hours, and at $30 per hour, your quantity supplied is 55 hours.

Quantity supplied, as we will see, is not the same as supply. **Quantity supplied** is a more limited concept — the quantity you actually plan to supply at a given price, taking into account everything that affects your willingness to supply work hours.

quantity supplied: quantity you actually plan to supply at a given price

As your eye goes down the two columns in Figure 3.1, notice that as the price rises, the quantity supplied increases. (What happens to quantity demanded as price rises?) In general, when prices rise, individuals and businesses devote more of their time or resources to producing or supplying — more money stimulates more product/service supplied. The two reasons for this are the quest for profits (higher prices usually mean higher profits) and the need for a higher price to cover higher marginal opportunity costs — your weekend time is worth more to you than your computer game time.

Let's take the economist's idea of supply and apply it to Paola's willingness to supply a particular quantity of piercings at a particular price.

Body Piercings or Nail Sets?

Businesses, like consumers, make smart choices based on economic advantage. Paola's first choice is *what to produce* with her resources — the labour and equipment she has in her shop. She can do body piercing, and she can also paint fingernails. Let's limit her choices to full body piercings and full sets of fingernails to allow the simple, made-up numbers below.

The PPF Parlour has special tools both for piercing and nail painting. There are four people working (including Paola). All four are equally skilled at piercing (the business started with just piercing), but their fingernail skills differ from expert (Paola) to beginner (Parminder). Figure 3.2 shows the different combinations of fingernail sets and piercings the PPF Parlour can produce in a day.

Figure 3.2	PPF Parlour: Maximum Daily Combination of Fingernails and Piercings Produced	
Combination	**Fingernails (full sets)**	**Piercings (full body)**
A	15	0
B	14	1
C	12	2
D	9	3
E	5	4
F	0	5

At one extreme (combination A) all four workers do fingernails only, so they can produce 15 fingernail sets and no piercings. If Paola starts shifting some of her staff from fingernails to piercings, she can move to combination B (14 fingernail sets and 1 full body piercing). Shifting more staff and equipment out of fingernails and into piercing gives her combination C (12 fingernail sets and 2 piercings), and then combinations D (9 fingernail sets and 3 piercings) and E (5 fingernail sets and 4 piercings). Combination F is the other extreme, where the PPF Parlour produces only piercings — 5 piercings and 0 fingernail sets. As we will see, the pattern of numbers in Figure 3.2 has a lot to do with differences in fingernail skills.

What Do Paola's Choices Cost Her?

So far, these numbers don't make much business sense — they are just the numbers of piercings and nail sets that the PPF Parlour can possibly produce. To make sense of the numbers for Paola's business supply decisions, we have to translate them into marginal costs. (And ultimately, in Chapter 7, profits.)

Remember that all costs are ultimately opportunity costs. The cost of acquiring or producing products/services is the value of the best alternative opportunity we must give up to get them. To get more body piercings, Paola gives up doing full nail sets. Opportunity cost is what we give up divided by what we get:

$$\text{Opportunity cost} = \frac{\text{Give up}}{\text{Get}}$$

Figure 3.3 shows, in the last column, the marginal opportunity costs to Paola of producing more piercings.

Figure 3.3	PPF Parlour's Marginal Opportunity Costs		
Combination	**Fingernails** (full sets)	**Piercings** (full body)	**Marginal Opportunity Cost of Producing More Piercings** (fingernail sets given up)
A	15	0	
			$\frac{(15 - 14)}{1} = 1$
B	14	1	
			$\frac{(14 - 12)}{1} = 2$
C	12	2	
			$\frac{(12 - 9)}{1} = 3$
D	9	3	
			$\frac{(9 - 5)}{1} = 4$
E	5	4	
			$\frac{(5 - 0)}{1} = 5$
F	0	5	

What is the marginal opportunity cost of producing the first full body piercing? To move from 0 to 1 piercing (from combination A to B), Paola must give up 1 fingernail set, because fingernail production drops from 15 to 14 sets as some staff time switches from fingernails to piercing. In exchange, she gets 1 piercing. So substituting into the formula, the marginal opportunity cost of the first piercing is

$$\frac{1 \text{ (fingernail set)}}{1 \text{ (piercing)}} = 1 \text{ (fingernail set per piercing)}$$

To produce a second piercing (moving from combination B to C), Paola must give up 2 fingernail sets (14 − 12 sets). The marginal opportunity cost of the second additional piercing is 2 fingernail sets given up per piercing. The third piercing (moving from combination C to D) has a marginal opportunity cost of 3 fingernail sets given up (12 − 9 sets) per piercing. In moving the last of her staff to piercing, for the fifth full body piercing she gives up 5 fingernail sets (5 − 0 sets). The marginal opportunity cost of the last additional piercing — the fifth — is 5 fingernail sets given up per piercing.

Costs Are Costs Are Costs — It's How You Look at Them

If you are wondering what the difference is between opportunity cost, marginal cost, and marginal opportunity cost — since they seem like the same thing — good for you! You are not confused. *All opportunity costs are marginal costs, and all marginal costs are opportunity costs.*

Opportunity cost and marginal cost are two sides of the same coin. Opportunity cost focuses on the value of the opportunity *given up* when you make a decision. On the flip side, marginal cost focuses on the *additional cost* that the decision produces. Paola must give up 5 fingernail sets in deciding to produce the fifth piercing. So the marginal opportunity cost of the fifth piercing is 5 fingernail sets. **Marginal opportunity cost** is the complete name for any cost relevant to a smart decision.

Figure 3.4 illustrates the economic sense of these numbers. Each finger measures the marginal opportunity cost of additional piercings produced (along the horizontal axis) in terms of fingernail sets given up per piercing (shown on the vertical axis).

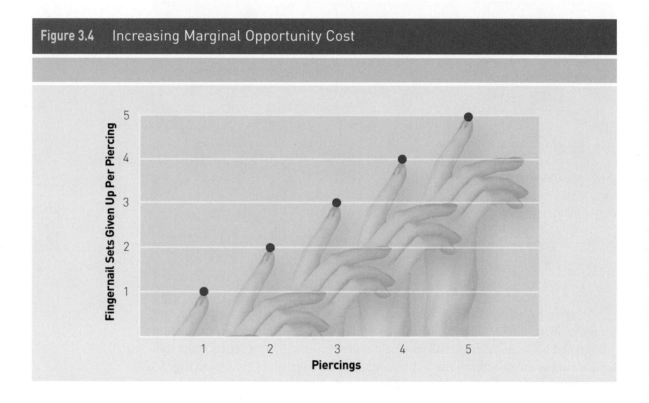

Figure 3.4   Increasing Marginal Opportunity Cost

Notice that as Paola produces additional piercings, her marginal opportunity costs increase, from 1 fingernail set given up for the first piercing to 5 fingernail sets given up for the fifth piercing. This is the same pattern we saw in the decision to shift your time away from alternative uses to working more hours — the marginal cost of additional time given up increases as you give up increasingly valuable uses of your time.

Are the reasons for Paola's increasing marginal opportunity costs the same as for your work decision? This is an important question, and the answer is not obvious. Paola's increasing marginal opportunity costs arise because her staff and equipment are not equally good at piercing and painting. Paola is better (more productive) at doing fingernails than is Parminder, and the tools can't be easily switched between tasks — nailpolish brushes and emery boards aren't much help in piercing.

Why Marginal Opportunity Costs Increase These differences in productivity cause increasing marginal opportunity costs. Think about Paola as she decides to reduce her fingernail output and produce the first piercing. Remember that all staff are equally skilled at piercing. Which staff member will she switch first to piercing? As an economizer, she will switch the person who is least productive for fingernails — Parminder. So her given up, or forgone, fingernail production is relatively small (1 set). To increase her piercing output more, she has to then switch staff who are slightly better at doing fingernails, so the opportunity cost is higher (2 fingernail sets). And who is the last person she switches when she moves entirely to piercing? Of course, it is Paola herself — the best nail painter — so the opportunity cost of that fifth piercing is the highest, at 5 fingernail sets given up.

Increasing marginal opportunity costs arise because inputs are not equally productive in all activities. There are always opportunity costs in switching between activities because time spent on piercing can no longer be spent on fingernails. But *increasing* opportunity costs arise because of the differing skill levels of the staff being switched. If all of Paola's staff and equipment were equally good at piercing and fingernail painting, the opportunity costs would always be the same, no matter what combinations of piercings and fingernails she produced. But in the real world, most inputs are not like that; they are different.

The reasons for Paola's increasing marginal opportunity costs are not quite the same as the reasons for your decision to supply more work hours as the price rises, but there is much overlap. For your work decision, increasing marginal opportunity costs arise from differences in the value of alternative uses of your time (from computer games to weekend fun). For Paola's decision to supply additional piercings, increasing marginal opportunity costs arise from differences in employee skill levels and equipment in producing alternative services. What is shared among the reasons is alternative uses (of time or inputs) with increasing opportunity costs.

Show Me the Money: Paying for Opportunity Costs

So far, all of the numbers in this example are measured in full body piercings or fingernail sets. But Paola, as a profit-seeking entrepreneur, will want to make a smart supply decision based on dollar prices. Luckily, there is an easy conversion here from body decorations to dollars. Suppose that fingernail full sets sell for $20. Then the marginal opportunity costs for producing additional piercings appear in Figure 3.5.

Figure 3.5 PPF Parlour's Supply of Piercings	
Price (marginal opportunity cost or minimum willing to accept per piercing)	**Quantity Supplied** (piercings)
$ 20	1
$ 40	2
$ 60	3
$ 80	4
$100	5

Increasing marginal opportunity costs arise because inputs are not equally productive in all activities.

Where inputs are equally productive in all activities, marginal opportunity costs are constant.

The marginal opportunity cost of producing the first piercing is $20 (the cost of 1 nail set given up); of the second piercing, $40 (2 nail sets given up); all the way up to $100 for the fifth piercing. So if Paola is to be willing to produce 1 piercing, she needs to receive a price of at least $20 to cover the costs of the alternative use of her inputs. To continue to produce more piercings, she needs to receive higher prices to cover her higher marginal opportunity costs. Paola won't produce the fifth piercing unless she receives at least $100 for it, because that is what she would be giving up from the best alternative use of her inputs (5 fingernail sets at $20 each). So the price of a piercing will determine what quantity of piercings Paola will decide to produce. The higher the price, the greater quantity of piercings Paola supplies.

The Law of Supply

Just as you are willing to supply more hours of work only if the price you are paid rises, Paola's business must receive a higher price in order to be willing to supply a greater quantity to the market. She needs the higher price to compensate for her increasing marginal opportunity costs as her production of piercings increases.

As the price offered for your time rises, you work more, first giving up the least valuable alternative use of time, and then giving up increasingly valuable time. Your willingness to work changes with circumstances, depending on the price offered and the cost — the value you place on alternative uses of your time.

As the price offered for piercings rises, Paola switches inputs from producing nail sets to piercings, first giving up the least productive inputs for nail sets, and then giving up increasingly productive inputs for nail sets. Paola's willingness to supply piercings changes with circumstances, depending on the price offered and the cost — the value of lost nail sets from the alternative uses of the inputs.

Usually, many businesses are willing to supply the market for any product/service. Like Paola's, each business tries to make a smart choice about *what* to supply, and *how much* to supply. Whether it is the output markets for piercings or nail sets, the input market for labour, or anything else, businesses and individuals always have alternative uses of their inputs, and will supply a larger quantity only at a higher price.

Market supply is the sum of the supplies of all businesses willing to produce a particular product/service. Suppose there were 100 piercing businesses exactly like Paola's. The market supply of piercings is the sum of the supplies of all piercing businesses, and looks like Figure 3.6.

In output markets, the left side of the circular-flow diagram (Figure 1.4, p. 12), businesses are suppliers, and households are demanders. In input markets, the right side of Figure 1.4 — individuals/households are suppliers, and businesses are demanders. On either side, higher prices increase quantity supplied.

market supply: sum of supplies of all businesses willing to produce a particular product/service

Figure 3.6	Market Supply of Piercings
Price (marginal opportunity cost or minimum willing to accept per piercing)	**Quantity Supplied** (piercings)
$ 20	100
$ 40	200
$ 60	300
$ 80	400
$100	500

Quantity Willing to Supply and Price Willing to Accept Recall that the general definition of supply is businesses' overall willingness to supply a product/service because the price covers all opportunity costs of production. Figure 3.6 shows, for each price, the particular quantity supplied by all piercing businesses combined.

If we read the numbers from left to right (from price to quantity supplied), the first row of the table tells us that at a price of $20 per piercing, all businesses together are willing to supply the quantity of 100 piercings. As your eye moves down the table and price rises, the quantity supplied also increases, until at a price of $100 per piercing the quantity supplied is 500 piercings.

Another way to read the numbers in Figure 3.6 is from right to left (from quantity supplied to price). Starting with the first row again, that reading tells us this: For businesses to be willing to supply 100 piercings, the minimum price they are willing to accept (that covers all opportunity costs of production) is $20 per piercing. To be willing to supply 500 piercings, the minimum price they are willing to accept is $100 per piercing (because of increased opportunity costs).

This positive relationship between price and quantity supplied (both go up together) is so universal that economists call it the **law of supply**: If the price of a product/service rises, the quantity supplied of the product/service increases. Higher prices create incentives for increased production through higher profits and by covering higher marginal opportunity costs of production.

The law of supply works as long as other factors besides price do not change. The next section will explore what happens when other factors do change.

law of supply: if the price of a product/service rises, quantity supplied increases

Refresh

3.3

1. Why does Paola need a higher price to be willing to supply more body piercings?

2. If you could spend the next hour studying economics or working at your part-time job, which pays $10 an hour, what is your personal opportunity cost, in dollars, of studying?

3. Suppose the PPF Parlour was producing only piercings and no fingernail sets. If Paola wanted to start producing some fingernail sets, which staff person would she switch to fingernails first? Who would she switch last? Explain your answers.

www.myeconlab.com

3.4 Changing the Bottom Line: What Can Change Supply?

Explain the difference between a change in quantity supplied and a change in supply, and list five factors that change supply.

The average price of a notebook computer in Canada fell from around $2000 in 2002 to under $1000 in 2007. But the quantity of notebook computers businesses sold *increased*.

Does that contradict the "law of supply"?

If nothing else changed except the price of notebooks, the answer would be yes. Why would notebook producers be willing to supply more notebooks at lower prices? Something is not right. But like evidence that appears to disprove the law of demand, a fall in price that leads to an increase in quantity supplied is a signal that something else must have changed at the same time.

Economists use the term *supply* to summarize all of the influences on business decisions. In the examples of your work decision or Paola's piercings, that willingness to supply depends on things like the value of alternative uses of time or inputs and marginal opportunity costs.

As long as these factors (and some others) do not change, the law of supply holds true: If the price of a product/service rises, the quantity supplied increases.

But when change happens, economists distinguish between two kinds of change:

- If the price of a product/service changes, that affects *quantity supplied*.
- If anything else changes, that affects *supply*.

This distinction is just like the distinction in Chapter 2 between quantity demanded and demand.

ECONOMICS Out There

Uncorking the Okanagan

In the Okanagan region of B.C. — an area known in particular for its fruit production — large excavation machines are ripping out apple trees to make way for a new crop: grapes. Local landowners hope the switch will allow them to make more profits from their property by jumping into the province's booming wine industry. Landowner Bryan Hardman says that in the past he has been a price taker, but is setting up his own winery because he "wants to be a price maker, and believes the wine business is the place to do it."

- This anecdote beautifully illustrates the law of supply. Higher prices and profits are creating incentives to increase quantity supplied of grapes and wine.

- It's also an illustration of how all inputs must be paid their opportunity costs. Even though the Okanagan Valley is a world-class area for apple-growing, landowners can make more money switching to grapes — more than covering their opportunity costs — so they do.

- If land is not equally productive for grape-growing, which apple orchards would you expect to be dug up and replanted with grapes first? Which will be replanted last?

- Consider Mr. Hardman's comment about wanting to be a price maker instead of a price taker. We will use those exact terms in Chapter 7 when we discuss competition among businesses in an industry.

Source: Wendy Stueck, in *The Globe and Mail* (Toronto), October 7, 2006.

Only a change in the price of a product/service itself changes *quantity supplied* of that product/service. There are five other important factors that can change market supply — the willingness to produce a product/service. They are:

- Technology
- Prices of inputs
- Prices of related products/services produced
- Expected future prices
- Number of businesses

Technology

Paola is ecstatic because she has just bought a newly invented piercing gun that allows her employees to double the number of piercings they do in a day. This increase in productivity from the new technology reduces her costs. Word spreads quickly, and all of the other piercing parlour owners realize that if they are to stay competitive, they, too, have to adopt the new technology. The result is an increase in market supply, which is shown in Figure 3.7.

Figure 3.7	Market Supply of Piercings Before and After a Technology Improvement	
Price (marginal opportunity cost or minimum willing to accept per piercing)	**Quantity Supplied** (before technology improvement)	**Quantity Supplied** (after technology improvement)
$ 20	100	200
$ 40	200	400
$ 60	300	600
$ 80	400	800
$100	500	1000

If we read the numbers from left to right, at any price, each business will make more profits given that its costs are lower, and so it will want to supply more piercings. At a price of $20, before the new technology, businesses were willing to supply 100 piercings (column 2). At an unchanged price of $20, with the new technology, businesses are now willing to supply 200 piercings (column 3). Economists call this an **increase in supply** — an increase in the overall willingness of businesses to supply at any price. This can be described in two equivalent ways. At any unchanged price, businesses are now willing to supply a greater quantity because costs are lower and profits are higher. Or, for producing any unchanged quantity, businesses are now willing to accept a lower price because costs are lower.

If we instead read the numbers from right to left, for any quantity supplied, after the new technology lowers costs, the minimum price businesses are willing to accept falls. In Figure 3.7, before the new technology, to be willing to supply 200 piercings businesses needed a minimum price of $40 per piercing (row 2). After the new technology, to be willing to supply 200 piercings, businesses now need a price of only $20 per piercing (row 1). The new technology has lowered Paola's and other piercers' marginal opportunity costs, so they can accept a lower price while still covering all costs. Either way, the result is an increase in supply.

increase in supply: increase in businesses' willingness to produce

An improvement in technology causes an increase in supply, not a change in quantity supplied.

Prices of Inputs

A fall in input prices causes an increase in supply.
A rise in input prices causes a decrease in supply.

Paola and other businesses have to pay a price for inputs that matches the best opportunity cost of the input owner. If those opportunity costs and input prices go down, Paola's costs decrease. At any price for piercings, lower costs mean Paola will earn higher profits, so she will want to supply more. The effect of lower input prices on market supply is the same as a technology improvement. In Figure 3.7, the last column of numbers for quantity supplied could also have been caused by lower input prices for studs, lower rent, or lower wages to employees. Lower input prices increase market supply.

In reverse, higher input prices mean higher costs for Paola and, at any price, lower profits. Therefore, market supply will decrease.

Prices of Related Products and Services

Lower prices for a related product/service a business produces cause an increase in supply.
Higher prices for a related product/service cause a decrease in supply.

The PPF Parlour can produce both piercings and fingernail sets. What happens to Paola's supply of piercings when the price of fingernail sets falls from $20 to $10 per set? Since Paola wants to earn maximum profits, which product will she produce more of, and which less of, when the price of fingernail sets falls? Take a minute to see if you can answer that question before reading on.

When the price of fingernail sets falls, Paola will supply more piercings and fewer fingernail sets. You probably reasoned that when the price of fingernail sets falls, they are less profitable to produce, so Paola will shift more of her resources to producing piercings. You are correct. A fall in the price of fingernail sets causes an *increase in supply of piercings*.

But there is another way to reason out the answer to the question. The lower price of fingernail sets lowers Paola's marginal opportunity cost of producing piercings. The real opportunity cost of producing more piercings is the fingernail sets Paola must give up. When those fingernail sets fall in price, Paola's marginal opportunity cost for producing piercings decreases. So the minimum price Paola needs to receive to be willing to supply any given quantity of piercings falls. In reverse, a rise in the price of fingernail sets causes a *decrease in supply of piercings*.

A change in the price of related products/services produced causes a business to reconsider its most profitable choices. A business will choose to supply more of one product/service when alternative products/services it produces fall in price, and supply less when alternative products/services it produces rise in price.

Expected Future Prices

A fall in expected future price causes an increase in supply today (better profits today).
A rise in expected future price causes a decrease in supply today (better profits in future).

What happens to the supply of a product/service when the expected future price of the product/service changes? Recall from Chapter 2 that consumer demand changes if consumers expect lower or higher prices in the future. The same holds true for businesses. If Paola expects falling piercing prices in the future, she will try to supply more now, while the price is relatively high. When future prices are expected to fall, supply increases in the present.

If Paola expects future prices to rise, she may reduce her current supply to the market and increase her supply when prices and profits are higher. When future prices are expected to rise, supply decreases in the present.

Number of Businesses

An increase in the number of businesses increases market supply. Figure 3.8 adds a third column to Figure 3.6 showing the quantity supplied after the number of businesses doubles.

Figure 3.8	Market Supply of Piercings with More Businesses	
Price (marginal opportunity cost or minimum willing to accept per piercing)	**Quantity Supplied** (100 businesses)	**Quantity Supplied** (200 businesses)
$ 20	100	200
$ 40	200	400
$ 60	300	600
$ 80	400	800
$100	500	1000

It is no surprise that with the additional businesses (column 3), at any price (column 1) the quantity supplied is greater than originally (column 2). The increased number of businesses causes an increase in supply, just as an improvement in technology or a fall in input prices causes an increase in supply. A decrease in the number of businesses causes a decrease in supply, just as a rise in the price of a related product/service or an increase in expected future prices causes a decrease in supply.

An increased number of businesses causes an increase in supply. A decreased number of businesses causes a decrease in supply.

Why would businesses enter (increase supply) or exit (decrease supply) a market? Typically, if profits are high, new competitors will enter a market, increasing the market supply. If profits are lower than available elsewhere in the economy, competitors will exit from the market, decreasing market supply. Those exiting businesses will search for more profitable uses of their resources.

Summary

Any increase (or decrease) in supply can be described in alternative ways. We have used these alternatives, in reading the tables of numbers from left to right (from price to quantity supplied) or from right to left (from quantity supplied to price). The left-to-right description of an increase in supply is:

- At any given price, businesses are willing to supply a larger quantity.

  The right-to-left description of an increase in supply is:

- At any given quantity supplied, businesses are willing to accept a lower price because their marginal opportunity costs of production are lower.

For an increase in supply, these two alternative descriptions of the connection between price and quantity supplied are summarized in Figure 3.9. Depending on the economic event you are trying to make sense of, sometimes you will use one description, and sometimes the other.

Figure 3.9	Relating Price and Quantity Supplied for an Increase in Supply	
Given price	⟷	Higher quantity supplied
Lower price	⟷	Given quantity supplied

Saving the Law of Supply

A change in quantity supplied (caused by a change in the price of the product/service itself) differs from a change in supply (caused by changes in technology, prices of inputs, prices of related products/services produced, expected future prices, and/or number of businesses). Can you now explain why, when notebook computer prices fell from $2000 to under $1000, the quantity of notebooks sold actually *increased*? Is the "law of supply" really a law?

If the price of a product/service falls, the quantity supplied decreases, *as long as other factors do not change*. The fall in notebook prices alone would have caused a *decrease* in quantity supplied, not an increase. But other things also changed. While a complete explanation involves demand factors from Chapter 2 as well as supply, major changes include technological improvements in computer chips and falling prices of inputs. These *increased the supply* of notebook computers. Using the right-to-left reading of an increase in supply in Figure 3.9, at any given quantity supplied, businesses were willing to accept a lower price because their marginal opportunity costs of production were lower. The impact of the increase in supply outweighed the impact of lower prices in decreasing quantity supplied.

Figure 3.10 is a good study device for reviewing the difference between the law of supply (focused on quantity supplied) and the factors that change supply.

Figure 3.10 Law of Supply and Changes in Supply	
The Law of Supply	
The quantity supplied of a product/service	
Decreases if:	*Increases if:*
■ price of the product/service falls	■ price of the product/service rises
Changes in Supply	
The supply for a product/service	
Decreases if:	*Increases if:*
——————	■ technology improves
■ price of an input rises	■ price of an input falls
■ price of a complement rises	■ price of a complement falls
■ price of a related product/service rises	■ price of a related product/service falls
■ expected future price rises	■ expected future price falls
■ number of businesses decreases	■ number of businesses increases

Refresh 3.4

1. Explain the difference between a change in quantity supplied and a change in supply, and distinguish the five factors that can change supply.

2. Suppose you are working at two part-time jobs, babysitting and pizza delivery. After many younger babysitters start offering to work for less, your babysitting clients will now pay only $6 per hour instead of $8 per hour. What will happen to your supply of hours for delivering pizzas? Explain.

3. When the price of nail sets falls, none of Paola's hard dollar costs change. Is there an effect on the quantity of piercings Paola chooses to supply?

3.5 How Far Will You Jump for the Money? Price Elasticity of Supply

Explain elasticity of supply and how it helps businesses avoid disappointed customers.

The Magic Christian, a 1969 movie written in part by Monty Python and starring Peter Sellers and Ringo Starr (of the Beatles), is a satire on greed. A wealthy man with a perverse sense of humour performs bizarre social experiments to see what respectable people will do for money. In a memorable scene, people dive into a pool of excrement because they can keep any of the gold coins they find at the bottom.

What would it take to get you to dive into that pool? In pondering your answer (and please do forgive me for placing this image in your mind's eye), you might also be wondering what on earth this has to do with smart supply decisions.

We know from the law of supply that (all other things unchanged), a rise in price causes an increase in quantity supplied. A smart business supply decision depends on *by how much* you increase quantity supplied when the price rises.

What might you do to earn a dollar? A thousand dollars? A million? What makes the difference?

What price would it take for you to "supply" a dive into the pool? By how much will you increase your work hours in response to your boss's higher wages? What determines by how much Paola increases her quantity supplied of piercings as the price of piercings rises?

The law of supply tells us that price and quantity supplied increase together and decrease together. The last question we will look at is this: What changes more, the price or the quantity? This *responsiveness* of quantity supplied to a change in price is related to greed and the quest for profits, but mostly it has to do with how easy or costly it is to increase production.

Responsiveness Again   I am hoping the word "responsiveness" reminds you of the concept of elasticity from Chapter 2. There, the price elasticity of demand measured the responsiveness of the quantity demanded by consumers to a change in price. **Elasticity of supply** measures by how much quantity supplied by businesses responds to a change in price.

Just as was the case for demand, the quantity supplied can be inelastic (unresponsive to a change in price) or elastic (very responsive). Let's look at some examples.

You are standing by the pool in *The Magic Christian,* but simply cannot bring yourself to jump. Even with an astronomical increase in the price — from only, say, a loonie at the bottom to a million gold coins — you stay put. Your "supply" of jumps is totally unresponsive to even a huge increase in price. This is inelastic supply in the extreme.

More realistically, consider an industry like gold mining. When the world price of gold rises, what happens to the quantity of gold supplied? Not much, and certainly not much quickly. Gold is hard to find, and prospecting for new gold fields is very expensive and takes years, even decades. The supply of new gold nuggets is *inelastic,* because quantity supplied is relatively unresponsive to even large rises in price. For **inelastic** supply, there is a small response in quantity supplied when the price rises.

At the other extreme, the supply of snow-shovelling services in most Canadian towns is relatively elastic. If the price offered rises even modestly, there is a willing supply of kids with shovels who don't have many other equally well-paying chances to work. And for anyone with a truck, it's not difficult or expensive to attach a plow and clear driveways in your spare time, before or after your regular job. Even a small rise in price causes a large increase in the quantity supplied of shovelling services, so supply is elastic. For **elastic** supply, there is a large response in quantity supplied when the price rises.

Measuring Business Responsiveness

This is the simple formula for calculating elasticity of supply:

$$\text{Elasticity of supply} = \frac{\text{Percentage change in quantity supplied}}{\text{Percentage change in price}}$$

The formula assumes that all of the other five factors that can affect supply are unchanged, so this is a controlled measurement of just the relationship (in the law of supply) between quantity supplied and price.

If the percentage change in quantity supplied (the numerator) is less than the percentage change in price (the denominator), elasticity of supply is less than 1 and is inelastic. Quantity supplied is relatively unresponsive to a change in price.

If the percentage change in quantity supplied (the numerator) is greater than the percentage change in price (the denominator), elasticity of supply is greater than 1 and is elastic. Quantity supplied is relatively responsive to a change in price.

Calculating Elasticity of Supply   Let's substitute some numbers into the formula, going back to your decision to work more hours for your boss. When she asked, you were willing to work 20 hours at $10/hour. When she then offered you $20/hour (a 100-percent increase), you agreed to supply 15 additional hours, for a total of 35 hours. If we convert the increase in quantity into a percentage (15 additional hours/20 original hours = 75 percent), your elasticity of supply is

$$\text{Elasticity of supply} = \frac{75 \text{ percent}}{100 \text{ percent}} = 0.75$$

That is a relatively inelastic response on your part (and your boss was disappointed!), as a 100-percent increase in pay led you to increase your supply of hours by only 75 percent.

As a comparison, imagine that the same offer of double time had gone to one of your co-workers who was not in school, was working 10 hours a week, and had just received a massive credit card bill. He offers to supply 50 more hours, for a total of 60 hours. His increase in quantity of hours supplied is 500 percent (50 more hours/10 original hours), so his elasticity of supply is

$$\text{Elasticity of supply} = \frac{500 \text{ percent}}{100 \text{ percent}} = 5$$

He has a relatively elastic response (good thing for you that your boss agreed to your triple-time hours first), as a 100-percent increase in pay would lead to a 500-percent increase in his supply of hours.

Gearing Up (Production) Can Be Hard to Do: Factors Determining Elasticity of Supply

What causes supply to be inelastic for some individuals and businesses and elastic for others? Two important causes are the availability of additional inputs and the time it takes to produce the product/service.

If Paola can easily hire more employees and buy more studs, all at the same prices, then her supply of piercings will tend to be elastic. Even a small rise in the price of piercings (in the denominator) will cause her to increase her quantity supplied (in the numerator) because her profits will increase. But if, as she tries to increase her quantity supplied, she faces higher opportunity costs and has to pay more for her inputs, it will take a big rise in the price of piercings (in the denominator) to get her to provide even a small increase in quantity (in the numerator). In that case, her supply is inelastic.

Availability of Input   Availability of inputs also helps explain the difference between supply elasticities for gold mining and snow shovelling. It is difficult to find new inputs for mining (gold deposits), while it is easy to attract new workers to snow shovelling. Easy availability of inputs makes for more elastic supply, while difficulty and costly availability of new inputs makes for more inelastic supply.

Time   To see the importance of time, compare Paola's supply with the supply in the gold-mining industry. When the price of piercings rises, Paola can quickly adjust her quantity supplied. When gold prices rise, it can take years or even decades for the quantity supplied to adjust, because it takes time to discover and exploit new mines. Industries with quick time to production tend to have more elastic supplies, and industries with slow time to production tend to have more inelastic supplies.

Supply is inelastic when the calculation of
$$\frac{(\% \text{ change in quantity supplied})}{(\% \text{ change in price})}$$
gives a value less than 1.

Supply is elastic when the calculation of
$$\frac{(\% \text{ change in quantity supplied})}{(\% \text{ change in price})}$$
gives a value greater than 1.

Elasticity of supply depends on availability of additional inputs and the time production takes.

Why Do We Care About Elasticity of Supply?

Elasticity of supply allows more accurate projections of future outputs and prices, (smart choices) helping businesses avoid disappointed customers.

In 2007, the Alberta housing market was booming. Oil revenues were raising incomes for everyone in the industry and beyond, and new workers were moving into the province to take well-paying jobs. New-home builders were expanding the quantity supplied of housing as fast as they could, but ended up disappointing many customers when they couldn't deliver the quantities or the prices promised. It is never good business to promise more than you can profitably deliver, and understanding elasticity of supply is important for avoiding such broken promises. Shortages and higher wages in the building trades limited the profitable availability of inputs. Housing construction, although not as time-consuming as mining, does take time to adjust to new price conditions. A smart entrepreneur can't change these business conditions, but he or she can use an understanding of elasticity of supply to make more accurate projections of outputs and prices, and avoid disappointed customers.

It is always a smart business decision to pay no more for an input than you have to. Your boss, in her desperate triple-time wage offer to you, might have paid more than she needed to for the extra work hours, compared to your co-worker who had a more elastic supply of labour. Knowing about elasticity of supply enables smart, informed choices, and can only help a business's bottom line.

Refresh

3.5

www.myeconlab.com

1. Explain the relationship between price and quantity supplied for inelastic supply and for elastic supply.

2. If your boss offers you a 20-percent raise, and in response you work 10 percent more hours, how would you describe your price elasticity of labour supply?

3. Your business is about to launch an advertising campaign boasting about your current low prices. You are hoping the ads will bring in many more customers. Explain why you need to be concerned about your elasticity of supply.

Show Me the Money

The Law of Supply

CHAPTER SUMMARY

3.1 WHAT DOES IT REALLY COST? COSTS ARE OPPORTUNITY COSTS

Businesses must pay higher prices to obtain more of an input because opportunity costs change with circumstances. The marginal costs of additional inputs (like labour) are ultimately opportunity costs — the best alternative use of the input.

- **Marginal cost** — additional opportunity cost of increasing quantity supplied, and changes with circumstances
  - For working example, you are supplying time, and marginal cost of your time increases as you increase quantity of hours supplied.
- Differences between smart supply choices and smart demand choices:
  - For supply, marginal cost increases as you supply more.
  - For demand, marginal benefit decreases as you buy more.
  - For supply, marginal benefit is measured in $ (wages you earn); marginal cost is opportunity cost of time.
  - For demand, marginal benefit is satisfaction you get; marginal cost is measured in $ (price you pay).

3.2 FORGET IT, IT'S HISTORY: SUNK COSTS DON'T MATTER FOR FUTURE CHOICES

Sunk costs that cannot be reversed are not part of opportunity costs. Sunk costs do not influence smart, forward-looking decisions.

- **Sunk costs** — past expenses that cannot be recovered.
- Sunk costs are the same no matter which fork in the road you take, so they have no influence on smart choices.

3.3 MORE FOR MORE MONEY: THE LAW OF SUPPLY

If the price of a product/service rises, quantity supplied increases. Businesses increase production when higher prices either create higher profits or cover higher marginal opportunity costs of production.

- **Supply** — businesses' willingness to produce a particular product/service because price covers all opportunity costs.
- **Quantity supplied** — quantity you actually plan to supply at a given price.
- **Marginal opportunity cost** — complete name for any cost relevant to a smart decision.
  - All opportunity costs are marginal costs; all marginal costs are opportunity costs.
- Increasing marginal opportunity costs arise because inputs are not equally productive in all activities.
  - Where inputs are equally productive in all activities, marginal opportunity costs are constant.
- **Market supply** — sum of supplies of all businesses willing to produce a particular product/service.
- **Law of supply** — if the price of a product/service rises, quantity supplied increases.
  - In output markets, businesses are suppliers and households are demanders.
  - In input markets, individuals/households are suppliers and businesses are demanders.
  - For both types of markets, higher prices increase quantity supplied.

3.4 CHANGING THE BOTTOM LINE: WHAT CAN CHANGE SUPPLY?

Quantity supplied is changed only by a change in price.
Supply is changed by all other influences on business decisions.

- Supply is a catch-all term summarizing all possible influences on businesses' willingness to produce a particular product/service.
- Supply changes with changes in technology, prices of inputs, prices of related products/services produced, expected future prices, number of businesses. For example, supply increases with:
  - improvement in technology.
  - fall in price of an input.
  - fall in price of a related product/service.
  - fall in expected future price.
  - increase in number of businesses.
- **Increase in supply** — increase in businesses' willingness to supply. Can be described in two equivalent ways:
  - At any unchanged price, businesses are now willing to supply a greater quantity.
  - For producing any unchanged quantity, businesses are now willing to accept a lower price.

3.5 HOW FAR WILL YOU JUMP FOR THE MONEY? PRICE ELASTICITY OF SUPPLY

Elasticity of supply measures how responsive quantity supplied is to a change in price, and depends on the difficulty, expense, and time involved in increasing production. With elastic supply, businesses can easily and inexpensively increase production; with inelastic supply, it is difficult and expensive to increase production.

- **Elasticity of supply** measures by how much quantity supplied responds to a change in price.
- The formula is:

$$\text{Elasticity of supply} = \frac{\text{Percentage change in quantity supplied}}{\text{Percentage change in price}}$$

- **Inelastic** — For inelastic supply, small response in quantity supplied when price rises.
  - Example: supply of mined gold.
  - Value for formula is less than 1.
- **Elastic** — For elastic supply, large response in quantity supplied when price rises.
  - Example: snow-shovelling services.
  - Value for formula is greater than 1.
- Elasticity of supply of a product/service is influenced by:
  - availability of additional inputs — more available inputs means more elastic supply.
  - time production takes — less time means more elastic supply.
- Elasticity of supply allows more accurate projections of future outputs and prices, helping businesses avoid disappointed customers.

TRUE/FALSE

Circle the correct answer.

3.1 COSTS ARE OPPORTUNITY COSTS

1. When higher-paying jobs are harder to find for workers, a business will have to pay more to hire labour. **True   False**

2. Any smart business supply decision involves a choice between a business's marginal benefit (or reward) from supplying (or selling) its product/service and the business's marginal opportunity cost of producing the product/service. **True   False**

3. Any smart worker supply decision involves a choice between a worker's marginal benefit (or reward) from supplying (or selling) her work and the worker's marginal opportunity cost of working. **True   False**

4. Gordie's marginal opportunity cost of spending an extra hour on Facebook increases if he suddenly has the opportunity to go on a date with his high school crush.

True   **False**

3.2 SUNK COSTS DON'T MATTER FOR FUTURE CHOICES

5. Businesses should consider the monthly rent when deciding whether to produce more of a product/service.

True   **False**

6. Sunk costs are part of opportunity costs.

True   **False**

3.3 THE LAW OF SUPPLY

7. Businesses need to receive higher prices to compensate for increasing marginal opportunity costs as output increases.

True   **False**

8. Opportunity cost equals what you get divided by what you give up.

True   **False**

9. As you shift your time *away* from watching TV in order to work more hours, the marginal opportunity cost of working decreases.

True   **False**

10. All opportunity costs are marginal costs, and all marginal costs are opportunity costs.

True   **False**

3.4 WHAT CAN CHANGE SUPPLY?

11. A rise in the price of inputs used by businesses decreases market supply.

True   **False**

12. A rise in the price of a related product/service a business produces increases market supply of the other product/service.

True   **False**

3.5 PRICE ELASTICITY OF SUPPLY

13. Supply is inelastic if a rise in price causes a very responsive change in quantity supplied.

True   **False**

14. The federal government of Canada introduced a Working Income Tax Benefit in its Budget 2007. This policy increases the return from working because it reduces the tax paid on earnings. We know that women's work-supply decision is more "elastic" to wages than men's, so women are more likely to benefit from this policy than are men.

True   **False**

15. If a 10-percent rise in price causes quantity supplied to increase by 40 percent, supply is elastic.

True   **False**

MULTIPLE CHOICE

Circle the correct answer.

3.1 COSTS ARE OPPORTUNITY COSTS

1. Your opportunity cost of watching *American Idol* increases if

A) it is your favourite TV show.

B) you have a very expensive television.

C) you have an exam the next day.

D) all of the above.

2. The opportunity cost of going to school is highest for someone who

A) has to give up a job paying $10 an hour.

B) has to give up a job paying $15 an hour.

C) loves school.

D) has to give up a volunteer opportunity.

3. Which statement is *false*?

A) Marginal costs are opportunity costs.

B) Opportunity costs are marginal costs.

C) Sunk costs are marginal costs.

D) Marginal opportunity costs increase as quantity increases.

3.2 SUNK COSTS DON'T MATTER FOR FUTURE CHOICES

4. Gamblers on slot machines often believe that the more they lose, the greater are their chances of winning on the next turn. However, the chances of winning on any turn are actually random — they do not depend on past turns. Therefore, the money lost on the previous turn is a(n)

A) total cost.

B) sunk cost.

C) smart cost.

D) opportunity cost.

5. Your friend Larry is deciding whether to break up with his current girlfriend, Lucy. He tells you that his number-one reason for wanting to stay with her is because of his tattoo, which says "I love Lucy." Based on economic thinking, you should advise him to ignore the fact that he has a tattoo because it is a(n)

A) opportunity cost.

B) marginal cost.

C) sunk cost.

D) total cost.

6. If all workers and equipment are equally productive in all activities, the opportunity cost of increasing output is always

   A) increasing.

   B) decreasing.

   C) the same.

   D) low.

7. The law of supply applies to an individual's decision to work because

   A) as the wage rises, the quantity of hours a worker is willing to supply increases.

   B) as the price workers receive rises, the quantity of hours a worker is willing to supply increases.

   C) workers need to be compensated with higher wages in order to work more hours to cover their increasing marginal opportunity costs.

   D) all of the above.

3.4 WHAT CAN CHANGE SUPPLY?

8. Which factor below does *not* change supply?

   A) Prices of inputs

   B) Expected future prices

   C) Price of the supplied product/service

   D) Number of businesses

9. The supply of a product/service increases with a(n)

   A) improvement in technology producing it.

   B) rise in the price a related product/service produced.

   C) rise in the price of an input.

   D) rise in the future price of the product/service.

10. The market supply of tires decreases if

    A) the price of oil — a major input used to produce tires — rises.

    B) tire-making technology improves.

    C) the expected future price of tires falls.

    D) new tire companies enter the market.

11. The furniture industry has shifted to using particle-board (glued wood chips), rather than real wood, which reduces costs. This

    A) increases supply.

    B) decreases supply.

    C) leaves furniture supply unchanged.

    D) impact on supply depends on demand.

12. The statement "Even after the reward was doubled, nobody volunteered for the mission" illustrates
    A) the law of supply.
    B) elastic supply.
    C) inelastic supply.
    D) inelastic demand.

13. Supply is most likely to be elastic for producing
    A) snow shovels.
    B) gold.
    C) houses.
    D) notebook computers.

14. There would be a high elasticity of supply for a business
    A) in a small town with no available workers.
    B) in a large town with many available workers.
    C) with workers who are lazy and unwilling to work additional hours.
    D) with workers who threaten to quit if their hours are reduced.

15. Since real trees take a very long time to grow, this year's supply of real Christmas trees is
    A) low.
    B) high.
    C) elastic.
    D) inelastic.

SHORT ANSWER

Write a short answer to each question. Your answer may be in point form.

1. Your boss asks you to work 20 additional hours next weekend. If you work those 20 hours, you will not be able to see your significant other. You really value the time you spend with your significant other, and the only time you've gone a weekend without seeing each other was when your friends offered to pay you $300 to spend the weekend with them instead. You agreed because this is the minimum amount you must be compensated for giving up a weekend with your significant other.
   A) Should you agree to work the 20 weekend hours if your boss pays your regular hourly wage rate of $10?
   B) Should you agree to work the 20 weekend hours if your boss pays the overtime rate of $15 per hour for the whole weekend?

2. Employees do not like working long weekdays and on weekends, so employers offer higher wages for the extra time in the form of "overtime pay," which could be up to three times the regular wage. Why is it important for businesses to offer overtime pay?

3. Suppose the government is considering raising income tax rates, which effectively reduces the wage that an individual earns. Research shows that women's decision to work is more sensitive to wage rates than is men's (women's decision to work is more elastic to wage rates). Explain how raising income tax rates will impact men and women differently. Who is less likely to work after the policy is implemented?

4. As wages go up, we work longer hours. Research indicates that some workers, such as medical surgeons, may work *fewer* hours in response to a wage increase. Why might surgeons make this decision? Would this violate the law of supply?

5. Your friend Pablo opens up a tattoo parlour because he thinks body art is a profitable industry. He is trying to forecast how different factors in the industry would affect supply in the market for tattoos. He knows you are taking a course in economics and asks you to verify whether his predictions are true or false.

   A) The entry of new businesses into the (hot) industry will increase supply.

   B) An increase in the minimum wage will increase supply.

   C) A rise in the price of piercings (a related service) will reduce supply of tattoos.

   D) An improvement in tattoo technology will increase supply.

   E) A rise in the price of tattoos will increase supply.

6. Dell tried to compete with Apple's iPod and invested millions of dollars into a factory to produce its own MP3 player. After months of poor sales, Dell started to look into the possibility of abandoning the player (which it eventually did). However, one of the top managers said it would be a mistake to abandon the project after so much money had been spent. What would be your advice?

7. A rise in oil prices causes many other products to become more expensive to produce, especially products with high transportation costs and oil-based plastics. How will the higher oil price affect the supply of these other products?

8. An unexpected fall heat wave makes consumers desperate to buy more air conditioners, but suppliers have none in stock. What factors might affect how quickly suppliers can restock their shelves? What does this have to do with the price elasticity of supply?

9. Rumour has it that Avril Lavigne is giving a concert in her home town of Napanee, Ontario. The first 50 fans get in free! You are 20 minutes away from Napanee and are considering speeding for the rest of the way. Speeding fines on Highway 401 outside Napanee are $110 for driving 120 km/hr, $143 for driving 130 km/hr, and $295 for driving 140 km/hr.

   A) If you are going 120 km/hour, what is the marginal cost if you speed up to 130 km/hour and get caught (assuming you *would* have been caught if you continued going at 120 km/hour)?

   B) If you are going 130 km/hour, what is the marginal cost of speeding up to 140 km/hour and getting caught (assuming you *would* have been caught if you continued at130 km/hour)?

   C) Compare the marginal cost of speeding up from 120 km/hour to 130 km/hour, with the marginal cost of speeding up from 130 km/hour to 140 km/hour. Why do you think the police have set up the fines this way?

10. List three things you have personally supplied in your life for someone else's consumption (for example, working at a summer job, donating blood, providing friendly advice, and so on). In each case, what were the most important considerations that affected your supply decision?

Chapter 4

Coordinating Smart Choices

Demand and Supply

LEARNING OBJECTIVES

After reading this chapter, you should be able to:

4.1 Describe how buyers and sellers compete and cooperate in markets.

4.2 Explain how shortages and surpluses affect prices.

4.3 Identify how market-clearing prices coordinate the smart choices of consumers and businesses.

4.4 Illustrate how changes in demand and supply affect market-clearing prices and quantities.

HAVE YOU EVER organized a big party and felt like it was a miracle everything worked out? There are so many details to look after and responsibilities to coordinate—who's bringing (or buying) the food and drinks, ice, music, toilet paper? Who's going to deal with crashers? Now imagine organizing one day in the life of a small town—or, if your imagination is up to it, in Toronto. Think about the millions of consumers who each make hundreds of decisions about what to eat or which movie to rent. Now think about the thousands of businesses that decide what to produce, where to find inputs, who to hire. Consumers find that, somehow, businesses have produced just about everything they want to buy—for a price. With no one in charge, it seems miraculous. How are all those billions of decisions coordinated so that you (and everyone else) can find the food you want for breakfast and the DVD you want at the video store, let alone places to live, water, jobs, and gas?

If all that doesn't seem enough of a miracle, consider that the coordination problem is a fast-moving target. Japanese food becomes fashionable, condos eclipse houses, new immigrants arrive with different tastes—and yet businesses adjust, and we all continue to find the changing items we are looking for.

Markets and prices are the keys to these apparent miracles. As consumers, we each make smart choices in our own interests. Businesses make smart choices in pursuit of profits. Markets, when they work well, create incentives that coordinate the right products and services being produced in the right quantities and at the right locations to satisfy our wants. This chapter explains how markets form prices, which provide signals and incentives coordinating the smart choices of consumers and businesses.

"It is not from the benevolence of the butcher, the brewer, or the baker that we expect our dinner, but from their regard to their own interest."

Adam Smith,
The Wealth of Nations, 1776

4.1 What's a Market?

Describe how buyers and sellers compete and cooperate in markets.

market:
the interactions of
buyers and sellers

Rolling Stone magazine named Jimi Hendrix the number-one rock guitarist of all time. Suppose you really want a vinyl copy of his first album, *Are You Experienced*. You can check out the local used album/CD stores, you can prowl garage sales for 60-something-year-olds cleaning out their basement album collections, or you can go online to eBay. These are all markets. A **market** is not a place (physical or virtual) or a thing: it's a process — the interactions between buyers and sellers. Markets exist wherever there is a process of competing bids (from buyers, or demanders) and offers (from sellers, or suppliers). What is common to all the markets above is a negotiation between a buyer and a seller that results in an exchange.

Markets Mix Competition and Cooperation

Markets are an unlikely mix of competition and cooperation. There is competition between buyers trying to get the same product. This is most obvious in auction markets like eBay, where you bid against other buyers and the highest bid wins. But even in a store with fixed prices or at a garage sale, you are competing with other potential buyers on a first-come, first-served basis.

Sellers also compete with each other for customers. Whether offering an album or artichokes, sellers try to get customers to buy from them by offering a lower price, better service, or higher quality than their competitors.

The cooperation in markets that is harder to see is between buyer and seller. Because any purchase or sale is voluntary, an exchange between a buyer and seller happens only when both sides end up better off. If you paid $100 for that rare Jimi Hendrix album, you must have felt that the benefit or satisfaction you would get is worth at least $100 (or you wouldn't have bought it). If the seller accepted $100, she felt that was at least the minimum she wanted to receive to give up the album (or she wouldn't have sold it).

Using the economist's terms for smart choices from Chapters 2 and 3, for you, the buyer, the marginal benefit of the album is at least as great as its price (marginal opportunity cost). For the seller, the price is at least as great as her estimate of marginal opportunity cost (the next best offer for the album). As long as the album — or any other product — sells voluntarily in a market, both sides are better off. Both buyer and seller have made smart choices.

Sure, you would have loved to pay less than $100, and the seller would have preferred to get $200. "Better off" doesn't require the buyer to get the lowest possible price or the seller to get the highest possible price. Both participants in the exchange are better off just as long each one has made a smart choice.

Voluntary exchange is cooperative at heart, and both sides win. Businesses want satisfied customers who will return, and they make money when they supply products/services that consumers want to buy. Consumers are better off when businesses supply products/services that provide satisfaction that is worth (or of greater value than) the price.

The Rules of the Game

For markets to work and voluntary exchanges to happen, some basic rules of the game are necessary. Through laws, government must define and protect property rights and enforce contracts between buyers and sellers. **Property rights** are rules that ensure that when you own something, no one can take it away from you by force. Property can be physical property (land, buildings, cars), financial property (stocks, bonds, savings), and intellectual property (music, books, or software resulting from creative effort, and protected by copyright and patents).

Without property rights, there would be no incentive to produce anything for exchange. Imagine that you operate a car-detailing business and have just finished a beautiful and time-consuming job on a 2009 Honda Acura. The owner of the car comes along, says thanks, and drives away without paying. If no laws protected you against theft, what incentive would you have to continue your business? While this example may sound outrageous, it's not much different from the case of a band that produces an album for sale, only to have it downloaded for free without the band or the record company being paid. Without property rights, most of our time and energy would have to go into protecting our property, rather than producing products/services.

While property rights are a prerequisite for anything to be produced, governments must also enforce agreements between buyers and sellers. For a successful exchange, both buyer and seller must deliver what they agreed to, and there must be some legal "referee" to settle disputes.

Consider the enormous amount of trust involved when you make an online purchase on eBay. The seller trusts you will pay. You trust the product will be delivered. This trust does not happen accidentally.

Part of the reason eBay has been successful is that it has implemented rules that foster the necessary trust. The PayPal system guarantees that payments made by the buyer are received by the seller. And the ability of buyers to give anonymous and public feedback about their experiences with a seller creates enormous incentives for sellers to "produce" happy customers. If these informal rules don't work, the legal system is still the ultimate referee. This enormous trust between complete strangers is the foundation for the billions of voluntary exchanges that happen every day in all markets. Even passionate supporters of "free markets" acknowledge that there is an important role for government in defining and enforcing property rights so that free and voluntary exchanges can happen in markets.

property rights: legally enforceable guarantees of ownership of physical, financial, and intellectual property

1. What is a market?

2. You are negotiating with a car dealer over the price of a new car. Explain where competition enters the process and where cooperation enters.

3. The Recording Industry Association of America's (RIAA) mission is "to foster a business and legal climate that supports and promotes our members' . . . intellectual property rights worldwide." Have you ever downloaded music? If so, what arguments do you use to counter RIAA's defence of property rights?

Refresh
4.1

www.myeconlab.com

4.2 Where Do Prices Come From?
Price Signals from Combining Demand and Supply

Explain how shortages and surpluses affect prices.

Why do most stores sell Gatorade for $3 a bottle, and doughnuts for 99 cents? Think back to the smart choices that consumers (Chapter 2) and businesses (Chapter 3) make: Prices play a central role. Consumers compare prices and marginal benefit *(buy if the marginal benefit is greater than the price)*, while businesses compare prices and marginal opportunity costs *(sell if the price is greater than the marginal opportunity costs)*. Where do these prices come from?

Prices are the outcome of a market process of competing bids and offers. These negotiations between buyers and sellers may be obvious on eBay or at garage sales, but when you buy Gatorade at the corner store or a coffee and bagel at Tim Hortons, the store has set the price and there is no negotiation. The only "process" seems to be the cashier swiping your debit card or making change. For most purchases we make as consumers, the answer to the question "Where do prices come from?" seems to be "Businesses set prices." What gives?

It's true that in a market economy, businesses are free to set any price they choose. But no one can force consumers to buy at any price, and competing businesses may set lower or higher prices. So why do prices settle at particular numbers?

The economist's short answer to these questions about where prices come from is . . . (drum roll) . . . the interaction of demand and supply, in markets with appropriate property rights! But that answer, while true, is pretty useless. We can point to anything that happens in an economy and say, in our best educated voice, "It is all determined by the laws of demand and supply." The longer and more useful answer exposes the hidden interactions between buyers and sellers, and also explains the miracles of markets in providing the products/services we want.

> *Prices are the outcome of a market process of competing bids (from buyers) and offers (from sellers).*

Rules of the Game Necessary for All Games, Not Just Markets

The game of football can be considered a model for how markets have developed. The earliest version, folk football, was played in medieval England—there were few rules, and the ones that were in place came about spontaneously and based on custom. There was "little skill . . . just muscle." The sport continued this way for centuries, until folk football morphed into soccer and rugby, and official rules were adopted. Skill started to matter, and the new forms of football were embraced the world over.

Typical markets grow in the way folk football did—evolving spontaneously, driven by participants, unstructured to the point when rules begin to develop. Only when the rules become formal does a market reach its full potential. "An absolutely free market is like folk football, a free-for-all brawl. A real market is like American football, an ordered brawl."

Like other markets, eBay is not a free-for-all brawl because of the rules and procedures that have evolved to ensure trust and enforce contracts. Instead of competition between two football teams, there is competition between thousands of buyers, and between thousands of sellers. But the rules allow cooperative deals to be struck.

Source: John McMillan, *Reinventing the Bazaar*, Norton, 2002, pp. 12–13.

Prices in Action

Paradoxically, the best way to understand why prices settle at particular numbers is to look at what happens in markets when prices have not settled. Let's begin the story of "Where do prices come from?" by looking at what happens when markets are not working to coordinate smart choices, leaving frustrated consumers and producers.

Since the story has to explain particular numbers, it will be helpful to have … particular numbers! Let's use a simple set of made-up numbers for the market for piercings (recall our example of Paola's Piercing and Fingernail Parlour, introduced in Chapter 3).

The best way to understand why prices settle at particular numbers is to look at what happens in markets when prices have not settled.

Figure 4.1	Market Demand and Supply for Piercings	
Price	**Quantity Demanded**	**Quantity Supplied**
$ 20	1200	200
$ 40	900	400
$ 60	600	600
$ 80	300	800
$100	0	1000

The three columns in Figure 4.1 show alternative market prices for piercings (column 1), and, for each price, the quantity of piercings demanded (column 2) and supplied (column 3). If you gaze down columns 1 and 2 together, you see that as the price rises, the quantity demanded decreases. This is the law of demand. As a product becomes more expensive, consumers economize on its use and search for cheaper substitutes. If you gaze down columns 1 and 3 together, you see that as the price rises, the quantity supplied increases. This is the law of supply. Higher prices increase business's willingness to supply, because higher prices mean higher profits and the ability to profitably cover higher marginal opportunity costs. While the particular numbers will be useful, all our stories really need is the general pattern of numbers. Higher prices generally lead to decreased quantity demanded and to increased quantity supplied in almost all markets.

We know from the law of demand that consumers prefer lower prices, and we know from the law of supply that businesses prefer higher prices. How do prices get set in a way that reconciles these opposing goals?

Frustrated Buyers What if the market price of piercings were $40 in parlours all around town? You might think that this relatively low price would make for happy consumers, but the number in Figure 4.1 tells another story. Look at row 2, where the price of a piercing is $40. Consumers want to buy 900 piercings, but Paola and her competitors are willing to supply only 400 piercings. While the 400 people who are able to buy a piercing for $40 will be happy, there are 500 frustrated buyers (900 − 400 = 500) who are willing and able to pay $40 but who can't get a parlour to do the piercing. This is a **shortage**, where quantity demanded exceeds quantity supplied. In markets with shortages, or **excess demand**, consumers experience long lineups and out-of-stock items at stores. Businesses experience products flying off the shelves and any inventories quickly dwindling to zero.

shortage or excess demand: quantity demanded exceeds quantity supplied

Shortages create pressure for prices to rise.

Shortages encourage competition among buyers. The consumers who most want the piercing will be willing to pay a bit more than $40, rather than being left with nothing. Buyers may bid for the scarce piercings (just like on eBay), driving up the price. Even if buyers don't actively bid up prices (when was the last time you offered to pay extra at Tim Hortons in hopes that they would find one more glazed doughnut for you?), sellers find that they can raise prices and still sell everything they have produced. Either way, shortages create pressure for prices to rise.

Rising prices provide signals and incentives, which are the key to how markets meet our wants. For businesses, higher prices are a signal, like a hand waving persistently in a classroom, saying, "Higher profits over here!" Higher prices and higher profits create an incentive for businesses to produce more and increase their quantity supplied. For consumers, higher prices mean we must revisit our smart choices. As prices go up, some consumers will give up on buying piercings and switch their planned purchases to some cheaper form of body decoration, like henna tattoos or costume jewellery. Quantity demanded decreases with higher prices.

Rising prices provide signals and incentives for businesses to increase quantity supplied and for consumers to decrease quantity demanded, eliminating the shortage.

Both adjustments — the increase in quantity supplied, and the decrease in quantity demanded — work to eliminate the shortage.

Frustrated Sellers Instead of $40, what if the market price of piercings was $80? Look at row 4 of Figure 4.1. At the relatively high price of $80, consumers want to buy only 300 piercings, but piercing parlours are eagerly willing to supply 800 piercings. So, all over town, parlours are expecting customers who don't show up, and idle piercers are sitting and reading newspapers. Parlours happily sell 300 piercings at $80, but are frustrated to the tune of 500 unsold piercings (800 − 300 = 500) they were willing to supply at that price. This is a **surplus**, where quantity supplied exceeds quantity demanded. In markets with surpluses, or **excess supply**, businesses experience underemployed resources, unsold products sitting on shelves, or rising inventories in warehouses. Those consumers willing and able to buy at the high price experience their choice of where to buy and sellers who are eager to please.

surplus or excess supply: quantity supplied exceeds quantity demanded

Surpluses encourage competition among sellers. The businesses that are most efficient or desperate for sales will cut their prices rather than be faced with empty piercing beds or unsold products. Some businesses will hold sales, or offer extras in trying to woo customers (free nail set with any piercing!). As discounts appear, consumers will be less willing to pay the $80 price. Surpluses create pressure for prices to fall.

Surpluses create pressure for prices to fall.

Falling prices also provide signals and incentives, but in the opposite direction to rising prices. For consumers, falling prices are an incentive to buy more of now less expensive products/services, switching from substitutes whose prices have not changed. And as prices fall, more people can afford to buy. More smart decisions result in buying products/services with lower prices. Quantity demanded increases. For businesses, falling prices are bad news — a warning signal of "lower profits ahead." They will decrease the quantities they are willing to supply, and switch inputs to more profitable opportunities. Paola will move some of her staff from piercing to fingernail painting. Quantity supplied decreases with falling prices.

Falling prices provide signals and incentives for businesses to decrease quantity supplied and for consumers to increase quantity demanded, eliminating the surplus.

Both adjustments — the increase in quantity demanded, and the decrease in quantity supplied — work to eliminate the surplus.

Adjusting Prices and Quantities   In these stories of shortages and surpluses, price adjustments play the key role. You may be thinking that the prices you observe in most markets don't adjust continuously and, in fact, settle for long times at particular values. Even the question I posed — "Why do prices settle at particular numbers?" — seems inconsistent with the stories about prices rising or falling in reaction to shortages and surpluses. There is a reconciliation, however.

Most businesses have some *market power* (a concept coming in Chapter 7), which means they have some control over setting prices. Businesses pick a price point that they expect will make the most profits, taking into account all cooperative and competitive forces. For a mutually beneficial exchange with a cooperating customer, price must be less than the customer's marginal benefit but also must profitably cover the business's marginal opportunity costs. The price point also must be competitive with what other similar businesses charge. Once a business picks a price point, it may turn out to be too low (shortages develop and products sell out quickly) or too high (resulting in surpluses, underemployed resources, and rising inventories). But over time, especially in the face of competition, businesses adjust price points in reaction to market conditions of shortages or surpluses.

Quantity adjustments also play an important role in the stories of how markets react to shortages or surpluses. When your favourite video store finds a popular movie is always out and frustrated customers come to the desk looking for it, the store orders more copies. Shortages lead to incremental increases in quantity supplied. If your local corner store regularly orders one case of Gatorade a week, but finds not all of the bottles are selling, it cuts back to ordering one case every other week. Surpluses lead to incremental decreases in quantity supplied. In response to excess demand or excess supply, businesses adjust quantities continuously, and can do so in small increments to match changing market conditions. When your boss asks you to work an extra shift next week, or your neighbourhood Tim Hortons bakes 10 dozen chocolate doughnuts a day instead of 13 dozen, those are quantity adjustments.

Even when prices don't change, shortages and surpluses also create incentives for frequent quantity adjustments to better coordinate smart choices of businesses and consumers.

What is remarkable about all of these price adjustments (not so frequent) and quantity adjustments (frequent) is that no consumer or business needs to know anything about anyone's personal wants or production capabilities. Prices (and quantities) serve as signals to both consumers and businesses, and all anyone has to do is consider his or her own self-interest. As long as an imbalance exists between quantity demanded and quantity supplied, prices will eventually adjust and send signals for consumers and businesses to change their smart decisions.

With excess demand, as long as prices are higher than marginal opportunity costs, businesses have an incentive to increase quantity supplied because there are profits to be made. And as long as the same prices are higher than consumers' marginal benefit (willingness and ability to pay), consumers have an incentive to search for cheaper substitutes and decrease quantity demanded.

With excess supply, as long as prices are lower than marginal opportunity costs, businesses have an incentive to decrease quantity supplied because they are losing money. And as long as the same prices are lower than consumers' marginal benefit, consumers will buy more of a product that feels like a bargain.

Consumers and businesses take all of these signals, and each make self-interested smart decisions based on the price. As a byproduct of all these individual decisions made by complete strangers, markets provide the products/services we want.

Refresh
4.2

www.myeconlab.com

1. Define a shortage, and explain who competes and what happens to prices.

2. Old Navy decides to price a new line of jeans at $75, which covers all marginal opportunity costs as well as a healthy profit margin. If Old Navy has priced the jeans too high, what signals does the company receive? What actions might Old Navy take next?

3. Most provincial parks charge a fixed price for a camping permit, and allow you to reserve specific campsites well in advance. By the time a summer holiday weekend arrives, all the permits are taken. There is excess demand, and no price adjustment. If you want to reserve your favourite campsite for next year, how do you compete, and who do you compete against?

4.3 When Prices Sit Still: Market-Clearing Prices Balancing Quantity Demanded and Quantity Supplied

Identify how market-clearing prices coordinate the smart choices of consumers and businesses.

So, after reading all these stories of rising prices (from shortages) and falling prices (from surpluses), you may be wondering, "When do prices finally sit still, and settle at particular values?" Indulge me one last time in looking at the numbers in Figure 4.1. Look at row 3, where the price of a piercing is $60. At $60, consumers want to buy 600 piercings, and all of the piercing parlours combined want to supply 600 piercings. At last, quantity demanded equals quantity supplied. With no shortages or surpluses, there are no competitive forces pushing prices up or down. Consumers are happy because every person who is willing and able to pay $60 gets a piercing. Businesses are happy because the $60 price profitably covers their marginal opportunity costs for the 600 piercings they are willing to supply.

There are consumers out there who would have demanded a piercing at $20, but think $60 is outrageous. They don't get pierced. But they have made a smart decision: For them, a piercing isn't worth $60, or $60 is more than they can reasonably afford. They make a smart choice to spend their money elsewhere, and thus are not putting pressure on piercing prices. Likewise, there are parlours out there that would have supplied more piercings if the price were $80, but $60 doesn't cover their marginal opportunity costs so they are using their resources to produce something else (nail sets? pedicures?) they can sell at a price that profitably covers marginal opportunity costs.

This price ($60 in our example) that coordinates quantity demanded and quantity supplied is so important that economists have two names for it. (Sort of like how you have at least two names — including nicknames — for people who are important to you.)

Market-clearing price is the first name for the market price that equalizes quantity demanded and quantity supplied. At the market-clearing price, there are no longer any frustrated buyers or sellers. There is a match for every buyer and seller, and all go home happy. Everyone who makes a voluntary exchange of $60 for a piercing (both the consumers buying and the parlours selling) is better off, or they wouldn't have bought and sold.

market-clearing price: the price when quantity demanded equals quantity supplied

The second name for the market price that equalizes quantity demanded and quantity supplied is **equilibrium price**. *Equilibrium* is a term from physics that means a balance of forces (see FYI in the margin). The equilibrium price exactly balances the forces of competition and cooperation to coordinate the smart choices of consumers and businesses. At the equilibrium price, there is no tendency for change (until some new event occurs to disturb the balance, as we will see in the next section) and no incentives for anyone — consumers or businesses — to change their own, self-interested, smart decisions. No one is kicking himself for making a mistaken purchase or missing a better opportunity. Everyone has done the best they can in their exchanges, given the wants and resources they started with.

Why is this particular "price that sits still" so important that it gets two names? It is the culmination of the forces of cooperation and competition that explains the miracle of the market. Ironically, when markets are functioning well and clearing, we don't pay much attention to this miracle. We find what we want for breakfast at Tim Hortons, the DVDs we like are on the shelf at the video store, and we find jobs, gas for our cars, and all the other products/services that satisfy our wants. And businesses find customers for all the products/services they want to profitably supply. Often, it's only when something goes wrong — perhaps a labour dispute or a natural disaster that disrupts supplies — that we realize how conveniently we usually find what we want to buy.

The fact that consumers find that businesses have produced just about everything they want to buy, and with no one in charge, and that billions of decisions get coordinated is due to . . . (drum roll reprise) . . . the interaction of demand and supply, in markets with appropriate property rights! The law of demand is shorthand for the smart choices of consumers. The law of supply is shorthand for the smart choices of businesses. Market-clearing prices (and quantities) result when smart choices are coordinated. The forces of competition (between consumers, and between businesses) are balanced with the forces of cooperation (voluntary, mutually beneficial exchanges between consumers and businesses). The key to this outcome is that price signals in markets create incentives so that while each person acts only in her own self-interest, the unintended consequence is the production of all the products/services we want.

Perhaps the most famous phrase in economics that describes this outcome is Adam Smith's "invisible hand" in his 1776 book, *The Wealth of Nations*:

> When an individual makes choices, "he intends only his own gain, and he is in this . . . led by an invisible hand to promote an end which was no part of his intention. . . . By pursuing his own interest he frequently promotes that of the society more effectually than when he really intends to promote it."

FOR YOUR INFORMATION

Definition of *equilibrium:* "A condition in which all acting influences are cancelled by others, resulting in a stable, balanced, or unchanging system." Synonym: *balance*.

Price signals in markets create incentives so that while each person acts only in her own self-interest, the unintended consequence is the production of all the products/services we want.

Refresh
4.3

1. Name and define the two other names for "prices that sit still."

2. Explain the balance between the forces of competition and cooperation at "prices that sit still." (I can't give away the answer to question 1, can I?)

3. In an attempt to promote the social good of energy conservation, Toronto Hydro introduced the Peaksaver Program. Participating households received a $25 reward for allowing a "peaksaver" switch to be installed on their central air conditioners, which briefly turns off the air conditioner during peak demand times on hot summer days. Do you think the program would work without the $25 reward? How does this illustrate the "invisible hand"?

www.myeconlab.com

We live in a fast-paced society where change happens regularly. Food and clothing go in and out of style, technology is constantly changing the way we communicate and how and what we produce, and business may boom in Alberta and bust in New Brunswick. Even if markets succeed in temporarily coordinating the plans of consumers and businesses and settle at market-clearing prices, what about when change happens? Will markets still coordinate the right products/services being produced in the right quantities at the right locations to satisfy our wants when the "right" target keeps moving?

Believe it or not, all the stories about shortages, surpluses, adjusting prices, and quantities actually had very limited change. Yes, prices and quantities changed, and smart decisions changed — but in the background, I was holding constant almost everything else.

All the stories began with the numbers in Figure 4.1, which illustrate the law of demand (when price rises, quantity demanded decreases) and the law of supply (when price rises, quantity supplied increases). We could focus carefully on those relationships between price and quantity because we were holding constant all other influences on consumers' choices and on businesses' choices.

Remember the Chapter 2 distinction between a change in quantity demanded (caused by a change in price) and a change in demand? Five factors can cause a change in demand. Name at least three and win a prize! Answers: changes in preferences, prices of related products, income, expected future prices, and number of consumers. All of those are unchanged in the numbers in Figure 4.1. And remember that Chapter 3 distinction between a change in quantity supplied (caused by a change in price) and a change in supply? The five factors that can cause a change in supply (changes in technology, prices of inputs, prices of related products produced, expected future prices, number of businesses) also are all unchanged in Figure 4.1.

Don't decide to give up on this chapter because you fear I plan to slog through changes in all 10 factors. To get you to break time faster, I'll combine the explanations into just four groups: what happens to market-clearing prices and quantities when there are increases or decreases in demand, and increases or decreases in supply.

Increases in Demand

For an increase in demand, market-clearing price rises, and quantity supplied increases.

When the Japanese food craze hit about 10 years ago, there was an increase in demand for sushi, triggered by a change in preferences. Increased demand drives up the market price, and restaurants responded to that signal of higher profits by increasing the quantity supplied of sushi. Any other factor that increases demand will cause a rise in the market-clearing price and an increase in the quantity supplied.

Decreases in Demand

For a decrease in demand, market-clearing price falls, and quantity supplied decreases.

With business booming in Alberta from oil revenues in 2007, many people moved from New Brunswick out west. What did this decrease in population do to the real estate market in New Brunswick? There was a decrease in demand, which drove down the market price, and there was a decrease in the quantity supplied of new housing. Any other factor that decreases demand will cause a fall in the market-clearing price and a decrease in the quantity supplied.

Increases in Supply

The relentless improvement in semiconductor technology makes it cheaper to produce computers and causes an increase in the supply of computers. Market price falls as Dell and HP compete for customers by lowering prices to reflect their lower costs of production. Consumers respond to lower prices by increasing their quantity demanded of computers. Any other factor that increases supply will cause a fall in the market-clearing price and an increase in the quantity demanded.

For an increase in supply, market-clearing price falls, and quantity demanded increases.

Decreases in Supply

The business boom in Alberta drove up wages, as businesses competed for scarce workers. The going wage, even in fast-food restaurants, rose from $10 to $15. For restaurants, this rise in inputs prices caused a decrease in supply. Restaurants were then willing to supply meals only at higher prices, and the market price of meals rose. Rising prices caused customers to rethink their smart food choices, and quantity demanded of restaurant meals decreased. Any other factor that decreases supply will cause a rise in the market-clearing price and a decrease in quantity demanded.

For a decrease in supply, market-clearing price rises, and quantity demanded decreases.

Still On Target

Markets are adept at reacting to change. Whether there are shortages, surpluses, or changes in any of the 10 factors affecting demand or supply, markets react quickly because prices create incentives for consumers and businesses to adjust their smart choices. Price signals in markets create incentives so that while each person acts only in her own self-interest, the result (coordinated through Adam Smith's invisible hand of competition) is the miracle of continuous, ever-changing production of the products/services we want.

Refresh 4.4

1. What happens to the market-clearing price and quantity when demand increases? When demand decreases? When supply increases? When supply decreases?

2. Predicting changes in market-clearing prices and quantities is harder when *both* demand *and* supply change at the same time. You run a halal butcher shop in Ottawa and expect an increase in the number of Muslims in Ottawa. Rents for retail space are also falling all over town. What do you think will happen to the market-clearing price for halal meat? What will happen to the quantity sold?

3. In response to the business boom in Alberta, the city of Edmonton offered $200 per month rent subsidies to low-income families so they could afford to live and work in the city. What impact would this effective *increase in income* have on rents? What do you think was the intention of the subsidies?

www.myeconlab.com

Coordinating *Smart* Choices

Demand and Supply

CHAPTER SUMMARY

4.1 WHAT'S A MARKET?

Markets connect competition between buyers, competition between sellers, and cooperation between buyers and sellers. Government guarantees of property rights allow markets to function.

- **Market** — the interactions of buyers and sellers.
- Because any purchase or sale is voluntary, an exchange between a buyer and seller happens only when both sides end up better off.
  - Buyers are better off when businesses supply products/services that provide satisfaction (marginal benefit) that is at least as great as the price paid.
  - Sellers are better off when the price received is at least as great as marginal opportunity costs.
- **Property rights** — legally enforceable guarantees of ownership of physical, financial, and intellectual property.

4.2 WHERE DO PRICES COME FROM?
PRICE SIGNALS FROM COMBINING DEMAND AND SUPPLY

When there are shortages, competition between buyers drives prices up. When there are surpluses, competition between sellers drives prices down.

- When the market price turns out to be too low:
  - **shortage,** or **excess demand** — quantity demanded exceeds quantity supplied.
  - shortages create pressure for prices to rise.
  - rising prices provide signals and incentives for businesses to increase quantity supplied and for consumers to decrease quantity demanded, eliminating the shortage.

- When the market price turns out to be too high:

  - **surplus,** or **excess supply** — quantity supplied exceeds quantity demanded.

  - surpluses create pressure for prices to fall.

  - falling prices provide signals and incentives for businesses to decrease quantity supplied and for consumers to increase quantity demanded, eliminating the surplus.

- Even when prices don't change, shortages and surpluses also create incentives for frequent *quantity adjustments* to better coordinate smart choices of businesses and consumers.

4.3 WHEN PRICES SIT STILL: MARKET-CLEARING PRICES
BALANCING QUANTITY DEMANDED AND QUANTITY SUPPLIED

Market-clearing prices coordinate the smart choices of consumers and businesses, balancing quantity demanded and quantity supplied.

- The price that coordinates the smart choices of consumers and businesses has two names:

  - **market-clearing price** — the price when quantity demanded equals quantity supplied

  - **equilibrium price** — the price that balances forces of competition and cooperation, so that there is no tendency for change

- Market-clearing prices balance the forces of competition (between consumers and between businesses) with the forces of cooperation (voluntary, mutually beneficial exchanges between consumers and businesses).

- Price signals in markets create incentives, so that while each person acts only in her own self-interest, the result (coordinated through Adam Smith's invisible hand of competition) is the miracle of continuous, ever-changing production of the products/services we want.

4.4 MOVING TARGETS:
WHAT HAPPENS WHEN DEMAND AND SUPPLY CHANGE?

When demand or supply change, market-clearing prices and quantities change. The price changes cause businesses and consumers to adjust their smart choices. Well-functioning markets supply the changed products and services demanded.

- For a change in demand (caused by changes in preferences, prices of related products, income, expected future prices, number of consumers)

  - an increase in demand causes a rise in market-clearing price, and an increase in quantity supplied.

  - a decrease in demand causes a fall in market-clearing price, and a decrease in quantity supplied.

- For a change in supply (caused by changes in technology, prices of inputs, prices of related products produced, expected future prices, number of businesses)

  - an increase in supply causes a fall in market-clearing price and an increase in quantity demanded.

  - a decrease in supply causes a rise in market-clearing price and a decrease in quantity demanded.

TRUE/FALSE

Circle the correct answer.

Apu Nahasapeemapetilon opens an outdoor iced cappuccino stand on his street in order to sell coffee to neighbours during peak hours of the day. Apu's product is unique enough that it allows him some choice in what price to charge. Use this scenario to answer questions 1 to 9.

4.1 WHAT'S A MARKET?

1. If customers are allowed to steal the iced cappuccinos without paying, this would still be a market.   **True**   **False**

2. The price should cover what it costs to make the iced cappuccinos, but not the cost of Apu's time.   **True**   **False**

4.2 PRICE SIGNALS FROM COMBINING DEMAND AND SUPPLY

3. In order for price and quantity adjustments to occur in this market, Apu needs to be aware of the personal wants of his neighbours.   **True**   **False**

4. If Apu prices above the maximum price that consumers are willing to pay, then he will end up with excess supply.   **True**   **False**

5. If Apu prices below the maximum price that consumers are willing to pay, then he will lose out on potential profits.   **True**   **False**

4.3 MARKET-CLEARING PRICES BALANCING QUANTITY DEMANDED AND QUANTITY SUPPLIED

6. If Apu sets a price that leaves him with no excess demand and no excess supply, he has found the equilibrium price.   **True**   **False**

4.4 WHAT HAPPENS WHEN DEMAND AND SUPPLY CHANGE?

7. An unexpected health warning links iced cappuccino consumption to severe obesity. The following causal chain of events would likely follow in the local coffee market: **True**   **False**

   (*Hint*: Assume that Apu's neighbours are not like Homer Simpson and *would* care about the health effects!)

   Demand $\downarrow$ → surplus → price $\uparrow$ → quantity supplied $\uparrow$ and quantity demanded $\downarrow$ → equilibrium (surplus disappears)

8. The Simpson family decides to also set up an iced cappuccino stand. The following causal chain of events would likely follow in the local coffee market:

Supply $\uparrow$ → shortage → price $\uparrow$ → quantity supplied $\uparrow$ and quantity demanded $\downarrow$ → equilibrium (shortage disappears)

True   **False**

9. Apu's wife gives birth to quintuplets, which increases the value of his time. The following causal chain of events would likely follow in the local coffee market:

Supply$\downarrow$ → shortage → price $\uparrow$ → quantity supplied $\uparrow$ and quantity demanded $\downarrow$ → equilibrium (shortage disappears)

True   **False**

10. Warmer weather appears to be giving cats a chance to mate three times each year instead of the usual two times a year (that is, due to global warming, more cats are on the prowl). The result has been a sharp increase in the cat population. The Humane Society last year had to find homes for roughly 6000 cats, compared with 3000 cats five years ago. Therefore, this is a good time to buy cats from the Humane Society.

True   **False**

11. Durham University researchers report Scottish grey seals are having more sex thanks to global warming. This is because, as drinking water becomes scarce, the females must travel farther distances and other males are able to seduce them. The market price for seal coat fur will likely increase.

True   **False**

12. Ontario had a ratio of 27 students for each full-time professor in 2005–06, while other provinces, on average, had a ratio of 18-to-one. Given that enrolment in Ontario universities is expected to continue to increase, it is estimated that Ontario needs 11 000 more professors by the end of the decade. If universities reduced qualification requirements to allow students with college degrees to teach introductory university courses, this action would help reduce the shortage.

True   **False**

13. In the early 2000s, many Canadians were worried about the "brain drain" (that is, Canada's most talented workers moving to the U.S. for jobs after obtaining a good education in Canada). Recent evidence suggests that the brain drain has been plugged, as more Canadians prefer to stay home and a lot more Americans are coming north. In 2005, almost 11 000 Americans came north, double the number in 2000, and more of them had at least a bachelor's degree. All else being equal, this will put upward pressure on the wages of workers in jobs requiring a bachelor's degree.

True   False

14. Canada Summer Jobs is an initiative by the federal government that provides wage subsidies to help small Canadian companies create career-related summer jobs for students between the ages of 15 and 30. This initiative will likely increase the demand for workers.

True   False

15. Organ donation saves hundreds of lives each year across Ontario, yet there are not enough available donors to meet the demand for organ transplants. In 2007, the Ontario government invested $4 million in a new plan to boost organ donations, which includes funding to reimburse living donors for pre-approved expenses, such as accommodation, meals, travel, and lost income. This new plan will likely lead to an increase in the quantity of organs supplied.

True   False

MULTIPLE CHOICE

Circle the correct answer.

4.1   WHAT'S A MARKET?

1. The place where buyers and sellers meet is called

   A) a store.

   B) an economy.

   C) a party.

   D) a market.

4.2   PRICE SIGNALS FROM COMBINING DEMAND AND SUPPLY

2. If a market is not at the market-clearing price,

   A) prices adjust.

   B) prices send signals for consumers and businesses to change their smart decisions.

   C) quantities adjust.

   D) all of the above.

3. Which of the following is *not* a quantity adjustment?

   A) Tim Hortons asking its workers to work overtime

   B) Blockbuster ordering extra copies of *Harry Potter*

   C) Leon's Furniture Ltd. eliminating sales tax on all patio furniture items

   D) a fish processing plant laying off 10 percent of its workers

4.3 MARKET-CLEARING PRICES BALANCING QUANTITY DEMANDED AND QUANTITY SUPPLIED

4. A price at which there are no shortages and no surpluses is a

   A) maximum price.

   B) minimum price.

   C) affordable price.

   D) market-clearing price.

5. In equilibrium,

   A) the price consumers are willing to pay equals the price suppliers are willing to accept.

   B) consumers would like to buy more at the current price.

   C) producers would like to sell more at the current price.

   D) all of the above.

4.4 WHAT HAPPENS WHEN DEMAND AND SUPPLY CHANGE?

6. If demand increased and supply decreased, this would lead to

   A) higher prices.

   B) lower prices.

   C) chaos.

   D) a shortage in the market.

7. The following will cause a reduction in prices:

   A) demand increases and supply decreases.

   B) demand increases and supply increases.

   C) demand decreases and supply decreases.

   D) demand decreases and supply increases.

8. A surplus can be eliminated by

   A) increasing supply.

   B) decreasing the quantity demanded.

   C) allowing the price to fall.

   D) allowing the quantity bought and sold to fall.

The Canadian Restaurant and Foodservices Association predicts a shortfall of 44 300 food and beverage workers in British Columbia by 2015. Use this information to answer questions 9 to 11.

9. This implies that, in British Columbia,

   A) demand for restaurant food exceeds supply of restaurant food.

   B) supply of restaurant food exceeds demand for restaurant food.

   C) demand is greater than supply for restaurant workers.

   D) supply is greater than demand for restaurant workers.

10. A shortage creates pressure for prices to change. In the British Columbia example, this may be represented through

    A) an increase in the price of labour (workers).

    B) an increase in the wage paid to employees in the restaurant business.

    C) an increase in labour costs for restaurant businesses.

    D) all of the above.

11. If the price offered to workers (that is, the wage) in restaurant businesses in B.C. increases, then

    A) the quantity of work supplied will increase.

    B) the quantity of work demanded will decrease.

    C) more workers will be looking for work.

    D) all of the above.

12. According to the Canadian Restaurant and Foodservices Association, "The labour shortage is the number one issue for restaurant operators in Alberta, who are coping with an estimated shortfall of 11 000 employees in the food-service industry alone." This implies that

    A) there is no demand for food service.

    B) the demand for food service is less than the supply of food service.

    C) the demand for food service is equal to the supply of food service.

    D) the demand for food service is greater than the supply of food service.

13. The Children's Fitness Tax Credit was introduced by the Government of Canada to provide parents with a tax credit (benefit) of up to $500 to register a child under the age of 16 in a program of physical activity. Therefore,

    A) demand for Harry Potter novels may increase.

    B) demand for Harry Potter novels may decrease.

    C) supply of Harry Potter novels may increase.

    D) supply of Harry Potter novels may decrease.

14. Recent research shows that the dramatic rise in obesity in the United States is due more to the overconsumption of unhealthy foods than it is to underactivity. As a result of this finding,

    A) the demand for potato chips is likely to increase.

    B) the demand for GoodLife Fitness gym memberships is likely to increase.

    C) the demand for nutrition-promoting foods will increase.

    D) all of the above.

15. Since 1960, there has been a dramatic increase in the number of working mothers. Based on this information alone, we can predict that the market for child-care services has experienced a(n)

    A) increase in demand.

    B) decrease in demand.

    C) increase in quantity demanded.

    D) decrease in quantity supplied.

SHORT ANSWER

Write a short answer to each question. Your answer may be in point form.

1. The price set in a market is much more than a number. What functions does a price perform for the buyers and sellers? And what is so special about the "market-clearing price"?

2. Apu wants to set the market equilibrium price, so he surveys all three families on his street in order to determine how many cappuccinos per day they are willing to buy at different prices. He gives them four price options. Their answers can be summarized on the following table.

Price per Iced Capuccino	Flanders Family Quantity Demanded	Van Houten Family Quantity Demanded	Simpson Family Quantity Demanded	Market Quantity Demanded
$1	2	5	5	12
$2	1	3	4	8
$3	0	1	3	4
$4	0	0	2	2

Apu also estimates his costs and determines how many iced cappuccinos he is willing to sell. Market demand and Apu's supply are summarized in the following table:

Price per Iced Capuccino	Market Quantity Demanded	Apu's Quantity Supplied
$1	12	7
$2	8	8
$3	4	9
$4	2	10

A) What is the market-clearing price? Explain.

B) If Apu sets the price above $2, will there be a shortage or surplus in the market? Explain.

C) If Apu sets the price above $2, will there be pressure for the price to rise or fall? Explain.

3. Rising housing prices in Alberta have motivated some Albertans to migrate to Saskatchewan. In fact, housing prices in Saskatchewan are at record levels. Using a demand and supply framework, explain why prices in Saskatchewan's housing market are rising.

4. Billions of dollars will be invested in energy-related projects across Alberta over the next 20 years, prompting Albertans to ask where the workers for these projects will come from. In 2007, the Alberta government warned that it is facing a shortfall of 100 000 workers by 2015, with at least 40 000 of those positions in the oil and gas sector. "It's in the whole economy . . . whether it's the Tim Hortons or a new restaurant that can't find people to serve coffee and food because there's not enough people to keep the restaurants or coffee shops open."

A) A union proposal calls for 14.5-percent wage increases over two years, barely above Alberta's nation-leading inflation rate of 6.5 percent. Explain why unions are asking for such high wage increases for their workers.

B) The skilled labour shortage is prompting many companies to look overseas for employees. If companies can hire many temporary foreign workers, how might this affect the wages that workers in Alberta receive?

5. Suppose a natural disaster increases the need for flashlights. Outline the steps the market will go through to communicate this information to not only the makers of flashlights, but also the makers of flashlight-making equipment.

6. High birth rates in the 1950s caused school overcrowding in the 1970s and 1980s, while the 1990s saw some schools closed down in the same neighbourhoods. If education is a product, identify: (a) the consumer, and (b) the supplier. Why do you think the school system keeps experiencing shortages and surpluses?

7. Temporary job placement agencies, such as Ontario Works, make it easier for workers to find jobs and for employers to find workers. Would the presence of a temporary job placement agency (in any given market) result in an increase, decrease, or uncertain change in the wages paid to workers?

8. Due to labour shortages, employers are allowed to hire temporary foreign workers (TFWs) once the employer proves the Canadian labour pool is exhausted. Between 1996 and 2005, the number of TFWs doubled in Canada to 145 871. If the Government of Canada eliminated this program, what would happen to the wages of Canadian workers who were previously competing with TFWs for jobs?

9. Suppose the Nudist Party wins the next federal election because all the clothed citizens forgot to vote. The Nudists pass a law making it illegal to produce clothes. The shift in party power causes a shift in preference away from buying clothes.

   A) The cost of supplying clothes is now very high given that it is illegal to do so. Assuming that the demand for clothes reduces only slightly (in comparison), how would this affect the market price for clothes?

   B) Now suppose that the police don't take the law seriously (where would officers pin their badges?), and put zero effort into enforcement. Assuming that the cost of supplying clothes is no different than it was before the election, how would the market price for clothes be affected?

10. In 2007, the Government of Canada proposed ending work permits for foreign strippers. According to a representative from the Adult Entertainment Association of Canada, "This is one of the professions where there is a worker shortage." Explain how the proposed legislative amendment would impact the price for adult entertainment if it were to be implemented.

What Gives When *Prices Don't?*

RENT CONTROL

Government Choices, Markets, Efficiency, and Equity

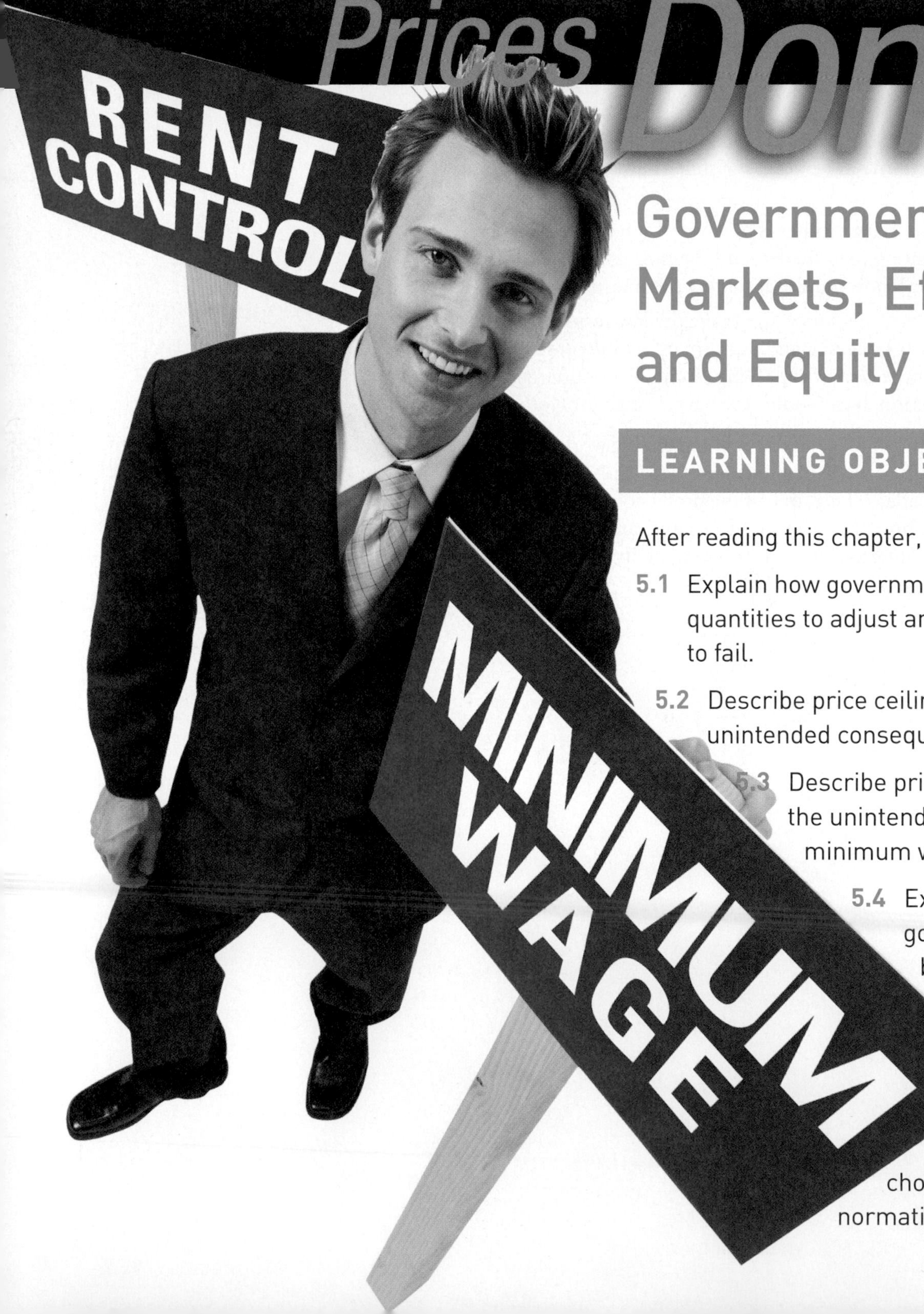

MINIMUM WAGE

EVERY TIME GAS PRICES JUMP above $1 per litre, the

complaints begin — the oil companies are price gouging, gas taxes
should be lowered, governments should do something. When motorists
(who are also voters) complain about prices, politicians notice.
Parliament holds hearings, and sometimes — like with the New
Energy Program in 1974 — governments actually fix oil prices,
making it illegal for suppliers to charge higher prices. The pattern
is similar when tenants (voters) complain that rents are too high, or
workers (voters) complain that wages are too low. Governments respond
with rent controls or minimum wage laws.

When high (or low) prices cause voters pain, governments are
tempted to fix prices. Despite good intentions, the consequences are
usually not what governments intended. Prices are the signals that
coordinate the smart decisions of consumers and businesses. Fixing
prices cripples the flow of information and incentives that make markets
effective at producing what we want. In this chapter, we look at what
happens when prices can't adjust.

Government choices, like choices for consumers and businesses,
involve trade-offs. When governments act to fix real problems around
affordability and fairness that markets can create, there is often a better
solution than fixing prices. We are also going to see that, despite the
unintended consequences, sometimes governments *might* still make
a smart choice to give up the benefits of flexible prices and markets in
order to promote more equitable outcomes.

5.1 Minding Your P's and Q's: Do Prices or Quantities Adjust?

Explain how government-fixed prices cause quantities to adjust and market coordination to fail.

If you have ever worked in retail sales, you know how rude customers can be. Even a simple "please" or "thank you" is hard to come by. But when a customer is polite and appreciative, you are motivated to give them better service. The exchange is easier and smoother, and both you and the customer feel good. Markets don't have manners, but when markets are working well (on good behaviour?), the voluntary exchanges are smoother and the outcomes better when prices and quantities (the market's P's and Q's) can easily adjust. We know from Chapter 4 that if the quantities demanded and supplied do not match, then prices adjust, and quantities follow, to coordinate the smart choices of consumers and businesses.

When Price Is Fixed Too Low, Quantities Adjust

Here's a markets-on-good-behaviour story. Suppose gas has been regularly selling for $1 per litre. That is a market-clearing price, matching the quantity of gas demanded and quantity of gas supplied at 85 million litres per month. Then, to no one's great surprise, some Middle East conflict destroys some oil refineries, and supply decreases.

If the price remained at $1 per litre there would be a shortage, as the unchanged quantity demanded would face a reduced quantity supplied. So begins the classic Chapter 4 shortage story of frustrated buyers. Consumers compete against each other for the now hard-to-find gasoline, and bid up prices. Gasoline suppliers respond to the rising prices by supplying increased quantities. Rising prices also lead to decreased quantity demanded, as consumers substitute away from more expensive gas, which fewer can afford (good thing you bought an iPod for those additional transit rides). Adjustments continue — with prices rising, increasing quantities supplied and decreasing quantities demanded — until the shortage is eliminated and the quantity of gas demanded again matches the quantity supplied. This is how well-functioning markets behave, resulting in the coordination of smart choices for both consumers and businesses.

What if the government, facing an election and worried about motorist/voter complaints, fixes gas prices at $1 per litre? A new law makes it illegal for anyone to sell gasoline for more than $1 per litre. The unchanged demand and reduced supply schedules appear in Figure 5.1. At the price of $1 per litre (row 2), the quantity of gas demanded stays at 85 million litres per month. But gasoline suppliers, now paying higher oil prices, are willing to supply only 55 million litres per month at the fixed price of $1 per litre. Governments have the power to fix prices, but they can't force businesses to produce if that price is not profitable.

Figure 5.1	Market Demand and Supply for Gasoline (after supply decrease)	
Price per litre	**Quantity Demanded** (millions of litres per month)	**Quantity Supplied** (millions of litres per month)
$0.80	95	35
$1.00	85	55
$1.20	75	75
$1.40	65	95

Frustrated Buyers   This frustrated buyer story does not have a happy ending. Now that prices can't adjust, the frustration will continue. Consumers who are lucky enough to get gas at the fixed price will either spend hours driving around looking for stations that still have some gas, wait in long line-ups, or try to bribe gas station owners to supply them first. Most will have to give up some driving — to the tune of 30 million litres less per month that is no longer supplied (85 million litres demanded – 55 million litres supplied). *Quantities adjust.*

Fixing prices does not change the voluntary nature of exchanges in a market economy. It is easier to smile and be on good behaviour when you are part of a mutually beneficial, voluntary exchange. Businesses are willing to supply only if price covers all opportunity costs of production. Consumers are willing to demand only if their smart choices make them willing and able to pay for the product/service at that price. For any price, set by the market or set by governments, businesses can always cut back output or shut down factories or move their inputs elsewhere. Consumers can always reduce their purchases or keep their wallets shut or buy something else (there are always substitutes).

Governments can legally fix prices, but consumers and businesses will *adjust quantities* to make their respective smart choices at the fixed price. But when prices can't adjust, the smart choices of consumers and the smart choices of businesses will not be coordinated, and both groups will be unhappy.

When Price Is Fixed Too High, Quantities Adjust

In Chapter 4, we discussed what happens in a well-functioning market when price is set too high. There would be a . . . (*Hint:* It's an *s*-word) . . . *surplus.* The quantity supplied (businesses are willing to produce more at higher prices — the "law of supply") is greater than the quantity demanded (consumers are less willing and able to buy at higher prices — the "law of demand"). This is the surplus story of frustrated suppliers who can't find willing buyers. If the price of gas is *above* the market-clearing price, businesses will compete against each other for hard-to-find customers, and cut prices. Falling prices lead to increased quantity demanded, as consumers buy more of the now-cheaper gas, which more can afford. Gasoline suppliers respond to the falling prices with decreased quantities supplied. Adjustments continue — with prices falling, increasing quantities demanded, and decreasing quantities supplied — until the surplus is eliminated and the quantity of gas demanded again matches the quantity supplied.

Frustrated Sellers   What if government stepped in to the gasoline market and fixed a higher-than-market-clearing price of $1.40 per litre? According to Figure 5.1 (row 4), gasoline suppliers are happy to supply 95 million litres per month, but consumers will demand only 65 million litres per month. There is a monthly surplus of 30 million litres of gasoline. Without price cuts, consumers will buy only 65 million litres, so the quantity actually sold will be 65 million litres, with 30 million litres stagnating in storage tanks around the country. Businesses will cut back on the quantity of gasoline produced in future months, until the unsold inventory finally disappears. *Quantities adjust.* But because prices can't adjust, the smart choices of consumers and the smart choices of businesses are not coordinated. Businesses are willing to supply more gasoline, but are frustrated because they cannot sell it. And in a voluntary market system, neither businesses nor governments can force consumers to buy more at the higher price.

When price is fixed below market-clearing, shortages develop (quantity demanded greater than quantity supplied) and consumers are frustrated.
Quantity sold = quantity supplied only.

When price is fixed above market-clearing, surpluses develop (quantity supplied greater than quantity demanded) and businesses are frustrated.
Quantity sold = quantity demanded only.

Fixed Prices = No Coordinated Prices When governments fix prices, either below or above the market-clearing price, the smart choices of consumers and businesses are not coordinated. The only way shortages or surpluses disappear is by quantities adjusting to whichever is less — quantity supplied (with a shortage), or quantity demanded (with a surplus). With fixed prices, either consumers or businesses are frustrated, and markets do not function as well as when prices and quantities (P's and Q's) are allowed to adjust.

Refresh 5.1

1. If government makes it illegal for businesses to lower their prices, and there is a surplus of products/services in the market, explain how consumers and businesses will react.

2. Tim Hortons charges the same price for coffee no matter what time of day it is. At your local Tim's, there are times of the day you walk right up to the counter and order, and other times when you have to wait in line. Explain how quantities supplied and quantities demanded are being coordinated.

3. You own a flower shop and usually sell roses for $25 a dozen. In the month before Valentine's Day, your suppliers charge you a higher price for roses. A politician who has many romantics in his riding gets Parliament to pass a private member's bill making it illegal to charge more than $25 for a dozen roses. Other flower prices are not fixed. What will be your smart business choice for Valentine's Day?

www.myeconlab.com

5.2 Do Rent Controls Help the Homeless? Price Ceilings

Describe price ceilings and explain the unintended consequences of rent controls.

rent controls: example of price ceiling: maximum price set by government, making it illegal to charge higher price

Not many citizens feel good seeing people sleeping out on the streets on a freezing winter night. Homelessness and a lack of affordable housing are serious problems in most big Canadian cities. To help solve these problems, compassionate and well-intentioned individuals, charitable organizations, and religious groups often ask governments to *do something* by controlling rents. **Rent controls** are a form of price fixing (rents are the monthly "price" of apartments). Governments can set a maximum rent (called a **price ceiling**) that limits how high rents can be raised, while allowing rents to be flexible downward. (The government-fixed price of $1 per litre of gasoline in the previous section is another example of a price ceiling.)

Governments introduce rent controls in response to concerns of many groups. Rent controls obviously have benefits for renters (in Toronto, 40 percent of voters are renters), but also appeal to citizens who believe government should help those who are less fortunate, simply because it is the right, or ethical, thing to do. Religious groups also share a belief in helping the poor. Social activists argue that in a relatively wealthy and enlightened society like Canada, governments should ensure that essential services like affordable housing, education, and health care are available to all citizens. These services are too important, they argue, to be left to impersonal markets alone to provide.

Benefits and Costs What are the perceived benefits of rent controls that lead governments to introduce them? A political benefit of rent controls to governments (not to renters) is that the government does not have to spend any money (which building schools or roads would require), yet voters perceive that the government is trying to do something to help. Rent controls, for those who can find apartments, reduce the amount of money tenants have to pay for housing, leaving them more money for food, clothing, and other necessities. Some citizens and politicians who believe in the "Robin Hood principle" — named after the famous character from medieval folklore — also see rent controls as a way of redistributing income from (relatively) rich landlords to (relatively) poor tenants.

Every choice, even a government choice, has an opportunity cost. What are the costs that must be weighed against the benefits to decide whether rent controls are a smart choice for helping the homeless?

While rent controls are introduced with the best of intentions, they have some undesirable and unintended consequences. Like any fixed price, rent controls cripple the coordinating forces of well-functioning markets. Rent ceilings are always set *below* the market-clearing rent, creating a classic shortage. (A rent ceiling above the market-clearing rent would be irrelevant. When apartments are readily available at $1000 per month, what good does it do to have a law preventing rents from rising above $1300?)

At the controlled rent ceiling, the quantity of housing supplied is less than it would be at the market-clearing rent. So while those who find apartments will be better off, there will be *fewer apartments available*. Quantities adjust. With a shortage of apartments at the rent ceiling (the quantity of apartments demanded will be greater than the quantity supplied), consumers who can no longer find apartments will be frustrated and worse off.

Consequences While governments can fix rents, they cannot force landlords to supply apartments if the rent does not cover all opportunity costs of "producing" or supplying housing. Remember, the opportunity cost of any input is its *best alternative use.* At the controlled rents, some landlords may see a better return by turning their building into condominiums, again reducing the supply of apartments. A homeowner who rents out a basement apartment in her house may decide it's not worth it at the lower rent ceiling and convert that space back to her own family's use. Smart choices change with changes in prices. With more time to adjust to the lower rent ceiling, fewer apartment buildings may be built (still more condos instead).

With tenants competing for scarce apartments, landlords have the upper hand. Landlords may allow the physical condition of their properties to deteriorate, since they can be sure of finding tenants given the shortage. Spending less on maintenance improves their profits in the short run. Let the tenants pay for painting and repairs! Landlords may also charge a potential tenant "key money," which is a polite term for a bribe, in exchange for giving that tenant (as opposed to the many other willing tenants) the key to the scarce apartment. Landlords are also in a position to discriminate against renting to tenants they don't like, both for legitimate reasons (are college students more likely to do property damage?) and illegitimate reasons (on the basis of race or religion).

The "Robin Hood principle" is to take from the rich and give to the poor.

Housing shortages, an unintended consequence of rent controls, give landlords the upper hand in dealings with tenants.

One final and clearly unintended consequence is that rent controls also subsidize the (relatively) rich! Rent controls apply to all apartments, not just apartments rented by those who have difficulty affording housing. Existing high-income tenants, who are both willing and able to pay more for their apartments, pay only the controlled rent.

So, are rent controls a smart choice for governments trying to ensure more affordable housing for the homeless? Almost every economist out there would give an emphatic *no* for an answer, and I hope I have convinced you, too. Rent controls, like any fixed price, sacrifice all the flexibility and advantages of well-functioning markets in producing the products/services we want, and directing them to those most willing and able to pay. As a way of trying to improve the supply of affordable housing, rent controls have many drawbacks, including the perverse, unintended results of reducing the total quantity of apartments on the market, and subsidizing housing for those who can well afford it.

If, as a society, we do want to help the homeless, much better choices are available. In a market economy, demand depends on willingness and ability to pay. No one has a greater willingness or desire for a service as basic as housing than someone who has none. The problem is ability to pay. Alternative policies to help the homeless would provide low-income people with government subsidies that could be applied to any housing they might find in the market. Or governments could build affordable housing and make sure it is available only to those who need it the most. While every government policy choice, including these, has opportunity costs that must be considered (will government bureaucrats do a better job of running a housing development than a private business?), these policies allow markets to flexibly coordinate the smart decisions of consumers and business, and result in more rental housing, without having landlords' losses subsidizing well-off tenants who do not need support.

A bigger policy question lurks behind this discussion of rent controls. Should governments make policy choices based on ethical concerns, even if those choices do limit the ability of markets to function well? We will address that important question at the end of this chapter, but only after looking at another form of government price fixing — minimum wage laws.

Refresh

5.2

1. What are rent controls?

2. Explain the unintended consequences of rent controls for the choices of tenants and of landlords.

3. Activists argue that education, like housing, is an essential service that should be affordable for all citizens. A tuition freeze (to keep college affordable) is another form of a price ceiling. What are the unintended consequences for students? What other policies might better provide a supply of affordable education?

www.myeconlab.com

5.3 Do Minimum Wages Help the Working Poor? Price Floors

Describe price floors and explain the unintended consequences of minimum wage laws.

Have you ever worked at a minimum wage job? Any proposal to "raise the minimum wage" sure sounds good to someone in a minimum wage job. It means a raise, right? What's not to like about that?

Minimum wage laws arose to protect the less fortunate and most vulnerable members of society. Unskilled and uneducated workers in 19th-century Canada were on their own. Employers paid workers as little as they wanted. Dangerous and poorly paid working conditions led to the rise of unions and, in 1918, to the first minimum wage laws in British Columbia and Manitoba. These early laws applied only to women and to limited kinds of jobs. Over time, minimum wage laws were extended to men, to more job categories, and to other provinces. Minimum wages for men were usually higher than for women, on the belief that the male breadwinner of the family deserved more pay. Gender differences in minimum wages ended in all provinces only in 1974!

Current (2008) hourly minimum wages in Canada range from $7.25 in New Brunswick, to $8 in Alberta, B.C., Manitoba, Ontario, and Quebec, and $8.50 in Nunavut. Earning $8 per hour translates into a yearly income of about $16 000, which is impossible to live on in a Canadian city. Many charitable, religious, and social activist groups support increases in minimum wages to $10 per hour. Ten dollars per hour is called a **"living wage"** because it is high enough to allow an individual to live above what Statistics Canada defines as the poverty line. Roughly 15 percent of all Canadian families have incomes below the poverty line, and about 2 million Canadians aged 20 or older are in full-time, low-paying jobs that leave them below the poverty line. These are the working poor. There is a vigorous debate in Canada about the pros and cons of an increased minimum wage for helping the working poor.

living wage: $10 per hour, enough to allow an individual in a Canadian city to live above the poverty line

The living wage proposal, like any minimum wage, is a fixed price for businesses hiring unskilled labour. It fixes a **price floor**, making it illegal for a business to hire anyone for a wage less than the minimum. From the discussion of the unintended consequences of the other form of price fixing by government (rent controls or price ceilings), and from your accumulating economics expertise, you can probably guess that minimum wages are not all good news.

minimum wage laws: example of price floor minimum price set by government, making it illegal to pay lower price

What are the perceived benefits of minimum wages? Like rent controls, a political benefit is that the government does not have to spend any money, yet voters perceive that the government is helping the working poor. More importantly, those workers who keep their jobs after the higher minimum wage becomes law are better off, earning a living wage. They get a raise.

Labour Markets Are Input Markets

Before looking at the costs of minimum wages in the labour market, I want to re-orient you by using the circular-flow map from Chapter 1 (Figure 1.4). Labour markets have an important difference from housing or gasoline markets. On the diagram, households and businesses interact in two sets of markets — input markets (on the right), where businesses buy the inputs they need from households to produce products/services, and output markets (on the left), where businesses sell their products/services to households.

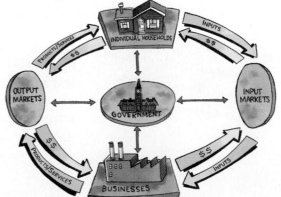

Circular-Flow Map of Economic Life

Housing and gasoline are outputs, so businesses are the sellers/suppliers and households are the buyers/demanders. Labour is different. Labour is an input, so the roles are reversed. Households are the sellers/suppliers, and businesses are the buyers/demanders. Governments (in the middle) set the rules of the game and, in this chapter, choose to interact in both output markets (rent ceilings) and input markets (minimum wages).

Minimum Wages The purpose of any minimum wage law is to set a wage that is *above* the current market-clearing price in the labour market. At the fixed minimum wage, like at any price above the market-clearing price, the quantity of labour demanded (by businesses) is less than it would be at the market-clearing wage. When any input to production, including labour, becomes more expensive, businesses reduce the input — hire fewer people and search for cheaper substitutes. If wages for janitors rise, businesses may switch from paper towels in washrooms to air dryers so they need fewer janitors. Businesses buying labour (in input markets) act like any smart consumer buying products/services (in output markets) — when the price rises, the quantity demanded decreases and the search is on for cheaper substitutes.

From Chapter 3, remember that if wages or other input costs go up, market supply of the output (check Figure 3.10) decreases. When supply decreases (check Chapter 4, Section 4.4), the price of output rises and quantity demanded decreases. Businesses will sell less output, which is why they cut back on employment. Consumers will pay higher prices for products/services.

When the minimum wage rises, those workers who are hired will be better off, but there will be *fewer jobs available.* Quantities adjust.

As wages rise, workers are willing to supply a greater quantity of labour. Remember in Chapter 3 how the number of hours you were willing to work increased as the boss offered you double time and then triple time? With a minimum wage above the market-clearing wage, there is a surplus of workers willing to work (meaning the quantity of labour supplied will be greater than the quantity demanded by employers). Workers who can no longer find jobs will spend more time and resources job searching, and will be frustrated and worse off. Statistics Canada defines workers who are willing to work but who cannot find jobs as "unemployed." Raising the minimum wage tends to increase unemployment.

Consequences of Minimum Wages While governments can fix minimum wages, they cannot force employers to hire workers if there are cheaper or better ways to produce output using different labour or different inputs.

So, are minimum wage laws a smart choice for governments trying to help the working poor? Many economists would say no, but not as strongly as to rent controls. Workers who get or keep jobs at the higher minimum wage will be better off. On the other hand, like any fixed price, minimum wages sacrifice the flexibility and advantages of well-functioning markets in coordinating the smart choices of consumers and workers and businesses. Minimum wages will cause some unemployment because, when prices are fixed, quantities adjust.

When governments set minimum wages above market-clearing wage, quantity of labour supplied by households will be greater than quantity of labour demanded by businesses, creating unemployment.

Quantity of unemployment created by increased minimum wage depends on the elasticity of business demand for unskilled labour.

How many workers will lose their jobs when minimum wages rise? Economists call this a factual or *empirical* question — the answer comes from real-world data. Those data are inconclusive. In some cases where minimum wages were introduced or increased, there were significant job losses. In others, there was not much change in employment among unskilled workers.

The number of jobs lost when the wage increases depends on the *elasticity of demand* for labour. When demand for unskilled labour is inelastic and businesses have few substitutes, a rise in the wage produces only a small response in decreased quantity demanded. The case is stronger for a living wage. But if demand for labour is elastic and businesses can easily substitute machines for people, a rise in the wage produces a large decrease in the quantity of labour demanded. The living wage policy then looks less beneficial. Elasticity is important not just for businesses deciding on sale prices, but also for social activists making the case for a living wage and for government officials deciding on smart policy choices.

Whatever the data show, a full answer to the question, "Do minimum wages help the working poor," requires us to compare the gains from the workers who remain employed and whose incomes go up, with the lost income of the workers who lose their jobs.

Are minimum wage laws the *best* way to help the working poor? Most economists believe better choices that do not sacrifice market's flexibility to coordinate smart decisions of consumers, workers, and businesses are available. For example, provide training to unskilled workers so they become eligible for higher-paying jobs or give direct wage supplements to raise their standard of living without risking higher unemployment. But these policy alternatives have opportunity costs: They are more expensive than minimum wages in helping the working poor.

ECONOMICS Out There

Hundreds of Economists Say Raise the Minimum Wage

Many economists believe the benefits of a minimum wage outweigh the costs. In a high-profile ad signed by 650 economists — including five Nobel Prize winners — the economists argued that:

- a modest increase in the minimum wage would improve the well-being of low-wage workers and would not have the adverse effects that critics have claimed.

- the weight of evidence suggests modest increases in the minimum wage have had very little or no effect on employment.

- while controversy about the employment effects of the minimum wage continues, research shows that most beneficiaries are adult, female, and members of low-income working families.

Alternative policies to help working poor are training programs and wage supplements. But all policies have opportunity costs to consider.

Refresh
5.3

1. Explain what a "living wage" is and how it works as a price floor.

2. Explain how a rise in the minimum wage will affect job losses when the demand for labour is inelastic, and when the demand for labour is elastic.

3. If you were a social activist arguing for a rise in the minimum wage to a "living wage," what data would support your argument that this policy will help the working poor? If you ran a business employing unskilled labour, what data would you need to counter the argument?

www.myeconlab.com

5.4 When Markets Work Well, Are They Fair? Efficiency/Equity Trade-offs

Explain the trade-offs in government policies between efficient and equitable outcomes.

To say that well-functioning markets produce products/services we value most means outputs go to those most willing and able to pay. Efficient market outcome may not be fair or equitable.

efficient market outcome: coordinates smart choices of businesses and consumers so outputs produced at lowest cost (prices just cover all opportunity costs of production) and consumers buy products/services providing most bang per buck (marginal benefit greater than price)

As an economist, I believe that when prices and quantities are allowed to adjust, well-functioning markets create incentives that balance the forces of competition (between consumers and between businesses) and the forces of cooperation (voluntary, mutually beneficial exchanges). When each consumer and business makes smart choices based only on self-interest, the coordinated result is the output of all the products/services we value most. I hope to convince you of the usefulness of markets in helping us all get the most out of life.

That appreciation for what markets can do does *not* translate into the conclusion that "Governments should always keep their hands off markets." Allowing markets to operate without government interaction is still a choice, and every choice has an opportunity cost. I also believe, like social activists, religious groups, and other economists, that the opportunity cost of allowing markets to work, even well, is sometimes unfairness or inequality.

Let me explain. Living in Toronto, I can't help but know some hard-core (and need I say long-suffering) Maple Leafs fans. Joe (not his real name) watches every hockey game on TV, attends games at the Air Canada Centre when someone gives him a ticket he usually can't afford, and has blue maple leaf logos tattooed on his . . . you don't want to know. If miracles happen and the Leafs ever make it to the seventh game of the Stanley Cup finals, there is no one more desperate, more willing, and more deserving to see the game. But poor Joe (literally and figuratively) won't be there. Tickets will go to the highest bidders, including many corporate executives who will write them off as business expenses.

When we say markets produce the products/services we value the most, we mean that outputs go to those most *willing and able to pay*. Joe is willing, but he is not able, and he gets no ticket. There is something about this outcome that does not seem fair. Economists use the word "efficient" to describe the outcome of a well-functioning market. An **efficient market outcome**, however, may not be fair or equitable.

The dictionary definition of *efficient* is "acting or producing effectively with a minimum of waste, expense, or unnecessary effort." When markets work well, businesses compete with each other, and successful, profitable businesses use inputs in the lowest cost combinations, and produce products/services that consumers demand. At market-clearing prices, businesses voluntarily produce the quantity of each product/service that consumers are willing and able to buy, and prices just cover all opportunity costs of production, including a normal profit.

Consumers compete with each other for the outputs of businesses, and products/services go to those most willing and able to pay. At market clearing prices, consumers voluntarily buy the quantity of each product/service that businesses have produced. Because consumers buy only when marginal benefit is greater than the market-clearing price (marginal cost), they get the most "bang per buck," spending their income to get maximum possible satisfaction from every dollar. This coordination of smart choices by both businesses and consumers is an efficient market outcome.

Who Is Excluded from Efficient Market Outcomes?

Consumers who do not buy at market-clearing prices can be put into two categories. The first doesn't find the product/service worth the price (marginal benefit is less than price) even though she can afford it. There are always substitutes. The second simply can't afford it, even though he wants it and finds the marginal benefit greater than the price. Joe, dejectedly watching the Stanley Cup on TV at home, is part of the second category.

In most people's eyes, Joe's misfortune is not a life-shattering tragedy. But what if, instead of the market for hockey tickets, we are talking about markets for what many consider to be essential services like housing, education, or health care? Are the benefits of an efficient market worth the sacrifice that might have to be made in terms of unfairness or inequality?

We have already seen the importance of ability to pay in formulating an equitable housing policy that will still help the homeless in a cost-effective or efficient way. Let's look again at the potential trade-offs between efficiency and equity, but in the market for health care.

Consumers who do not buy at market-clearing prices are unwilling because marginal benefit is less than price, even though they can afford to buy, or are unable to afford to buy even though they are willing and marginal benefit is greater than price.

Health Care

Federal and provincial governments set the prices paid to the doctors, nurses, and hospitals who supply health care services. The Canadian government also guarantees free access to most health care services to all permanent residents and citizens, paying for those services through tax revenues. Governments fix the price of each health care service (how much a doctor gets paid for an office visit, how much a hospital gets paid for providing a bed with nursing services, and so on), but governments cannot force doctors or nurses to work or force hospitals to admit patients. Each health care practitioner can choose the quantity of services to provide at the fixed price. Some choose not to supply services in Canada at all, going instead to work in the United States, where prices are higher. There are usually alternatives for suppliers as well as for consumers.

Many dedicated and talented healthcare workers in Canada work hard to provide fine medical care. But have you ever waited to get an appointment with a medical specialist in Canada? Do you know someone who is on a waiting list for a CAT scan or a surgical procedure? Of course the answer to these questions is "yes." When prices can't adjust, quantities will, and waiting lists are the most visible form of a quantity adjustment.

At the fixed price to consumers of zero, and a government-set price to suppliers, it is no surprise that the quantity demanded of medical services is far greater than the quantity supplied. As with any shortage, the market will produce only the quantity that suppliers are willing to provide, and frustrated consumers seeking/demanding medical care end up on waiting lists. This is one inefficiency that exists in the health care system in Canada.

In the public Canadian health care system, everyone has relatively equal access to health care services. Prices paid by consumers (zero) and to suppliers are fixed by governments, resulting in shortages and inefficiencies because quantity demanded exceeds quantity supplied.

Is Inefficient Health Care All Bad?

Having said all this, does it mean that Canadian governments have made a not-smart policy choice? Not necessarily.

Consider the alternative of allowing a private market for health care services, where consumers pay the bills; doctors, nurses, and hospitals set prices; and governments do nothing more than set the rules of the game and enforce property rights. The United States health care system has many of these qualities. With shortages, prices would rise, quantities demanded would decrease, quantities supplied would increase, and waiting lists would disappear. But the fortunate people who receive health care services would be those most willing and able to pay. Anyone not able to afford the market-clearing price would not receive medical care. They would be part of the same category as Joe. But since these consumers will include families desperate for life-saving surgeries who simply cannot afford to pay, their tragedies will be real. There are 46 million people in the United States who do not have health care benefits.

A switch in Canada to a private market in health care services would add flexibility and incentives, and end waiting lists. Doctors, nurses, and health care services would flow to where they are most valued, which means to those consumers most willing and able to pay. Many doctors would return to Canada from the United States. Market-driven health care would likely be more efficient, but the "haves" will get excellent care, and the "have-nots" may get no care at all. The U.S.-style private market outcome may be efficient, but at the cost of being less fair and less equitable. The Canadian-style outcome is more equitable, but at the cost of being less efficient.

In making these comparisons between health care in Canada and in the United States, I am leaving out many details of both systems. The Canadian system has some market-based incentives and flexibility, and the U.S. system has some role for government through the Medicare and Medicaid programs. Private insurance companies set many prices and limit quantities of services. But, as we learned in Chapter 1, a useful map must leave out less important details to focus attention on the most important information. I believe the simplifications help to show the key issue, which everyone acknowledges — the trade-off between efficiency and equity.

So how do governments, or you as a citizen voting for governments, choose between efficiency and equity? They are both desirable outcomes. Economics alone does not provide the answer.

In the private U.S. health care system, anyone willing and able to pay has access to health care services. Prices are set efficiently in markets, in that price adjustments match quantities demanded and supplied. Those unable to pay do not receive health care services, resulting in inequality.

This simplified comparison of health care in Canada and the U.S. leaves out many details to highlight the trade-off between efficiency and equity.

Refresh

5.4

1. Describe what an "efficient market outcome" means for businesses and for consumers.

2. What are the trade-offs between efficiency and equity in comparing a private market for health care services with government provision of health care services?

3. If you had to choose between a health care system run by the market or run by government, which would you prefer? How might your choice be influenced by your income?

www.myeconlab.com

5.5 Can Opinions Be Right or Wrong? Positive versus Normative Claims

Illustrate how positive economic thinking identifies the smartest choices for achieving a normative goal.

Who is the greatest hockey player of all time? My wife, who is a bigger fan than I am, claims it is Bobby Orr. Ian Howe, my co-author, claims it is Wayne Gretzky. I have heard them argue for hours about this. Do you think it's someone else? Will it eventually be Sidney Crosby? Who is right? How do you choose?

Let's take a different perspective. Who scored more lifetime points, Bobby Orr or Wayne Gretzky? That question is easier to evaluate. It is an empirical question — you can go check the facts. You'll find that the facts show Bobby Orr scored 915 points over 14 seasons; Wayne Gretzky scored 2857 points over 20 seasons. Those facts certainly help Ian's claim.

But facts alone will not conclusively answer the greatest player claim. That's because greatness has many different dimensions — points, goals versus assists, offensive versus defensive contributions, leadership, sportsmanship, toughness, and so on. Bobby Orr and Wayne Gretzky had different strengths and weaknesses, and played in different eras in the NHL. To come to a summary judgment requires placing a relative *value* on each dimension, and those *values are a matter of opinion*. There is no hard-and-fast, universally agreed upon definition of "greatness" in a hockey player.

Empirical claims or statements are also called **positive statements** by economists. Empirical or positive statements (like about lifetime points) can be evaluated as true or false by checking the facts.

Claims or statements that involve value judgments or opinions are called **normative statements** by economists. (A norm is a standard — a normative statement depends on which value or standard or ethic you believe is most important.) If you place the highest value or weight on the scoring dimension, Wayne Gretzky might be the greatest. If you place the highest value on defensive contributions, it might be Number 4, Bobby Orr.

What is the connection to government policy choices about rent controls, minimum wages, or health care? Glad you asked. *Should* the government implement rent controls to help the homeless? *Should* the government pass minimum wage laws to help the working poor? *Should* the government push a health care system that emphasizes equity over efficiency (Canadian style), or one that emphasizes efficiency over equity (U.S. style)? All these policy choices involve trade-offs between efficiency and equity. Your answer to these questions, or any politician's answer, depends on the *relative value* or weight placed on efficiency versus equity.

A conservative politician on the right of the political spectrum might oppose minimum wage laws because she believes the efficiency of markets is most important for generating the economic prosperity that will ultimately help people who are poor. She also might believe that markets are already equitable because they provide everyone with *equal opportunities* (and she fully expects that each person's income and accomplishments in life will differ with differences in talents, initiative, and luck). A left-leaning politician might favour minimum wage laws because he believes equity is more important than efficiency (and would accept some inefficiency and less economic prosperity for all). He is concerned with improving the equality of incomes, and does not believe that poor children have the same opportunities as rich children. You cannot decide that one politician is right and the other wrong just on the basis of facts. What you can decide is which politician's *values* best match your own values.

If you are not a hockey fan, pick any sport or profession — writer, artist, filmmaker, actor, band — and make the case for who is/was the greatest.

positive statements: about what is; can be evaluated as true or false by checking the facts

normative statements: about what you believe should be; involve value judgments

What Economics Can and Cannot Do for You   Economic thinking alone won't allow you to decide on policy choices. You must choose based on your own values and opinions. But once you decide on a particular policy choice or "end" you support, economic thinking is all about finding the most effective and efficient means to that end.

Economists excel (if I may say so) at evaluating empirical, or positive, claims. Economic thinking allows you to find right and wrong answers to questions like "Will a low fixed gasoline price create shortages and line-ups at the pumps?" We can observe what actually happened in Canada in 1974 when governments fixed prices. Or take the law of demand — the claim that a rise in price will cause a decrease in quantity demanded. That is an empirical claim, and by looking at factual evidence of prices and quantities, we can decide whether it is true or false.

What is the most efficient policy for helping the homeless find housing? That is actually a positive, or empirical, question. Once you or the government have decided that equity is an important "end," economic thinking can help in picking the policy "means" that provides the most bang for the buck or that involves the least amount of waste. On the other hand, "*Should* the government develop policies to help the homeless?" is a normative question involving value judgments. Normative questions and claims often use the word *should*. Watch for it to help distinguish positive from normative claims.

Economic thinking will help you intelligently evaluate claims you hear from politicians or administrators or parents. Most politicians make claims about what they will do if elected, but leave out the opportunity costs of their plans. Every plan, every policy, every choice has an opportunity cost. Figure out what that is before passing judgment. And when a politician's policy claim does make clear the opportunity cost or sacrifice (often, tax increases are the opportunity cost of government spending programs), look to see if there is a better, more efficient way to achieve the same end.

Governments, when they function well, should be making smart choices. The policy objectives, or ends, that they choose may be efficient markets, affordable housing, equitable incomes, environmental sustainability, or minimal taxes. Citizens' opinions will differ reasonably about those normative, value-based ends that are properly set for a society by democratically elected politicians. Those are not the smart choices. Once an end is chosen, economic thinking can help with the smart choices — finding the most efficient and effective means to the end. Being an informed, economically literate citizen will help you help governments make smart choices.

Normative statements often use the word "should" and cannot be evaluated as true or false by checking the facts.

Once you pick a political position or social goal to support based on your values, economic thinking helps identify the smartest choice of action to efficiently achieve that goal. Always weigh benefits against opportunity costs.

Refresh

5.5

1. Explain the difference between a positive statement and a normative statement.

2. Is the statement "Government taxes on tobacco will reduce smoking" positive or normative? If you answered "positive," rewrite the statement so that it becomes normative. If you answered "normative," rewrite the statement so that it becomes positive.

3. Arguments often end with someone saying "Everyone is entitled to an opinion." Does that mean that all opinions are equally valid? (The positive/normative distinction can help answer this question.)

www.myeconlab.com

What Gives When Prices Don't?

Chapter 5

Government Choices, Markets, Efficiency, and Equity

CHAPTER SUMMARY

5.1 MINDING YOUR P'S AND Q'S: DO PRICES OR QUANTITIES ADJUST?

When government fixes prices, quantities adjust. Smart choices of consumers and businesses are not coordinated. Either consumers or businesses will be frustrated.

- When price is fixed below market-clearing:
  - shortages develop (quantity demanded greater than quantity supplied) and consumers are frustrated.
  - quantity sold = quantity supplied only.
- When price is fixed above market-clearing:
  - surpluses develop (quantity supplied greater than quantity demanded) and businesses are frustrated.
  - quantity sold = quantity demanded only.
- Governments can fix prices, but can't force businesses (or consumers) to produce (or buy) at the fixed price.
  - Businesses can reduce output or move resources elsewhere.
  - Consumers can reduce purchases or buy something else (there are always substitutes).

5.2 DO RENT CONTROLS HELP THE HOMELESS? PRICE CEILINGS

Rent controls fix rents below market-clearing levels, and quantity adjustment takes the form of apartment shortages. The unintended consequences are reduced quantity of housing supplied and subsidized, well-off tenants.

- **Rent controls:** example of **price ceiling** — maximum price set by government, making it illegal to charge higher price.
- Rent controls sometimes justified by *Robin Hood principle* — take from the rich (landlords) and give to the poor (tenants).
- Rent controls have unintended and undesirable consequences:
  - create housing shortages, giving landlords the upper hand over tenants.
  - subsidize well-off tenants willing and able to pay market-clearing rents.

- Alternative policies to help the homeless that do not sacrifice market flexibility are
  - government subsidies to help those who are poor pay rent.
  - government-supplied housing.
- All policies have opportunity costs.

5.3 DO MINIMUM WAGES HELP THE WORKING POOR? PRICE FLOORS

Minimum wage laws fix wages above market-clearing levels, and quantity adjustment takes the form of a surplus of workers. The benefit of these laws is higher wages to the employed, but the unintended consequence is fewer are employed.

- **Minimum wage laws:** example of **price floor** — minimum price set by government, making it illegal to pay a lower price.
  - **Living wage** — estimated at $10 per hour, enough to allow an individual in a Canadian city to live above the poverty line.
- When governments set minimum wages above market-clearing wage, quantity of labour supplied by households will be greater than quantity of labour demanded by businesses, creating unemployment.
- Quantity of unemployment created by raising minimum wage depends on elasticity of business demand for unskilled labour.
  - When demand for unskilled labour is inelastic and businesses have few substitutes, rise in minimum wage produces *small* response in decreased quantity demanded.
  - When demand for unskilled labour is elastic and businesses can easily substitute machines for people, rise in minimum wage produces *large* response in decreased quantity demanded.
  - Minimum wages help the working poor if gains from workers who remain employed and whose incomes go up are greater than losses of incomes of workers who lose their jobs.
- Alternative policies to help the working poor that do not sacrifice market flexibility are
  - training programs to help unskilled workers get higher-paying jobs.
  - wage supplements.
- All policies have opportunity costs.

5.4 WHEN MARKETS WORK WELL, ARE THEY FAIR? EFFICIENCY/EQUITY TRADE-OFFS

The outcomes of well-functioning markets, while efficient, are not always equitable. Government may smartly choose policies that create more equitable outcomes, even though the trade-off is less efficiency.

- To say that well-functioning markets produce products/services we value most means outputs go to those most willing and able to pay.
  - Efficient market outcome may not be fair or equitable.
  - **Efficient market outcome** — coordinates smart choices of businesses and consumers so outputs produced at lowest cost (prices just cover all opportunity costs of production), and consumers buy products/services providing the most bang per buck (marginal benefit greater than price).

- Consumers who do not buy at market-clearing prices are:
  - unwilling because marginal benefit is less than price (even though they could afford to buy), and/or
  - unable to afford to buy, even though they are willing (marginal benefit is greater than price).
- Allowing markets to operate without government interaction is a choice that has an opportunity cost — unfairness, inequity, or inequality. There is a trade-off between efficiency and equity. In comparing U.S. market-driven health care with Canadian universal, government-run health care:
  - Canadian-style government outcome is more equitable, but at the cost of being less efficient.
  - U.S.-style private market outcome may be efficient, but at the cost of being less fair and less equitable.

5.5 CAN OPINIONS BE RIGHT OR WRONG? POSITIVE VERSUS NORMATIVE CLAIMS

Once you choose to support a political position or social goal based on your values, positive economic thinking helps identify the smartest choices to efficiently achieve that goal.

- **Positive** (or empirical) **statements** — about what is; can be evaluated as true or false by checking the facts.
- **Normative statements** — about what you believe *should* be; involve value judgments.
  - Cannot be evaluated as true or false by checking the facts.
- For any policy, always weigh benefits against opportunity costs.

TRUE/FALSE

Circle the correct answer.

5.1 DO PRICES OR QUANTITIES ADJUST?

1. Fifty-six percent of young workers in Canada live at home with their parents. More young adults are remaining home or are "doubling up" in apartments. Doubling up is a quantity adjustment by tenants in the rental house market.   **True   False**

5.2 PRICE CEILINGS

2. The following statement — with which 93 percent of economists from the American Economic Association were in agreement — is a positive statement.   **True   False**

   A ceiling on rents reduces the quality and quantity of housing.

3. The following statement by the Sheldon Chumir Foundation for Ethics in Leadership is a positive statement.

Calgary's homeless population grew 740 percent between 1994 and 2006.

True   False

4. The following statement by the Manhattan Institute (an independent think tank in New York) is a positive statement.

Examining investment in previously rent-controlled buildings, we find that the removal of rent controls increased the construction of new units and the renovation and repair of existing ones by approximately 20 percent over what would have been the case in the absence of decontrol.

True   False

5. Rent ceilings are usually applied to only part of the market. Tenants in the controlled market hold on to their apartments, forcing everyone else to shop in the more expensive uncontrolled market. In New York, 88 percent of tenants living in rent-controlled apartments have not moved in more than 25 years. According to demand and supply analysis, rental prices in the uncontrolled market will be lower as a result of a rent ceiling in the controlled market.

True   False

5.3 PRICE FLOORS

6. The following statement by the Organisation for Economic Co-operation and Development (OECD) is a positive statement.

A moderate minimum wage is generally not a problem.

True   False

7. The following statement by the Arthurs Commission on Canadian federal labour standards is a positive statement.

The government should accept the principle that no Canadian worker should work full-time for a year and still live in poverty.

True   False

8. The following statement — with which 46 percent of economists from the American Economic Association were in agreement (27 percent disagreed) — is a positive statement.

A minimum wage increases unemployment among young and unskilled workers.

True   False

9. There is evidence that minimum wage laws significantly increase teen unemployment, slightly increase young adults' unemployment, and have no impact on employment for workers aged 25 or older. This suggests that elasticity of demand for labour is highest for workers aged 25 or older.

True   False

10. Canadian researchers found that the benefits of minimum wages go primarily to individuals in families that are less well off than the average. This suggests a minimum wage would reduce wage inequality and increase equity.

True   False

11. Suppose you just graduated and your provincial government has raised its minimum wage from $8 to $10. Assuming you were not working before, this would increase your incentive to look for work. However, you may be less likely to find work because businesses are now more likely to cut back on hiring workers in this wage range.

True   False

5.4 EFFICIENCY/EQUITY TRADE-OFFS

12. The Canadian Medical Association found 40 percent of Canadians grade their health care system as a "C" or worse, partly due to unhappiness with long waiting times. Therefore, longer waiting times are a trade-off that Canadians make in order to have a more *efficient* health care system.

True   False

13. The following statement by The Center for American Progress is a positive statement.

   Americans who were poor as children — and there are now 37 million of them — are much more likely than other citizens to commit crimes, to need more health care, and to be less productive in the workforce.

True   False

5.5 POSITIVE VERSUS NORMATIVE CLAIMS

14. The following statement by many student associations across Canada is a positive statement.

   Tuition fees should be reduced.

True   False

15. Canada's progressive income tax system, which requires those who earn more to pay a higher percentage of their income to taxes, is based on a principle of equity.

MULTIPLE CHOICE

Circle the correct answer.

1. In 1973, oil price controls led to long gas lines and rationing at the pumps. The price controls were a

   A) price ceiling, set above the market-clearing price.

   B) price ceiling, set below the market-clearing price.

   C) price floor, set above the market-clearing price.

   D) price floor, set below the market-clearing price.

2. If the government set gas prices above the market-clearing price,

   A) this would be a price floor.

   B) gasoline suppliers would respond to the lower-than-market-clearing price by decreasing quantity supplied.

   C) gasoline consumers would respond to the lower-than-market-clearing price by increasing quantity demanded.

   D) this would result in long line-ups at the pumps.

3. Most of the employment impact of minimum wages will not come from businesses terminating workers whose wages now rise. Rather, the impact will be businesses hiring fewer low-wage workers in the future. This response, or quantity adjustment, occurs because when wages rise businesses

   A) increase supply.

   B) decrease quantity supplied.

   C) go out of business.

   D) search for cheaper input substitutes.

5.2 PRICE CEILINGS

4. Rent ceilings imposed by governments

   A) keep rental prices below the market-clearing price.

   B) keep rental prices above the market-clearing price.

   C) keep rental prices equal to the market-clearing price.

   D) increase the quantity of rental housing.

5. Rent ceilings are likely to

   A) reduce the quantity of private rental construction.

   B) reduce the quantity of existing rental units.

   C) lower the quality of existing rental units.

   D) all of the above.

6. After rent controls were imposed, the supply of apartment units in Winnipeg declined between 1998 and 2005 — from 54 924 units to 53 046. Which of the following impacts on Winnipeg's rental housing market are also consistent with economic thinking?

   A) No affordable units were added by the private sector for years and many existing units were withdrawn from the market.

   B) Subsidized public housing programs have been the only source of new units in the low-to-medium price range.

   C) Maintenance expenses fell, decreasing the quality of rental housing.

   D) All of the above.

7. According to the Frontier Centre for Public Policy, "The most recent information on apartment rents and vacancy rates on the Prairies provides sufficient evidence that the best friend of tenants is the free market: Saskatchewan, with no controls, enjoys lower rents and substantially more supply. It is time to learn from Saskatchewan and end rent control in Manitoba." If rent controls were removed, which of the following would occur?

   A) Prices would fall.

   B) Shortages would increase.

   C) Supply would increase.

   D) All of the above.

8. In Canada, some provinces have relaxed rent controls by permitting landlords to charge market rents *when the original occupants move out*. This provides

   A) tenants with an incentive to stay in their apartments as long as possible.

   B) landlords with an incentive to let the quality of existing apartments deteriorate.

   C) governments with an incentive to pass strong anti-eviction laws so that landlords cannot remove current tenants without justified cause.

   D) all of the above.

9. Ontario built about 27 000 apartment units per year in the six years before rent ceilings were introduced in 1974, and that dropped to around 4200 units per year after rent ceilings were introduced. Before rent ceilings were introduced in Ontario, provincial government helped subsidize 27 percent of all rental units; by the early 1990s, it was more than 75 percent. This demonstrates that rent ceilings

   A) create shortages of housing.

   B) are costly for governments.

   C) reduce incentives for private-sector investment.

   D) do all of the above.

5.3 PRICE FLOORS

10. Minimum wages in Canada vary, and are listed below (2008 figures).

Jurisdiction	Wage Rate
Alberta	$8.00
British Columbia	$8.00
Manitoba	$8.00
New Brunswick	$7.25
Newfoundland and Labrador	$7.00
Northwest Territories	$8.25
Nova Scotia	$7.60
Nunavut	$8.50
Ontario	$8.00
Prince Edward Island	$7.50
Quebec	$8.00
Saskatchewan	$7.95
Yukon	$8.37

Based on this information, which of the following statements is *false*?

A) Nunavut had the highest minimum wage.

B) Newfoundland and Labrador had the lowest minimum wage.

C) A minimum wage below $7.00 would be irrelevant.

D) A minimum wage above $10.00 would be irrelevant.

11. Raising the minimum wage may have limited impact on reducing overall poverty rates because

A) many minimum-wage workers are young people or earners who live in families that do not fall below the poverty line.

B) many individuals who are in poverty are not working.

C) raising the minimum wage is still not enough to help workers working part-year or part-time out of poverty.

D) all of the above.

5.4 EFFICIENCY/EQUITY TRADE-OFFS

12. In markets without any government interaction, the question of who gets an apartment is decided by who is

A) most willing to pay.

B) most able to pay.

C) most willing and able to pay.

D) most willing and able to dance.

13. Which of the statements is a positive (empirical) statement?

A) People who work for minimum wage should be able to feed their families.

B) The minimum wage level should meet standards where, in a just society, individuals working full-time would not find themselves in poverty.

C) Minimum wage increases can significantly improve the lives of low-income workers and their families, without the adverse effects that critics claim.

D) All of the above.

5.5 POSITIVE VERSUS NORMATIVE CLAIMS

14. Which of the following statements is *not* normative?

A) Something should be done about the homeless.

B) Rent ceilings would reduce the number of homeless people.

C) Rent ceilings should be introduced to reduce the number of homeless people.

D) All of the above.

15. In 1997, Canadian family incomes near the top of the income distribution were four times higher than family incomes near the bottom of the distribution. In the United States, the ratio is about five to one, while in Sweden and Finland the ratio is about three to one. The country with the most unequal distribution of income is

A) Canada.

B) the United States.

C) Sweden.

D) Finland.

SHORT ANSWER

Write a short answer to each question. Your answer may be in point form.

1. The gains from the economic expansion of the 1990s went mainly to higher-income families, while earnings of poorer families remained the same. The result was a moderate increase in family income inequality.

A) The Canadian Centre for Policy Alternatives argues that raising the minimum wage is a useful tool to create greater social justice in the distribution of income because it decreases family income inequality. Explain how increasing the minimum wage to a level that is above the poverty line would decrease family income inequality.

B) Business groups such as the Canadian Federation of Independent Businesses argue that raising the minimum wage causes upward pressure on the entire wage structure. Think of the worker working for $10 an hour who then suddenly sees co-workers who were previously making less get a raise to $10. Explain why business groups think that raising the minimum wage may have no impact on reducing family income inequality.

C) Poor families received 28 percent of the additional earnings from a 35-percent increase in the Ontario minimum wage, but individuals from rich families received an even higher share (31 percent) of the additional earnings. Why would individuals in rich families benefit from a policy that increases wages only for those earning minimum wages?

2. In Canada, a person who works full-time throughout the year for minimum wage is considered a low-paid worker. However, a low-paid worker in a family with a high family income would not be considered a *low-income* worker, nor would he be considered part of the "working poor." The working poor are considered to be in poverty if their family income falls below a certain income threshold. In Canada, the most widely used measure of poverty is Statistics Canada's Low Income Cut-offs (LICO). The LICO takes into account both family size and city size to establish income thresholds. For a family of four living in a city with more than half a million people (like Toronto), the LICO is about $40 000.

A) As TD Economics frames the issue, "The question policy makers need to ask themselves is whether they want to help workers with low earnings independent of their family economic situation, or help workers who live in poverty." Would a minimum wage help workers with low earnings independent of their family economic situation, or help only those workers who live in poverty? In other words, are minimum wages aimed at assisting low-paid workers or low-income workers?

B) Consider the argument by the Canadian Centre for Policy Alternatives: "It's true that 45 per cent of low-wage employees are students, what's wrong with paying students adequately … tuition has doubled between 1993 and 2003." Does this argument support helping workers with low earnings independent of their family economic situation, or does it support helping only workers who live in poverty (the "working poor")?

C) Evidence suggests that the 35-percent increase in the Ontario minimum wage only reduced Ontario's poverty rates from 16.9 percent to 16.6 percent. If raising the minimum wage does have a big negative impact on employment, as some predict, is it possible for it to actually increase poverty? Why or why not?

3. An alternative policy to help the working poor is to give a tax break (an income tax credit) to workers in families that are poor. This idea is promoted by the Canadian Policy Research Network (CPRN), the Caledon Institute of Social Policy, and the Task Force on Modernizing Income Security for Working-Age Adults (MISWAA). In the U.S., the federal Earned Income Tax Credit helps more working parents and children move out of poverty than any other government program.

A) Why would businesses be more likely to support these alternatives rather than minimum wages?

B) What are the opportunity costs of these government tax credits?

4. Some have argued that an increase in the minimum wage, because it affects all employers equally, will not increase unemployment. The Canadian Centre for Policy Alternatives argues that "in the real world it doesn't work out that way." The dry-cleaning industry, with many low-wage workers, is an example: "You raise the minimum wage and the cost of dry cleaning will go up slightly. But all of the dry cleaning companies across Ontario are going to have their cost structures changing in exactly the same way. And the last time I checked, people don't take their laundry to Buffalo to get it cleaned."

   A) What is the simplest way for businesses to adjust to the rising costs, assuming that the economy is doing well and individuals are not cutting back on their spending on laundry?

   B) Some businesses may not be able to afford to pay their workers the new minimum wage. List solutions (other than laying off current workers) that the laundry business could consider in response to the minimum wage.

5. In one minimum wage study, "Job loss was minimal when higher wages were forced on businesses. About 97 per cent of all minimum wage workers were better off when wages went up." Part of the reason why most minimum wage workers benefit is because of a small reduction in hours worked.

   A) What would you say if your employer asked if you were willing to work one fewer hour per week in return for a 10-percent hourly wage increase?

   B) If your employer asked you this same question near exam time, would you be more or less likely to say yes? What does this imply about your labour supply responsiveness (elasticity of supply) to a change in wage?

   C) Are there any reasons to believe that increasing minimum wages could actually benefit businesses?

6. Many question whether the market can provide affordable housing for those most in need. What are the equity concerns with allowing the market to provide rental housing to Canadians?

   A) What does a rent ceiling do, and how is it intended to increase equity?

   B) Why does a government-imposed rent ceiling reduce efficiency in the rental housing market?

   C) What is the unintended consequence?

7. Explain whether or not the following groups will be negatively affected by rent controls.

   A) Poor individuals/families

   B) Those who occupy rental units when rent controls are imposed

   C) Private construction companies and workers in private construction companies

8. Alternative polices to rent control for affordable housing are

   • government housing (which only low-income persons can qualify for); and

   • cash that can be used only for housing ("housing vouchers").

   A) Which policy affects the demand side of the housing market, and which affects the supply side?

   B) A housing voucher increases tenants' ability to pay for rental housing. How would it affect the incentive of builders' supply of new rental accommodation?

   C) In your opinion, should government improve the housing situation in Canada by concentrating more on increasing the supply of affordable housing or by improving the purchasing power of low-income households?

9. One policy cost that we have not explored in this chapter is the cost of *not* helping the homeless or the working poor. These costs of inaction may come in the form of higher crime rates and higher health care costs.

   A) Is reducing homelessness a smart choice economically? The British Columbia government found that while it costs money to house the homeless, doing so is cheaper than the indirect costs of neglect — paid for through the criminal justice system, expensive visits to emergency rooms, and other social services. If housing the homeless is actually cheaper than the indirect costs of not housing the homeless, should we definitely do it?

   B) Is reducing child poverty a smart choice economically? The Centre for American Progress estimated that the costs to the U.S. in crime, health care, and reduced productivity associated with childhood poverty amount to $500 billion a year — $170 billion in increased crime, $160 billion in increased health care costs, and $170 billion in decreased productivity.

      i) If Canada has one-tenth the population, assuming that Canadian children growing up in poverty are just as likely to grow up to be criminals or to need health care, what would be Canada's cost savings from eliminating child poverty?

      ii) Canada's public health care system is very different from the U.S. health care system. Would this imply that the cost savings from eliminating child poverty in Canada would be actually higher or lower than what you stated in the previous answer?

10. The health care system in Canada provides free coverage for medically necessary care for all Canadians. Canadians and Americans often debate which health care system is better.

A) If the government did not participate in the market for health care services, what would be the equity issue?

B) Since health care patients (consumers) in Canada do not pay user fees for medically necessary services, do you think that the number of doctor and hospital visits is efficient? Why or why not?

C) How would shortages be eliminated in the U.S. health care system if it resembles a private health care market?

D) What is the efficiency–equity trade-off in the Canadian health care system?

Chapter 6

Finding *the* Bottom Line

Opportunity Costs, Economic Profits and Losses, and the Miracle of Markets

After reading this chapter, you should be able to:

6.1 Describe accounting profits, and explain why they miss hidden opportunity costs.

6.2 Define normal profits and economic profits, and explain their differences.

6.3 Explain how economic profits signal smart business decisions and coordinate consumer and business choices.

HAVE YOU EVER HAD a teacher or a boss who acted like a little dictator? Have you ever fantasized about life without a boss and opening your own business? ("Yes" to the first question often leads to "yes" to the second question.)

Once college and part-time jobs are distant memories, your success in life will depend largely on how you spend your time and your money. Business success has a clear and simple measure—the bottom line, or the profits that remain once you subtract all your costs from your revenues.

But finding the bottom line and making smart business choices are not as simple as hiring an accountant to crunch the numbers. It turns out that economists have something valuable to add to the accountant's calculation of profits. Our old friend "opportunity cost" is the hidden key to smart choices about spending your time and money, whether you are running your own business, working for others, or even investing your lottery winnings—the other (fantasy) way to avoid having a boss.

In this chapter, we will revisit the Three Keys to Smart Choices. Key 1 says "Choose only when additional benefits are greater than additional opportunity costs." Here you will learn the importance of adding *implicit costs* in Key 3: "Be sure to count *all* additional benefits and costs, including *implicit costs* and externalities." Key 3 not only will help you make smart business choices, but also will expose the importance of economic profits in directing markets to produce the products/services we value most.

6.1 What Accountants Miss: Obvious Costs, Accounting Profits, and Hidden Opportunity Costs

Describe accounting profits, and explain why they miss hidden opportunity costs.

After suffering too many bosses, Wahid listens to the entrepreneurial voice inside his head and decides to set up his own web design business. He has been saving for a while, and a small inheritance from his grandfather brings his total ($30 000) high enough to get started. Trying to make smart choices, he develops a business plan for Wahid's Web Wonders (www.www.com). Let's see what the plan looks like to an accountant.

Obvious Costs and Accounting Profits

depreciation: tax rule for spreading cost over lifetime of long-lasting equipment

Depreciation also means decrease in value because of wear and tear and because equipment becomes obsolete.

obvious costs: costs a business pays directly

The details of Wahid's business plan appear in Figure 6.1. With the contacts he has made from part-time web design jobs, he *expects* (this word will be important later on) that he can generate $60 000 in revenues for his first year.

Wahid has to buy computer hardware and software that costs $20 000. Because that equipment lasts many years, Canada Revenue Agency does not allow accountants to treat it all as a cost in the first year. The rule for spreading the cost over the lifetime of long-lasting equipment is called **depreciation**. If the equipment lasts four years, then the allowable depreciation cost is $5000 per year ($20 000 divided by four years).

Wahid has found an office to rent in the design district for $14 000 per year, has a web access and hosting package for $3000 per year. He figures yearly phone expenses will be $1000 and advertising will cost $2000. These total costs (including depreciation) are $25 000 per year.

These are "**obvious costs**" in the sense they are plain to see — Wahid must pay them out of his own pocket.

Figure 6.1	Accountant's Business Plan for Wahid's Web Wonders (1 year)		
Total Expected Revenues			**$60 000**
Obvious Costs	Depreciation	$5 000	
	Rent	$14 000	
	Web Hosting	$3 000	
	Phone	$1 000	
	Advertising	$2 000	
Total Obvious Costs			**$25 000**
Accounting Profits			**$35 000**

accounting profits: revenues minus obvious costs (including depreciation)

To calculate profits, accountants subtract obvious costs from revenues:

Accounting Profits = Revenues − Obvious Costs (including depreciation)

So, for Wahid,

Accounting Profits = $60 000 − $25 000 = $35 000

Not bad for a first year in business. Or is it?

Your Time's Opportunity Cost

Accountants do not account for the hidden opportunity costs, of what the business owner could earn elsewhere with the time and money invested in the business. Economists call these hidden opportunity costs **implicit costs**.

The obvious, or out-of-pocket, cost of Wahid's time in his new business is zero — he is working for himself and not paying himself money. But in working for himself, he is giving up the best alternative use of his time. If the best job he could have (working for a boss) would pay $40 000, then that is the hidden opportunity cost, or implicit cost, of Wahid's time invested in his own business.

Your Money's Opportunity Cost

If Wahid had borrowed money to start up the business, the interest he would have to pay to the bank would be an obvious cost to be subtracted from his revenues. But the $30 000 Wahid invests in his business has no obvious cost. Since he did not have to borrow the money, the obvious cost of borrowing is zero — he is loaning the money to himself. Nonetheless, by investing his money in his business, he is giving up the best alternative use of the money. Wahid could have put the money in the bank and earned interest for a year, or invested it elsewhere. The interest, or return on investing elsewhere, that Wahid gives up is the hidden opportunity cost — the implicit cost — of using his own money. He cannot use the same money in two different places at the same time.

Calculating the precise opportunity cost of investing your own money is tricky because returns from business investing are *risky*, while returns from the bank are *guaranteed*. Let me explain this unequal comparison of returns.

Consider the numbers in the following choice. If you (or Wahid) invest $30 000 in a bank GIC (guaranteed investment certificate) that pays 5-percent interest, at the end of the year you will get your $30 000 back and a guaranteed 5-percent return of $1500. If you instead invest $30 000 in your own business (or any other business), suppose the *expected* return is 5 percent if things go according to plan. Let's say there is only an 80-percent chance that things will go well. Which alternative would you choose? Of course, you choose the safe 5-percent return from the bank instead of the risky 5-percent return from the business.

The more important question is: What *expected* return would it take for you to go for the risky business investment? You need to *expect more* than the safe 5 percent you will get from the bank in order to compensate for the risk of the business investment. Your personal risk compensation depends on your personality and your assessment of just how risky the investment is. Let's say you (and Wahid) believe an *extra expected* 15-percent return would just compensate for the risk.

implicit costs: hidden opportunity costs of what business owner could earn elsewhere with time and money invested

If you are a gambler at heart (economists call you "risk loving"), you might not require much risk compensation to go for the uncertain investment as long as the returns are just a bit higher than the guaranteed return. (Did you ever think economists would have a technical term that includes the word *love*?) If you are more cautious (*risk-averse*), it would take a very high risk compensation to get you to go for the uncertain investment over the guaranteed bank investment. How big a gambler are you?

Then you and Wahid would be equally pleased with the two forks, one with a *guaranteed* 5-percent return, the other with an *expected* 20-percent return (the same 5 percent from the bank plus 15 percent more to compensate for the risk of the uncertain return).

In investing $30 000 of his own money, Wahid would be equally pleased with a *guaranteed* 5-percent return of $1500 or an *expected* 20-percent return of $6000. Since Wahid's business plan *expects* (I told you this word would be important) revenues of $60 000 in the first year, the return is not guaranteed. So the precise number to use for the hidden opportunity cost of using and risking his own money is not just the bank return of 5 percent; it is that rate plus risk compensation of 15 percent. The total *expected* return needs to be 20 percent, or $6000 on his $30 000 risky investment.

In section 6.2 let's look at Wahid's "profits" once we consider these hidden opportunity costs of his time and money — the implicit costs of investing his time and money.

Wahid's hidden opportunity cost (implicit cost) of investing his own $30 000 in his risky business is 20 percent expected return, or $6000 — sum of guaranteed bank return of 5 percent plus risk compensation of 15 percent.

ECONOMICS Out There

Which Mortgage Is Right for You?

If you own a home, should you pick a variable-rate mortgage or a fixed-rate mortgage? The answer has much to do with your attitude toward risk.

- The interest rate on a variable-rate mortgage varies as market interest rates change. The interest rate on a fixed-rate mortgage is fixed for the entire term.

- Historical data show that a variable-rate mortgage is cheaper — you almost always pay less interest over the full term of your mortgage if you go with a variable rate. But there is a risk involved as rates go up and down. If rates go down, you benefit and pay less, if rates go up, you lose and pay more. Your total interest cost is uncertain — it varies as rates vary.

- Financial advisers suggest a variable-rate mortgage *if* your personality or wealth can handle the uncertainty and risk. But if the risk will keep you awake at night, they advise you to go for a fixed rate. You will pay for that certainty, but you get peace of mind.

- People who are risk-averse need to be paid more to take risk — or will pay more to avoid risk—than risk-loving individuals.

Refresh
6.1

1. Explain how to calculate accounting profits.

2. The interest rate is 5 percent and you borrow $10 000 from the bank as well as invest $20 000 of your own money in a new business for a year. Identify the obvious costs and hidden opportunity costs.

3. You are deciding between safely investing your lottery winnings in the bank or taking a chance on a friend's business venture. What factors would lead you to invest in your friend's business? In what ways did your attitude toward risk affect your decision?

www.myeconlab.com

**What Economists Find:
Normal Profits and Economic Profits**

Define normal profits and economic profits, and explain their differences.

Accountants, economists, and ordinary people all think of profits as revenues minus costs. Profits are what's left over when all costs have been paid. And if costs are greater than revenues, there's a loss. But a more precise definition of profits — and losses — depends on what gets included in costs. And a precise definition is important for making smart business decisions.

Recall the accountant's definition of profits:

Accounting Profits = Revenues − Obvious Costs (including depreciation)

Economists have two more-precise definitions: normal profits and economic profits.

Normal Profits

Normal profits are compensation for the use of a business owner's time and money, the sum of the hidden opportunity costs. The *time component* of normal profits is the value of the best alternative use of the owner's time. For Wahid, that is the $40 000 he could have earned elsewhere. The *money component* of normal profits is the best alternative return on investment, including risk compensation. For Wahid, that is the $6000 he *expects* on his $30 000 investment. So, normal profits for the first year of Wahid's Web Wonders business are $46 000 ($40 000 + $6000). Normal profits are what a business owner must earn to do as well as he could have been doing in the best alternative uses of his time and money.

normal profits:
- *compensation for business owner's time and money*
- *sum of hidden opportunity costs (implicit costs)*
- *what business owner must earn to do as well as best alternative use of time and money*

Economic Profits

The economist's definition of profits is "revenues minus *all opportunity costs*." Like accountants, economists subtract all obvious costs from revenues. These out-of-pocket costs are also opportunity costs. The best alternative use of the $25 000 Wahid spends on obvious rent, phone expenses, and so on is still $25 000 worth of different business-related items he could have bought instead.

▼

Can the salesperson in this comic expect to make profits?

The key difference between economists and accountants is that economists also subtract hidden opportunity costs from revenues:

Economic Profits = Revenues − All Opportunity Costs

= Revenues − (Obvious Costs + Hidden Opportunity Costs)

Since the sum of hidden opportunity costs is defined as normal profits, the definition of economic profits can also be written as

Economic Profits = Revenues − (Obvious Costs + Normal Profits)

With all these definitions and equations, you are no doubt thinking, "Why is he bothering with these picky distinctions? Isn't this just splitting hairs?" No one should be subjected to picky distinctions *unless those distinctions are important for understanding.* Let me show you why the definition of economic profits matters for making smart business choices.

Figure 6.2 revisits Wahid's business plan, but as it would look to an economist.

Figure 6.2	Economist's Business Plan for Wahid (1 year)		
Total Expected Revenues			**$60 000**
Obvious Costs	Depreciation	$5 000	
	Rent	$14 000	
	Web Hosting	$3 000	
	Phone	$1 000	
	Advertising	$2 000	
Total Obvious Costs			**$25 000**
Hidden Opportunity Costs	Wahid's Time	$40 000	
	Wahid's Money	$6 000	
Total Hidden Costs			**$46 000**
Economic Profits			**($11 000)***

*On business plans and balance sheets, losses are indicated with parentheses: (11 000) is an eleven thousand dollar loss.

According to the economist's calculation, when you subtract all of Wahid's opportunity costs ($25 000 in obvious costs and $46 000 in hidden opportunity costs) from his expected revenues ($60 000), Wahid is suffering **economic losses** of $11 000! What this means is that Wahid is *not* covering all of his opportunity costs.

economic profits: revenues minus all opportunity costs (obvious costs plus hidden opportunity costs)

economic losses: negative economic profits

What Economists Find Recall that Wahid's accounting profits are $35 000. But if, instead of working and investing in his business, he had worked elsewhere and invested his money either in the bank or in an investment equally as risky as his business, he would have earned between $41 500 (guaranteed) and $46 000 (expected). The amount of $35 000 in accounting profits might sound attractive, but it is not as good as Wahid's best alternative uses of his time and money. With these numbers, *Wahid has not made a smart choice* (other than avoiding having a boss). He is worse off after a year running his business than if he had been working and investing his money elsewhere.

Refresh 6.2

1. Explain how to calculate economic profits.

2. If your business earns accounting profits of $50 000 and economic profits of $20 000, what are your hidden opportunity costs?

3. You earn a good salary, but you hate your boss. You develop a plan for a new business that projects economic profits of $5000 at the end of the year. Before you start the business, someone offers you a job for $15 000 more than you were earning before. Does that change your projected economic profits?

www.myeconlab.com

6.3 How Economic Profits Direct the Invisible Hand

Explain how economic profits signal smart business decisions and coordinate consumer and business choices.

Economic profits are the only signal — the key bottom line — that allows us to judge smart business decisions. Accounting profits provide some useful information, but not enough. To illustrate, let's look at three alternative end-of-year scenarios for Wahid. While his business plan was based on *expected* revenues, what happens if his *actual* revenues turn out to be $60 000, $71 000, or $80 000? In each of the three alternative scenarios, his obvious costs and hidden opportunity costs (normal profits) are the same as before (see Figure 6.3).

In each of the three scenarios Wahid has positive accounting profits, seeming to indicate that he is doing well. But the economic profits calculations tells a different story.

Figure 6.3	Alternative Profit Scenarios for Wahid's Web Wonders		
Scenario	**One**	**Two**	**Three**
Revenues	$60 000	$71 000	$80 000
Total Obvious Costs	$25 000	$25 000	$25 000
Total Hidden Opportunity Costs	$46 000	$46 000	$46 000
Accounting Profits	$35 000	$46 000	$55 000
Economic Profits	($11 000)	$0	$9 000

In the first scenario, with revenues of $60 000, Wahid's economic profits are negative — economic losses of $11 000. Wahid is kicking himself because he is worse off than if he had chosen the best alternative uses of his time and money.

In the second scenario, with revenues of $71 000, Wahid's economic profits are zero. That doesn't sound good, but what it means is that Wahid's revenues are just covering all his opportunity costs of production (obvious costs and hidden opportunity costs). If Wahid's revenues turn out to be $71 000, he will be content. He did as well as he could have done with the best alternative uses of his time and money (and he was his own boss!). He is not kicking himself.

In the third scenario, with revenues of $80 000, Wahid's economic profits are positive, to the tune of $9000. Wahid is one happy web designer. Any amount of positive economic profits indicates he is doing better than the best alternative uses of his time and money. Wahid has made a smart choice.

Looking at economic profits makes it easy to identify whether you have made a smart choice, combining Keys 1 and 3 of the Three Keys to Smart Choices. Key 1 says, "Choose only when additional benefits are greater than additional opportunity costs." Key 3 says, "Be sure to count *all* additional benefits and costs, including *implicit costs* and externalities." For Wahid's business, revenues in the first year are "additional benefits." And all of the business's additional opportunity costs in the first year must include both obvious costs as well as implicit costs, or hidden opportunity costs.

So the combination of Keys 1 and 3 for business decisions can be written as "Choose only when revenues are greater than all opportunity costs," or, even more simply,

"Choose only when economic profits are positive."

Rule for smart business decisions: Choose only when economic profits are positive.

Economic Profits Signal the Way

More than just a signal for smart business decisions, economic profits create the incentive for businesses to supply the products/services that consumers demand. In Chapter 4 we saw how markets coordinate the smart choices of consumers and businesses. Markets form prices (through the interaction of demand and supply), which provide signals and incentives that affect everyone's smart choices. When there are imbalances between demand and supply, prices adjust to coordinate smart choices.

When businesses focus on bottom line — pursuing economic profits — unintended consequence is markets produce what consumers want.

For a business, changing prices affect both revenues (prices of products/services sold) and costs (prices of inputs bought). While a well-run business tries to keep track of all of that changing information, if it just focuses on the bottom line — on pursuing economic profits — the unintended consequence is that markets will produce the products/services consumers want.

Just like traffic signals keep drivers moving smoothly to their different destinations quickly and safely, economic profits direct businesses to produce what consumers want. Simply look back at Wahid's three alternative scenarios for economic profits.

Economic losses are red lights, signalling not-smart business decision — get off that road.

breakeven point: business just earning normal profits (no economic profits, no economic losses)

Economic profits are green light signalling smart business decision — get on that road.

Scenario One   In the first scenario, Wahid's economic profits are negative — he has suffered economic losses. This is a red light to a business. Because Wahid could have done better on an alternative road, the red light of economic losses is telling him to get off this road and direct his energy, talent, and money elsewhere, where they will be more valued. For any business or industry, economic losses are a signal of not-smart choices to avoid.

Scenario Two   In the second scenario, Wahid's economic profits are zero. He is just covering all his opportunity costs (including earning normal profits). This is a yellow light — proceed with caution. Economists also call this scenario a business's **breakeven point** because Wahid is doing as well as he could have with the best alternative uses of his time and money.

Scenario Three   In the third scenario, Wahid is earning positive economic profits. These economic profits are *over and above* the best alternative uses of his time and money (normal profits). This is a green light. It says to Wahid that he has made a smart choice and should continue on this road, investing more time and money in expanding his business. When outsiders see economic profits in a particular line of business, they shift their time and money out of industries that are yielding economic losses or just breaking even, and into green-light industries.

Market Equilibrium   The flows of time and money following the signals for economic profits bring market demand and supply into balance.

When economic losses occur, it indicates that prices (the most important influence on revenues) are not covering all businesses' opportunity costs of production. Consumers don't value the product/service enough to pay the price that will allow businesses to cover all their costs (including hidden opportunity costs, or normal profits). Smart businesses get off that road, leave the industry, and move their time, money, and inputs elsewhere to a promise of economic profits. When businesses exit from the industry, there is a decrease in supply (Chapter 3), which pushes prices up. Businesses keep exiting, prices keep rising, and quantities demanded and sold keep decreasing, until prices and revenues just cover all opportunity costs of production (including normal profits), and economic profits are zero.

When businesses are breaking even, and economic profits are zero, there is no strong incentive for any change. Businesses are doing as well as they could elsewhere. Economists describe an industry where businesses have zero economic profits as being in **market equilibrium**. Equilibrium is a situation where there is a balance of forces, with no tendency for change. Business owners in this industry are not jumping for joy, but they are also not jumping out of windows because of financial ruin. They are not kicking themselves.

A market equilibrium exists when the forces of demand and supply are in balance. The price consumers are willing to pay just covers businesses' opportunity costs of production. Without excess demand or excess supply, the market is providing the quantity of products/services that consumers are willing and able to buy at that price.

market equilibrium: quantity demanded equals quantity supplied, economic profits zero, no tendency for change

Economic Profits Signal A "Go"   When there are economic profits, the message is that consumers are willing to pay a price that is greater than businesses' opportunity costs of production. This green light directs existing businesses in the industry to increase their output, and signals new businesses to turn onto this road. As businesses enter the industry supply increases, which pushes prices down. But as long as economic profits remain, businesses keep entering, prices keep falling, and the quantities demanded and sold keep increasing. Traffic stabilizes only once prices have fallen enough to just cover all opportunity costs of production, and economic profits have fallen to zero.

On the supply side of markets, economic profits are the key signal directing the self-interest of businesses to produce the products/services that consumers want. Changes in economic profits trigger changes in supply, which changes prices, bringing demand and supply into balance.

By finding the real bottom line, we expose the invisible hand directing business owners' self-interest to unintentionally produce the miracle of markets.

Changes in economic profits trigger changes in supply, changing price and bringing demand and supply into balance. On the supply side, economic profit is the key signal coordinating smart choices of businesses with smart choices of consumers.

Refresh
6.3

1. What signal does it send to new businesses considering entering an industry when economic profits are negative? Zero? Positive?

2. Explain how the rule "Choose only when additional benefits are greater than additional opportunity costs" is the same as "Choose when economic profits are positive."

3. Businesses in the beachball market are currently earning zero economic profits. A heat wave strikes and demand for beachballs skyrockets, so a shortage develops, driving up beachball prices. Using economic profits as the key, explain all the choices that will be made before the beachball market once again returns to market equilibrium with zero economic profits.

www.myeconlab.com

Finding the Bottom Line

Opportunity Costs, Economic Profits and Losses, and the Miracle of Markets

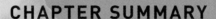

CHAPTER SUMMARY

6.1 WHAT ACCOUNTANTS MISS: OBVIOUS COSTS, ACCOUNTING PROFITS, AND HIDDEN OPPORTUNITY COSTS

Accounting profits equal revenues minus all obvious costs, including depreciation. But accounting profits miss the hidden, implicit, opportunity costs of a business owner's time and money.

- **Obvious costs** (**explicit costs**) — costs a business pays directly. Accountants account for all obvious business costs and include **depreciation**:
  - tax rule for spreading cost over lifetime of long-lasting equipment.
  - decrease in value because of wear and tear and because equipment becomes obsolete.
- **Accounting profits** — Revenues − Obvious Costs (including depreciation).
- **Implicit costs** — hidden opportunity costs of what business owner could earn elsewhere with time and money invested.
  - Opportunity cost of time — best alternative use of business owner's time.
  - Opportunity cost of money — best alternative use of business owner's money invested in the business; must include compensation for risk.

6.2 WHAT ECONOMISTS FIND: NORMAL PROFITS AND ECONOMIC PROFITS

Smart business decisions return at least normal profits — what a business owner could earn from the best alternative uses of her time and money. There are economic profits over and above normal profits, when revenues are greater than all opportunity costs of production, including hidden opportunity costs.

- **Normal profits:**
  - compensation for business owner's time and money; or
  - sum of hidden opportunity costs (implicit costs); or
  - what business owner must earn to do as well as best alternative use of time and money.
- **Economic profits** equal
  - Revenues minus all Opportunity Costs
  - Revenues − (Obvious Costs + Hidden Opportunity Costs)
  - Revenues − (Obvious Costs + Implicit Costs)
  - Revenues − (Obvious Costs + Normal Profits)
- Key difference between economists and accountants is that economists subtract *hidden opportunity costs* when calculating profits.
  - Economic profits are less than accounting profits.
- **Economic losses** — negative economic profits.
  - If revenues are less than all opportunity costs, business owner has not made a smart decision and would be better off in alternative uses of time and money.
  - With economic losses, business owner not even earning normal profits.

6.3 HOW ECONOMIC PROFITS DIRECT THE INVISIBLE HAND

The simplest rule for smart business decisions is "Choose only when economic profits are positive." When businesses pursue economic profits, the unintended consequence is that markets produce the products/services consumers want.

- Economic profits (and losses) serve as signal for smart business decisions.
  - With economic losses (red light): businesses leave industry, supply decreases, pushing quantities sold down and prices up, until prices just cover all opportunity costs of production and economic profits are zero.
  - With **breakeven point** (yellow light): businesses just earning normal profits. Market equilibrium with zero economic profits or losses. No tendency for change.
  - With economic profits (green light): businesses expand and enter industry, supply increases, pushing quantities sold up and prices down, until prices just cover all opportunity costs of production and economic profits are zero.
- **Market equilibrium** — quantity demanded equals quantity supplied, economic profits zero, no tendency for change. The price consumers are willing and able to pay just covers businesses' opportunity costs of production (including normal profits).
- Changes in economic profits trigger changes in supply, changing price and bringing demand and supply into balance. On supply side, economic profits are key signal coordinating smart choices of businesses with smart choices of consumers.

TRUE/FALSE

Circle the correct answer.

6.1 OBVIOUS COSTS, ACCOUNTING PROFITS, HIDDEN OPPORTUNITY COSTS

1. The rule for spreading the cost of purchases of long-lasting machinery and equipment over their useful life is called depreciation.   **True**   **False**

2. The cost of a self-employed worker's time, in any given year, is zero.   **True**   **False**

3. If you can borrow money from your parents for free, the opportunity cost of using that money to start a business is zero.   **True**   **False**

4. Returns from investing in stocks are *guaranteed,* while returns from saving money in the bank are *risky.*   **True**   **False**

5. Individuals who are risk averse need to be paid more to take a risk than risk-loving individuals would.   **True**   **False**

6. The best alternative use of your money could be the interest earned if you put the borrowed money in a savings account.   **True**   **False**

6.2 NORMAL PROFITS AND ECONOMIC PROFITS

7. The time component of normal profits is the value of the best alternative use of the owner's money.   **True**   **False**

8. The money component of normal profits is the best alternative return on investment, including risk compensation.   **True**   **False**

9. The interest rate is 10 percent per year. You invest $50 000 of your own money in a business and earn accounting profits of $20 000 after one year. Assume the opportunity cost of time is zero. Therefore, economic profits will be $30 000.   **True**   **False**

10. It is a smart choice to remain in business if accounting profits are greater than zero.   **True**   **False**

6.3 HOW ECONOMIC PROFITS DIRECT THE INVISIBLE HAND

11. If revenues increase, business owners will be more likely to stay in the industry.   **True**   **False**

12. If prices fall, business owners will be more likely to stay in the industry.   **True**   **False**

13. You should always listen to your accountant when she tells you to stay in business.   **True**   **False**

14. Businesses are at the breakeven point when revenues equal hidden opportunity costs.   **True**   **False**

15. Businesses will leave an industry when economic profits are zero.   **True**   **False**

MULTIPLE CHOICE

Circle the correct answer.

6.1 OBVIOUS COSTS, ACCOUNTING PROFITS, HIDDEN OPPORTUNITY COSTS

1. What do accountants miss?
   - A) Opportunity costs
   - B) Obvious opportunity costs
   - C) Hidden opportunity costs
   - D) Everything

2. Success should be measured by
   - A) revenues.
   - B) costs.
   - C) accounting profits.
   - D) economic profits.

3. Abdul operates his own business and pays himself a salary of $20 000 per year. He refused a job that pays $30 000 per year. What is the opportunity cost of Abdul's time in the business?
   - A) $0
   - B) $20 000
   - C) $30 000
   - D) $50 000

4. If you borrow money from the bank to start up a business, the interest you pay to the bank is
   - A) an obvious cost.
   - B) subtracted from revenues.
   - C) included in the calculation of accounting profits.
   - D) all of the above.

5. An economist would consider someone who is a gambler and does not need much compensation to go for an uncertain investment to be
   - A) crazy.
   - B) risk loving.
   - C) risk averse.
   - D) all of the above.

6.2 NORMAL PROFITS AND ECONOMIC PROFITS

6. Normal profits include
   - A) compensation for the use of a business owner's time and money.
   - B) the sum of hidden opportunity costs.
   - C) what a business owner could have earned elsewhere.
   - D) all of the above.

7. Which of the following is *not* another way of saying "hidden opportunity costs"?

   A) Explicit costs

   B) Implicit costs

   C) Normal profits

   D) The sum of the opportunity costs of time and money

8. The key difference between economists and accountants is that economists

   A) are always smarter.

   B) are always better looking.

   C) subtract hidden opportunity costs when calculating profits.

   D) add opportunity costs when calculating profits.

9. The definition of economic profits can also be written as

   A) Economic Profits = Revenues − (Obvious Opportunity Costs + Normal Profits).

   B) Economic Profits = Revenues − (Obvious Opportunity Costs + Hidden Opportunity Costs).

   C) Economic Profits = Accounting Profits − Hidden Opportunity Costs.

   D) All of the above.

10. If your business earns accounting profits of $50 000 and economic profits of $20 000, what are your hidden opportunity costs?

   A) $20 000

   B) $30 000

   C) $60 000

   D) $70 000

11. If your business earns accounting profits of $50 000 and economic losses of $20 000, what are your hidden opportunity costs?

   A) $20 000

   B) $30 000

   C) $60 000

   D) $70 000

6.3 HOW ECONOMIC PROFITS DIRECT THE INVISIBLE HAND

12. A business owner should enter an industry when

   A) economic profits are positive.

   B) additional benefits are greater than additional opportunity costs.

   C) revenues are greater than all opportunity costs.

   D) all of the above.

13. Which of the following "signals the way" when making decisions to enter or exit an industry?

A) Revenues

B) Normal profits

C) Economic profits

D) Yield signs

14. When economic profits are zero, businesses are

A) breaking even.

B) not kicking themselves.

C) likely to remain in the industry.

D) all of the above.

15. All of the following are "red lights," signalling that a business owner should probably leave an industry, *except*

A) economic losses.

B) rising prices.

C) falling prices.

D) rising opportunity costs.

SHORT ANSWER

Write a short answer to each question. Your answer may be in point form.

Lenny is an accountant and Lex is an economist. One day at a shopping mall, they meet an old school friend, Angelina. She informs them that she is starting a business and would appreciate their advice. Lenny and Lex immediately hand over their business cards.

1. One week later, Angelina sends Lenny and Lex an email, asking them what her expected profits will be for the year, given the following information:

Expected revenue	$50 000
Cost of renting equipment	$10 000
Cost of web access and hosting	$3 000
Cost of phone, cable, and internet (combined)	$5 000
Cost of advertising	$2 000

A) Will Lenny and Lex agree on the amount of Angelina's obvious costs?

B) Will Lenny and Lex agree on the amount of Angelina's accounting profits?

C) What are Angelina's obvious costs for the year?

D) What are Angelina's accounting profits for the year?

2. The next day, Lenny replies to Angelina's email: "You should definitely go for it. This business venture will provide you with some sweet profits."

On the other hand, Lex (being an economist) isn't yet convinced that pursuing this business opportunity is the smart choice. Lex sends Angelina an email suggesting they chat by instant messaging as soon as possible in order to discuss it further. The following discussion takes place.

Angelina: Hi Lex! Thank you for your help. What's next?

Lex: Although the accounting profits are nice, you have to remember that the accounting profits are really your take-home pay. In order to determine if this is a smart choice, you have to compare these profits with how much you would get paid if you were to work in another job. Do you have any other opportunities?

Angelina: Well, the last three years I've worked for a marketing company and I'm sure they would hire me back for $25 000 a year.

Lex: Before deciding whether to pursue this business opportunity you have to consider your opportunity cost of time.

Angelina: Oh, okay . . . . So, "Mr. Economist" big shot, I need to know three things then:

i) In dollar terms, how much is this "opportunity cost of time" that you speak of?

ii) How would this affect my accounting profits and economic profits?

iii) Should I still stay in business if I take the opportunity cost of my time into consideration?

How would you answer Angelina if you were Lex?

3. After Lex gives his "opportunity cost of time" lesson to Angelina, he remembers that the opportunity cost of time is not the only hidden opportunity cost. The next time he sees Angelina online, they have the following exchange:

Lex says: Me again! I forgot to tell you . . . you also have to think about your opportunity cost of money — that is, what else you could have done with the money you borrowed. I can help you understand why this is important to your business decision, but first I have to know two things:

i) Where did you borrow your money from?

ii) How much money did you borrow?

Angelina: My parents said they would give me $20 000 at the beginning of every year for as long as I had my own business. And they don't expect me to pay them back.

Lex: But, instead of spending your parents' money on this business opportunity, you can put the money in the bank and let the interest grow at the current interest rate of 10 percent a year.

Angelina: Hmm ... okay, well, now I have the same three questions!

i)   In dollar terms, how much is this "opportunity cost of money" that you speak of?

ii) How would this affect my accounting profits and economic profits (if I take the opportunity cost of both my *time and money* into consideration)?

iii) Should I still stay in business if I take the opportunity cost of my *time and money* into consideration?

Provide answers to Angelina's three questions.

4. One year goes by without any communication between Lex and Angelina. Then, out of the blue, Angelina signs in to instant messaging and sends Lex a message.

Angelina: Sorry I haven't been online much. I've been super busy with the business, which has been going great by the way! In fact, the marketing company noticed my success and offered to hire me for a salary of $28 000 next year — this is $3000 higher than what they were offering me last year.

Lex: That's cool. FYI — even if your revenues, obvious opportunity costs, and hidden opportunity costs of money stay the same as last year, your economic profits will be different this year.

Angelina: OK — so let me try to figure this out. You tell me if I'm right.

i)   Since my outside job option is now offering me $3000 more than last year, this means that my "economic profits" from continuing with this business opportunity are $3000 lower, right?

ii) Since my economic profits will be zero next year, I should not go ahead with this business opportunity then, right?

Reply to (i) and (ii).

5. Just before the end of last year, Angelina's industry experienced a huge increase in demand.

A) How will this affect prices?

B) How will this affect economic profits and her decision to stay in the industry?

6. Since Angelina made economic profits at the end of last year, an economist would predict that this would signal to other businesses that the return here is higher than elsewhere, which would encourage other businesses to enter the industry.

   A) Explain what will happen to market prices if businesses enter the industry.

   B) If Angelina doesn't adjust her price to the market price, what do you expect to happen to her sales? What do you expect will happen to her revenues?

   C) If she does adjust her price so that it is equal to the market price, what do you expect will happen to Angelina's revenues?

7. Angelina is so impressed with Lex's skills that she decides to hire him as her financial adviser. She offers to pay him an annual salary of $24 000. She also decides to hire a worker at the minimum wage of $8 per hour (which would be an annual salary of about $16 000) to help reduce the amount of work that she previously had to do on her own.

   A) Since Lex would very much enjoy working with Angelina, he is tempted to continue to offer his financial advice for free. From an opportunity cost of time perspective, should Lex offer his time for free (assuming he makes a smart choice)?

   B) Given that Angelina is now paying a worker $16 000 and Lex $24 000, how will this affect her obvious costs and accounting profits?

   C) Can you think of a reason why Angelina may profit from hiring a worker and Lex, even though they represent a large cost?

8. Angelina's parents decide that it's time for Angelina to start borrowing money from the bank rather than from her parents. The current interest rate is 10 percent.

   A) Will Angelina's obvious costs increase? Why or why not?

   B) Will the opportunity cost of money increase? Why or why not?

9. Suppose that the New Democratic Party gets elected and forms the federal government. Also suppose that they introduce two laws:

   1) They raise the minimum wage from $8 to $10 (which raises annual minimum wage income from $16 000 to $20 000).

   2) They remove rent ceiling controls.

   A) How will the rise in the minimum wage affect economic profits (all else being equal)?

   B) How will the removal of rent ceilings affect economic profits if the market rent is higher than the rent ceiling imposed by the government (all else being equal)?

   C) Suppose that Angelina's economic profits for the year were expected to be $5000 before the New Democratic Party was elected. Is staying in business still a smart choice if rent increased by $100 a month ($1200 a year) and the minimum wage rose from $16 000 to $20 000?

10. Explain how each of the following events would affect economic profits.

   A) Government decides that web access and hosting fees are too high, so it puts a maximum ceiling on how high they can be.

   B) A competitor gets sued for fraud, and consumers reduce their demand for all products/services sold by your industry.

   C) The scare of an influenza pandemic makes the city's population afraid to leave their homes. People start spending a lot more time surfing the internet for products/services to buy, which increases the demand for your product/service.

Chapter 7

The Power to Price

Monopoly and Competition

After reading this chapter, you should be able to:

7.1 Differentiate between monopoly and extreme competition, and explain what businesses aim for and what businesses fear.

7.2 Identify three characteristics of market structure and explain their influence, with elasticity of demand, on a business's ability to set prices.

7.3 Identify the four main market structures, and explain the differences among them.

7.4 Explain how businesses compete, and why the process of creative destruction improves productivity and living standards.

DO YOU PREFER LOW PRICES OR HIGH PRICES?

This is a trick question. If you answered "low prices," you were thinking as a consumer who buys Gatorade, or iPods, or doughnuts. If you answered "high prices," you were thinking as a businessperson who sells piercings, or web services, or your own hours of labour. In Canada's market economy, we each play dual roles — as a buyer (of products/services we need) and as a seller (of inputs earning income).

As consumers or businesses, we rarely get to choose the prices of our products/services. Prices are determined through the interaction of demand and supply in markets. Prices settle somewhere between the maximum consumers are willing to pay (marginal benefit) and the minimum businesses are willing to accept (covering all marginal opportunity costs of production). Businesses generally seek higher prices (with economic profits); consumers seek lower prices (bargains that leave zero economic profits for businesses).

What determines exactly where market prices end up between the two extremes? Why are economic profits high in some markets and non-existent in others? The answers, which we will explore in this chapter, have to do with how much competition there is, which influences a business's power to price products/services. And that *power to price* depends on what substitutes are available to consumers and on the elasticity of demand.

Since we all sell something to earn income, whether as a business or a worker, knowing about competition will help you make smart choices in pricing your products/services, negotiating a salary, or competing with other sellers in your market.

7.1 Price Makers and Price Takers: Dreams of Monopoly and Nightmares of Competition

Differentiate between monopoly and extreme competition, and explain what businesses aim for and what businesses fear.

monopoly:
only seller of
product/service;
no close substitutes
available

market power:
business's ability to
set prices

price maker:
pure monopoly with
maximum power to
set prices

Think of yourself as a seller hoping to set high and profitable prices. Let's look at the competitive situations you might face, starting with the extremes of your best case and worst case. Then we'll look at the situations in between.

Pure Monopoly

For a seller's best case, let's go back to the example in Chapter 3, where it's Sunday night and your boss calls in a panic, begging you to work as many hours as possible next week. All your co-workers are sick and you are the only person who knows how to run the store. As the *only seller* of labour trained for that store, an economist would say you have a **monopoly**. The word *monopoly* comes from the Greek words *mono* (meaning "one") and *poly* (meaning "seller"). A monopoly is the *only seller* of a product/service — *no close substitutes are available.*

Instead of asking how many hours you will work at different wages, suppose your boss says, "I desperately need you to work 60 hours next week. I have no one else. Name your price." (Don't you wish life were always like that?) That power to set prices is called **market power**. If we think of market power on a scale of 0 to 10, a pure monopoly scores a 10, the maximum power to set prices. As the only seller of a product/service that has no close substitutes, you are a **price maker**. You can name your price.

When Xerox Corporation invented the first photocopy machine in 1959, it had a monopoly. There were no other quick and inexpensive ways to copy a document. The only (poor) substitutes available involved copying by hand, using carbon paper between two sheets of paper on a typewriter (when the typewriter keys pounded the first sheet, they also created a carbon copy on the paper behind), or going to a printing company. The original Xerox 914 machine leased for $95 per month ($700 in today's dollars) and made enormous profits for Xerox. During the years before other photocopy machines appeared, Xerox earned profits at rates of 1000 percent — for every dollar you invested in Xerox, you got back $1000! Xerox was a highly profitable price maker with a score of 10 on the market power scale.

▲
The name Xerox 914 came from the copier's ability to copy document sizes up to 9×14 inches. At the time this machine entered the market, this was a major benefit to consumers.

While price makers have maximum power to set prices, their market power is still limited by what buyers are willing and able to pay. The law of demand always operates — higher prices mean lower quantity demanded. So the trade-off of setting a higher price is lower sales. The price maker's goal is to find the price and quantity combination that yields the greatest profits. When your boss asks you to name your selling price, you could answer "one million dollars." It's a free country, and you can charge any price you want. But freedom exists for buyers, too — no one can be forced to buy. Your boss would likely laugh and close the store for the week because she would lose less by closing than by paying you $1 million. If Xerox set the price of its photocopiers much higher, customers might find it cheaper to go to printing companies or to pay for handwritten copies, or even to do without copies. The fall-off in sales from even higher prices could more than offset the higher price, so profits could be lower. Even monopoly price makers must live by the law of demand.

Businesses can set any price they choose, but can't force consumers to buy. Even monopoly price makers must live by law of demand.

Extreme Competition

A small wheat farmer in Saskatchewan is a worst-case example of a seller's market power. Although the farmer is proud of the #1 quality wheat he has grown, thousands of other farmers in Canada and around the world are selling the identical product. Perfect substitutes for the farmer's wheat are instantly available.

If the market price of #1 quality wheat is $3 per bushel, what chance does this farmer have of setting and getting a price higher than that? Even $3.01? The answer is zero. No buyer will pay even a penny more because he can easily get the identical product for $3. The farmer is a **price taker**, with a score of zero on the market power scale. This is a case of **extreme competition**, where many sellers are producing identical products (perfect substitutes). Profit margins are razor thin — the best this farmer, or any business in extreme competition, can hope for is to recover all of his opportunity costs of production (including normal profits). Economic profits are zero. With no ability to raise prices, his only hope for economic profits is to produce at a lower cost than his competitors.

Every business, or seller, dreams of being a price maker like a pure monopoly (market power of 10) and dreads the prospect of extreme competition, where it is a passive price taker (market power of zero). Most business decisions are motivated by the desire for the economic profits and market power of a monopoly, yet the forces of competition are usually pushing businesses back toward their nightmare of extreme competition.

price taker: business with zero power to set price different from market price

extreme competition: many sellers producing identical products/services

FOR YOUR INFORMATION

Adam Smith nicely summed up the difference between monopoly and competition when it comes to pricing power:

"The price of monopoly is ... the highest which can be squeezed out of the buyers, or which ... they will consent to give."

"The natural price, or the price of free competition, on the contrary, ... is the lowest which the sellers can commonly afford to take, and at the same time continue their business."

Refresh 7.1

1. Explain the differences in market power between pure monopoly and extreme competition.

2. Besides wheat, what products/services do you think have markets that are like extreme competition?

3. Sellers generally prefer higher prices. When might a seller earn more revenues by cutting prices instead of raising them? [*Hint:* Think elasticity of demand.]

www.myeconlab.com

7.2 How Much Competition Is Going On? Market Structure

Identify three characteristics of market structure and explain their influence, with elasticity of demand, on business's ability to set prices.

The markets for newly invented products (photocopiers in 1959, or Apple's iPhone in 2007) and for wheat are extreme cases. Most businesses fall somewhere in between these extremes of all-powerful price makers and passive price takers. What factors in the real world are common to all markets and affect all businesses' power to price? Economists have a shorthand term for the answer. It is **market structure** — the characteristics of a market that affect competition and the ability of businesses to set prices. Market structure has three main characteristics: availability of substitutes, number of competitors, and barriers preventing new competitors from entering the market. Let's look at each of these before re-examining the concept that best sums up a business's power to price — elasticity of demand.

market structure: characteristics that affect competition and pricing power — availability of substitutes, number of competitors, barriers to entry of new competitors

"What's a Market" Depends on "What's a Substitute"

Since we are going to describe the characteristics of a market, let's review what a market is (Chapter 4, Section 4.1). A market is not a place or a thing, it's a process — the interaction between buyers and sellers. A market brings together buyers and sellers of a *particular* product/service (*particular* is an important word).

For example, the 2007 market for iPhones, like the 1959 market for photocopiers, involved a single seller (Apple) and thousands of buyers. The market for wheat involves thousands of sellers and thousands of buyers (in Canada and around the world).

Markets can be defined narrowly or broadly. More broadly = more substitutes and competitors. More narrowly = fewer substitutes and competitors.

But how we define a market depends on how we define a *particular* product/service. In 2007, the iPhone was unique because of Apple's touchscreen software and its distinctive design. Even so, other products existed that combined cell phones, music players, and web browsers — for example the RIM BlackBerry and the Palm Treo. If we shift from a narrow definition of the market for iPhones to a broader definition of the market for handheld, combined cell/music/web devices, then Apple was no longer the single seller, and buyers had a wider variety of choices. There are always substitutes, and the more broadly we define a market the more substitutes there are — and the more competitors there are. For consumers who wanted only an iPhone (that's particular!), Apple had a monopoly and was a price maker. But for consumers who wanted a handheld, combined cell/music/web device, there were more substitutes and more sellers with less pricing power.

Narrow Markets Mean Fewer Substitutes   The reverse is also true. The more narrowly we define a market, the fewer substitutes there are — and the fewer competitors. For the broadly defined wheat market, our Saskatchewan farmer has thousands of competitors, and consumers have the choice of thousands of identical substitute bushels of wheat. But the definition of the market gets narrower if the "buy and eat local" movement (which advocates eating only foods grown within 200 kilometres of where you live) becomes fashionable in Saskatoon and Regina. Then farmers within a 200-kilometre radius of those cities have far fewer competitors, and "buy local" consumers in those cities have fewer substitutes. The local farmers gain market power, and we would expect to see higher prices for locally grown wheat.

If your boss will hire only workers specifically trained for her store, you are the only seller. But if she defines the labour market more broadly, she might bring in workers from similar chain stores elsewhere in the city, or go to a temporary agency, hire workers with some retail experience, and spend a day training them. The more broadly she defines the labour market, the more substitutes she has, the more competitors you face, and the lower is your price power as a seller.

One more example for the coffee addicts. Do you have a favourite brand, Tim's, Second Cup or Starbucks? If you are a die-hard Tim's addict, then you don't consider other brands as substitutes, and there is a limited number of sellers you'll buy from (probably only one or two Tim's in your neighbourhood). But if all you want is hot caffeine there are substitutes in abundance and many sellers with less price power.

ECONOMICS Out There

Product Differentiation   Businesses/sellers are always trying to develop brand loyalty among customers, because when customers rule out other substitutes, the seller faces less competition and has more ability to raise prices. Any attempt by a business to distinguish its product from its competitors' products is called **product differentiation**. If the wheat farmer tried raising prices to (non-local) customers, his sales would fall to zero. But Tim's can charge a higher price than 7-Eleven can for coffee, and Apple can charge a higher price than Palm can, in part because of brand loyalty. The more you, as a seller, can convince potential buyers that there are fewer substitutes out there, the more likely you will be a price maker rather than a price taker.

Product differentiation can take the form of actual product differences (cell phones may have different features, styles, pricing plans) or of advertising that attempts to convince you that one coffee brand is better, even though the coffee tastes pretty much the same. (See *FYI* in the margin.)

product differentiation: attempt to distinguish product from competitors' products

FOR YOUR INFORMATION

Molson Canadian or Labatt Blue? Beer companies spend millions in advertising to convince you that their particular beer tastes better, and many consumers prefer one brand to the other. But in tests where beer drinkers were given different beers to try, most could not taste or tell the difference between brands. That's product differentiation without actual product differences!

Counting Competitors: Number of Businesses

Once you define your market and identify which products/services are substitutes, the second characteristic affecting competition and the power to price is the number of other businesses selling similar products/services. As we just saw, the more broadly we define the market, the more competitors there are, and the more narrowly we define the market, the fewer competitors there are. But whatever the definition of your market, some markets have more sellers competing, and other markets have fewer sellers competing. The extremes are pure monopoly (one seller) and extreme competition (countless sellers). For all the market structures in between, in general, the fewer competitors, the more price power; the more competitors, the less price power.

Why do businesses often try to buy or merge with other businesses in their market? One reason is to reduce the number of competitors, and thereby increase pricing power and potential economic profits.

Counting your competitors is not always as easy as it seems. Some markets are mostly local. If you are a business selling piercings, dry cleaning, or fruits and vegetables, most of your customers and competitors are in a limited geographical area around you. You can easily identify your main competitors.

But other markets are not bound by geography, and counting competitors is hard. Wahid, in Chapter 6, located his web design business in the design district of the city because that's where most of his city customers expect to find design services. It's also where most of Wahid's local competitors are. But the internet, digital technologies, videoconferencing, and inexpensive airfares have exploded the geographical boundaries of competition.

This explosion of competition is good and bad for businesses. The good news for Wahid is that he can extend his market, sell his services anywhere in the world, and increase his sales. The bad news is that design companies anywhere in the world can compete for Wahid's customers, which limits his pricing power. If you are selling design services, books, or DVDs, your competitors are not just local businesses, but also Chapters, Amazon, and sellers anywhere in the world connected through eBay or craigslist or other websites. Counting competitors is hard!

For consumers, the explosion of competition is generally good news — more choices and lower prices.

Consider the internet. Although you probably can't imagine life without it, the web has been around only since 1995 — less than 15 years! Before then, advertising played, and still plays, the same role in increasing competition. For a business, advertising extends your market to new customers. Even local businesses — like Paola's Piercing, or restaurants — can attract new customers from far away with advertising and if their reputation is good (think how a listing in a guidebook like *Lonely Planet* attracts tourists). But competitors elsewhere can do the same, with the happy result (for us in our consumer roles) of expanding choices and reducing the pricing power of businesses.

> Fewer competitors = more price power; more competitors = less price power.

Keeping Competitors Out and Profits In: Barriers to Entry

Competitors may be *actual* businesses already selling in your market, or they may be *potential* sellers who decide to enter your market because they are attracted to your high economic profits. When Xerox was earning profits at rates of 1000 percent per year, you can bet other businesses were very interested in figuring out a way to start producing photocopy machines and getting a piece of that hugely profitable action.

And, as we saw in Chapter 6, supply increases as new businesses enter a market and prices and economic profits fall. New businesses continue to be attracted as long as there are economic profits, and stop trying to enter only when economic profits are competed down to zero. If that finally happens, businesses in the market are earning normal profits only — the average rate of return on investment that covers all opportunity costs.

For a monopoly to continue to earn economic profits over a long period of time, there must be some way to keep out potential competitors. Economists call the ways to keep out competitors **barriers to entry**. There are two main types of barriers — legal barriers and economic barriers.

Legal Barriers to Entry Governments can keep new competitors out of a market by passing laws giving a business the exclusive right to supply a product/service. New inventions, like Xerox's photocopy machine or Apple's iPhone, or new methods of production can be protected against competition by legal patents. A patent gives an inventor the exclusive right to supply his new product/service or to license it to other businesses in exchange for royalty payments for 20 years in Canada. Apple took out more than 200 patents on the iPhone before the product appeared. Similarly, a legal copyright gives exclusive rights to the creator of a literary, musical, dramatic, or artistic work. **Patents** and **copyrights** give inventors property rights over what they have produced, part of the rules of the game that are necessary for markets to work well.

Why, I hope you are wondering, would the government do this? Why would the government restrict competition and help guarantee economic profits for certain businesses and artists? It's done to create incentives, encouraging the research, development, and creation of inventions and art that improve our standard of living and quality of life.

To understand why patents and copyrights are necessary to create incentives, imagine if they did not exist. Inventing new products can take lots of time and money, with no guarantee of success. Pharmaceutical companies can spend decades and invest tens of millions of dollars developing and producing new lifesaving drugs, like antibiotics, or other costly drugs that end up failing. Without patents, competitors could buy the successful drugs, analyze their chemical composition, and, through reverse engineering, create comparable drugs that they are more than willing to sell at a much lower price. Competition would drive the price of the drugs down to the cost of production, and the inventing company would never recover the research and development investment. As a business, why would you spend money on research and development ever again?

barriers to entry: legal or economic barriers preventing new competitors from entering market

patents and copyrights: exclusive property rights to sell or license creations, protecting against competition

Patents and copyrights give businesses short-term monopoly power (incentive for invention) but eventually expire (balancing consumers' desire for reasonably priced products/services).

FOR YOUR INFORMATION

Patent or Trade Secret?
Patents have a downside for businesses. To acquire a patent, an inventor must publicly specify all the details of the product and process. This may allow competitors to come up with similar products or processes that are just different enough to not violate the patent. For this reason, many businesses choose not to file for patents, and instead keep the information as a *trade secret*. The Colonel's recipe for *Kentucky Fried Chicken* is a trade secret, not a patented invention.

The same incentives apply to artistic works. Without copyright, the millions of dollars that go into the production of a film would never be recovered, and there would be no hope of profits. If it were legal for anyone to copy the finished film and sell it (for little more than the cost of the blank DVD), no studio would ever start another movie.

Patents and copyrights attempt to balance businesses' and artists' need for "incentives to invent" with consumers' desires for reasonably priced innovative products/services. That is why patents and copyrights eventually expire — once businesses and artists have had a chance to recover their investments and earn economic profits, the entry of competitors will be able to force down prices to where more consumers benefit. After patents expire, generic versions of drugs appear at much lower cost (you can buy no-name ibuprofen for much less money than patented Advil).

One last example of a legal barrier to entry is Canada Post's exclusive right to deliver first-class mail. Did you ever wonder why competitors haven't tried to provide better daily mail delivery? They would be breaking the law, which exists to ensure that all Canadians have access to inexpensive mail service. Without the law, competitors would jump into the profitable locations — like densely populated cities — and abandon the rural and remote communities where delivery costs are high and potential profits are low.

Economic Barriers to Entry A business may be able to keep competitors out and economic profits in simply by being big. For most products, the total production cost per unit (average cost) falls as the business produces larger quantities of output. Economists describe this benefit of being big as **economies of scale** — average costs fall as the scale of production increases. If a big business is already supplying most of a market, a new competitor trying to enter will start with smaller sales and therefore higher costs. The new business simply can't compete on price.

In the most extreme cases, one business can supply the entire market at a lower cost per unit than can two or more businesses. That means there is room for only one low-cost business. Examples are utilities like water or electricity or cable television. There are huge costs of creating the distribution network of pipes or wires or cables (these are the **sunk costs** of Chapter 3, which economists also call **fixed** costs — they do not change with changes in quantities of output produced). Once the network is in place, the **marginal cost** of delivering the water or electricity or programming is quite low. (These are **variable costs** — costs that change with changes in the quantities of output produced.) As the quantity of output increases, the network costs are spread over more and more customers, and the **average total costs** fall.

$$\text{Average Total Costs} = \frac{(\text{Fixed Costs} + \text{Variable Costs})}{\text{Quantity of Output}}$$

economies of scale: average cost of producing falls as quantity (scale) of production increases

FOR YOUR INFORMATION

Economists, businesspeople, and accountants use a variety of cost definitions:

Sunk costs or fixed costs: Costs that do not change with changes in quantity of output.

Marginal costs: Additional costs of producing one more unit of output = change in variable costs as output increases.

Variable costs: Costs that do change with changes in the quantity of output.

Total costs: Sum of fixed costs and variable costs.

Average total costs: Total costs / quantity of output.

Average variable costs: Variable costs / quantity of output.

Average fixed costs: Fixed costs / quantity of output.

Natural Monopolies   If there were competing businesses, each building its own expensive network, each would never reach the scale of output that would allow lowest costs. Economists call these kinds of businesses **natural monopolies**. To achieve lowest cost, the technology of production allows only a single seller. We will discuss natural monopolies further in Chapter 9. Governments allow natural monopolies to exist in order to achieve lowest costs, but often step in and regulate them to be sure the low costs are passed on to consumers, instead of allowing the monopoly to act like a price maker and earn high economic profits.

natural monopolies: one business can supply entire market at lower cost than can two or more businesses

How Do You Spell Competition? E-L-A-S-T-I-C-I-T-Y of Demand

The three characteristics of market structure — available substitutes, number of businesses, and barriers to entry — make up the competitive environment for a business and determine its market power — its ability to be a price maker rather than a price taker. Market power helps determine where price settles, between the maximum consumers are willing to pay and the minimum businesses are willing to accept (covering all opportunity costs of production). All three characteristics of market structure relate to elasticity of demand, which gives us a shortcut for understanding market power.

Market power is inversely related to the elasticity of demand for your product/service.

Highest market power in markets with lowest elasticity of demand: Consumers have few substitutes or strong brand loyalty.

Businesses with the highest market power (price maker score of 10) tend to have the lowest elasticity of demand (most inelastic demand). In 1959, Xerox had enormous flexibility in setting a high price for its photocopy machines. Like the extreme case of inelastic demand for insulin by diabetics, a rise in price caused almost no decrease in quantity demanded, because few good substitutes were available. With fewer substitutes, consumers have less choice and are in a weaker bargaining position. Businesses have more market power to be able to raise prices (that is, be more of

Here, control of the market is depicted as coming from aggressive ownership. Is this a natural monopoly?

a price maker) and still keep selling. Product differentiation can create the same market power and lower elasticity of demand. If a business can develop brand loyalty, that makes demand for its product more inelastic.

The flip side of high market power for businesses is that consumers have less choice and a weaker bargaining position the fewer businesses there are, or the higher the barriers to entry. With fewer competitors (actual or potential), there are fewer substitutes and less choice for consumers. Market power tends to be high when elasticity of demand is low. Price is limited on the upside only by customers' ability to pay.

Lowest market power in markets with highest elasticity of demand: consumers have many substitutes or no brand loyalty.

Businesses with the lowest market power (price taker score of 0) tend to have the highest elasticity of demand (most elastic demand). Take the extreme case of the demand for wheat. No supplier/farmer can raise its price without losing all sales because many perfect substitutes are available. With more substitutes, consumers have more choice and are in a stronger bargaining position. Businesses have no market power to raise prices. With perfect substitutes there is no product differentiation or brand loyalty, so the demand for every supplier's particular bushel of wheat is perfectly elastic.

Consumers have more choices and a stronger bargaining position the greater the number of businesses, or the lower the barriers to entry. With more competitors (actual or potential), there are more substitutes and greater choice for consumers. Market power tends to be low when elasticity of demand is high. Price is limited on the downside only by the business's opportunity costs of production, with only normal profits.

While the photocopy (1959) and wheat markets are extremes, the rule applies to the entire continuum of market structures in between, which we will explore in the next section. **In general, the higher the market power, the lower the elasticity of demand. The lower the market power, the higher the elasticity of demand.**

Figure 7.1 summarizes the relationships between market structure, competition, pricing power, and elasticity of demand for monopoly and extreme competition.

Higher market power = lower elasticity of demand. Lower market power = higher elasticity of demand.

Figure 7.1	Market Structure and Pricing Power Monopoly and Extreme Competition	
Market Structure Characteristic	**Monopoly**	**Extreme Competition**
Pricing Power (scale 0 – 10)	Price Maker (10)	Price Taker (0)
Product Substitutes	No Close Substitutes	Many Perfect Substitutes
Number of Sellers	1	Many, Many
Barriers to Entry	High	None
Elasticity of Demand	Low/Inelastic	High/Elastic

Refresh 7.2

1. What is market structure, and what are its three main characteristics?

2. Even after patents expire, brand-name drugs like Advil and Tylenol sell for more than chemically identical no-name generic drugs. Why would consumers spend more for brand names? What do the companies that produce the brand names do to keep sales away from generic substitutes?

3. What counts as a substitute product depends on how broadly or narrowly you define the market. Pick any specific product/service. Argue that it is a monopoly. Then argue that it is *not* a monopoly.

www.myeconlab.com

7.3 Mash-ups of Market Structure: Oligopoly and Monopolistic Competition

When my eight-year-old daughter saw black-and-white television for the first time (I didn't consider her education complete until she had seen *I Love Lucy*), she described it as "grey TV." If pure monopoly is black and extreme competition is white, most real-world market structures are some shade of grey. The markets in which you sell and buy as a business, worker, or consumer are almost all on a continuum somewhere between the end points of pure monopoly and extreme competition.

Identify the four main market structures, and explain the differences among them.

From Figure 7.1, you know how the characteristics of market structure tend to change as we move from pure monopoly to extreme competition. Pricing power moves from price maker to price taker, available substitutes go from none to many, number of sellers goes from one to many many, entry barriers go from high to low, and elasticity of demand goes from low to high.

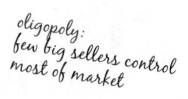

As with any continuum, it can be helpful to group ranges together that have similar characteristics. Age is also a continuum, between birth and death. When you have to identify someone's age, you can try to be precise (she is 22 but acts like she's 15), or you can generalize. She is 20-something, he is middle-aged, they are seniors. Economists have found it helpful to group some of the market structures in between the extremes into groups called oligopoly and monopolistic competition. Both groups are mash-ups, in that they combine some characteristics of pure monopoly and some of extreme competition.

Oligopoly   An **oligopoly** is a market structure with a few big businesses that control most of the market. The word *oligopoly* again comes from the Greek, *oligos* ("few") and *poly* ("sellers"). The gaming hardware market is an oligopoly, with Microsoft, Sony, and Nintendo as the major sellers. Oligopolists are price makers, but don't have as much pricing power as a pure monopolist. Any time one of the major sellers changes its price, the others usually make a similar change. While there is product differentiation (playing with a Wii wand is different from playing on an Xbox), the products are often fairly close substitutes — a characteristic closer to extreme competition. The cola market (Pepsi and Coke) is another example of an oligopoly. With available substitutes, demand is more elastic than for pure monopoly, but more inelastic than extreme competition. Finally, there are usually barriers to entry in an oligopolistic market. The sellers are usually big, with economies of scale that make it hard for new competitors to enter. These characteristics of oligopoly are summarized in Figure 7.2 on the next page.

oligopoly: few big sellers control most of market

Monopolistic Competition   **Monopolistic competition** is, by name, a mash-up of monopoly and extreme competition. Restaurants, piercing parlours, dry cleaners, and hair salons are all examples of monopolistic competition. Many small businesses are making similar but slightly differentiated products. Like extreme competition there are no barriers to entry, so the only hope for economic profits comes from the product differentiation that gives each business some slight pricing power, or from producing at lower cost. Businesses might differentiate their products/services to compete on quality, service, marketing, or price. Pricing power and elasticity of demand are closer to extreme competition than to pure monopoly.

monopolistic competition: many small businesses make similar but slightly differentiated products/services

Figure 7.2	Market Structure and Pricing Power			
Market Structure Characteristic	**Monopoly**	**Oligopoly**	**Monopolistic Competition**	**Extreme Competition**
Pricing Power (scale 0 – 10)	Price Maker (10)	Price Maker (5–9)	Price Maker (1–4)	Price Taker (0)
Product Substitutes	No Close Substitutes	Differentiated Substitutes	Differentiated Substitutes	Many Perfect Substitutes
Number of Sellers	1	Few	Many	Many, Many
Barriers to Entry	High	Medium	None	None
Elasticity of Demand	Low/Inelastic	Low/Inelastic	High/Elastic	High/Elastic

Figure 7.2 is a great study tool. Keep in mind a particular real-world industry for each structure (gaming hardware sellers for oligopoly, restaurants for monopolistic competition).

The characteristics are summarized in Figure 7.2 — it gives you the differing characteristics of the full range of market structures, from the extremes of pure monopoly and extreme competition to the mash-ups in the middle of the continuum of oligopoly and monopolistic competition. (The numbers I used on the 0–10 scales for pricing power are just to give you a rough idea — they are not precise calculations.) These groupings of market structure are often used in media reporting of economic events, and we will use them again in Chapter 9 to talk about government policies to deal with abuses of competition and monopoly.

Refresh 7.3

1. What is an oligopoly? What is monopolistic competition?

2. What characteristics of extreme competition appear in oligopoly? In monopolistic competition? What characteristics of monopoly appear in oligopoly? In monopolistic competition?

3. Suppose you are thinking of opening a gardening business — you will cut, weed, rake, and water lawns. What market structure would you be competing in? What might you do to differentiate yourself from other sellers in the market?

www.myeconlab.com

7.4 To Compete Is a Verb: How Do Businesses Compete?

The 1980 Wimbledon Men's Final was one of the greatest tennis matches in history. Bjorn Borg, the icy, methodical, four-time reigning champion from Sweden, defeated the brash young American challenger John McEnroe 1–6, 7–5, 6–3, 6–7 (16–18 in the tiebreaker), 8–6 to win his fifth consecutive Wimbledon title. This was a classic competitive battle, with each player using every shot in his arsenal, matching winning shot for winning shot in a heroic quest for victory. TV coverage of subsequent Borg/McEnroe matches often played the then-popular Police song "Every Breath You Take," emphasizing the words in the song that say I will be watching every move that you make and every step that you take.

Competition among sellers in markets is much like sports competitions — take any shot or action to gain a competitive advantage. Every business, or seller, dreams of winning the market power and economic profits of pure monopoly. The businesses and individuals that succeed or triumph do more than dream — they *take actions* (make smart choices) to make those dreams come true. What actions do sellers take to compete? What do businesses and individuals do to compete? Competition is an active process of trying to find an advantage over your competitors, to capture more sales in the market, to beat out other candidates for a job. But (sing along here) *every choice you make, every action you take* happens in the context of a market, where all your competitors have the same dream of winning and all are taking similar actions while watching yours. The consequences for the market and the economy as a whole are not necessarily what the competitors hoped for.

Explain how businesses compete, and why the process of creative destruction improves productivity and living standards.

Business competition takes many forms (cutting costs, improving quality, innovating, advertising, buying competitors, erecting barriers to entry), but is always an active attempt to increase profits and gain the market power of monopoly.

What Do Businesses Do to Compete?

Competition takes many forms, but it is always an active attempt to increase profits and gain the market power of monopoly.

competition: active attempt to increase profits and gain market power of monopoly

Cutting Costs   Cutting costs is a key competitive weapon. If your business can reduce waste, find lower-cost raw materials, or develop new technologies that use less energy, you gain competitive options. With its ruthless efficiency, size, and buying power, Wal-Mart is legendary for forcing suppliers to cut "to the bone" the prices of products they provide to Wal-Mart. You can earn higher profits while matching your competitors' prices, or you can profitably cut your prices to attract new sales away from your competitors.

Improving Quality   Instead of competing on price, you may want to compete by providing a higher *quality* product/service ("Paola's Piercing uses only platinum studs") or by offering better service or warranty protection. These actions differentiate your product/service from those of your competitors, earning you some pricing power and inelasticity of demand. It's just like how taking this course and getting a post-secondary education differentiates you from high-school graduates and earns you more pricing power in labour markets.

Innovating and Advertising   "To compete" may mean developing innovative new products like the photocopy machine or the iPhone, or advertising to expand your market and establish brand loyalty that gives you some pricing power. Does your computer have "Intel Inside"? Would you be caught dead in a pair of Gap jeans instead of Tommy Hilfiger? Advertising not only can make your demand more inelastic, but also can increase the demand for your product/service by stealing customers from competitors, or by finding consumers who just didn't know about your product/service.

Eliminating Competition   Businesses also compete by buying out or merging with competitors to reduce substitutes and gain economies of scale. In 2007 the Walt Disney Company bought out the children's website Club Penguin, eliminating a competitor and enhancing the scale of its child-focused web products/services.

Erecting Barriers to Entry   Businesses can also gain market power by erecting barriers to entry. Have you ever wondered why there seems to be a Starbucks on every corner in some neighbourhoods? Is there really enough coffee business to go around? Don't more sales at one Starbucks come from fewer sales at the Starbucks down the block? Maybe. But the Starbucks business strategy is to *take as many good locations as possible to prevent competitors from setting up at those locations.* Densely spaced locations serve as a barrier to entry for other coffee competitors.

Here's another example of surprising barriers to entry. The market for laundry detergent seems very competitive, with many, many substitute products — Tide, Ivory, Gain, Downy, Cheer. But all these products are made by the same company, Procter & Gamble (P&G). What about Wisk and All? Both made by Unilever. While the detergent market appears to be highly competitive, it is in fact an oligopoly, with just a few major players and many generic or no-name products.

Why does P&G make so many competing brands? The variety serves as a barrier to entry to new businesses. If P&G made only one brand, a new supplier could target advertising against a single competitive product and get noticed. But with five P&G products, each with advertising and brand loyalty, the chances of success for a new detergent are much less, so most businesses don't even try.

What is common to all these competitive actions is the attempt to beat your rivals using every tactic in your business arsenal that can increase your profits.

The Invisible Hand, Like Gravity, Is Unforgiving: Freedom Meets Competition

Unlike sports, business competition is not always "winner takes all." Many businesses in a market can make profits, but to do so each must at least match — or in some way better — the actions of all other competitors. As a result of that pressure to match the competition, most businesses in a market adopt similar tactics.

The results of business competition still have some sports parallels. If the best players develop new physical conditioning routines that are superior (Borg outlasted McEnroe in the fifth set largely because of superior conditioning), or adopt new technologies like carbon fibre racquets (or hockey sticks) that are superior to wooden versions, all players have to follow suit or risk falling from that competitive level. (I will be watching every move that you make and every step that you take.) Individual competitive actions by businesses spread quickly throughout a market, unless there are barriers to entry like patents or trade secrets. Those businesses that don't keep up with the competition will suffer economic losses and eventually go bankrupt or out of business — they cease to be players. Only the successful businesses survive the competitive struggle.

Economic Freedom One of the great ironies of the market economy is that it provides all of us with extraordinary economic freedom — freedom to make business decisions, to invest and spend our money as we please, to choose our occupations, to pursue our own self-interest (however we define it, within the bounds of legal rules of the game). These freedoms are greater than in any other economic system in history. And yet, because we all, whether as businesses or individuals, play the role of sellers who depend on the market to earn a living, we must play by the market's competitive rules.

A market economy provides extraordinary economic freedom, but as sellers who depend on markets to earn a living, we must play by the market's competitive rules.

Competitive Pressure That competitive pressure limits the choices we can make if we want to succeed as a seller. For example, Wahid may believe advertising for his web design business is a waste of money. But if all his competitors advertise, and his sales suffer, he will be forced to advertise. As a boss, Paola may feel strongly about paying her piercing employees generous wages. But if her competitors pay less and can undercut her piercing prices and take all her customers, she has no choice but to pay lower wages. After the successful introduction of Apple's iPhone, imagine the "choice" that competitors had about whether or not to innovate and attempt to match the iPhone's features. And even if you don't expect to run a business but dream of being a writer or an artist, if you can't sell your work you'll continue to be a restaurant server who does some art as a hobby.

Businesses must adopt or better successful techniques and innovations of competitors.

The market economy gives us tremendous freedom of choice, but the pressure of competition is an unforgiving taskmaster. All businesses, if they want to succeed, must adopt the successful techniques and innovations of their competitors. All sellers must provide a product/service that consumers in the market are willing to buy, and at a price as low as consumers can get from a competitor.

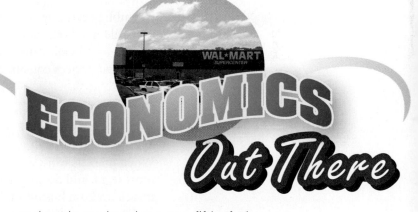

Higher Wages=Lower Costs?

There are different ways to achieve low costs. One Deutsche Bank business analyst looked at the high wages and generous benefits Costco pays it employees, and claimed there is no way Costco can compete with Wal-Mart, which pays much less, offers fewer benefits, and vigorously opposes attempts at unionization, which would increase its labour costs. "At Costco, it's better to be an employee or a customer than a shareholder," he said.

But *BusinessWeek* magazine found that "by compensating employees generously to motivate and retain good workers, one-fifth of whom are unionized, Costco gets lower turnover and higher productivity." Costco also has less "shrinkage" (the polite term for employee theft) and lower training costs from lower turnover, which reduce total labour costs.

The bottom line: Costco has lower labour costs and higher productivity than Wal-Mart, even though Costco pays its employees much more.

Source: Based on "Commentary: The Costco Way," *BusinessWeek*, April 12, 2004.

The bottom line of matching competitors' actions usually means matching price cuts on existing products/services. Once a business serves up a competitive action or tactic that generates economic profits, the forces of competition pull those profits back down to earth. Just like gravity pulls down anything above the ground, competitive forces are always pulling prices down toward the level of extreme competition, where businesses earn only normal profits. The only resistance to the downward pull of competitive prices comes from the market power your business develops because of product differentiation or barriers to entry. If prices are not forced down by the actions of competitors within your market, economic profits will attract new competitors (unless there are barriers to entry), and the increased competition and increased supply will pull down prices and profits to those of extreme competition. To repeat the Adam Smith quote from earlier in the chapter, "the price of free competition . . . is the lowest which the sellers can commonly afford to take, and at the same time continue their business."

Once a business takes an action that produces economic profits, competition pulls profits back toward normal profits and pulls prices back toward extreme competition.

Back to Equilibrium   That price toward which competition is always pulling businesses is the market-clearing price of Chapter 4, which balances quantity demanded and quantity supplied. It is also an equilibrium price that coordinates the smart choices of consumers and businesses. At the equilibrium price, no consumer is kicking himself for paying too much, and each business is earning the same rate of profits being earned in any other market (adjusted for risk and other market structure differences).

Paradoxically, the competitive actions businesses take in pursuit of the economic profits of monopoly pull each market back to a stable equilibrium situation, where most businesses and products and prices are similar, prices just cover all opportunity costs of production, and businesses earn only normal profits. No business dreams of extreme competition. Yet dreams of monopoly market power and profits generate competitive actions that ultimately yield outcomes resembling extreme competition. Competition is the force behind Adam Smith's invisible hand, channelling business self-interest — the dream of monopoly profits — to yield the unintended consequence of the production of all the products/services consumers want, at the lowest possible costs.

Competition as Creative Destruction: Breaking Free of Equilibrium

When markets work well, businesses supply the products/services that consumers most want, and do so efficiently, at lowest cost. Not surprisingly, you have heard this claim from business leaders and wealthy individuals who have benefited from markets. But even Karl Marx (1818–1883) was a great admirer of the productivity of the market economy!

Marx was the most famous and most severe critic of the market economy due to the inequalities in wealth he observed. He called it the capitalist system, referring to the capitalists who ran it as "the bourgeoisie" and the workers he observed being exploited as "the proletariat." In the call to revolution in the *Communist Manifesto* (1848, co-authored with Friedrich Engels), Marx wrote that "The bourgeoisie, during its rule of scarce one hundred years, has created more massive and more colossal productive forces than have all preceding generations together."

What makes market economies so enormously productive? Why are we so much better off than our great-grandparents were? What accounts for these continual increases in our ability to produce products/services and the impressive increases in standards of living (whether those increases are spread equitably or inequitably across the population)? The answers lie in the same competitive forces of Adam Smith's invisible hand that channel the restless energy of profit-seeking self-interest into the public good.

The competitive actions that businesses take do much more than pull prices back to competitive levels, pull economic profits back to zero, and bring demand and supply into equilibrium. Remember, competition is about figuring out new ways to *beat* your rival suppliers in the market, not just match their moves. In the short run, businesses can earn economic profits by innovating and differentiating themselves from competitors — by cutting costs, developing new technologies of production, inventing new products, advertising to expand to new markets and exploit economies of scale, or finding new or cheaper sources of raw materials. These economic profits keep flowing until, if ever, competitors match their moves.

Over a longer period of time, these competitive innovations, which result from the endless quest for monopoly profits, make businesses more productive and improve living standards and product choices for consumers. Joseph Schumpeter (1883–1950) was a brilliant economist who recognized that these competitive actions were behind the ever-changing and ever-more-productive market economy. In his book *Capitalism, Socialism and Democracy,* he wrote the following:

> Capitalism . . . is by nature a . . . method of economic change [that] never can be stationary. . . . The fundamental impulse that sets and keeps the capitalist engine in motion comes from the new consumers, goods, the new methods of production or transportation, the new markets, the new forms of industrial organization that capitalist enterprise creates.

Schumpeter's Creative Destruction   Schumpeter saw that the competitive actions of businesses "incessantly revolutionize[s] the economic structure from within, incessantly destroying the old one, incessantly creating a new one. This process of **creative destruction** is the essential fact about capitalism." (Is that not a great phrase — *creative destruction*?) Competitive innovations not only generate economic profits for the winners, but also can destroy the losers while making the world a better place for consumers. Computers destroyed typewriters and carbon paper — have you ever used a typewriter at all, let alone to make carbon copies? DVDs destroyed VHS tapes, digital downloads and music players like iPods will soon destroy CDs, fluorescent and LED lights are eliminating incandescent bulbs, robotic assembly lines destroyed the jobs of craftsmen and -women who used to make cars and clothing and bread. All these innovations and more were introduced in the competitive quest for monopoly profits, but ended up improving living standards while destroying the less productive or desirable products/services and production methods.

This incessant process of change is behind many of the controversial competitive trends we see today. Jobs in Canada are being destroyed as corporations move manufacturing to the Far East and "off-shore" their computer programming and call centre jobs to India. We will discuss these trends more fully in macroeconomics when we examine the pros and cons of globalization. But there is no denying that the outcome is more efficient, with cheaper products/services for most of us (understanding that a win for consumers as a whole can still have individual losers — sellers and workers in the destroyed markets).

FOR YOUR INFORMATION

Schumpeter, who was born the year Marx died, was greatly influenced by Marx, but instead emphasized the positive side of the relentless, competitive forces of capitalism in improving living standards.

Rather than focus on price competition, which pulls prices back down to competitive levels, Schumpeter focused on "the competition from the new commodity, the new technology, the new source of supply, the new type of organization (the largest-scale unit of control for instance) — competition which commands a decisive cost or quality advantage and which strikes not at the margins of the profits and the outputs of the existing businesses but at their foundations and their very lives. This kind of competition is as much more effective than [price competition] as a bombardment is in comparison with forcing a door, and so much more important that it becomes a matter of comparative indifference whether [price] competition . . . functions more or less promptly; the powerful lever that in the long run expands output and brings down prices is in any case made of other stuff."

Source: Quote from Joseph A. Schumpeter, *Capitalism, Socialism and Democracy* (New York: Harper & Row, 1962), p. 84.

creative destruction: competitive business innovations generate economic profits for winners, improve living standards for all, but destroy less productive or less desirable products and production methods

The BlackBerry innovations of the Canadian business RIM (Research In Motion) have revolutionized business communication, making it faster and more efficient, while earning handsome profits for shareholders. But RIM's success has destroyed jobs among competitors (what ever happened to Palm?), reduced business profits in competing forms of communication, and eliminated jobs for secretaries who used to handle business correspondence.

The inherent and incessant change and growth of the market economy comes from unleashing the power of self-interest in all humans, but channelling it through competition and the invisible hand to improve living standards.

The restless energy of self-interest and competition that is the strength of a market economy is also a weakness. Sometimes the quest for monopoly power is so excessive and successful that it is not in the public good. When competition fails, governments step in with competition laws, which we will examine in Chapter 9. And that restless energy can also contribute to "boom and bust" cycles of economic activity (which economists call **business cycles**), which are the focus of much of macroeconomics. But before we get to all of that, we will look more closely in the next chapter at how businesses that have at least some price-making power (the majority of "grey" markets) make smart choices of the precise combination of price and quantity that yields maximum profits.

business cycles: ups and downs of overall economic activity

Refresh 7.4

1. What actions can businesses take to compete?

2. Explain Schumpeter's process of creative destruction.

3. Markets combine freedom of choice with tremendous competitive pressure to supply products/services the market values. This combination is connected to the age-old philosophical question about whether humans have free will, or whether our choices are all determined by other forces in society. Argue that your choice of "what you want to be when you grow up" is an example of free will. Then argue that the freedom of your choice is an illusion and that your choice is determined by economic forces in society.

The Power to Price

Monopoly and Competition

CHAPTER SUMMARY

7.1 PRICE MAKERS AND PRICE TAKERS:
DREAMS OF MONOPOLY AND NIGHTMARES OF COMPETITION

A business's market power to set prices ranges from a maximum for monopoly to a minimum for extreme competition. Businesses aim for the economic profits and market power of monopoly. Competitors usually push businesses toward the normal profits and price taking of extreme competition.

- **Monopoly** — only seller of product/service; no close substitutes available.
- **Market power** — business's ability to set prices.
- **Price maker** — pure monopoly with maximum power to set prices.
- Businesses can set any price they choose, but cannot force consumers to buy. Even monopoly price makers must live by law of demand.
- **Extreme competition** — many sellers producing identical products/ services.
- **Price takers** — businesses with zero power to set prices.

7.2 HOW MUCH COMPETITION IS GOING ON?
MARKET STRUCTURE

Pricing power depends on the competitiveness of a business's market structure. The characteristics of market structure are availability of substitutes, number of competitors, and barriers to the entry of new competitors. The power to set prices is inversely related to a business's elasticity of demand for its products/services.

- **Market structure** — characteristics that affect competition and pricing power:
  - availability of substitutes
  - number of competitors
  - barriers to entry of new competitors
- Broader definition of market = more substitutes and competitors.
- Narrower definition of market = fewer substitutes and competitors.

- **Product differentiation** — attempt to distinguish product/service from competitors' products/services:
  - allows a seller to reduce competition and increase market power.
  - can take the form of actual differences or perceived differences.
- Fewer competitors = more price power.
- More competitors = less price power.
- **Barriers to entry** — legal or economic barriers preventing new competitors from entering market.
  - Legal barriers: **patents** and **copyrights** — exclusive property rights to sell or license creations, protecting against competition.
  - Economic barriers: **economies of scale** — average cost of producing falls as quantity (scale) of production increases.
  - **Natural monopolies** — one business can supply entire market at lower cost than can two or more businesses.
- Higher market power = lower elasticity of demand.
  Lower market power = higher elasticity of demand.

7.3 MASH-UPS OF MARKET STRUCTURE: OLIGOPOLY AND MONOPOLISTIC COMPETITION

The four main market structures are monopoly, oligopoly, monopolistic competition, and extreme competition. The market structures are different in pricing power, available substitutes, number of sellers, barriers to entry, and elasticity of demand.

- **Oligopoly** — few big sellers control most of market.
- **Monopolistic competition** — many small businesses make similar but slightly differentiated products/services.
- In moving across the continuum of market structures from pure monopoly to extreme competition:
  - pricing power moves from price maker to price taker
  - available substitutes go from none to many
  - number of sellers goes from one to many, many
  - entry barriers go from high to low
  - elasticity of demand goes from low to high

7.4 TO COMPETE IS A VERB: HOW DO BUSINESSES COMPETE?

Businesses' quest for economic profits and the market power of monopoly generates actions — cutting costs, improving quality, innovating, advertising, buying competitors, erecting barriers to entry. When competitors respond, prices are driven toward levels of extreme competition. Competitors who do not adequately respond are driven out of business. This process of creative destruction unintentionally improves productivity and living standards for all.

- **Competition** — active attempt to increase profits and gain market power of monopoly.
- While a market economy provides extraordinary economic freedom — to make business decisions, to invest and spend as we please, to choose our occupations — as sellers who depend on markets to earn a living we must play by the market's competitive rules.

- **Creative destruction** — competitive business innovations generate economic profits for winners, improve living standards for all, but destroy less productive or less desirable products and production methods.
- Competitive actions by businesses can have the unintended consequence of **business cycles** — ups and downs of overall economic activity.

TRUE/FALSE

Circle the correct answer.

7.1 PURE MONOPOLY AND EXTREME COMPETITION

1. Monopolists have market power and do not have to live by the law of demand.   True   False

2. A worker who is the only one with a particular skill in her community has a monopoly over that skilled labour in her community.   True   False

3. The only seller of a product/service that has no close substitutes is a price maker.   True   False

4. Sellers always prefer selling at higher prices.   True   False

5. Businesses would prefer to have a pure monopoly over extreme competition.   True   False

7.2 MARKET STRUCTURE

6. Of all market structures, barriers to entry are highest for monopoly.   True   False

7. If McDonald's were to buy Wendy's, this would reduce McDonald's economies of scale.   True   False

8. The higher the market power, the lower the elasticity of demand.   True   False

7.3 OLIGOPOLY AND MONOPOLISTIC COMPETITION

9. In monopolistic competition there are many perfect substitutes.   True   False

10. Businesses in monopolistic competition have some pricing power.   True   False

11. The elasticity of demand is higher for oligopoly than for monopolistic competition.   True   False

12. The gaming hardware industry is an example of monopolistic competition.   True   False

7.4 HOW DO BUSINESSES COMPETE?

13. Dreams of monopoly market power and profits generate competitive actions that ultimately yield outcomes resembling extreme competition.   True   False

14. Competition is about figuring out ways to match your rival suppliers in the market.   **True   False**

15. Every choice you make, every action you take happens in the context of a market.   **True   False**

MULTIPLE CHOICE

Circle the correct answer.

7.1 PURE MONOPOLY AND EXTREME COMPETITION

1. A monopolist
   A) is the only seller of a product/service.
   B) is a price maker.
   C) has no close substitutes.
   D) is all of the above.

2. The trade-off to setting a higher price is
   A) higher sales.
   B) lower sales.
   C) higher revenues.
   D) nothing — there is no trade-off.

3. The impact on the nearby farming industry of the "buy and eat local" movement will
   A) make it more competitive.
   B) increase the number of substitutes available.
   C) reduce the number of substitutes available.
   D) all of the above.

7.2 MARKET STRUCTURE

4. Monopolies can exist even though economic profits are supposed to attract entry from new businesses, if there are
   A) natural monopolies.
   B) legal barriers that prevent new businesses from entering.
   C) economic barriers that prevent new businesses from entering.
   D) all of the above.

5. Patents and copyrights increase market power by
   A) increasing the number of buyers.
   B) increasing the number of sellers.
   C) preventing other businesses from competing.
   D) making it easier for other businesses to compete.

6. Which of the following could receive a patent?

   A) A song

   B) A poem

   C) An iPhone

   D) All of the above

7.3 OLIGOPOLY AND MONOPOLISTIC COMPETITION

7. Which of the following is *not* a market structure?

   A) Monopoly

   B) Oligopoly

   C) Competitopoly

   D) Extreme competition

8. Which market structure has the lowest barriers to entry?

   A) Monopoly

   B) Oligopoly

   C) Monopolistic competition

   D) Extreme competition

9. Which market structure has the highest elasticity of demand?

   A) Monopoly

   B) Oligopoly

   C) Monopolistic competition

   D) Extreme competition

10. Which market structure has the most number of sellers?

    A) Monopoly

    B) Oligopoly

    C) Monopolistic competition

    D) Extreme competition

11. Which market structure does not have pricing power?

    A) Monopoly

    B) Oligopoly

    C) Monopolistic competition

    D) Extreme competition

12. Which market structure does not have close substitutes?

    A) Monopoly

    B) Oligopoly

    C) Monopolistic competition

    D) Extreme competition

13. How do businesses compete?

    A) Lower prices

    B) Better product quality

    C) Better service quality

    D) All of the above

14. Advertising

    A) makes demand more elastic.

    B) makes demand more inelastic.

    C) reduces demand for a product/service.

    D) does all of the above.

15. Automated assembly lines reduce the jobs available for assembly-line workers. This phenomenon is called

    A) karma.

    B) destructive creationism.

    C) creative destruction.

    D) the handmaid's tale.

SHORT ANSWER

Write a short answer to each question. Your answer may be in point form.

1. Does Apple have a monopoly on iPhone production? Explain how the answer to that question can be yes, and how it can be no.

2. Canadian beer companies spend millions of dollars a year on advertising.

    A) Why do they do it?

    B) Suppose the government were to ban all beer advertising. How do you think beer businesses in Canada would compete?

    C) What kind of barriers to entry are there in the beer industry?

3. Sometimes substitutes are not easily defined. In fact, the degree of substitutability can vary across consumers — some consumers may be addicted to a particular brand and may not be willing to switch.

    A) Name some brands for which there (technically) are substitutes but for which in your mind there is no such substitute.

    B) What is the term that means you have a tendency to purchase a certain type of brand?

    C) Name some advertisements that try to make you think there are no substitutes available.

4. Why is it important for the government to offer the monopoly protection of patents and copyrights?

5. In 2006, the Government of Canada considered interacting in the telecommunications market. It was concerned by the market power of existing companies, and wanted to reduce their market power by buying some of their shares and creating a new company. Why would consumers be expected to benefit from this?

6. Consider the labour market, where workers sell labour and employers buy labour. Explain how workers can increase their power to price (for their labour).

7. In one of the most popular YouTube videos of 2007, a man from Brooklyn expressed his distaste toward Starbucks, noting how expensive their coffee is. One reason why Starbucks has so much pricing power (and, hence, can succeed in keeping prices high) is because of how effective it is at creating barriers to entry.

   A) Name a barrier to entry.

   B) Do you think Starbucks has more or less pricing power in Canada compared to the United States? Why or why not?

   C) Do you think the elasticity of demand for Starbucks is higher or lower for Canadian consumers compared to American consumers? Why?

   D) Suppose Starbucks wanted to increase its market power in Canada. What is one strategy it can use to increase its market power?

8. Explain how the following would affect your power to price:

   A) The entry of a competitor

   B) A legal barrier to entry into your industry imposed by the government

   C) Designing a menu of prices that makes it difficult for your customers to determine whether a change in price has occurred (for example, bundling together items on the menu).

9. Jimmy stands outside the entrance to Best Buy in Regina. His job is to listen to people as they talk to their friends about what they intend to purchase while walking into the store. The two most common comments are

   • I want to buy an electronic device today.

   • I want an iPod and I want it now.

   Jimmy's boss hands him a stack of coupons and says, "If a customer uses the coupon to purchase an iPod they get 25 percent off. You have 20 coupons, so use them smartly. If we sell 20 more iPods today than usual I will give you a raise!"

   How should Jimmy hand out these coupons smartly?

10. Provide your own example of "creative destruction" and discuss what market was destroyed, what market was created, and why the destruction was good (from a social perspective).

Chapter 8

Pricing for Profits

Marginal Revenue and Marginal Cost

LEARNING OBJECTIVES

After reading this chapter, you should be able to:

8.1 Define marginal revenue, and explain how it depends on market structure and when it differs from price.

8.2 Explain when marginal cost increases and when it is constant as a business increases output.

8.3 Explain quantity and price decisions in the recipe for maximum profits, and show the importance of marginal revenue and marginal cost.

8.4 Define price discrimination, and explain how it leads to higher profits by taking advantage of differences in elasticity of demand.

IMAGINE YOU RUN A BUSINESS and have some pricing power. How do you find the combination of price and quantity sold that yields the greatest profits? There are so many variables to consider. On the demand side, how much are your customers willing to pay, and how much will your sales decrease as you raise prices? On the supply side, what are your costs, and are they rising, falling, or constant as you increase quantity? And what about the competition — what substitutes are available, how many other businesses are you competing against, and what barriers are keeping out new competitors?

Making a smart business choice about price and quantity sounds complicated. Do you need to hire an economist? Actually, you don't — business owners make these decisions on their own all the time. In business, as in cooking, if you're not sure what to do, follow a recipe. In this chapter you will learn the recipe for pricing for profits. It's simple enough to state in one sentence, and it yields smart choices no matter how much or how little pricing power a business has. In the rest of this chapter, I will explain each "ingredient" and how to combine them.

Here's the recipe: Estimate marginal revenues and marginal costs, and then set prices that allow you to sell all quantities for which marginal revenue is greater than marginal cost. The basic ingredients are marginal revenue and marginal cost, and they are combined in the recipe for pricing for profits. Because *marginal* means "additional," Key 2 of the Three Keys for Smart Choices plays a key role: "Count only *additional* benefits and *additional* opportunity costs."

8.1 Is the Price You See the Revenue You Get? Marginal Revenue

So, the business recipe for maximum profits is this: Estimate marginal revenues and marginal costs, and then set prices that allow you to sell all quantities for which marginal revenue is greater than marginal cost.

The recipe sounds far more complicated than it really is. Cookbooks often provide a photo of the completed dish to give you a feel for what you are about to make. Before we get into the full recipe, let's look at a simple business decision to get a feel for the intuition behind the basic ingredients of marginal revenue and marginal cost.

Basic Ingredients

Suppose Paola's Piercing and Fingernail Parlour is open weekdays, from 10:00 a.m. to 7:00 p.m. Paola's customers tell her it would be more convenient if the shop stayed open later, until 10:00 p.m. Is it smart for Paola to stay open later?

How would you make the decision? Well, smart business decisions will increase Paola's profits, and profits increase when revenues are greater than costs. If Paola stays open later, we need to know her *additional revenues* (how much additional money she will take in selling piercings and nail sets during those three extra hours), and her *additional costs*. Additional revenues are easy to estimate — the value of all sales Paola will make during those additional three hours. Economists call additional revenues **marginal revenue**.

marginal revenue: additional revenue from selling one more unit or from extension of sales

But be careful about estimating additional costs. The additional three hours of wages Paola must pay her employees clearly count, as do costs of additional studs, nail polish, and extra hydro costs from operating lights and equipment. Additional costs Paola must pay as a consequence of staying open later are marginal costs. But sunk costs (Chapter 3, Section 3.2), like rent or insurance, do not change with the decision to stay open later. Economists also call these sunk costs **fixed costs** — costs that do not change (they are fixed) with changes in the quantity of output a business produces. Fixed costs do not affect smart decisions; only marginal costs do.

fixed costs (sunk costs): do not change with changes in quantity of output

If Paola's estimated marginal revenues are greater than her marginal costs, then her profits will increase by staying open later. It's a smart decision and she, and her customers, will be happy. But if her estimated marginal costs are greater than her marginal revenues, her profits will decrease. If marginal costs are greater than marginal revenues, she should continue to close at 7:00 p.m., even though it means a few disappointed evening customers.

Businesses always compare marginal revenues and marginal costs in making smart decisions. Whether it's extending their hours, introducing a new product/service, opening a new location, launching an advertising campaign, hiring new employees (more on this in Chapter 11) — all these decisions are smart as long as estimated marginal revenues are greater than marginal costs.

With that simple snapshot of the basic ingredients of any smart business decision, let's look in more detail at a business's pricing decision.

One Price Rules When Buyers Can Resell

You walk into Tim Hortons, order a medium double-double, and pay the usual $1.25. How would you feel if the next customer ordered the same coffee and was charged only 75 cents?

Most products/services have one price, not a different price for each customer. Why is that? First, it's not a good idea to make your customers angry and resentful. Second, competitive economic forces tend to equalize prices. Tim's customers like you, who paid $1.25, would save money by not buying at the counter, but instead by offering to buy coffee from the low-price customers for less than $1.25. Low-price customers would make easy money by reselling their coffees to customers like you for more than 75 cents. Self-interest and competition between coffee drinkers would push the price toward a single price.

Most products that can easily be resold tend to have a single price. We will see in Section 8.4, however, that sometimes businesses can charge different customers different prices for the identical product/service in an attempt to increase profits. Here, we are going to stick to examples where a business has to charge all customers the same price for the same product/service. The one-price rule has a big impact on a business's marginal revenue.

Products easily resold tend to have single price in market.

Marginal Revenue

Marginal revenue, or additional revenue, can also be defined as the revenue you get from selling one more of your product/service. Marginal revenue depends on market structure — how competitive your industry is, and whether your business is a price taker or a price maker.

For price-taking businesses (extreme competition), marginal revenue = price.

When Marginal Revenue Equals Price In the market structure of extreme competition, like the wheat market, every business is a price taker. You can't raise your price because thousands of other businesses are selling identical products at the market price. And there is no incentive to lower your price, because you are so small relative to the market you can sell as much as you can produce at the market price. Your decision about what quantity to produce has no effect on the market because as a bit player — one of thousands of suppliers — your increase in supply does not affect market supply or market price.

Because you can sell each additional unit at the market price, your marginal revenue from each additional unit sold is the same as the price. For businesses in extreme competition, *marginal revenue equals price for price takers.* This sounds obvious, but it turns out not to be true for price makers.

When Marginal Revenue Is Less Than Price What about businesses with some price power? Price makers — whether monopolies, oligopolies, or small monopolistic competitors like Paola's Piercing and Fingernail Parlour — can raise prices without losing all their sales to competitors. Barriers to entry, brand loyalty, or advertising all can create pricing power. But price makers still face the law of demand. They will sell less if they raise their prices. And *to sell more, they must lower their prices.*

ECONOMICS Out There

iResentment
Less than three months after introducing the iPhone in 2007 at US$599, Apple cut the price by one-third, to $299. This was an attempt to increase sales to those not willing to pay the original price.

This caused so much resentment among original customers that Apple was forced to back-pedal. Steve Jobs quickly apologized and offered original customers a US$100 credit.

- This is the kind of resentment that enforces the one-price rule among products that can be easily resold (which iPhones can).

Calculating Marginal Revenues

Calculating Marginal Revenues   This is where the one-price rule becomes important. As long as a product can be resold and a business does not want to anger its customers, in order to sell more, price makers must lower the price *on all units,* not just on new sales. The result is that *marginal revenue is less than price for price makers.* Let's look at a simple example.

Figure 8.1   Calculating Marginal Revenues

Row	Price	Quantity Demanded	Total Revenue (Price × Quantity)	Marginal Revenue (Difference in Total Revenue)
A	$20	0	$ 0	—
B	$18	1	$18	$18
C	$16	2	$32	$14
D	$14	3	$42	$10
E	$12	4	$48	$ 6
F	$10	5	$50	$ 2

Figure 8.1 shows how many piercings Paola expects her customers to demand at different prices, and the revenues she will collect. (We will add costs in the next section.) The second column shows the different prices Paola is thinking about setting for a single nose piercing. The third column shows her estimate of how many piercings her customers will demand at each price. The fourth column calculates her total revenues, or price multiplied by quantity. If Paola charges $20 (row *A*), she will have no customers and no revenues. If instead she sets a price of $18 (row *B*), she will sell one piercing and get total revenues of $18 ($18 × 1). If she sets a price of $16 (row *C*), she will sell two piercings and get total revenues of $32 ($16 × 2). Paola must lower her price to sell more piercings — that is the law of demand.

To understand marginal revenue — the last column in Figure 8.1 — let's compare two prices that Paola is considering in rows *B* and *C*. In planning her price-making strategy, if she wants to increase her sales from one to two piercings, she must drop the price from $18 to $16. If she does so, total revenues increase from $18 to $32, shown in column 4. So what is Paola's additional, or marginal, revenue from selling the second piercing? Her additional revenue is the difference between $18 for one piercing and $32 for two piercings, or $14 ($32 − $18). Are you surprised?

If Paola is selling the second piercing in row C for $16, why is her marginal revenue only $14, and not the $16 price? The answer lies in the one-price rule. To sell the second piercing at the lower price of $16, Paola must also drop the price of the first piercing from $18 to $16. So *while Paola gets an additional $16 from the second piercing, she has to subtract the $2 less she gets on the first piercing:* $16 − $2 = $14. That is why Paola's marginal revenue from selling the second piercing is only $14, not $16.

Paola, like most business owners, has to make a price-making decision *before* sales start. Customers want to know the prices when they walk into the store. So think about this calculation of marginal revenue (which is less than price) as being *planned* — on paper, or in discussions, *before the selling begins.*

The bottom line is this. As price-making businesses consider setting lower prices to increase sales, with the one-price rule, marginal revenue also falls, and marginal revenue falls faster than the falling price. Don't get confused between total revenue and marginal revenue. When price-making businesses make smart decisions to cut their prices to increase sales, their total revenue (price × quantity) will increase. But their *marginal revenue*, from each *additional* unit sold, will be decreasing as sales increase. Smart choices are made at the margin — Key 2 of the Three Keys to Smart Choices.

Refresh 8.1

1. What is marginal revenue?

2. The connection between marginal revenue and price depends on a business's competitive environment. Why are marginal revenue and price the same for a business that is a price taker in extreme competition? Why is marginal revenue less than price for a business that is a price maker?

3. Most businesses have to lower the price on all units sold to sell more. But transit systems and movie theatres violate the one-price rule to sell more tickets, lowering prices for students and children while keeping higher prices for adults. How do these businesses get away with this discriminatory policy?

www.myeconlab.com

8.2 Marginal Cost

The profits from any new business decision depend on whether marginal revenue is greater than marginal cost. For a price-making business facing the one-price rule, marginal revenue falls as a business cuts prices to increase its quantity of sales. What happens to marginal cost as quantity increases?

Just as marginal revenue depends on market structure (marginal revenue is constant-and-equal-to price for price takers and falling-and-less-than price for price makers), so does marginal cost. Marginal cost depends on the supply side of businesses behind market structure. Price makers cover a wide range of businesses in the "grey" market structures of monopolistic competition and oligopoly — between the black-and-white extremes of extreme competition and pure monopoly. Different businesses have different marginal cost patterns. To answer the question of what happens to marginal cost, we have to shift our focus from the demand side (which determines revenues) to the supply side, which depends on costs. Let's look at the two most likely patterns of what happens to marginal cost as quantity increases — increasing marginal cost and constant marginal cost.

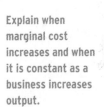

Explain when marginal cost increases and when it is constant as a business increases output.

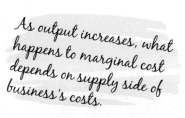

As output increases, what happens to marginal cost depends on supply side of business's costs.

Increasing Marginal Cost

Paola's shop is busy, with all her employees either piercing or nail painting. If a busload of tourists shows up all wanting piercings, what happens to Paola's marginal costs as she tries to increase piercing output?

There is not enough time to call in additional employees, so the only way for Paola to supply more piercings is to shift employees away from nail painting.

We saw in Chapter 3 that as she switches employees from nail painting to piercing her marginal opportunity costs increase. Do you remember why? Because she switches her worst nail painters first and doesn't lose much, but eventually has to switch her best nail painters and loses more nail revenues. Of course, she is earning more revenues on the piercing side to offset the reduced revenues on the nail side, and her ultimate choice, as we will see, depends on a comparison of marginal revenues and marginal costs. But for now, we are just looking at the cost side, and Paola has increasing marginal costs as she increases her output of piercings.

Many businesses face increasing marginal costs. Most businesses operating close to capacity have increasing marginal costs as they try to increase output. Increasing output can mean adding more employees, often at more expensive overtime rates. In some businesses, like oil drilling, to increase output you have to shift to more expensive sources of inputs, such as from easily drilled oil wells to more difficult and costly oil sands extraction. Many price makers in the grey range of market structures have increasing marginal costs.

Businesses operating near capacity, or shifting to more expensive sources of inputs, have increasing marginal costs to increase output.

Constant Marginal Cost

If Paola's shop is not very busy when the busload of piercing-seeking tourists arrives, what happens to her marginal costs?

If Paola is already paying her employees for being at work, those wages are a sunk cost. What are Paola's *additional costs* in increasing her output of piercings? Remember, fixed costs like rent and insurance do not change with increases in output. Paola's additional costs, or the marginal cost of one more piercing, is just the cost of the stud and the additional electricity used by the piercing gun. That is a small, constant amount for each additional piercing.

Most businesses that are *not* operating near capacity have constant marginal costs as they increase output. Think of an airline. If a plane is not full, what is the marginal cost of adding one more passenger to the plane? A very small amount — the cost of snacks served (if any, these days!), and the tiny increase in fuel consumption for the extra weight of the passenger and luggage. All other costs of flying this passenger (salaries, airport landing fees, advertising, cost of purchasing new airplanes) are fixed costs — they do not change with one additional ticket. The same goes for the constant marginal cost of a seat in a movie theatre. Many price makers in the grey range of market structures, as well as monopolies, have constant marginal costs.

Businesses not operating near capacity have constant marginal costs to increase output.

In making a smart business decision, you need to identify whether your business is in the increasing marginal cost group, or the constant marginal cost group. But no matter whether your marginal costs are increasing or constant, the same recipe applies for pricing for maximum profits.

Refresh
8.2

1. What is marginal cost?

2. What if, when the busload of piercing-seeking tourists arrives at Paola's shop, she has employees on standby she could bring in within 15 minutes, and who would be paid their regular hourly wage? What difference, if any, would that make to Paola's marginal cost of increasing piercing output?

3. Pick a business and figure out whether marginal costs are increasing or constant. What factors are important to consider?

8.3 Recipe for Profits: Marginal Revenue Greater Than Marginal Cost

Now that we have examined the basic ingredients of marginal revenue and marginal cost, it's time to combine them using the recipe of pricing for profits.

The recipe is as follows: **Estimate marginal revenues and marginal costs and then set prices that allow you to sell all quantities for which marginal revenue is greater than marginal cost.**

Once we have estimated marginal revenues and marginal costs, a smart business "cook" needs to make two related decisions about quantity and price:

- Find all quantities for which marginal revenue is greater than marginal cost.
- Set prices.

It is easiest to follow the recipe if we make the quantity decision first, and follow it with the price-setting decision. Any experienced business owner (or economist) will tell you that you can't pick a price for your product/service unless you have some idea of the quantity you expect to sell. The price you pick if you are expecting to sell 10 units will be different from the price you pick if you are expecting to sell 10 000 units. As we have seen, marginal revenues and marginal costs can change as quantities change.

The Quantity Decision

For the quantity decision, let's continue to use the simple numbers in Figure 8.1. Figure 8.2 (on next page) reproduces those numbers, showing how many nose piercings Paola expects her customers to demand at different prices, and the revenues she will collect. Like any business with pricing power, Paola must lower her price to sell more. Because the one-price rule applies, that means Paola's marginal revenue falls with each increase in piercings sold, and marginal revenue falls faster than the falling price — compare columns 2 (Price) and 5 (Marginal Revenue).

Marginal cost may be increasing or constant. Let's look at the case of constant marginal cost, because the numbers are simpler. But the recipe works the same even if marginal cost is increasing with increased output.

Column 6, Marginal Cost, shows that Paola's marginal cost of each additional nose piercing is constant at $8, no matter what the quantity. This is the case where Paola is not operating near capacity, and is already paying her employees for being at work. The only additional costs for a nose piercing are the costs of the stud and the additional electricity used by the piercing gun. Paola estimates those marginal costs to be $8 per piercing.

What is Paola's smart quantity decision — how many nose piercings should she produce to get maximum profits? The recipe says to find all quantities for which marginal revenue is greater than marginal cost. Let's look at the quantities one by one, starting with the first piercing (row *B*).

If Paola produces one piercing, her marginal revenue is $18 and her marginal cost is $8. That is clearly a smart decision because marginal revenue is greater than marginal cost. The last column in Figure 8.2 shows the net impact on Paola's total profits from producing that first piercing. Total profits go up by $10, which is the amount by which marginal revenue ($18) exceeds marginal cost ($8).

Explain quantity and price decisions in the recipe for maximum profits, and show the importance of marginal revenue and marginal cost.

Recipe for maximum profits is easiest to follow by first looking at quantity decision, then price decision.

Figure 8.2 has constant marginal costs, but recipe for maximum profits same even if marginal costs increase with increased output.

Row	Price	Quantity Demanded	Total Revenue	Marginal Revenue	Marginal Cost	Impact on Total Profit
A	$20	0	$0	$0	$0	$0
B	$18	1	$18	$18	$8	+ $10
C	$16	2	$32	$14	$8	+ $6
D	$14	3	$42	$10	$8	+ $2
E	$12	4	$48	$6	$8	– $2
F	$10	5	$50	$2	$8	–$6
G	$8	6	$48	– $2	$8	– $10

Figure 8.2 Paola's Marginal Revenues and Marginal Costs for Nose Piercings

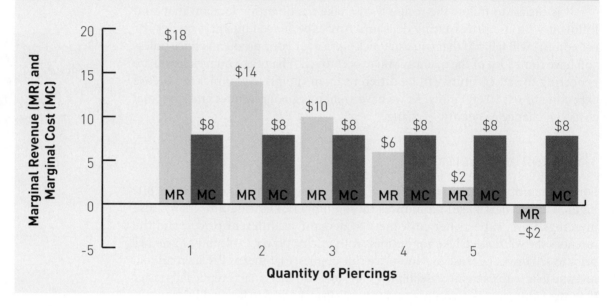

Look in sequence at each quantity — first piercing, second piercing, and so on. For each quantity, compare marginal revenue and marginal cost. If marginal revenue greater than marginal cost, produce. Total profits will increase. Stop increasing quantity when marginal revenue less than marginal cost.

In row *C*, if Paola increases output to two piercings, her marginal revenue is $14 and her marginal cost is $8. Total profits increase by a further $6, so this is still a smart decision. In row *D*, if Paola continues to increase output to three piercings, total profits increase by a further $2 — still smart.

Things change in row *E*. If Paola were to increase output to four piercings, her marginal revenue is $6, which is less than her marginal cost of $8. Total profits would start to *decrease by $2* if Paola were to produce the fourth piercing. Not smart.

Things get even worse in rows *F* and *G*. If Paola were to produce a fifth piercing, her total profits would fall by an additional $6. The sixth piercing would drag down total profits by a further $10!

If Paola follows the recipe of *producing all quantities for which marginal revenue is greater than marginal cost,* she will produce three nose piercings (row *D*). If she produces fewer than three piercings, she is forgoing potential profits. If she produces more than 3 piercings, her profits will start falling.

The Price-Making Decision

Once we have all the information for the quantity decision, the price-making decision is a piece of cake. Like any business, Paola wants to **set the highest possible price that allows her to sell her target quantity** of three nose piercings. Look at row *D* in Figure 8.2. From Paola's estimates of her customers' demand in columns 2 (Price) and 3 (Quantity Demanded), the highest price she can charge and still sell three piercings is $14. If she were to set a higher price customers would not buy as much (the law of demand), and she doesn't need to set a lower price to sell three piercings.

Once you choose (target) quantity with maximum profits, set highest possible price allowing you to sell target quantity.

The Proof Is in the Pudding: Pricing for Maximum Total Profits

When Paola applies the recipe for maximum profits, her smart business decision is to produce three nose piercings and to set her price at $14. How do we know this is the combination of price and quantity that yields *maximum total profits* when we haven't yet looked at her total profits? We have looked at marginal revenues and marginal costs, and how Paola's decisions *change* total profits, but what about Paola's fixed costs, like rent and insurance? And what about the normal profits Paola needs to earn on her investment if she is to do as well as she could in any other business? Just as the success of any recipe is judged by how the dish tastes, the success of the recipe for pricing for profits is judged by whether total profits are indeed at a maximum, with *all costs* taken into consideration.

FOR YOUR INFORMATION

Do you like dessert? The British word for dessert is *pudding*. Ever wonder what the saying "The proof is in the pudding" means? It's a shortened version of "The proof of the pudding is in the eating." It means the true value of something can be judged only when it is put to use, or tried and tested.

Figure 8.3 reproduces all the information on revenues and costs from Figures 8.1 and 8.2 and adds two more columns at the end. The Total Costs column adds Paola's fixed costs to her marginal costs. To keep the numbers very simple, we are assuming that Paola divides her fixed costs, like rent, among her different product lines — nose piercings, full-body piercings, nail sets, and so on. She has estimated that the portion of her fixed costs for nose piercings is $10. That number also includes the normal profits she must earn on her investment in just nose piercing to be doing as well as in any other line of business.

Figure 8.3	Paola's Calculation of Total Profits for Nose Piercings							
Row	Price	Quantity Demanded	Total Revenue	Marginal Revenue	Marginal Cost	Impact on Total Profits	Total Costs (Fixed Costs + Marginal Costs)	Total Profits (Total Revenue — Total Costs)
A	$20	0	$0	$0	$0	$0	$10 (Fixed Costs)	$10 (Losses)
B	$18	1	$18	$18	$8	+ $10	$18	$0
C	$16	2	$32	$14	$8	+ $6	$26	$6
D	$14	3	$42	$10	$8	+ $2	$34	$8
E	$12	4	$48	$6	$8	– $2	$42	$6
F	$10	5	$50	$2	$8	–$6	$50	$0
G	$8	6	$48	– $2	$8	– $10	$58	– $8 (Losses)

In row *A*, if Paola produces no nose piercings, she has no revenues and still has fixed costs of $10, so her total profits (last column) would be losses of $10 in this line of business. In row *B*, if Paola sells one piercing for $18, her total revenues are $18 and her total costs are $18 ($10 fixed costs plus $8 marginal cost for one piercing), so her total profits are zero. In row *C*, if Paola sells two piercings for $16 each, her total revenues are $32, her total costs are $26 ($10 fixed costs plus $8 marginal cost for the first piercing and $8 marginal cost for the second piercing), so her total profits are $6.

According to the recipe, row *C* should yield maximum profits. If Paola sells three nose piercings for $14 each, her total revenues are $42 and her total costs are $34 ($10 fixed costs plus $8 marginal cost for each piercing), so her total profits are $8. That is the highest total profits so far, but what if Paola — thinking that more has been better so far, so why not keep producing — were to push her output higher?

Look at row *E* to see why that would be a mistake, like burning the cake by keeping it in the oven too long. If Paola sells four piercings for $12 each, total revenues are $48 and total costs are $42, so her total profits are $6. That is *less than* the smart choice of 3 piercings at a price of $14, which yields total profits of $8. As you can see from rows *F* and *G*, total profits get even worse for five piercings ($0 total profits) or six piercings ($8 total losses).

Back to the Three Keys to Smart Choices

The original version of our recipe for maximum total profits is this: **Estimate marginal revenues and marginal costs and then set prices that allow you to sell all quantities for which marginal revenue is greater than marginal cost.**

When we arrange the steps in the order that businesses actually do them, with the quantity decision first, the recipe looks more like this:

- Find all quantities for which marginal revenue is greater than marginal cost.
- Set the highest possible price that allows you to sell all quantities for which marginal revenue is greater than marginal cost.

The quantity decision is much like the decision about whether Paola should keep her shop open in the evenings. In that decision, which did not involve setting prices, the only question was whether marginal revenues were greater than marginal costs.

In the quantity decision about how many nose piercings to produce, Paola compares marginal revenue and marginal cost for each additional piercing. If she were making a similar detailed decision about hours, it would be like comparing marginal revenues and marginal costs for staying open one extra hour, from 7:00–8:00 p.m., then making the same comparison for an additional hour from 8:00–9:00 p.m., and finally comparing marginal revenues and marginal costs for the 9:00–10:00 p.m. hour. The principle is the same — keep increasing your output or extending your business as long as marginal revenue is greater than marginal cost. The principle applies to all business decisions.

I am hoping this recipe for pricing for profits reminds you of the "map" to smart choices from Chapter 1. Just to remind you, the map consists of Three Keys to Smart Choices:

1. Choose only when additional benefits are greater than additional *opportunity costs.*
2. Count only *additional* benefits and *additional* opportunity costs.
3. Be sure to count *all* additional benefits and additional opportunity costs, including *implicit costs* and *externalities.*

Our recipe for pricing for profits is much like Keys 1, 2, and 3. Paola's business "benefits" are her profits. A smart, profit-maximizing business decision is to produce only when *marginal* revenues (*additional* benefits) are greater than *marginal* costs (*additional* opportunity costs). Differences in fixed costs (including *implicit costs* from Key 3) would not change Paola's decision.

As Key 2 says, focus only on *marginal* revenues (*additional* benefits) and *marginal* costs (*additional* costs). If Paola had focused instead on *total* revenues, which are at a maximum ($50) in Figure 8.3 for five piercings, her total profits would have been zero — not a smart decision. If Paola had focused on *total* costs, which are at a minimum ($10) in Figure 8.3 for producing no piercings at all, her total profits would have been losses of $10 — again, not smart.

By producing all quantities for which marginal revenue is greater than marginal cost, three piercings, and then setting the highest possible price that allows her to sell all three piercings, Paola maximizes her total profit ($8) and makes a smart choice. The proof of this recipe is not in the pudding, but in maximum total profits.

The recipe for pricing for profits works well for any business that has to follow the one-price rule. But what happens if businesses can set different prices for different customers for the very same product/service? Check out Section 8.4 to find out.

Recipe for maximum total profits focuses on marginal revenues and marginal costs. Focus on highest total revenues or lowest total costs does not give maximum profits — not-smart decision.

Refresh

8.3

1. What are the steps in the recipe for maximum total profits, in the order that businesses actually do them?

2. Suppose Paola's marginal revenues and fixed costs are the same as in Figure 8.3, but her marginal costs are increasing: $1 for the first piercing, $2 for the second, $3 for the third, $4 for the fourth, $5 for the fifth, and $6 for the sixth piercing. What quantity and price will Paola choose if she is making a smart decision? Does the recipe still work? [*Hint:* Create a table like Figure 8.3.]

3. You have been working too many hours at your part-time job (which pays $10 per hour), and your Economics marks are suffering. Your father, who wants you to do better in school but recognizes your desire for cash, offers you this deal. For every 1-percent increase in your mark on the next test, he will pay you $6. You estimate that one additional hour of studying will raise your mark 5 percent; a second hour of studying will raise your mark 4 percent; a third hour, 3 percent; a fourth hour, 2 percent; and a fifth hour, 1 percent. If all you are trying to do is make the most money, how many hours do you study?

www.myeconlab.com

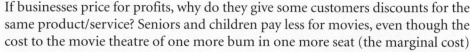

8.4 Divide and Conquer: Price Discrimination for Higher Profits

Define price discrimination and explain how it leads to higher profits by taking advantage of differences in elasticity of demand.

If businesses price for profits, why do they give some customers discounts for the same product/service? Seniors and children pay less for movies, even though the cost to the movie theatre of one more bum in one more seat (the marginal cost) is the same, regardless of age. For the same airline ticket from Vancouver to Montreal, you can pay much less if you book at least two weeks in advance and stay over a Saturday. And your cell phone plan gives away evening and weekend minutes for free, when for your provider the cost of delivering those phone calls is exactly the same as for daytime minutes.

Are these discounts really smart business pricing decisions, or are the businesses being charitable? How can a business be pricing for maximum profits if it is not charging the higher price to all customers? These differential prices are definitely smart and not at all charitable — they actually *increase a business's total profits*. Economists call this practice of charging different customers different prices for the same product/service **price discrimination**.

Would it bother you to hear how little I paid for this flight?

price discrimination: charging different customers different prices for same product/service

Price discrimination is possible when business can prevent low-price buyers from reselling to high-price buyers and can control resentment among high-price buyers.

Breaking the One-Price Rule

Price discrimination breaks the one-price rule, and is possible only when a business can

- prevent low-price buyers from reselling to high-price buyers, and
- control resentment among high-price buyers.

It's easy to resell a physical product like an iPod or a camera or a textbook — think eBay. So it's not accidental that most examples of price discrimination involve services (getting pierced, viewing a movie, flying on an airline, using cell phone minutes) that cannot be easily resold. (Want to buy my noise piercing?) Ticket takers at movie theatres will not let in a 20-year-old holding a senior or child ticket. Airlines were checking ID long before the post-9/11 security concerns — you always had to prove you were the person named on the ticket. And while new cell phone plans allow you to share minutes with selected friends, you generally cannot resell your minutes to someone else.

How do businesses control resentment among the high-price buyers? It's all in the marketing, and the key word is *discount*. Businesses describe the higher price as the "regular" price, and the lower price as the "discounted" price. They could just as easily call the lower price the regular price, and the higher price a "premium" price. You don't need to be a marketing guru to understand why businesses choose the word *discount*!

Discriminate (Cleverly) by Elasticity

So why charge lower prices to some customers? The answer goes back to the concept of elasticity of demand. In Chapter 2 we asked whether it is a smart choice for a business to hold a sale and cut prices. From the point of view of revenues (price × quantity), it is a smart choice as long as the increase in quantity more than makes up for the decrease in price. Remember: "You make it up in volume." That happens when demand is elastic — even a small change in price produces a large, responsive (elastic) change in quantity demanded. Customers with elastic demands have a lower willingness to pay and respond well to discounts.

But if demand is inelastic — a change in price produces only a small, unresponsive (inelastic) change in quantity demanded — then the smart choice is to *raise* price to increase revenues. The higher price more than makes up for the small decrease in quantity. Customers with inelastic demands have a higher willingness to pay and won't all disappear if you raise prices.

So *if* you can break the one-price rule and set more than one price for your service, it would be smart to set a lower price for the customers who have elastic demands, and a higher price for the customers with inelastic demands.

But how do you identify customers with different elasticities of demand, and get them to voluntarily pay different prices? This is where price discrimination schemes are so clever. Obviously, you can't ask each potential customer about his or her elasticity of demand. (And if you did, they would look at you with a blank stare: "Er, what's elasticity?") Even if customers could describe their willingness to pay, none would volunteer their high willingness to pay if they knew you would then charge them a higher price. That would be as foolish as going to a car dealership dressed in a tuxedo and announcing how desperately you want the car whose price you are about to haggle over. The clever business strategy is to set conditions that divide your customers into groups roughly approximating elastic demanders and inelastic demanders, and then charging the elastic demanders a lower price and the inelastic demanders a higher price. How do businesses accomplish what sounds like another complicated recipe for pricing for profits?

Price Discrimination at the Movies Let's start with movies. Seniors often have fixed income and are less willing and able to pay $13 for a movie. And parents, who pay for most of the children's tickets purchased, are less willing to pay for a child (especially if they have more than one child) than for themselves. This group (seniors and children) has, generally speaking, more elastic demand. A lower price will lead to a relatively large increase in quantity demanded, increasing total revenues. For other adults, especially the prime 18- to 35-year-old moviegoers, movies are an important part of social life, and they (Is this you?) are more willing and able to pay for a movie. You don't need to offer them a discount to get them into the seats. Society accepts these price differences, as it seems fair that people who are less able to pay get a lower price.

Smart strategy sets lower price for customers with elastic demand, and higher price for customers with inelastic demand.

Customers do not volunteer high willingness to pay. Clever price-discrimination strategies divide customers into elastic demanders (lower price) and inelastic demanders (higher price).

Price discrimination — discounts for seniors and children — profitable because of more elastic demand, ability to prevent resale, and lack of resentment from full-price customers.

People accept price discrimination at the movies.

Price Discrimination on Airplanes   For airlines and cell phone providers, the secret for successful price discrimination is to distinguish business customers from non-business customers, and set higher prices for the business customers (oops, I mean give discounted prices to non-business customers).

How do the airlines get away with that, since no customer will voluntarily tell you she is a business traveller if she knows it means you will charge her a higher price? What the airlines do is to set restrictions (advance purchase and Saturday stay-over) on the cheaper tickets, which makes them unattractive to business travellers but poses few problems for holiday travellers. Businesspeople often have to travel at the last minute — if the client is demanding, you usually have to go. And while business travel may sound exciting if you haven't done it, ask anyone who has. It's hard to be on the road. Most business travellers, especially if they have families, do not want to be away for the weekend if they can help it (and they don't get paid for the weekend!). Businesses are also willing to pay more for tickets because they are a legitimate cost that can be charged back to the customer. For all these reasons, the airline restrictions identify the travellers whose demand is more inelastic, and who are more willing and able to pay.

On the other hand, if you are planning a holiday, buying an airline ticket in advance is no big deal. You have to ask your boss for the days off in advance anyway. And you want to stay over the weekend because it adds days to your holiday beyond the workweek. Do you really want to go to Cuba in February but be back by Friday night? And holiday travellers are much more price sensitive. There are no customers to ultimately pay for your airfare. If the price of an airline ticket is too much, you might take a driving vacation instead. The advance purchase and Saturday stay-over restrictions are just fine for the holiday travellers whose demand is more elastic, and who are less willing and able to pay. Discounted tickets mean far more holiday trips, and higher revenues from non-business customers.

Plan Name	Basic	Enhanced	Super Plus
Monthly fees	$17	$25	$35
Minutes (Billed by the second)	60	90	300
Text messages sent	70	200	Unlimited
Text Messages received	Free	Free	Free
Evenings & Weekends	n/a	n/a	n/a

(Weeknights from 7 p.m. to 8 a.m. and weekends Friday 7 p.m. to Monday 8 a.m.)

▲

Price discrimination is all around us. Cell phones and airline ticket prices are two obvious examples. Where else do you see price discrimination? Do you agree with it?

Why Evening and Weekend Minutes Are Free   How do Bell and Telus separate business customers from others, since customers will not voluntarily reveal that they want a business rate plan if they know that means a higher price? Cell providers charge "regular" prices for core business hours, and offer discounted prices for evenings and weekends. While business is increasingly becoming a 24-hour-a-day experience (ask anyone who has to carry a BlackBerry), core business hours are still 9:00 a.m. to 5:00 p.m. Because everyone in business has to be available during normal business hours, businesses must have phone service during the day, and are willing and able to pay for it. Phone bills, like airfares, are a legitimate business expense that can be recovered in the prices customers pay for whatever your business produces or sells. Businesses have a relatively inelastic demand, and a high willingness to pay for daytime minutes.

For many of us making personal calls, it's no big deal to make the call in the evening or on the weekend. And no one is giving us a tax break for our phone bills — non-business consumers are less willing and able to pay, and have more elastic demand. Discounted plans with free evening and weekend minutes are a bargain that will lead us to use our phones more and lead to higher revenues for the phone companies.

Recipe for Price Discrimination   The basic recipe for using price discrimination to increase profits is as follows:

- prevent resale of product/service;
- charge lower price to elastic demand group (lower willingness to pay);
- charge higher price to inelastic demand group (higher willingness to pay);
- control resentment among higher price buyers.

Price discrimination is a way of lowering the price to attract additional customers who are more sensitive to price (elastic demanders) without lowering the price to everyone else (inelastic demanders).

Doubling Up the Recipe for Profits

While I hope the basic recipe and examples of price discrimination make sense, they do not tell you *exactly* where a business should set its prices. A business that can prevent resale and control resentment should charge lower prices to elastic demanders and higher prices to inelastic demanders. *But exactly which higher price and exactly which lower price?*

Luckily, you already have the answers to those questions. Remember the business recipe for maximum profits? Estimate marginal revenues and marginal costs, and then set prices that allow you to sell all quantities for which marginal revenue is greater than marginal cost. That more precise recipe also applies to price-discriminating businesses.

To set exact prices *for each separate group,* the price-discriminating business estimates marginal revenues and marginal costs, and then sets prices that allow the sale of all quantities for which marginal revenue is greater then marginal cost. If a business has correctly separated the groups according to elasticity, and applied the precise recipe, the result will be a lower price for the elastic group, a higher price for the inelastic group, and higher total profits than the one-price strategy. We could go through two more detailed tables of numbers for Paola's Piercing and Fingernail Parlour, but I think you get the idea without the extra tables.

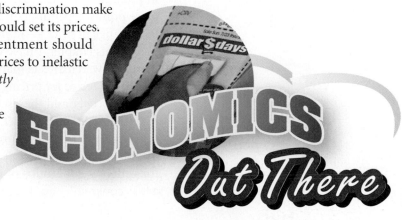

Are You a Coupon Clipper?

Why do stores offer discounts for customers who have coupons, instead of just lowering prices for everyone?

Coupons are a form of price discrimination. Two customers (one with coupon, one without) pay different prices for the same product. Coupons are the smarter, more profitable business strategy. Bargain-conscious customers with lower willingness and ability to pay will take the time and effort to find the coupons. Customers who are less price conscious will pay the full price rather than spend time clipping coupons.

Because everyone has the option of using coupons, there is no resentment among the full-price customers.

Why Stop at Two?   Speaking of more detail, price-discrimination strategies are not limited to two groups. The more finely a business can successfully subdivide its customers by elasticity, the more profits it will earn. Airlines have different prices for 14-day advance purchase, 7-day advance purchase, 3-day advance purchase, and so on. Think about the overwhelming number of different cell phone rate plans. All these clever price-discriminating strategies are finely tuned attempts by businesses to match prices with willingness to pay, lowering prices to attract additional customers who are more sensitive to price (elastic demanders) without lowering prices to everyone else (inelastic demanders).

Putting It All Together

Back in Chapter 2, I said, "All businesses have to live by the law of demand — a rise in price causes a decrease in quantity demanded. Smart businesses choose their price points depending on how much consumers' quantity demanded responds to a change in price — in other words, on price elasticity of demand."

In this chapter, I have combined that information about price elasticity of demand (which affects marginal revenue) with cost information (marginal cost) to find the recipe for pricing for maximum profits: Estimate marginal revenues and marginal costs, and then set prices that allow you to sell all quantities for which marginal revenue is greater than marginal cost. For businesses with price-setting power, price discrimination fine-tunes that recipe, if they can get around the law of one price, prevent resale, and control resentment to set different price points for different subgroups of consumers. Pricing for profits can be as much of an art as cooking!

Refresh 8.4

1. In your own words, write the basic recipe for successful price discrimination.

2. Compare the cell phone plan you have chosen with more expensive plans. What factors went into your decision to select your plan?

3. Devise a successful price discrimination plan for Paola's Piercing and Fingernail Parlour. What "groups" have different elasticities of demand, and what conditions lead them to voluntarily reveal their higher willingness and ability to pay?

Pricing *for* Profits

Marginal Revenue and Marginal Cost

CHAPTER SUMMARY

8.1 IS THE PRICE YOU SEE THE REVENUE YOU GET? MARGINAL REVENUE

Marginal revenue equals price for price takers and is less than price for price makers. Smart businesses choose actions when marginal revenue is greater than marginal cost.

- **Marginal revenue** — additional revenue, from selling one more unit or from extension of sales.

- **Fixed costs** (sunk costs) — do not change with changes in quantity of output.

- Marginal revenue depends on market structure (how competitive industry is) and whether business is a price taker or a price maker.

  - Marginal revenue *equals* price for price-taking businesses in extreme competition.

  - Marginal revenue *less than* price for price-making businesses in all other market structures.

- One-price rule — products easily resold tend to have single price in market.

  - When price-making business lowers price, must lower price *on all units* sold, not just new sales.

  - The "one-price rule" is why marginal revenue is less than price for price makers.

8.2 MARGINAL COST

As output increases, marginal cost increases for businesses operating near capacity or when businesses' additional inputs cost more. Marginal cost is usually constant for businesses not near capacity.

8.3 RECIPE FOR PROFITS:
MARGINAL REVENUE GREATER THAN MARGINAL COST

A smart business decision for maximum profits involves both quantity and price decisions. The quantity decision is this: produce all quantities for which marginal revenue is greater than marginal cost. The price decision is this: set the highest possible price that allows you to sell that quantity. Key to maximum profits is to focus on marginal revenues and marginal costs, not on total revenues and total costs.

- Recipe for maximum profits easiest to follow by looking at quantity decision first, then price decision.
  - Increase in quantity yields increase in profits if marginal revenue greater than marginal cost.
  - Stop increasing quantity when marginal revenue less than marginal cost.
- Once you choose quantity with maximum profits (target quantity), price part of recipe is to set highest possible price that allows you to sell target quantity.

8.4 DIVIDE AND CONQUER:
PRICE DISCRIMINATION FOR HIGHER PROFITS

Price discrimination is a business strategy that divides customers into groups. Businesses increase profits by lowering the price to attract additional price-sensitive customers (elastic demanders), without lowering the price to others (inelastic demanders).

- **Price discrimination** — charging different customers different prices for same product/service.
- Price discrimination breaks one-price rule, possible only when business can:
  - prevent low-price buyers from reselling to high-price buyers; and
  - control resentment among high-price buyers.
- Most examples of price discrimination involve *services* (for example, flying on an airline), which cannot easily be resold.
- Price discrimination increases profits by:
  - charging lower price to elastic demand group (lower willingness to pay).
  - charging higher price to inelastic demand group (higher willingness to pay).
- Price-discriminating business estimates marginal revenues and marginal costs for each separate group, then sets prices allowing sale of all quantities for which marginal revenue is greater than marginal cost.

TRUE/FALSE

Circle the correct answer.

8.1 MARGINAL REVENUE

1. If your business decision results in marginal revenue being greater than zero, profits will increase.   **True**   **False**

2. For oligopolies and businesses in extreme competition, price equals marginal revenue. True False

3. Products that can easily be resold tend to have a single price. True False

4. To sell more, monopolists must lower the price on new sales only. True False

8.2 MARGINAL COST

5. Fixed costs are relevant for deciding whether to stay open for an extra hour. True False

6. If a store offers its employees a commission that is the same percentage for each unit sold, and all its other marginal costs are constant, it has constant marginal costs. True False

7. Marginal costs tend to be constant as output increases if the business is operating below capacity. True False

8. The marginal cost of adding passengers on a plane increases with every ticket sold. True False

9. Constant marginal cost means total costs are always the same. True False

8.3 RECIPE FOR PROFITS

10. If marginal costs are greater than marginal revenues, then profits will decrease. True False

11. An increase in the cost of rent will change the profit-maximizing quantity of output for a business. True False

12. The price your business chooses does not depend on the quantity you expect to sell. True False

8.4 PRICE DISCRIMINATION FOR HIGHER PROFITS

13. Price discrimination occurs when a business charges different customers different prices for the same product/service. True False

14. Price discrimination occurs more frequently among products than services. True False

15. Price discrimination increases profits when businesses can provide discounts to the inelastic demand group. True False

MULTIPLE CHOICE

Circle the correct answer.

8.1 MARGINAL REVENUE

1. Marginal revenue is the additional
   A) sales revenue from staying open later.
   B) profit from staying open later.
   C) cost from staying open later.
   D) all of the above.

2. Self-interest and competition would most likely push the price toward a single price for
   A) haircuts.
   B) coffee.
   C) tennis lessons.
   D) Broadway show tickets.

3. A business facing extreme competition has no ability or incentive to
   A) raise prices.
   B) lower prices.
   C) affect market supply.
   D) all of the above.

4. The additional revenue, or marginal revenue, from selling the second textbook is the difference in
   A) price between one and two textbooks.
   B) total revenue between one and two textbooks.
   C) marginal revenue between one and two textbooks.
   D) marginal revenue between two and three textbooks.

5. Which of the following statements about prices and marginal revenues is *true*?
   A) Marginal revenue equals price for monopolists.
   B) Marginal revenue equals price for businesses in extreme competition.
   C) Marginal revenue is greater than price for monopolists.
   D) Marginal revenue is greater than price for businesses in extreme competition.

8.2 MARGINAL COST

6. The marginal cost of staying open an extra hour would include
   A) additional wages.
   B) additional costs of hydro/electricity.
   C) additional costs of time.
   D) all of the above.

7. To increase output, marginal costs will increase when a business must

   A) shift to more expensive sources of raw materials.

   B) switch workers from jobs they are good at to jobs they are not so good at.

   C) use more workers at overtime rates.

   D) do all of the above.

8. A business probably has constant marginal costs if

   A) workers are sending text messages and checking Facebook instead of working.

   B) customers are angry that wait times at the check out are ridiculously long.

   C) it is offering workers increased overtime-pay rates.

   D) it is selling Christmas trees and it is the Christmas season.

8.3 RECIPE FOR PROFITS

9. With each additional item sold by a monopolist under the one-price rule,

   A) total revenue falls.

   B) marginal revenue falls by less than price.

   C) marginal revenue falls by the same amount as the fall in price.

   D) marginal revenue falls by more than price.

Use the information from question 3 of the "Refresh" summary at the end of Section 8.3 (repeated here) to answer questions 10 through 12.

You have been working too many hours at your part-time job (which pays $10 per hour), and your Economics marks are suffering. Your father, who wants you to do better in school but recognizes your desire for cash, offers you this deal. For every 1-percent increase in your mark on the next test, he will pay you $6. You estimate that one additional hour of studying will raise your mark 5 percent; a second hour of studying will raise your mark 4 percent; a third hour, 3 percent; a fourth hour, 2 percent; and a fifth hour, 1 percent. If all you are trying to do is make the most money, how many hours do you study?

10. If all you are trying to do is make the most money, and you have only five hours in total to divide between studying and working, how many hours should you *work*?

    A) 1

    B) 2

    C) 3

    D) 4

11. You have only five hours in total to divide between studying and working. Suppose your boss gets desperate and offers to pay you $15 an hour. How many hours will you now *study*?

    A) 1

    B) 2

    C) 3

    D) 4

12. You have only five hours in total to divide between studying and working. Suppose your boss gets desperate and offers to pay you $15 an hour. How many hours will you now *work*?

    A) 1

    B) 2

    C) 3

    D) 4

8.4 PRICE DISCRIMINATION FOR HIGHER PROFITS

13. Price discrimination increases profits when businesses can

    A) charge lower prices to consumers with elastic demand.

    B) charge higher prices to consumers with inelastic demand.

    C) control resentment among higher-price buyers.

    D) do all of the above.

14. The secret for successful price discrimination is to set

    A) higher prices for customers with elastic demand.

    B) higher prices for all customers.

    C) lower prices for customers with elastic demand.

    D) lower prices for customers with inelastic demand.

15. The passenger next to you who paid more than you did for her airline ticket is probably

    A) smarter than you.

    B) older than you.

    C) travelling for business.

    D) all of the above.

Write a short answer to each question. Your answer may be in point form.

1. Explain how each of the following decisions will be a smart choice by comparing estimated marginal revenues with marginal costs.

   A) Launching an advertising campaign

   B) Hiring a new employee

   C) Extending business hours

2. You are trying to determine how many people to invite to your wedding reception. So far, 100 people are on the list. You are trying to decide whether to add a friend you have known since high school. Describe all the additional costs and benefits to inviting this extra person. *Note:* Sometimes the additional *benefits* extend beyond the additional *revenues* that should factor in to whether this is a smart decision.

3. Ori the ice cream truck driver knows he can sell 50 single-scoop ice cream cones on a hot, sunny day if his price is $3 each. His brother, who used to be in the ice cream business, tells him he can probably sell 80 single-scoop ice cream cones if he lowers his price on all cones to $2. What is Ori's marginal revenue if he lowers the price to $2?

4. The Vanherk family has a pig farm in a small town near Stratford, Ontario. The family currently charges the market price because the pig market is extremely competitive. Explain why the Vanherk family has no ability or incentive to raise or lower its pig prices.

5. Refer to Figure 8.2, on page 192, about Paola's marginal revenues and marginal costs for nose piercings.

   A) Explain why producing three piercings is Paola's smart, profit-maximizing choice.

   B) Explain why charging a price of $14 is Paola's smart, profit-maximizing choice.

   C) Increasing quantity from zero units to one unit has the largest additional impact on profits. Explain why producing one unit is not Paola's smart, profit-maximizing choice.

   D) If Paola increases quantity from three units to four units, she makes an additional $6. Explain why producing four units is not Paola's smart, profit-maximizing choice.

6. For question 5 and Figure 8.2, if Paola had increasing marginal costs instead of constant marginal costs, do you think this would increase or decrease her smart, profit-maximizing quantity of piercings?

7. Explain whether we need information about fixed costs or total profits to determine the profit-maximizing choices of output and price.

8. Let's revisit the example from multiple-choice questions 10–12 above, but with one change. Instead of assuming that the marginal cost of studying is always $10 per hour (the wage you could have earned working), now assume *increasing marginal opportunity costs* — the cost of studying increases for each additional hour of studying.

A) Explain why the cost of studying could feel like it is increasing for each additional hour of studying.

B) Fill in column two in the table below using the information above. Fill in column three by *making up* dollar estimates of the marginal cost of your time. Any numbers are OK, as long as the *marginal cost of studying is increasing*. Fill in column four based on your answers in columns two and three.

Hours of Study	Marginal Revenue from Studying	Marginal Cost of Studying	Impact on Studying on Total Profits
1		10	
2			
3			
4			
5			

C) If you have only five hours in total to divide between studying and working, how many hours should you *study*?

D) If you have only five hours in total to divide between studying and working, how many hours should you *work*?

9. Tifo works for Infamous Players cinemas and wants to look smart during his next staff meeting. Suppose all movie ticket customers currently pay the same price.

A) Explain how Tifo can win the respect of his fellow employees by having different groups pay different prices.

B) Suppose Infamous Players likes the idea of lowering the price to the age group most sensitive to price, but it would prefer to do this in an indirect way — that is, by lowering the price of movie tickets during the *time of day* the price-sensitive group watches movies. Explain how this could be done.

10. Prior to airline deregulation in 1978, the U.S. government set domestic air fares. All airlines were required to charge the same price for flights of the same length. Today, prices are determined by the forces of demand and supply, but airline companies have enough pricing power to offer different prices to different customers.

A) To divide consumers into groups, airlines offer discounted tickets to consumers who book well in advance and prefer to travel for more than a week. What types of consumers are willing to pay full price and why?

B) The airline industry provides price discounts through the use of frequent-flyer programs. Is this a form of price discrimination? Explain why or why not.

Chapter 9

Monopoly *Rules*

Government Regulation, Competition, and the Law

LEARNING OBJECTIVES

After reading this chapter, you should be able to:

9.1 Describe natural monopolies, and explain the challenge they create for policymakers.

9.2 Explain how strategic interaction between competitors complicates business decisions, creating two smart choices.

9.3 Explain why cartels form and why they are unstable and illegal.

9.4 Explain arguments for and against government regulation, and describe three of its forms.

9.5 Differentiate between the public-interest view and the capture view of government regulation.

ARE YOU HAPPY WITH YOUR LOCAL CABLE TV

company's prices and service? Did you know that the Canadian Radio-television and Telecommunications Commission (CRTC) willingly gives your cable company a legal monopoly on providing services in your neighbourhood? Why would the CRTC *prevent* competition? Why not just allow the competitive market to operate?

Markets usually work to provide the products/services we value most. Adam Smith's invisible hand can channel smart choices for you into smart choices for all. But sometimes markets fail to produce outcomes that are in society's best interests. In the next three chapters we will explore *market failures* that result in problems, such as natural monopolies (like cable TV) and cartels (like OPEC), pollution (Chapter 10), and poverty and inequalities (Chapter 11). When markets fail, governments often step in to correct the failures. Regulations, Crown corporations, and competition laws are all attempts by governments to produce more efficient and desirable outcomes for society.

No matter how well-intentioned, these government policies may actually do more harm than good, making the outcome *less* efficient and *less* desirable. Like rent controls, government regulations can have negative, unintended consequences. When that happens, we call it *government failure* rather than market failure. Sometimes policies designed to protect the public good work well, but sometimes government policies end up promoting the special interests of the very businesses being regulated.

In this chapter, we will examine the trade-offs involved in using government policies to deal with monopoly-style market failures. That understanding will help you make better choices as a citizen in voting for politicians supporting regulation policies you agree with — and may even reduce your frustration with your cable company!

9.1 Size Matters: Natural Monopoly and Regulation

Describe natural monopolies and explain the challenge they create for policymakers.

For cable TV suppliers, fixed costs are high and variable costs low. Average Total Costs (= [Fixed Costs + Variable Costs] / Quantity) keep falling as quantity of subscribers increases.

Imagine a world where many cable TV companies compete for your business. Sounds like a consumer's dream come true, doesn't it? Competitors provide choices, which consumers value. And just like the downward pull of gravity, competitive forces pull prices down toward levels of extreme competition, where businesses cover all opportunity costs but earn only normal profits. While the dream of cable competitors sounds wonderful, be careful what you wish for. Let's describe what would happen if your dream came true.

It's called cable TV because television signals are delivered to households through . . . wait for it . . . cables. By far the largest cost for cable companies is the network of thousands of kilometres of fibre-optic cable running under the streets or paralleling hydro wires above ground. Once the network is in place and the company has paid for programming, the *marginal cost* of supplying a signal to an additional subscriber is almost zero — the cost of their flipping a switch. While the fixed costs of the network are high, the variable costs of adding subscribers are very low. The result is that average total costs (Average Total Costs = [Fixed Costs + Variable Costs] / Quantity) keep falling as the high fixed costs are spread over a larger number of subscribers (quantity).

Right now in your neighbourhood, there is only one such cable network because the CRTC has granted a local monopoly to Rogers, Eastlink, Shaw, or whichever company is your provider. If there were competition in the cable TV industry, every entering competitor would have to dig or string a complete network. And every time you or a neighbour decided to switch providers, there would be digging or rewiring. Besides those higher variable costs, each cable company would end up with fewer subscribers in your neighbourhood over which to spread costs, so average total costs would be higher for all. The benefit of competition is to tend to force prices down to levels just covering average total costs and normal profits. But if average total costs are higher with multiple competing cable companies, *prices will be higher compared to a single cable company.*

▶ Cable companies operate with a government-granted monopoly. Many consider this a natural monopoly. Do you think the government should force the cable companies to share their cables with potential rivals?

The cable TV business, like water and electricity utilities, has **economies of scale** — average total costs fall as a business produces increasing quantities of output. Economists call these kinds of businesses **natural monopolies**. To achieve lowest average total cost, the technology of production allows only a single seller.

Even if competition were allowed in the cable TV industry, because of the nature of the technology and high fixed costs, eventually the biggest company could under-price the smaller companies — forcing them out of business or into takeovers or mergers. The same competitive forces that force down prices would yield a single seller with monopoly power! This type of monopoly seems inevitable, like a force of nature.

economies of scale: average total costs fall as quantity of output increases

natural monopoly: technology allows only single seller to achieve lowest average total cost

The Government Policy Challenge

In businesses with economies of scale, the only way to achieve the efficiency of lowest cost production is to have a single large business supply the entire market. Size matters. But, of course, that private business, for example your local cable provider, will act like any other profit-maximizing monopoly. While its costs may be low, no competitors are forcing it to pass on those cost savings to consumers in the form of lower prices. The monopolist with economies of scale will follow the same recipe for profits as any other business with pricing power: estimate marginal revenues and marginal costs, and then set the highest price that still allows it to sell all quantities for which marginal revenue is greater than marginal cost. The outcome, compared to competitive outcomes, will be that the monopolist will restrict output and raise prices. Instead of passing on cost savings to consumers, the monopolist will keep the price well above average total costs to earn the highest possible economic profits.

This is the challenge facing government policymakers: **How do you gain the low-cost efficiencies of economies of scale, but avoid the inefficiencies of monopoly's restricted output and higher price?**

The two major policies that governments around the world use to deal with this challenge are public ownership and regulation.

With natural monopoly, challenge for policymakers is to gain low-cost efficiencies of economies of scale but avoid inefficiencies of monopoly's restricted output and higher price.

Public Ownership: Crown Corporations   In Canada, public ownership of businesses with economies of scale takes the form of **Crown corporations**. Crown corporations are created by the federal or provincial governments, which own 100 percent of the corporation's assets. Crown corporations can be created from scratch, or from buying out the assets of private businesses. There are Crown corporations in electricity, water, and gas, as well as in industries that don't necessarily have economies of scale but are deemed to be publicly important for other economic, political, or social reasons (culture, alcohol control, lotteries, agriculture, fisheries). Here are some of the Crown corporations in Canada:

Crown corporations: publicly owned businesses in Canada

- BC Hydro
- Canada Post
- Canadian Broadcasting Corporation (CBC)
- GO Transit
- Hydro-Québec
- Saskatchewan Liquor and Gaming Authority
- VIA Rail Canada

While Crown corporations such as utilities (water, gas, electricity) can achieve economies of scale, they are not a perfect solution to the policy challenge. The disadvantages stem from the lack of competitive pressure. Incentives are weak to further reduce costs or increase efficiency or explore new innovative technologies. And there are the usual risks of a large, bureaucratic organization — waste, lack of performance incentives, and red tape.

Regulated Private Monopoly The other government response to the policy challenge of economies of scale is to allow a single private business, but subject it to government regulation. This is what the CRTC does in regulating the cable TV industry. Each cable provider is granted a monopoly for its assigned neighbourhoods, but the price it can charge subscribers is regulated by the government. Here are some of the industries in Canada where businesses are regulated private monopolies:

- banks
- air transportation, including airports
- railway and road transportation across borders
- telephone, telegraph, and cable systems
- grain elevators, feed and seed mills
- uranium mining and processing
- fisheries as a natural resource

In principle, government regulators try to set prices that just cover average total costs and normal profits. In practice, regulators do not directly observe costs, and can't tell how hard the business is trying to keep costs low, so they use a technique called **rate of return regulation**. The regulated monopoly is allowed to charge a price that earns it the normal rate of return, or normal profits — the average rate of profits in other industries.

Rate of return regulation is not a perfect solution to the policy challenge either. The "normal rate of return" policy creates an incentive for managers of the regulated businesses to exaggerate their reported costs, since they are guaranteed a normal rate of return on all costs. "Costs" may include luxury consumption for management, such as a private box at the Air Canada Centre (justified in the name of entertaining clients), limousines, company jets, international travel, entertainment, and so on.

In the final section of this chapter, we will look again at the advantages and disadvantages of unregulated monopolies and at government alternatives for dealing with the challenges of natural monopolies.

What's So Natural about Natural Monopoly?

The term "natural monopoly" implies there is something inevitable about these technologies that will always produce a monopoly, like a law of nature that never changes. Natural monopolies arise when the technology has inherent economies of scale that can be efficiently exploited only by a single seller. But technologies change. Before 1990, the only way to place a long-distance call from Canada to Europe was through the single undersea cable that linked the continents. Phone companies had a natural monopoly. But the development of new technologies changed the industry to a more competitive market structure.

Advances in fibre optics and VoIP (Voice over Internet Protocol) technologies mean that now phone company cables can carry television signals, and cable companies can also provide phone services. And satellites provide yet another technology for delivering phone and television signals. So what has been a regulated monopoly is in the process of changing. Natural monopolies are only as natural as the current technology.

Refresh

9.1

www.myeconlab.com

1. What is a natural monopoly, and how does it help consumers?

2. If you were to manage a regulated private monopoly (like New Brunswick Power) governed by rate of return regulation, explain the incentives you would personally face for delivering electricity at the lowest cost to consumers.

3. Identify one regulated private monopoly you buy services from. Find out from its website everything you can about its costs and the regulations under which it operates. Do you think its services could be improved? Explain your answer.

9.2 Cooperate or Cheat? Prisoners' Dilemma and Cartels

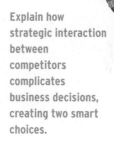

Explain how strategic interaction between competitors complicates business decisions, creating two smart choices.

Every Thursday before a long weekend, gas prices seem to rise simultaneously at filling stations across Canadian cities. By Saturday or Sunday a few stations cut their prices, and within a few days prices fall everywhere. This odd pricing behaviour repeats in regular cycles.

Gasoline Price Wars and Conspiracies

Gasoline price-swings often cause motorists to complain so bitterly that governments strike committees to investigate whether the oil companies are conspiring unfairly to raise prices. The investigations rarely find any clear evidence of conspiracy.

My wife (who is not an economist, thank goodness) always asks, "So if it's not a conspiracy, and the price of oil certainly doesn't change that much over a weekend, why do gas prices rise and fall like that, and why don't the stations learn to keep prices steady?" I, the economist, actually have answers to her questions. (Why she never accepts or remembers my answers is another story, but I am counting on you to do better.)

Both simultaneous gasoline price rises *and* gas price wars result from strategic, competitive decisions by the stations and the oil companies that own them. Gas prices fluctuate wildly on long weekends not because of changes in the cost of oil used to produce gasoline, but because of a tension that exists between stations trying to agree to keep prices high, but being tempted to cheat on the agreement in order to sell more gas. Is this quick explanation as clear to you as it is to my wife? Let me elaborate using the unlikely example of police interrogation tactics.

The Prisoners' Dilemma: Game Theory and Strategic Behaviour

game theory: *mathematical tool for understanding how players make decisions, taking into account what they expect rivals to do*

Strategic, competitive decisions, like gas pricing, can be better understood using **game theory**. Game theory began as an abstract mathematical tool developed in the 1940s by John von Neumann and Oskar Morgenstern. It was extended by John Nash, a Princeton professor who won the Nobel Prize in Economics in 1994 and was the subject of the 2001 movie *A Beautiful Mind*. The beauty of game theory is its simplicity in helping us understand any strategic situation where the players of the game have to make decisions while worrying about what their rivals will do. Game theory is used by economists and political scientists to understand the OPEC oil cartel, nuclear arms races between countries, and even gasoline price wars.

prisoners' dilemma: *game with two players who must each make a strategic choice, where results depend on other player's choice*

The simplest example of game theory is called the **prisoners' dilemma**, which describes a scenario you have seen on countless TV detective shows. Two criminals, Bonnie and Clyde, have been caught in the act of robbing a bank. The police suspect the pair of murdering a bank teller in a previous robbery, but don't have the evidence to prove it. The detective in charge has a plan to get Bonnie *or* Clyde to confess to the murder. He places the prisoners in separate rooms, with no ability to communicate with each other. He then sets up rewards (reduced jail time) for cooperating with the police by confessing, and penalties (more jail time) for denying the murder charge if the other prisoner confesses. The detective's plan is to build up mistrust between Bonnie and Clyde, and to get each one to worry the other will confess.

The rewards and penalties are illustrated in Figure 9.1. Let me explain how to "read" the figure. The two players are Bonnie and Clyde. Each has a single strategic choice — to *confess* to the murder, or to *deny* the murder. The payoff to each choice depends on the other prisoner's choice. Bonnie's payoffs are in orange, Clyde's payoffs are in brown. Look at payoff box *A*. If Bonnie and Clyde both confess to the murder, they each get 10 years in prison for both crimes — armed bank robbery and murder. Look at payoff box *B*. If Bonnie confesses but Clyde denies, Bonnie gets rewarded with only a 5-year sentence for both crimes, while Clyde gets hit with the maximum 25-year sentence. Payoff box *C* is the reverse of *B*. If Clyde confesses but Bonnie denies, Clyde gets the lower 5-year sentence and Bonnie gets 25 years. And if both deny the murder, they can be convicted only of bank robbery and get 7 years each (box *D*).

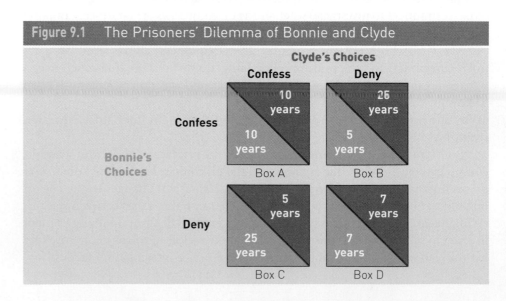

Figure 9.1   The Prisoners' Dilemma of Bonnie and Clyde

Nash Equilibrium

What choices are Bonnie and Clyde likely to make? We need to figure out Bonnie's best choice *given Clyde's choice*, and Clyde's best choice *given Bonnie's choice*. This is called a **Nash equilibrium** (after John Nash), and will tell us the outcome of the game.

Let's start with Bonnie (Bonnie's payoffs are in orange). If Clyde confesses, Bonnie's best choice is to confess, because 10 years in jail (box *A*) is better than 25 years (box *C*). If Clyde denies, Bonnie's best choice again is to confess, because 5 years in jail (box *B*) is better than 7 years (box *D*). No matter what choice Clyde makes, the detective has set up the outcomes so Bonnie's best choice is to confess.

What about Clyde (Clyde's payoffs are in brown)? If Bonnie confesses, Clyde's best choice is to confess, because 10 years in jail (box *A*) is better than 25 years (box *B*). If Bonnie denies, Clyde's best choice again is to confess, because 5 years in jail (box *C*) is better than 7 years (box *D*). No matter what choice Bonnie makes, the detective has set up the outcomes so Clyde's best choice is to confess.

So both Bonnie and Clyde confess, each gets a 10-year jail sentence, and the detective gets promoted. This outcome (except for the promotion) is the Nash equilibrium of the game.

The "dilemma" part of the prisoners' dilemma comes from the fact that each prisoner is motivated to confess, when each would be better off if they could trust each other to deny (7 years instead of 10 years). Game theory exposes a complication to our rule for smart choices — choose only when additional benefits are greater than additional opportunity costs. There seem to be *two* smart choices for the prisoners, hence the dilemma. The smart choice is to *confess if you don't trust the other*. But the other smart choice is to *deny if you can trust the other*. Smart choices are complicated by considering what your rivals will do, and whether or not you can trust them.

Game Theory and Gas Prices

So (my wife might ask), what does all this have to do with gas prices? Everything! Gas station owners face the same dilemma. Their strategic choice is not to deny or confess, but to *cooperate* with an implicit agreement to keep prices high, or to *cheat* on the agreement and cut prices. There is no need for a clever detective to set the incentives of the game. Self-interest, the quest for profits, and competition do the trick.

If station owners can trust each other to raise prices before the weekend and *cooperate* with the agreement to keep them high (this is the equivalent of box *D*, where both prisoners deny and get their best outcome), profits will be maximized for all. But each owner has an incentive to *cheat* on this agreement (confess), hoping that if his is the only station to lower prices just a little, he will sell far more gasoline at what is still a relatively high price. But once cheating begins, trust breaks down and all owners are driven to the Nash equilibrium outcome, where everyone cheats (the equivalent of box *A*, where both prisoners confess).

Nash equilibrium: outcome of game where each player makes own best choice given the choice of the other

The "dilemma": each prisoner is motivated to confess, but both would be better off if they could trust each other to deny. Two smart choices: confess if don't trust; deny if trust.

For gas station owners, strategic choice is to cooperate with implicit agreement to keep prices high, or to cheat on agreement and cut prices.

Key insight of game theory is tension between Nash equilibrium outcome (players who can't trust each other's best choice is to cheat/confess) and better outcome (if both players could trust each other and cooperate/deny). With complication of trust, now two smart choices.

Prices fall and profits are reduced. Eventually, reduced profits lead owners to take a chance on trusting each other again, since they figure it couldn't be worse than the existing low prices and profits. All stations raise their prices, and the cycle of pricing behaviour begins again. But hopefully, now that you know some game theory, the pricing behaviour doesn't seem quite so odd — the instability of price and profit outcomes can be explained by the cycle of trust and non-trust.

The important insight of game theory is the *tension* between the Nash equilibrium outcome (where players who can't trust each other's best choice is to confess or cheat) and the fact that both players could make themselves better off if they *could* trust each other (and deny or cooperate). With the complication of trust, there are now two smart choices. When gas prices are simultaneously high, that is one smart choice based on trust. When gas price wars break out, that is another smart choice based on non-trust. Is that clear enough for you to explain it to my wife (or to your friends)?

Refresh

9.2

www.myeconlab.com

1. Describe the scenario for the prisoners' dilemma.

2. What is a Nash equilibrium?

3. Explain the tension in the key insight of game theory.

9.3 C-Words Everywhere: Cartels, Collusion, Cheating, Competition Law

Explain why cartels form and why they are unstable and illegal.

There may be no solid evidence of conspiracy in fixing gasoline prices, but economists, consumers, and governments have long worried about businesses secretly cooperating to improve profits by fixing prices and restricting output.

Well-Dressed Thieves

Cooperate is a polite, friendly sounding word. However, the other c-words generally used to describe these business agreements are *collusion* by a *cartel*. The dictionary definition of **collusion** is "secret or illegal cooperation or conspiracy, especially in order to cheat or deceive others." A **cartel** is an association of manufacturers or suppliers with the purpose of maintaining prices at a high level and restricting competition.

collusion: conspiracy to cheat or deceive others

cartel: association of suppliers formed to maintain high prices and restrict competition

The best known international cartel today is OPEC — the Organization of Petroleum Exporting Countries. OPEC was formed in 1961 and gained world prominence in 1973, when the 12 member countries successfully agreed to restrict their combined outputs, reducing the supply of oil and driving up the world price. The collusive agreement set individual production quotas, so each country had to restrict its output below its previous production levels. By managing to trust each other to stick to the quotas in the agreement (it is hard to monitor precisely the quantity of oil produced by every oil well), OPEC acted much like a single monopoly. The rise in price and restricted output transferred billions of dollars of wealth out of the pockets of consumers and businesses in oil-consuming countries and into OPEC's pockets.

But just like the prisoners or the gas station owners, OPEC members had — and continue to have — an ever-present temptation to cheat on the agreement. Over time, energy conservation efforts and new oil suppliers (attracted by the economic profits and not part of OPEC) caused prices to fall. The recession of 1981–1983, which reduced economic activity and decreased demand for oil, caused a more dramatic fall in price. Even with cutbacks in quotas, OPEC could not raise prices. Members began to cheat and increase output, causing oil prices to fall further. Since that time, OPEC has swung between periods of trust and high oil prices, and periods of mistrust, cheating, and lower oil prices. Just as game theory predicts!

There is great temptation for businesses to form cartels because the payoffs to collusion are high. Cartels generally transfer money from consumers to business profits. Collusive agreements to fix prices are a clear and knowing conspiracy against consumers. To put it bluntly, consumers get robbed. An Australian government official said it well: "Cartels are theft — usually by well-dressed thieves."

"People of the same trade seldom meet together, even for merriment and diversion, but the conversation ends in a conspiracy against the public, or in some contrivance to raise prices."

— Adam Smith

Competition Law

The OPEC cartel does not break the law, but only because there is no international law on cartels that crosses national borders. But almost every country, including Canada, has national laws prohibiting collusion among businesses to fix prices and restrict competition.

In Canada in the late 1800s, there were cartels in a wide range of industries, from biscuits to coal to coffins to fire insurance. These cartels (called *combines* or *trusts* at the time) attracted consumer and government concerns. Parliament passed the first anti-combines (also called anti-trust) act in 1889, making it illegal for businesses to combine to form monopolies or near-monopolies. The act also forbade collusion among businesses to raise prices or restrict supplies to customers, or to do anything that would "unduly lessen" competition.

Similar laws were passed in most industrialized countries, becoming part of the legal *rules of the game* (with property rights and the enforcement of contracts discussed in Chapter 4) governing economic activity and markets. Such laws make it illegal for businesses to communicate about fixing prices, and prevent them from drawing up legal contracts to enforce cartel cooperation. Anti-combines laws drive price-fixing agreements underground, making it harder for colluding businesses to monitor each other's actions, making it harder to trust others, and leaving no legal penalties for cheating on agreements. These laws serve much the same purpose as the detective putting prisoners in separate rooms and preventing communication. No cooperation is legally possible. The result is to encourage businesses to be competitors, each one acting only in its individual self-interest. The goal is to try to achieve invisible hand outcomes that are better for consumers and society as a whole.

Today's anti-combines law is called the *Competition Act*, passed by Parliament in 1986. Its stated intent is "to maintain and encourage competition in Canada in order to promote the efficiency and adaptability of the Canadian economy."

This intent sounds desirable and clear, but all competition laws have to walk a fine line in distinguishing *competitive* business behaviour from *collusive* behaviour. Competition takes many forms, but it is (as we saw in Chapter 7) always an active attempt to increase profits and gain the market power of monopoly. When businesses buy or merge with other competitors in their markets, they can increase their profits and pricing power by eliminating substitute products.

The 1986 Competition Act was passed by Parliament "to maintain and encourage competition in Canada in order to promote the efficiency and adaptability of the Canadian economy."

Desirable competitive behaviour — always an active attempt to increase profits and gain market power of monopoly — is hard to distinguish from undesirable collusive behaviour.

Competition may be reduced. But if the merger also provides economies of scale that lower costs or allow the business to better compete internationally, that promotes "efficiency and adaptability."

The *Competition Act* attempts to address this fine line by distinguishing between two kinds of anti-competitive offences or practices with different legal penalties.

- *Criminal offences* include price fixing, bid rigging (see Economics Out There), and false or misleading advertising. Trials are held by the courts, and penalties include prison sentences and fines.

- *Civil offences* include mergers, abusing a business's dominant market position, and other actions that lessen competition. Charges are heard by a quasi-judicial Competition Tribunal composed of federal judges and business experts. Penalties include fines and legal prohibitions of mergers and anti-competitive business practices.

Canada, along with Australia, Britain, France, Germany, Ireland, Japan, and the U.S., uses prison time to penalize business executives convicted of price fixing. When large, sophisticated businesses enter into secret agreements to fix prices, this is a planned conspiracy against consumers. Because these underground agreements are both highly profitable and hard to discover, harsh penalties like prison terms serve as a deterrent to make businesses think twice. The *Competition Act* raises the expected costs to businesses of price fixing relative to the expected benefits (profits). Fines also raise the expected costs of price fixing, but a fine alone that would be high enough to work as a deterrent could financially cripple a business, reducing competition and unintentionally penalizing innocent bystanders like suppliers to the company (who might lose sales) and workers (who might lose their jobs).

The threat of prison terms also helps governments uncover secret cartels. Like the detective in the Bonnie and Clyde case, *Competition Act* government officials can offer reduced sentences or amnesty to whistle-blowers who reveal the cartel agreement. This sets up a Nash equilibrium similar to the prisoners' dilemma because each conspirator can make herself better off by confessing to the agreement and escaping punishment. The tougher the prison penalties, the greater the incentive to be the first to confess.

Civil, or non-criminal, offences like mergers are reviewed by a Competition Tribunal. The Tribunal must first determine whether the merger will lessen competition in that market. The Tribunal must then *also* determine whether the merger will yield any increased efficiencies. Any decision must be justified by weighing the costs of the merger (decreased competition) with the benefits (increased efficiencies). Does this sound familiar? It is Key 1 of the Three Keys to Smart Choices! The Competition Tribunal will prohibit the merger if expected costs are greater than expected benefits, and will allow the merger if expected benefits are greater than expected costs.

ECONOMICS Out There

Colluding Mills

Three large flour mills in 1990 — Maple Leaf Mills, Ogilvie Mills, and Robin Hood Mills — rigged bids to buyers of flour for the Third World. They secretly agreed on the price each would charge and the quantity each would supply to the Canadian International Development Agency (CIDA), which was distributing the flour for hunger relief.

The Competition Bureau filed criminal charges, and the courts slapped the guilty businesses with the largest fines for bid rigging in Canadian history — $1 million each.

1. What is a cartel?

2. Explain the two kinds of anti-competitive offences in the 1986 Competition Act.

3. Construct a payoff matrix (similar to Figure 9.1) for two oil companies forming a cartel, where the single strategic choice is to *collude* (stick to an agreement to restrict output and raise prices) or to *cheat* on the agreement. Your payoffs should be made-up numbers of the expected $ profits of each combination of player choices. Explain the difference between the Nash equilibrium of the game and the outcome that would be best for the two oil companies.

9.4 Master or Servant? Regulatory Agencies in Canada

It was a bad year for the safety of consumer products in Canada in 2007. Hundreds of dogs and cats died from eating tainted pet food that contained polyvinyl. Mattel and Hasbro recalled thousands of toys because they contained lead paint that was potentially poisonous for children. And inexpensive toothpastes imported from China contained a toxic ingredient that was cheaper than the proper ingredient. It was discovered only when the few unfortunate people who were the first to use the toothpaste died.

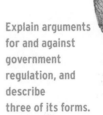

Explain arguments for and against government regulation, and describe three of its forms.

Should the Buyer Alone Beware?

In the pursuit of lower costs, competitive advantage, and higher profits, private businesses may use cheaper, even dangerous, materials and compromise workers' and consumers' safety. The same economic forces behind the invisible hand may produce deadly results when channelled through the hands of unscrupulous businesses and individuals.

The discipline of market competition ensures that, *eventually,* as word gets around, consumers will stop buying from businesses that produce harmful products. But few citizens want to be the guinea pigs who serve as the signal to future consumers to beware, so they call on their elected representatives in government to do something. That usually takes the form of regulating the questionable industry.

◄ Sometimes, in the pursuit of profit, businesses may put the public at risk. How closely should governments monitor private companies?

*caveat emptor:
"let the buyer beware" — buyer alone responsible for checking quality of products before purchasing*

Should the government play the role of regulator for products/services? If so, how effective will that regulation be? The debate over this question goes back centuries, to the beginning of trade. You can tell the debate is ancient because the phrase used to describe it — *caveat emptor* — is from Latin. **Caveat emptor** means "Let the buyer beware."

One answer to the question is that it is the responsibility of consumers, not government, to monitor the quality of what they buy. Far too many products/services exist for government to be able to monitor them all. Even if the government were capable of such an enormous task, the required bureaucracy would cost far more than the benefits of screening out the minority of products that are dangerous (additional costs of regulation greater than additional benefits — Key 1 for smart choices).

The other answer is that there are certain products — nuclear power, medicines, poisonous insecticides, and so on — that the average consumer is simply not capable of evaluating. Similarly, there are professional services — from doctors, lawyers, accountants, tradespeople — where most of us will not know whether those professionals are doing a good job or whether they are quacks pretending to do a good job. No consumer wants to be the one to be deceived, especially if the deception could cost us our health, our fortune, or even our life (additional benefits of regulation greater than additional costs).

Forms of Regulation

Major forms of government regulation in Canada: government departments, government-appointed agencies/boards, professional self-governing bodies.

There is no single right answer to the regulation question. As a result, there are some products/services that are regulated, and many others that are not. There are three major forms of government regulation in Canada.

Government Departments   Federal and provincial government departments, headed by ministers, are responsible for specific industries or roles. For example, the Department of Labour is responsible for enforcing workplace safety standards. These departments enforce the regulations designed to prevent businesses from compromising worker safety in attempting to keep costs down.

Government-Appointed Agencies and Boards   Governments appoint independent agencies and boards, usually called commissions (Public Service Commission, Canadian Dairy Commission, Canadian Transport Commission), boards (Nova Scotia Board of Public Utility Commissioners, Canadian Wheat Board, Atomic Energy Control Board), or tribunals (Ontario Commercial Registration Appeal Tribunal) to regulate industry. Senior bureaucrats and employees are usually experts in the industry, and often are recruited from the regulated businesses. These agencies and boards often have processes involving public input. But the guiding principles the government legislation provides — act "in the public interest," or allow only "just and reasonable rates" — are sufficiently vague that regulators have considerable leeway in forming specific regulations.

Professional Self-Governing Bodies   Because professions like medicine or law or certain trades involve specialized training, they can be knowledgeably regulated only by a member of the profession or trade. Governments grant professional associations, like the Canadian Medical Association and the Canadian Bar Association, and some trade unions, like the International Brotherhood of Electrical Workers, the authority to regulate themselves. This involves certifying who is qualified to practise, and disciplining members who fail to live up to professional standards.

But there is a fine line between ensuring quality service and ensuring the self-interest of the profession. For example, rules that guarantee a certain level or type of training also rule out professionals who have trained in different countries. The net effect is to restrict the supply of doctors or lawyers or tradespeople, which, as we know from Chapter 4, tends to restrict competition and raise the price paid for services.

All these well-intentioned attempts at regulation are capable of serving the public interest. But do they? The guiding principles are vague, and there are close relationships between the regulatory bodies and the industries they regulate. Therefore, it is also possible for regulators to serve the interests of businesses in the industry at the public's expense — the subject of the final section of this chapter.

Refresh 9.4

1. What are the three forms of regulation in Canada?

2. Explain the arguments for and against the principle of *caveat emptor*.

3. Suppose you are a successful dairy farmer recruited to serve on the Canadian Dairy Commission. You understand well the industry from a producer's perspective, but your mandate is to regulate the industry in the public interest, where the public consists mostly of consumers. What conflicts might you face in doing your job?

www.myeconlab.com

9.5 Pick Your Poison: Market Failure or Government Failure?

Differentiate between the public-interest view and the capture view of government regulation.

In most situations, market outcomes serve the public interest. Thanks to the competitive pressures of the invisible hand, markets provide the products/services we value most, and do so efficiently, at the lowest possible cost. But as we have seen in this chapter, markets can fail when there are natural monopolies with economies of scale, when there is monopolistic collusion among competitors, and from unscrupulous behaviour among profit-seeking businesses. When markets fail, consumers call on governments for action, believing that government regulation will improve the outcome. Consumers-as-citizens speak up to say, "Government *should* regulate industries where there is market failure."

Should Governments Regulate? Public-Interest View or Capture View

If you recall the positive/normative distinction from Chapter 5, the word *should* signals that the statement "Government *should* regulate industries where there is market failure" is normative. Normative statements involve value judgments or opinions — as opposed to positive statements, which can be evaluated as true or false by checking the facts.

Even the most careful economic thinking cannot answer the *normative* question, "Should government regulate industries where there is market failure?" That answer, as we will see, will be different for different individuals, and depends on the values they hold. Where economic thinking is helpful is in answering a related *positive* question, "When will government action improve market failure outcomes, and when will government action produce an outcome that is actually worse than market failure?"

Public-Interest View of Government Regulation

Public-Interest View of Government Regulation   When government actions improve on market (failure) outcomes, they contribute to the public interest. Economists call this the **public-interest view** of government regulation. According to this view, government regulations act to eliminate waste, achieve efficiency, and promote the public interest, just like the invisible hand of markets usually does when markets work well.

Capture View of Government Regulation   When government actions turn out to be worse than the market (failure) outcomes, it is usually because industry interests subvert the regulatory process to their own advantage. Economists call this the **capture view** of government regulation. The regulators have been "captured" by the industry they are supposed to regulate. The regulations are set and enforced in ways that promote the self-interests of businesses in the industry instead of the public interest.

Evidence and Explanations

Which view of government regulation is correct? It depends on which regulated industry we examine. Overall, the available evidence is mixed — some supports the public-interest view, some supports the capture view. Let's look at a few examples of the evidence. And since the evidence necessary to evaluate these views as true or false is not always available or clear, it is also useful to look at the explanations behind the two views.

Evidence   Regulated natural monopolies tend to earn higher rates of return than the average rate of profits in the economy. For example, the regulated cable TV industry earns a more than 10-percent rate of return per year, almost double the economy average. The fact that the rate of return is greater than the economy average supports the capture view. On the other hand, the public-interest view gets some support as long as the 10-percent rate of return is less than what a private monopolist would earn running the industry. We don't know what the private returns would be, since there are no private cable TV businesses.

Do Crown corporations operate as efficiently as private businesses? A number of research studies have tried to answer this question by comparing two similar businesses, where one is run publicly and one privately. Comparisons have included a Canadian public railway (Canadian National — CN) with a private railway (Canadian Pacific — CP), and an Australian public domestic airline (Trans Australia Airlines — TAA) with a private domestic airline (Ansett Australia). The studies found that costs for the Crown corporations were significantly higher than for the private businesses, for example. CN's costs were 14 percent higher than CP's costs.

Another research strategy for evaluating the competing views of government regulation is to look at what has happened to regulated industries when they are deregulated. The airline and trucking industries used to be heavily regulated by Transport Canada, and long-distance phone industries (among others) were regulated by the CRTC. In the 1980s, many governments around the world removed regulations and allowed businesses to compete in the marketplace. If the public-interest view were true, we would expect prices and profits to rise after deregulation. If the capture view were true, we would expect prices and profits to fall.

public-interest view: government regulation eliminates waste, achieves efficiency, promotes public interest

capture view: government regulation benefits regulated businesses, not public interest

Evidence mixed on government regulation — some supports public-interest view, some supports capture view.

Deregulation sometimes brings unintended results. Do you think this cartoonist is for or against deregulation of the airline industry?

WE SHOULD HAVE READ THE FINE PRINT MORE CAREFULLY BEFORE PURCHASING THESE REALLY CHEAP AIRFARES!!

Mixed Results   The evidence is mixed over all industries, but for the airline, trucking, and long-distance industries prices fell and outputs increased after deregulation. This supports the capture view, suggesting that the regulated industries were operating like a cartel, restricting output and raising prices.

Much of the strongest evidence supporting the capture view comes from the Canadian agricultural sector. The National Farm Products Council (NFPC) regulates the production of eggs, chickens, and turkeys, much like a cartel, establishing production quotas for each producer and setting prices. These regulations are justified in terms of promoting "efficient, competitive Canadian agriculture," "a stable supply of poultry and eggs for Canadian consumers," and "stable farm incomes." One study estimated that the regulated prices of the NFPC transferred over $100 million a year from Canadian consumers to 4600 individual chicken producers, in much the same way that OPEC transfers money from consumers and businesses in oil-consuming countries into OPEC's pockets. See Economics Out There for a similar story from the Canadian dairy industry.

The evidence on the effectiveness of the *Canadian Competition Act* is much more uniform. Most economists agree that legislation has served the public interest well.

For many regulated industries, there simply isn't conclusive evidence that allows us to evaluate whether the public-interest view or the capture view more accurately describes the outcomes. For that reason, it is also helpful to understand the explanations behind each view, so you can at least think a bit more carefully about whatever information is available.

Explanations   There is a straightforward explanation behind the public-interest view of government regulation. Government regulators are presumed to have the public's interest in mind, and to make decisions on the basis of what is best for society.

Most economists agree the Competition Act serves the public interest well.

ECONOMICS Out There

Milking Cows or Consumers?
The Canadian dairy industry is intensely regulated by the federal government. In December 2007, it implemented a change requiring the country's cheese makers to include more whole milk in their products. Cheese-making companies argued the new rule would raise their production costs. Coincidentally, also in December 2007, Statistics Canada reported on the country's farming incomes: B.C. was home to the country's best-off dairy farmers, with "average net assets: $5.6-million; average net cash income: $155 000." Dairy farmers, the report showed, were significantly better off than the country's average farmer. Critics charge that the new cheese standard — although not nutritionally significant — would divert millions of dollars per year from consumers to "the richest farmers," in proportions based on each farmer's milk quota.

The extra costs ultimately will be recovered from the consumer in the form of a rise in cheese prices of 25 cents per kilogram. There's also the matter of politics: Quebec produces almost half the country's milk output, dominating the dairy industry and heavily influencing federal policy — inspiring the suggestion in *The Globe and Mail* that minority governments wishing to win seats in rural Quebec "must keep the province's cows as contented as they can."

Source: Neil Reynolds, "Sacred Cows: Guess Who's Getting Milked," *The Globe and Mail*, Feb. 1, 2008.

The explanation behind the capture view of government regulation is more complicated. The capture view seems to imply that government regulators collude with those in the industry being regulated, and conspire against the public interest. The actual explanation is not so sinister. In fact, it is basically a cost–benefit explanation.

According to the capture view, even if government regulators begin with the public interest in mind, the decisions they end up making are influenced by the lack of competitive incentives, vague legislative mandates, and necessary close relations between the regulators and the industry being regulated.

It's not just the regulators who are influenced. Regulations that favour industry producer interests over the public interest are passed and supported by elected politicians who can succumb to political pressure. When the Canadian Dairy Commission is considering a rise in the regulated price of cheese, think about the potential political reactions. If you are a consumer, how important is the extra 25 cents per kilogram that you will have to pay? If you even hear about the price rise, will it cause you to change your vote for your member of parliament or make a large campaign contribution to make sure your interests are represented? Not likely.

But if you are one of the average B.C. dairy farmers described in Economics Out There, with net assets of $5.6 million and average net cash income of $155 000, that 25 cents per kilogram means tens of thousands of dollars every year, and even more in terms of the value of your assets. As a producer in the industry, you have a very, very strong incentive to be politically active when regulations are discussed.

Politicians support regulations that favour producers in response to political pressures generated by the unequal distribution of costs and benefits. The tiny cost to many consumers generates only weak political pressure to lower prices. The huge benefits for the relatively few producers in the regulated industry make it worth their while to exert enormous political pressure (votes, political actions, campaign contributions) to "capture" the interests of the politicians to raise prices.

Those same unequal costs and benefits lead "captured" politicians to support regulations, like those in the dairy industry, that enforce cartel-style collusion within the industry, keep out new (and lower-cost) potential competitors, and monitor prices to avoid cheating on quotas. All these regulations are passed in the name of protecting quality or safety or promoting a "stable supply" in the public interest. But the businesses in the industry benefit the most.

Trade-offs:
Market Failure or Government Failure?

We began this chapter by identifying a key challenge facing government policymakers: How do you gain the low-cost efficiencies of economies of scale, but avoid the inefficiencies of monopoly's restricted output and higher price? The policy responses to that challenge include Crown corporations, regulated natural monopolies, and competition laws to discourage collusion and cartels.

All these government attempts to deal with market failure involve trade-offs. It's important for you as a citizen who elects the politicians who put these policies in place to understand the trade-offs. As you know only too well (I hope!), every choice, even a policy choice to leave the market alone, has an opportunity cost. What we have been trying to do here is to expose those opportunity costs so that you can make smart political choices based on the values you hold.

What are the trade-offs? First, you want to compare any choice with the next best alternative. It is not useful to compare a market failure outcome with an ideal but unattainable government policy outcome. Keep it real!

Cost–benefit explanation of capture view is that concentrated benefits to businesses make regulations worth lobbying for, while small costs to individual consumers do not generate political pressure for regulators to serve the public interest.

When comparing a market failure outcome with a government regulation outcome, weigh the costs and benefits of the actual outcomes. That means evaluating whether the government outcome is better or worse than the market failure outcome. If the public-interest view applies to that industry, the government outcome may be superior to the market failure outcome. If the capture view applies, it is more difficult to tell. It may be a case of comparing market failure with what economists call **government failure**. Government failure occurs when regulations fail to serve the public interest and instead benefit the industry being regulated.

- Sometimes the market outcome, even with monopoly power, will be better than the government regulation outcome if there is significant government failure.

- Sometimes the government outcome, especially with public-interest regulations, will be better than the market outcome if there is significant market failure.

In comparing industry outcomes, we can often make positive statements about which is better for consumers in terms of costs of production, prices, and rates of return.

But there are other aspects of the outcomes that are not so easy to compare. What is the value of public safety? How much is it worth to you to know that you will not be poisoned by the toothpaste you buy, or that nuclear power plants are operated safely, or that your doctor is well-trained and not a quack? If governments step in and regulate those industries, and the cost of the products/services goes up, is that a worthwhile trade-off? That is a normative question — it depends how you value low prices relative to the risk of occasional dangerous products (one nuclear accident sure can ruin your day) or wrong medical advice.

Economic thinking cannot make those normative choices for you. As a citizen, your views on regulation will depend on the relative values you place on many outcomes, including efficiency, low costs to consumers, public safety, and quality control. Where economic thinking can be helpful is in answering the related *positive* question, "When will government action improve market failure outcomes, and when will government action fail and actually produce an outcome that is worse than market failure?" The answer to that positive question depends on available evidence and how well (or badly) you think markets and government regulations function. Which failure is worse — market failure or government failure? No option is perfect; each has an opportunity cost. Pick your poison.

Economic thinking cannot make normative policy choices for you, but can help answer the positive question, "Will government action improve market failure outcomes, or will government action fail and produce a worse outcome than market failure?"

Refresh 9.5

1. Explain the public-interest and capture views of government regulation.

2. If a previously regulated industry is de-regulated, and we observe that prices rise and output falls, which view of government regulation does that evidence support? Explain why.

3. In Chapter 5, we observed that a conservative politician on the political right might tend to value efficiency more than equity, while a left-leaning politician might value equity more than efficiency. Which of the two views on government regulation — public-interest or capture — do you think a conservative politician is more likely to hold? Which view is a left-leaning politician more likely to hold? Explain your answers.

www.myeconlab.com

Monopoly Rules

Government Regulation, Competition, and the Law

CHAPTER SUMMARY

9.1 SIZE MATTERS: NATURAL MONOPOLY AND REGULATION

Natural monopolies create a challenge for policymakers — gain the low-cost efficiencies of economies of scale, but avoid the inefficiencies of monopoly's restricted output and higher price.

- **Economies of scale** — average total costs fall as quantity of output increases.

- **Natural monopoly** — technology allows only single seller to achieve lowest average total cost.

  - Natural monopolies are based on current technology. When technology changes, natural monopoly may change to more competitive market structure.

- The two major policies governments use to deal with challenge of natural monopoly are public ownership and regulation.

  - **Crown corporations** — publicly owned businesses in Canada. Achieve economies of scale, but lack of competition weakens incentives to reduce costs or innovate.

  - **Rate of return regulation** — set price allowing regulated monopoly to just cover average total costs and normal profits.

9.2 COOPERATE OR CHEAT? PRISONERS' DILEMMA AND CARTELS

Strategic interaction among competitors complicates business decisions, creating two smart choices — one based on trust and the other based on non-trust.

- **Game theory** — mathematical tool for understanding how players make decisions, taking into account what they expect rivals to do.

  - Gasoline pricing is a strategic decision that can be understood using game theory.

- **Prisoner's dilemma** — game with two players who must each make a strategic choice, where results depend on other player's choice.
- **Nash equilibrium** — outcome of game where each player makes own best choice given the choice of the other player.
- Two smart choices exist in a prisoners' dilemma game: one based on *non-trust* and one based on *trust*.
  - If other player cannot be trusted, smart choice is cheat/confess; all players driven to Nash equilibrium outcome where everyone cheats/confesses.
  - If other player can be trusted, smart choice is cooperate/deny; all players driven to equilibrium outcome where everyone cooperates/denies.
  - The prisoners' "dilemma" is that each player (prisoner) is motivated to cheat (confess), yet both would be better off if they could trust each other to cooperate (deny).

9.3 C-WORDS EVERYWHERE: CARTELS, COLLUSION, CHEATING, COMPETITION LAW

Cartels collude to raise prices and restrict output to increase economic profits. Cartels are unstable because members can increase their individual profits by cheating on the others.

- **Collusion** — conspiracy to cheat or deceive others.
- **Cartel** — association of suppliers formed to maintain high prices and restrict competition.
  - OPEC (Organization of Petroleum Exporting Countries) is international cartel that acts like a monopoly.
- Desirable competitive behaviour — always an active attempt to increase profits and gain market power of monopoly — is hard to distinguish from undesirable collusive behaviour.
- The *Competition Act*, introduced by government to prevent anti-competitive business behaviour, raises expected costs to business of price fixing (through prison time, fines, legal prohibition) relative to the expected benefits (profits).
  - Criminal offences (punished by prison time, fines): price fixing, bid rigging, false/misleading advertising.
  - Civil offences (punished by fines, legal prohibitions): mergers, abusing dominant market position, lessening competition. Competition Tribunal weighs costs of lessening competition against benefits of any increased efficiencies.

9.4 MASTER OR SERVANT? REGULATORY AGENCIES IN CANADA

The discipline of market competition eventually eliminates dangerous products, but in the process people may be harmed. Three major forms of government regulation in Canada address this problem.

- **Caveat emptor** ("let the buyer beware") — buyer alone responsible for checking quality of products before purchasing.
- Certain products — nuclear power, medicines, poisonous insecticides — regulated by government because average consumer not capable of knowing product's quality.

- Major forms of government regulation in Canada: government departments, government-appointed agencies/boards, professional self-governing bodies.

9.5 PICK YOUR POISON: MARKET FAILURE OR GOVERNMENT FAILURE?

There are two views of government regulation. The public-interest view suggests government actions improve market failure outcomes. The capture view suggests government actions produce government failure.

- **Public-interest view** — government regulation eliminates waste, achieves efficiency, promotes public interest.
- **Capture view** — government regulation benefits regulated businesses, not public interest.
- Evidence mixed on government regulation — some supports public-interest view, some supports capture view.
  - Most economists agree *Competition Act* serves public interest well.
- **Government failure** — regulation fails to serve public interest, instead benefits industry being regulated.
  - Sometimes market outcome, even with monopoly power, will be better than government regulation outcome if there is significant government failure.
  - Sometimes government outcome, especially with public interest regulations, will be better than market outcome if there is significant market failure.

TRUE/FALSE

Circle the correct answer.

9.1 NATURAL MONOPOLY AND REGULATION

1. Natural monopolies occur in industries with high fixed costs. **True   False**

2. Crown corporations occur only in industries where there are economies of scale. **True   False**

9.2 PRISONERS' DILEMMA AND CARTELS

Use the following information to answer questions 3 through 5.

Suppose that two characters in the TV series *Prison Break*, Michael Scofield and Alex Mahone, find themselves in a prisoners' dilemma. Each character has a single strategic choice — to confess to a murder, or to deny a murder. (*Note:* Breaking out of jail is not an option in this example!)

3. The payoffs to each choice do **not** depend on the other prisoner's choice. **True   False**

4. The Nash equilibrium outcome in this game is that both characters confess. **True   False**

5. Each character is better off confessing. **True   False**

9.3 CARTELS, COLLUSION, CHEATING, COMPETITION LAW

6. OPEC is an illegal international agreement (or cartel).　　**True**　　**False**

7. The *Competition Act* is intended to prevent anti-competitive business behaviour, such as the collusion to raise prices and restrict output in cartels.　　**True**　　**False**

8. Competition Tribunals will prevent a merger if the benefits of increased efficiencies exceed the costs of decreased competition.　　**True**　　**False**

9. *Competition Act* penalties for civil offences include prison sentences.　　**True**　　**False**

9.4 REGULATORY AGENCIES IN CANADA

10. The principle of *caveat emptor* means that government is responsible for monitoring the quality of products/services.　　**True**　　**False**

11. The discipline of market competition ensures that, *eventually,* consumers will stop buying from businesses that produce harmful products.　　**True**　　**False**

12. The additional costs of regulation always exceed the additional benefits of regulation.　　**True**　　**False**

9.5 MARKET FAILURE AND GOVERNMENT FAILURE

13. If the public-interest view is true, we would expect prices and profits to rise after deregulation. If the capture view is true, we would expect prices and profits to fall.　　**True**　　**False**

14. For the airline and trucking industries, prices fell and outputs increased after deregulation. This supports the public-interest view.　　**True**　　**False**

15. Evidence supporting the public-interest view of government regulation would show that profit rates in regulated industries are higher than profit rates in non-regulated industries.　　**True**　　**False**

MULTIPLE CHOICE

Circle the correct answer.

9.1 NATURAL MONOPOLY AND REGULATION

1. Crown corporations exist in all the following industries except
   A) diamonds.
   B) electricity.
   C) water.
   D) gas.

2. A natural monopoly is likely to have
   A) low fixed cost and low marginal cost.
   B) low fixed cost and high marginal cost.
   C) high fixed cost and low marginal cost.
   D) high fixed cost and high marginal cost.

3. Which of the following is *least* likely to be a natural monopoly?
   A) Electric utility
   B) Taxi service
   C) Water and sewer service
   D) Cable TV service

4. The challenge facing government policymakers is
   A) who will be the next *Canadian Idol*.
   B) how to gain the low-cost efficiencies of economies of scale, but avoid the inefficiencies of monopoly's restricted output and rise in price.
   C) how to avoid the low-cost efficiencies of economies of scale, but gain the inefficiencies of monopoly's increased output and lower price.
   D) how to gain the low-cost efficiencies of economies of scale, but avoid the inefficiencies of monopoly's increased output and lower price.

9.2 PRISONERS' DILEMMA AND CARTELS

5. John Nash, who extended the idea of game theory, was the subject of what Academy Award–winning movie?
   A) *Beauty and the Beast*
   B) *A Beautiful Economist*
   C) *A Beautiful Mind*
   D) *A Beautiful Body*

6. In the prisoners' dilemma with Bonnie and Clyde, each prisoner would be best off if
   A) both prisoners confess.
   B) both prisoners deny.
   C) Bonnie denies and Clyde confesses.
   D) Clyde denies and Bonnie confesses.

9.3 CARTELS, COLLUSION, CHEATING, COMPETITION LAW

7. Gas prices fluctuate wildly on long weekends because of
   A) changes in the cost of oil used to produce gasoline.
   B) changes in the cost of gasoline.
   C) the cycle of trust and non-trust among gasoline station owners.
   D) the cycle of trust and non-trust between parents and teenagers.

8. According to game theory,

   A) businesses within cartels are tempted to cheat.

   B) businesses within cartels have incentives to cooperate.

   C) prison penalties help governments uncover secret cartels.

   D) all of the above are true.

9. Anti-combines (or anti-trust) laws attempt to

   A) support prices.

   B) establish Crown corporations.

   C) prevent monopoly practices.

   D) regulate monopolies.

10. Criminal offences in the *Competition Act* include:

    A) price fixing.

    B) bid rigging.

    C) false advertising.

    D) all of the above.

9.4 REGULATORY AGENCIES IN CANADA

11. Which of the following is *not* a federal regulatory agency?

    A) Atomic Energy Control Board

    B) Canadian Radio-television and Telecommunications Commission

    C) Petro-Canada

    D) Canadian Transport Commission

12. The Canadian Radio-television and Telecommunications Commission (CRTC) is an example of regulation through

    A) public ownership.

    B) government departments.

    C) government-appointed agencies.

    D) self-governing bodies.

9.5 MARKET FAILURE AND GOVERNMENT FAILURE

13. Which of the following is an example of a *government failure*?

    A) Deregulation in the airline industry has resulted in lower prices and has changed the price–quality mix in a pro-consumer way.

    B) Previous regulations in the airline industry led airlines to provide more luxuries than consumers would choose to pay for.

    C) Routes that airlines were once required to service are no longer being serviced under deregulation because they are unprofitable.

    D) Competition in the telecommunications sector has moved prices closer to marginal cost.

14. Which of the following statements about government regulation is/are true?

   A) The public-interest view suggests government actions improve market failure outcomes.

   B) The capture view suggests government actions produce government failure.

   C) Government failure can be worse than market failure because the regulators act on behalf of the regulated industry instead of consumers.

   D) All of the above.

15. Economic thinking can be helpful in answering the following question(s):

   A) "When will government action improve market failure outcomes?"

   B) "When will government action fail?"

   C) "When will government action produce an outcome that is worse than market failure?"

   D) All of the above.

SHORT ANSWER

Write a short answer to each question. Your answer may be in point form.

1. We are often told that, in business, size matters.

   A) Explain why size matters in the context of economies of scale.

   B) When is it efficient to have one seller (a monopoly)?

2. Consider the strategic game that your local gas station owners play.

   A) Explain why gas station owners cooperate.

   B) Explain why collusion hurts consumers.

   C) Explain why collusion rarely lasts.

   D) Try to summarize the strategic game and outcome in one sentence using as many c-words as you can.

3. Reconsider the *Prison Break* example used for questions 3 to 5 in the True/False section, where two characters find themselves in a prisoners' dilemma.

   A) What would be the outcome if the two characters are brothers who trust each other? Why?

   B) What would be the outcome if the two characters don't trust each other? Why?

   C) What would be the outcome if the two characters don't know whether to trust each other? Why?

4. Jack and Jill, who are high school sweethearts, are going away to college in different cities. Jack and Jill both have two options: they can cheat (on one another) or be faithful.

Values (or levels of happiness) can be assigned to these strategic choices. Suppose that both of them rank the outcomes of the strategic choices as follows:

- 1st best outcome: they cheat but their partner is faithful
- 2nd best outcome: both are faithful
- 3rd best outcome: both cheat
- 4th best outcome: they are faithful but their partner cheats

Since it makes sense to assign higher values to outcomes that give greater happiness, assume that Jill receives:

- 4 happy-points if she cheats but Jack is faithful
- 3 happy-points if she is faithful and Jack is faithful
- 2 happy-points if she cheats and Jack cheats
- 1 happy-point if she is faithful but Jack cheats

A) Assuming that Jack assigns the same units of happiness to each strategic outcome as Jill does, construct a table that is similar to Figure 9.1.

B) Suppose that Jill gets some inside information and finds out Jack cannot be trusted. What strategic choice would give her more happiness: cheating or being faithful? Why?

C) Suppose Jill gets some inside information and finds out Jack *can* be trusted. What strategic choice would give her more happiness: cheating or being faithful? Why?

D) Explain what the Nash equilibrium outcome is in this game.

E) Explain how this game and outcome is similar to two businesses deciding whether to cheat or cooperate on a collusive agreement.

5. Retail alcohol stores were privatized in Alberta in 1993. Privatization led to an average 8.5-percent rise in the price of all alcohol from October 1993 to January 1996. A rise in retail prices over the short term is an effect of privatization that has also been found in other jurisdictions. But despite higher average prices, which reduce consumption, all else being equal, evidence from Canada and elsewhere shows that privatization typically results in an increase in alcohol consumption (per person).

A) Why might competitive forces lead to higher rates of alcohol consumption?

B) In Alberta, there is evidence that privatization led to less enforcement of laws preventing underage purchases. And, within Canada, Alberta continues to have some of the highest rates of alcohol-related problems, such as drunk driving. Why might the profit motive lead to market failure?

6. In Ontario, where tuition fees in professional programs were deregulated in 1998, tuition fees rose dramatically in three professional programs (medicine, dentistry, and law) from 1998 to 2002. In contrast, Quebec and British Columbia largely maintained their policy of regulating fees, and tuition fees *fell* among these programs. Does this support the public-interest view or the capture view? Explain.

7. The telecommunications regulatory body in Canada — the Canadian Radio-television and Telecommunications Commission (CRTC) — has supported the move toward greater competition but retains control over telecom prices.

    A) Until the late 1990s, prices of telecommunication services were set by the CRTC at levels that covered total costs. Explain why linking prices with costs would have reduced supplier incentives to develop cost-saving technology.

    B) The telecommunications industry experienced a slow rate of entry of new competitors into local residential service. Some argue that if prices were allowed to rise, more competitors would enter. Explain why price regulation holds back the progress toward a more competitive industry.

8. In April 2008, the president and CEO of Québecor told the Canadian Radio-television and Telecommunications Commission that it's "time to deregulate the broadcasting system."

    A) Explain the reason for maintaining a natural monopoly in the cable TV industry, using the economies of scale argument.

    B) Québecor's president and CEO favours deregulating advertising rules: "If there is too much advertising, [a distributor or broadcaster] would lose its viewership." With deregulation, what do you think would happen to the amount of advertising, assuming that viewers' needs are met?

9. In 1995, the Government of Ontario commissioned the Macdonald Committee to study the Ontario electricity market. The Committee recommended eliminating Ontario Hydro (a government-owned monopoly) and opening the electricity market to competition. The Ontario government listened, and opened electricity to competition in May 2002.

    A) Politicians promised that electricity reform would lower prices immediately. If the generation of electricity is not a natural monopoly, would competitive forces likely lower prices? Why or why not?

    B) Would the public-interest view or the capture view support the politician's position above? Why or why not?

    C) When the market opened in May, wholesale prices averaged 3.01 cents per kilowatt hour. By July, prices had more than doubled, due to an especially hot summer, a reduction in domestic generating capacity, and an increasing reliance on a limited import capacity. The Ontario government reacted in December 2002 by capping retail prices at 4.3 cents per kilowatt hour, with transmissions and distribution rates being frozen at their existing levels. Some have argued that the regulated prices were below the marginal opportunity cost of producing electricity. If this is the case, how might private electricity suppliers respond to the price freeze?

10. In 2008, Canada Post was reviewed to determine whether postal service should be deregulated and opened to competition. Canada Post had the exclusive right to deliver letters coast to coast. The price of a stamp in Dease Lake, B.C., was exactly the same as in Glace Bay, Nova Scotia.

A) If postal service were deregulated, why would a private business charge different prices in different regions of the country? What regions would likely experience a price increase?

B) Some international evidence suggests that deregulation would not lead to cheaper rates or better service. In Sweden, deregulation almost immediately led to the doubling of the price of a stamp. Would this evidence support the public-interest view or the capture view of government regulation?

Chapter 10

Acid Rain on Others' Parades

Externalities, Carbon Taxes, Free Riders, and Public Goods

LEARNING OBJECTIVES

After reading this chapter, you should be able to:

10.1 Describe how externalities make smart private choices different from smart social choices.

10.2 Explain the rule for coordinating private choices that cause negative externalities, with smart social choices.

10.3 Identify how government policies can internalize externalities for polluters to create smart social choices.

10.4 Explain how positive externalities create the free-rider problem and cause markets to fail.

10.5 Identify how government subsidies can internalize positive externalities to create smart social choices.

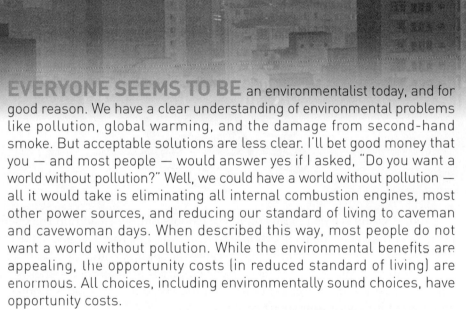

EVERYONE SEEMS TO BE an environmentalist today, and for good reason. We have a clear understanding of environmental problems like pollution, global warming, and the damage from second-hand smoke. But acceptable solutions are less clear. I'll bet good money that you — and most people — would answer yes if I asked, "Do you want a world without pollution?" Well, we could have a world without pollution — all it would take is eliminating all internal combustion engines, most other power sources, and reducing our standard of living to caveman and cavewoman days. When described this way, most people do not want a world without pollution. While the environmental benefits are appealing, the opportunity costs (in reduced standard of living) are enormous. All choices, including environmentally sound choices, have opportunity costs.

So how do we, individually and collectively, make smart choices in deciding how much pollution to tolerate? Economists have a concept called *externalities* — costs or benefits affecting people external to the original activity — that brings clarity to making smart choices about pollution. When your cigarette smoke causes your non-smoking housemate to develop cancer in 20 years, the cost of treating that cancer is a *negative externality* you don't consider in your decision to smoke. *Positive externalities* exist when others benefit from your actions without paying. For example, if most people pay for flu shots, even those who don't get shots benefit from the reduced likelihood of catching the flu. When externalities exist markets fail, producing too much of things we don't want (like pollution, traffic jams, and second-hand smoke) and too little of things we do want (like vaccinations, education, and good public transit). In this chapter, you will learn how to clear the confusion and, as a voter, identify the costs and benefits of smart policy choices for reducing pollution and other externality-based market failures.

10.1 Handcuffing the Invisible Hand: Market Failure with Externalities

Describe how externalities make smart private choices different from smart social choices.

Chapter 4 was about how market-clearing prices coordinate the smart choices of consumers and of businesses. Here's the last sentence of the chapter to refresh your memory: "Price signals in markets create incentives so that while each person acts only in her own self-interest, the result (coordinated through Adam Smith's invisible hand of competition) is the miracle of continuous, ever-changing production of the products/services we want."

But if markets are so good at producing the "goods" (products/services) we want, why does market coordination of economic activity also produce "bads" like pollution and traffic jams? The answer, in a word, is externalities, which drive a wedge between smart choices for individuals and smart choices for society as a whole.

How Much Does That Honda Civic Really Cost?

After years of riding the bus, even with the comfort of an iPod to block out others' mind-numbing cell phone conversations, you are ready to buy a car. You've had your eye on a blue Honda Civic, and are crunching the numbers to see if you can afford it. Your private additional costs include monthly payments, insurance, gas, repairs, and maybe parking. If you can afford it, and if the additional benefits of driving versus taking transit make you willing to pay those costs, then buying the car is a smart choice for you. Remember the Three Keys to Smart Choices:

Your decision is based mostly on Key 1: Choose only when additional benefits are greater than additional *opportunity costs*. The money you pay (above the cost of transit) represents *opportunity costs* because that money could have been spent on other things. And Key 2 enters with the emphasis on *additional* benefits and costs. (The cost of the driver's education course you took years ago is a *sunk cost* and doesn't influence your smart choice.)

There are also social costs you don't have to consider when choosing your Honda Civic. The exhaust from your driving will contribute to air pollution, to global warming, and — depending on your choice of muffler or sound system — to noise pollution that might drive your neighbours crazy. You are also adding one more car to the roads, which will (marginally) worsen traffic jams and increase other drivers' commute time. But while your choice creates these real costs to others and to society as a whole, *you don't have to pay them.*

negative externalities (external costs): costs to society from your private choice that affect others, but that you do not pay

Negative Externalities Economists call these additional social costs **negative externalities**, or **external costs**. They are costs to society from your private choice that affect others, but that you do not pay. External costs affect people *external to* the original activity — others not involved in the exchange between you and the Honda dealer.

This brings us to Key 3 for smart choices (which we haven't had to discuss much, except for implicit costs in Chapter 6), which emphasizes the word *all*: Be sure to count *all* additional benefits and additional opportunity costs, including *implicit costs* and *externalities*. When there are negative externalities, opportunity costs include both private costs and external costs. So, social costs are greater than private costs.

Social Costs = Private (Opportunity) Costs + External (Opportunity) Costs

◀

Often unintended costs attach to events. Producing much-needed energy, living in a car-oriented society, or communicating with friends create negative externalities. Should those costs be built into the products/services we use?

Cell phone conversations you are trying to avoid overhearing on the bus are another example of a negative externality. The talker is simply having a "private" conversation with the person on the other end of the line, and pays her cell provider in exchange for the call. While she is not out to irritate you, an unintended consequence of that private conversation is what you experience as "noise pollution," or an external cost. One final negative externality example is of an electrical utility using a coal-burning generator that emits sulphur dioxide as a byproduct. The utility does not have to pay for the external costs from the damage caused by the resulting global warming and acid rain. Can you see why economists also refer to negative externalities as "spillover effects"?

The Invisible Hand Fails
Based only on your private costs, buying the Honda may be a smart choice for you. But when we calculate in the external costs, it may not be a smart choice for society as a whole. Say the local electrical utility decides to produce a thousand kilowatt hours using coal instead of hydro power. That may be a smart, profit-maximizing private business choice, but it's not a smart choice from a social or environmental point of view. When there are negative externalities, smart private choices (using Keys 1 and 2) are different from smart social choices (Keys 1, 2, and 3). Because they don't pay the external costs, private individuals or businesses do not have an incentive to make choices that are good for society as a whole. The invisible hand fails to coordinate individual choices to balance social benefits with social costs.

If somehow we could all be forced to pay the external costs as well as the usual private costs of our choices, then we would buy fewer cars, have fewer public cell phone conversations, and produce less coal-generated electricity. But because we generally do *not* pay external costs, consumers buy, and businesses produce, too many products/services with negative externalities.

Was It Good Just for You?

Externalities come in two flavours — negative and positive. While negative externalities involve external costs, *positive* externalities involve external *benefits*. Key 3 says to be sure to count *all* additional benefits as well as additional opportunity costs.

Think about your decision to go to college or university. You're here, so clearly you decided the additional benefits from school were greater than the additional opportunity costs. The opportunity costs include money spent on tuition and books — money that could have been spent on other things. Forgone income from working fewer hours than if you were not in school is also an opportunity cost for your decision. Those are all private costs to you — there are no external costs.

The positive externality happens on the *benefits* side. Your additional private benefits include the significantly increased lifetime income you will earn compared to high school graduates, and the satisfaction from acquiring more knowledge. You obviously estimated that those additional private benefits to you were greater than your additional opportunity costs of attending school.

But there are also social benefits you did *not* consider when making the choice to go to school. Because you have acquired skills in school, employers will not have to spend as much money and time training you. Educated citizens, who can make informed political choices and participate in public debate and election campaigns, also improve the functioning of a democracy, to the benefit of all citizens. And evidence shows that citizens with higher levels of education are less likely to commit crimes or depend on social assistance payments, saving money for government.

Economists call these additional social benefits **positive externalities**, or **external benefits**. They are benefits to society from your private choice that affect others, but that others do not pay (you) for. External benefits go to people *external to* the original activity — others not involved in the exchange between you and your school.

Look at Key 3 again. This time, focus on the benefits side instead of the costs side. Be sure to count *all* additional benefits and additional opportunity costs. When there are positive externalities, benefits include both private benefits and external benefits. So, social benefits are greater than private benefits.

Social Benefits = Private Benefits + External Benefits

Public transit is another example of a service with positive externalities. If you decide against the Honda Civic and continue to take public transit, your private benefits include the ability to get around inexpensively, without all the expenses of owning a car. But by keeping one more car *off* the roads, you unintentionally reduce pollution for everyone, (marginally) reduce traffic jams, and decrease other drivers' commute time.

Free-Riders   Based only on your private benefits and costs, choosing school over work may be a smart choice for you. But many workers out there would also switch their choices to school *if only they were paid for the external benefits of that choice*. Similarly, taking public transit may be a smart choice for you. But many drivers out there would also switch to public transit *if only they were paid for the external benefits of that choice*. When there are positive externalities, smart private choices (using Keys 1 and 2) are different from smart social choices (Keys 1, 2, and 3). Because they don't get paid for the external benefits of their choices to others, private individuals or businesses do not have the proper incentive to make choices that are best for society as a whole. External benefits allow others to "free ride" on our private choices.

If there were some way to force the free-riders to pay students and transit riders for the benefits the free-riders receive (which is what taxes to subsidize public education do — more in Section 10.5), then there would be more education and more public transit. But because free-riders have no incentive to pay us for the external benefits our choices produce, consumers buy, and businesses produce, too few products/services with positive externalities. Once again the invisible hand fails to coordinate individual choices to balance social benefits with social costs.

No Ownership, No Incentives, No Coordinated Choices

What is it about externalities, both negative and positive, that causes such problems for markets and for the invisible hand? Here's the answer: *lack of clear property rights*. Property rights — government's legal protection of property and enforcement of contracts (again from Chapter 4) — are part of the necessary "rules of the game" for markets to work. Without property rights, you have no incentive to produce for exchange because customers could walk away with your work for free by simply taking it. Property rights give us the incentive to make smart choices because we have to pay for costs and because we are legally entitled to receive rewards for producing products/services others value.

For both negative and positive externalities, no clear property rights exist. Who has rights to the atmosphere, where pollution is dumped and global warming occurs? Individuals and businesses own legal title to pieces of land, but that doesn't prevent others from pumping pollution into the air above, which then spills over into all of the atmosphere. There is no easy way to charge for the costs imposed on others by the pollution. The flip side of no property rights is that when you *reduce* pollution by taking public transit instead of driving, you don't get credit for the benefits you provide to others. Without property rights, there is no way for you to claim title to the cleaner air you have helped create, so there is no way to be paid for your contribution to a greener planet.

Whether as an individual or a business, if you don't pay a cost or receive a payment because no property rights exist, you don't consider those costs or payments in your decision. External costs are someone else's problem, and external benefits are someone else's windfall. So you, quite reasonably, ignore them all.

As a result, you do more activities that generate external costs than if you had to pay those costs. If you had to pay for the costs of pollution and global warming every time you turned the key on your car, you would probably drive less since it would be more expensive. Also as a result of no clear property rights, you do fewer activities that generate external benefits than if you were paid for those benefits. If everyone received payment for reducing pollution every time they took transit, they would take more transit rides.

Because free-riders do not have to pay for external benefits, consumers buy, and businesses produce, too few products/services with positive externalities.

Externalities occur when no clear property rights exist.

When externalities exist, prices don't accurately reflect all social costs and benefits, preventing markets from coordinating private smart choices with social smart choices.

Wrong Prices   Without clear ownership and legally enforceable property rights, there's no payment of costs or collection of revenues. Those missing costs and revenues affect prices, which are the incentives we all respond to in making smart choices. When there are negative externalities, prices are too low because of missing costs. When there are positive externalities, prices are too high because of missing benefits and revenues.

The invisible hand helps markets coordinate private smart choices to be smart choices for society as a whole, *when prices adjust to reflect all costs and all benefits.* Without ownership and property rights, externalities arise, and prices don't accurately reflect all social costs and benefits. The invisible hand is handcuffed.

Refresh

10.1

www.myeconlab.com

1.   What is a negative externality? A positive externality?

2.   Talking in large lecture halls is a problem, both for instructors who can't concentrate and attentive students who can't hear. Can you explain this problem in terms of externalities? Why is this problem hard to solve?

3.   Many condominiums have strict rules about the colour of window coverings. Why do these rules arise? Is it fair to restrict the choices of property owners?

10.2   Why Radical Environmentalists Dislike Economists: Negative Externalities and Efficient Pollution

Explain the rule for coordinating private choices that cause negative externalities, with smart social choices.

Economists — including me — argue that a smart society should choose an "efficient" amount of pollution. This position appalls many environmentalists. The environmentalists' principled position is that *any* amount of pollution is too much — zero pollution is the goal.

The Price (Opportunity Cost) of Pollution

Here's a good illustration of the economist's argument. Suppose I offered you $1 to drink a tall glass consisting of rats that had been liquefied in a blender. Would

you? I'm guessing not. But what if you were a contestant on a television show like *Fear Factor*, where contestants are offered large sums of money to do unimaginably horrible and frightening tasks? Suppose you are offered $1 million? People on those shows say yes to offers like this all the time. A choice about an action that in principle is disgusting or wrong turns out to depend on the price.

So, while a world with zero pollution sounds good, most of us are unwilling to do what it takes to achieve it because the associated standard of living would be unacceptably low.

▶ Money becomes an incentive for people to do things they would never normally do. How much money would it take to get you to drink a tall glass of disgusting "stuff"?

Trade-offs Between Pollution and Living Standards   Once we admit our willingness to live with some pollution, the problem becomes the acceptable trade-off between our standard of living (good) and the associated pollution (bad) that is created unintentionally as a negative externality. Where do we draw the line — like between $1 and $1 million? How low a standard of living are we willing to "pay" in order to reduce pollution? How much do you need to be paid to drink the rats?

While we want to eliminate pollution, the actions required to do so have a cost. As usual, opportunity cost is the key. Small reductions in pollution are relatively inexpensive — eliminating lead from gasoline and paint, conserving energy to reduce output from coal-fired electrical plants, and so on. But achieving zero pollution would mean eliminating all cars and airplanes, outlawing all power except solar and hydroelectric power, and shutting down most factories. Pollution and global warming are unintentional byproducts of the benefits we receive from driving or flying, from enjoying the comfort of air conditioning in summer and heat in winter, and from enjoying products produced in factories. The opportunity cost of eliminating all pollution is enormous. As we eliminate more and more pollution, there comes a point when the additional (opportunity) costs become greater than the additional benefits from further pollution reductions.

Therefore, economists conclude, some level of pollution is "efficient" — which means there is a smart choice that balances the benefits of a higher standard of living against the costs of the associated levels of pollution. A simple rule that adds in the cost of negative externalities to market prices based on demand and supply allows us to find efficient combinations of quantities, pollution, and prices. Let's see how to smartly draw the line for acceptable levels of pollution — the equivalent of the line between the offers of $1 and $1 million — and hopefully convince all environmentalists not to turn away in disgust from the economists. (Incidentally, David Suzuki agrees with the economist's position — see Economics Out There on page 252.).

As we reduce pollution, "efficient pollution" balances additional environmental benefits with additional opportunity costs of reduced living standards.

ECONOMICS Out There

A Useful Poison?

DDT is an effective, potent pesticide that persists in the environment — it accumulates in animals that eat insects and is now banned in many countries, including Canada. So should DDT be banned everywhere, just like the goal of zero pollution? Without more information, we tend to think, yes, it should be banned. But all choices have opportunity costs.

DDT is by far the most effective tool in fighting malaria because it kills the mosquitoes that spread the disease. In the 1950s and 1960s, widespread use of DDT all but eliminated malaria in most countries, and saved an estimated 500 million lives by 1970.

Since then, DDT has been banned in many countries, and malaria outbreaks have increased significantly. In Mozambique, malaria infection

rates are 20 to 40 times higher than in neighbouring Swaziland, which never stopped using DDT. The World Health Organization estimates that roughly 500 million people currently suffer from malaria, most in sub-Saharan Africa. About 2 million die per year.

So, should DDT be banned everywhere?

Never make a choice, including environmentally friendly choices, without considering opportunity costs.

Source: Based on "A Useful Poison," *The Economist*, December 14, 2000.

Efficient Combinations of Output and Pollution

The rule for finding an efficient combination of output and pollution is a simple refinement of Key 1 to take into account all costs, including negative externalities. For any product/service (output) whose production also generates a negative externality, the rule for smart choices is as follows:

Choose the Quantity of Output Where

Marginal Social Cost = Marginal Social Benefit

$(MSC) = (MSB)$

marginal social cost: marginal private cost plus marginal external cost

We need to explain the two new concepts in the rule — **marginal social cost** and **marginal social benefit** — which are related to the definitions of *social cost* and *social benefit* in Section 10.1. Let's start with marginal social cost.

When there are negative externalities, social costs are greater than private costs. When we focus on *additional* costs and benefits (Key 2), that relationship is

| Marginal Social Cost (MSC) | = | Marginal Private Cost Directly Paid by Producers (MPC) | + | Marginal External Cost Imposed on Others |

Marginal external cost = price of preventing or cleaning up damage to others external to original activity.

Let's look at the example of a pulp mill. There are opportunity costs the mill pays directly, for labour, wood, power, and so on. (These costs include normal profits for the use of the owner's time and money.) These privately paid costs are the only ones the business uses in deciding on prices to charge and quantities to produce. But the mill's smokestacks also emit sulphur dioxide — causing acid rain and contributing to global warming. If we could put a price, per tonne of pulp produced, on the cost of preventing or cleaning up the damage from the pollution, that would be the marginal external cost. The marginal social cost (MSC) is the sum of the marginal private cost and the marginal external cost.

When there are positive externalities (more in Section 10.4), social benefits are greater than private benefits.

marginal social benefit: marginal private benefit plus marginal external benefit

| Marginal Social Benefit (MSB) | = | Marginal Private Benefit Directly Received by Consumers (MPB) | + | Marginal External Benefit Enjoyed by Others |

Your post-secondary education provides you with private benefits like an increased lifetime income. But there are also external benefits, like reduced training costs for employers and reduced government expenditures on crime fighting and social assistance. Section 10.4 looks more closely at marginal social benefit. But the pulp mill in our example here does *not* produce positive externalities, so the marginal social benefit is the same as the marginal private benefit. It is the value of the pulp bought and sold in markets.

Figure 10.1 provides some hypothetical numbers for the daily output of all the mills producing for the pulp market. The table is related to Figure 4.1 (reprinted in the margin), which shows market demand and market supply data, but with a few key differences.

Figure 4.1	Market Demand and Supply for Piercings	
Price	Quantity Demanded	Quantity Supplied
$ 20	1200	200
$ 40	900	400
$ 60	600	600
$ 80	300	800
$100	0	1000

Let's look at the six columns of Figure 10.1. The left three columns show market demand, and the right three columns show market supply. The first column on both the demand and supply sides is *Output*, showing the different quantities of pulp the businesses might choose to produce. The rule focuses on making a smart choice about the *quantity to produce and the associated levels of pollution*. That's why the first column on both the demand and supply sides is quantity, instead of price (as in Figure 4.1).

Figure 10.1 Pulp Market: Demand, Supply, and Externalities

DEMAND			SUPPLY		
Output (tonnes/day)	Marginal Private Benefit (MPB)	Marginal Social Benefit (MSB)	Output (tonnes/day)	Marginal Private Cost (MPC)	Marginal Social Cost (MSC)
1	$140	$140	1	$50	$80
2	$120	$120	2	$60	$90
3	$100	$100	3	$70	$100
4	$80	$80	4	$80	$110
5	$60	$60	5	$90	$120

Demand   The second column, *Marginal Private Benefit*, shows the maximum price consumers or buyers are willing to pay for each quantity of pulp. Notice that the private benefit of the first tonne of pulp (output = 1) is $140, but that marginal benefit diminishes for each successive tonne; $120 for the 2nd tonne, $100 for the 3rd tonne, and so on. (Remember your willingness to pay for the first Gatorade after a workout, compared to a second or third bottle?)

If you think of column 2 as *the price buyers are willing to pay* for the different quantities of pulp in column 1, then you can see (I hope!) the law of demand in the pattern of numbers. Start at the top. When the price is $140 per tonne, quantity demanded is only 1 tonne. As the price falls to $120, $100, down to $60, the quantity demanded increases to 2, 3, up to 5 tonnes of pulp. As a product becomes cheaper, we buy more of it.

The 3rd column, *Marginal Social Benefit*, is the same as *Marginal Private Benefit* in column 2 because there are no positive externalities.

Supply   Column 4 repeats the quantities of output choices from column 1. Column 5, *Marginal Private Cost*, shows the costs the pulp mills actually pay for additional labour, wood, power, and other inputs for each additional tonne of pulp. Notice the pattern of increasing marginal cost as output increases, from $50 for the 1st tonne, to $60 for the 2nd tonne, up to $90 for the 5th tonne. (Remember Paola's increasing marginal costs in Chapter 3 as she increased output of piercings?) Marginal private costs represent the minimum price the business needs to receive to be willing to supply that additional quantity — price must cover all marginal opportunity costs of production. If you think of column 5 as *the minimum price businesses are willing to accept*, you can see the law of supply in the pattern of numbers. As the price rises, the quantity supplied increases.

Pulp mill has no external benefits, so marginal social benefit = marginal private benefit. All action happens on marginal social cost side.

Marginal External Cost/Negative Externality/Marginal Social Cost

So far, the pattern of numbers for demand and supply is similar to Chapter 4, where the invisible hand works well. The big difference is in the last column, *Marginal Social Cost.* Let's say each tonne of pulp generates $30 of external costs — the costs of either preventing or cleaning up the damage from the pollution associated with that tonne of pulp. The pulp mills do not pay for these external costs, which is why they do not enter into the supply decisions of the previous columns. But these are costs to society as a whole that must be added to the marginal private costs to calculate marginal social cost. Notice that the numbers in the last column are equal to the numbers in the *Marginal Private Cost* column, plus $30.

Putting It All Together   Figure 10.1 shows us what the market outcome will be, and what the smart social choice should be.

Because consumers and businesses do not pay external costs, and there are no external benefits, externalities do not enter into anyone's private decisions. So the only columns that determine the market output are marginal private benefit (market demand) and marginal private cost (market supply).

Markets coordinate choices of consumers and businesses through prices so that quantity demanded and quantity supplied are equal. Looking only at the three columns in Figure 10.1 of *Output, Marginal Private Benefit,* and *Marginal Private Cost,* you can see (highlighted in red) that the market-clearing price of a tonne of pulp is $80, and at that price businesses will supply, and consumers will buy, a quantity of 4 tonnes per day.

In Figure 4.1, we instead found the market-clearing price, or equilibrium price, by seeing where the quantity demanded and quantity supplied were equal. Here, we are finding the market-clearing quantity, where the price buyers are willing to pay and the price sellers need to receive are equal. When those two prices are equal we have also found the market-clearing price, or equilibrium price, in the pulp market.

What about the smart choice for society, which should also take into account external costs? The rule says choose the quantity of output where marginal social benefit equals marginal social cost. That means in Figure 10.1, look only at the three columns of *Output, Marginal Social Benefit,* and *Marginal Social Cost.* The smart output (highlighted in green) is 3 tonnes per day, where marginal social benefit and marginal social cost are both equal to $100.

Understanding the Smart Social Choice   To understand why this rule gives us a smart choice of quantity of output (and associated level of pollution), look at the choice for pulp, one tonne at a time. Reading across the row for Output = 1, you see that the first tonne has a marginal social benefit of $140 and a marginal social cost of $80 (including the external cost). Since the additional benefits are greater than the additional costs, it's a smart choice (Key 1). Tonne 2 has a marginal social benefit of $120 and a marginal social cost of $90 — still a smart choice. For tonne 3, the marginal social benefit and cost are equal to $100, so society at least breaks even. But to increase output to tonne 4, marginal social benefit of $80 is less than marginal social cost of $110. Tonne 5 is even worse, with marginal social benefit of $60 and marginal social cost of $120. Society should draw the line at 3 tonnes of pulp, accepting the associated "efficient" amount of pollution.

For market-clearing quantity and price in Figure 10.1 (red), look at columns Output, Marginal Private Benefit, Marginal Private Cost.

For smart social choice for quantity and price in Figure 10.1 (green), look at columns Output, Marginal Social Benefit, Marginal Social Cost.

Compared to the market outcome, the smart choice for society means producing less of a product with a negative externality (3 tonnes of pulp instead of the market's 4 tonnes) and charging a higher price ($100 per tonne instead of $80 per tonne). These numbers illustrate the general result that *markets tend to overproduce products/services that have negative externalities and the price charged is too low* (because it does not incorporate the external costs).

Markets overproduce products/services with negative externalities; price is too low because does not incorporate external costs.

Refresh 10.2

1. What is the rule for finding efficient combinations of output and pollution?

2. If the marginal external cost of pollution in Figure 10.1 were $60 per tonne instead of $30 per tonne, what would be the smart choice for society of pulp output? What would be the smart price of a tonne of pulp?

3. What position on DDT do you support (see story from Economics Out There, page 245)? What additional information do you need before you decide?

www.myeconlab.com

10.3 Liberating the Invisible Hand: Policies to Internalize the Externality

When there are negative externalities, markets fail. The market prices we pay do not reflect the external costs associated with producing products/services we desire. Smart choices for individual consumers and businesses are not the same as smart choices for society as a whole.

Because there are no clear property rights to the environment, individuals and businesses do not have to pay for the external costs their choices create. In fact, businesses will usually save money and improve profits by ignoring external costs like pollution, soil contamination, and global warming, which means businesses actually have *incentives to take actions that make society worse off* instead of, like Smith's invisible hand, those that make society better off. Businesses that can produce at lower cost because they ignore external costs will be rewarded with more sales to price-conscious consumers. And without having to pay for your personal contribution to global warming, individuals like you and I are more likely to buy Honda Civics instead of choosing to take transit.

When markets work well, our self-interest leads us to make smart choices that turn out also to be good for everyone else, and markets produce the products/services we desire at lowest possible cost. With negative externalities, markets fail and self-interest leads to pollution and global warming.

What can be done to restore the power of the invisible hand?

Identify how government policies can internalize externalities for polluters to create smart social choices.

Without property rights to the environment, businesses have incentives to save money and improve profits by ignoring external costs like pollution and global warming.

Government Support for the Invisible Hand

Just as government enforcement of private property and contracts are necessary rules of the game for markets to function at all, government has a crucial role to play in remedying the market failures caused by externalities.

Roads are a commonly shared space, just like the environment. If there were no traffic laws — no rules of the (road) game — self-interested individual drivers would not have to stop at intersections, signal turns, or obey speed limits. Traffic chaos would prevail as each driver tried to get where she was going without any concern for other drivers. Government traffic laws improve the functioning of roadways to the benefit of all drivers.

Government can also improve the functioning of the environment: It can effectively create social property rights by making it illegal to pollute the atmosphere or waterways. Once polluting becomes illegal, governments can protect the environment by "punishing" those who pollute. The punishment might be criminal penalties (jail time) or, more commonly, financial penalties (fines or taxes).

The key principle for any government policy is to set the environmental rules of the game in a way that aligns smart private choices with smart social choices. Smart government policies and taxes will lead self-interested individuals and businesses to choose the outcomes that are also best for society as a whole. For any product/service with negative externalities, that means implementing policies that get everyone to voluntarily choose the quantity of output where marginal social benefit equals marginal social cost.

Carbon Taxes and Cap-and-Trade System for Emissions

Two important environmental polices that induce individuals and businesses to choose the quantities of outputs (and associated levels of pollution) that are best for society are

- carbon taxes, and
- cap-and-trade system for emissions.

Both policies are designed to force polluters to pay the cost of preventing or cleaning up the external damage they cause to others.

Carbon Taxes Noxious emissions into the environment cause negative externalities, whether in the form of carbon dioxide causing global warming; sulphur dioxide, causing acid rain; or harmful chemicals, causing cancers and birth defects. **Emissions taxes** are designed to pay for the external cost of preventing or cleaning up the damage to others from these emissions. **Carbon taxes**, which must be paid by anyone using carbon-based fossil fuels (like oil, gas, or coal) are the most well-known kind of emissions tax.

Let's look at how a government carbon tax would affect the choices of the pulp mills in our previous example. A smart carbon tax will be set at an amount equal to the marginal external cost of the damage associated with a tonne of pulp. If that marginal external cost is $30 per tonne, the tax should be $30 per tonne.

Figure 10.2 reproduces the numbers in Figure 10.1, with one change. The last column is now labelled *Marginal Private Cost + Tax*. This column lists the costs the mill must now pay for each additional tonne of pulp it produces. For the first tonne (output = 1), the mill pays $50 in marginal private costs for inputs like labour, wood, and power, and the $30 emissions tax to the government, for a total of $80. This last column is the sum of the marginal private costs that pulp mills must now pay for producing the first tonne of pulp.

Figure 10.2 Pulp Market with $30/tonne Emissions Tax

DEMAND			SUPPLY		
Output (tonnes/day)	Marginal Private Benefit (*MPB*)	Marginal Social Benefit (*MSB*)	Output (tonnes/day)	Marginal Private Cost (*MPC*)	Marginal Private Cost + Tax
1	$140	$140	1	$50	$80
2	$120	$120	2	$60	$90
3	$100	$100	3	$70	$100
4	$80	$80	4	$80	$110
5	$60	$60	5	$90	$120

Given the new tax, which changes the rules of the game, what is the market-clearing output and price for the pulp industry?

Looking only at the three columns in Figure 10.2 of *Output, Marginal Private Benefit,* and *Marginal Private Cost + Tax,* you can see (highlighted in green) that the market-clearing price of a tonne of pulp is $100, and at that price businesses will supply, and consumers will buy, a quantity of 3 tonnes per day. This is also the smart choice for society, where marginal social benefit equals marginal social cost (See Figure 10.1).

By forcing producers to pay the external marginal cost of the negative externalities, emissions taxes get producers to voluntarily choose the socially best combination of output and price and associated level of pollution. There is a wonderfully descriptive and catchy (for an economist) phrase that describes how emissions taxes induce the best social outcome — we say that the emissions tax **internalizes the externality**. Remember that phrase. The tax transforms the external cost into a cost the producer must pay privately, directly to the government.

internalize the externality: transform external costs into costs producer must pay privately to government

Cap-and-Trade System for Emissions   A smart social choice of an efficient amount of pollution involves a combination of output, price, and associated levels of pollution. While emissions tax policies focus on increasing the price (and cost) of products/services to reflect internal and external costs, cap-and-trade policies focus on the level or *quantity of emissions.*

In a **cap-and-trade system** for emissions, the government (or an international agreement among governments, like the Kyoto Accord) establishes property rights to the environment and restricts the emission of pollutants. The system sets a limit, or *cap,* on the quantity of emissions that businesses can release into the environment. Businesses must have permits to pollute, which the government auctions off to the highest bidders. The total quantity of emissions allowed by the permits is set equal to the government target for emissions.

A market for emissions permits is established, where businesses can buy and sell (that is, *trade*) permits. Businesses that can reduce their emissions will be able to sell permits to other businesses, which are willing to pay the costs of additional pollution permits because the associated product/service is sufficiently valuable to them and their consumers. The cap-and-trade system gives businesses a choice of reducing pollution themselves or buying pollution permits.

cap-and-trade system: limits emissions businesses can release into environment

Government auctions off permits to pollute to highest bidders. Total quantity of emissions allowed by permits = emissions target.

In theory, the price of an emissions permit will reflect the marginal external cost of the pollution produced. Since this becomes a private cost to the business that must buy the permits, a smart cap-and-trade system *internalizes the externality,* just like an emissions tax, and leads to the choice of output, prices, and pollution that is best for society.

Although the initial focus of the cap-and-trade system is on the quantity of emissions, the additional costs businesses pay for emissions permits will eventually be reflected in higher prices for consumers.

A common objection to the cap-and-trade system is that it allows businesses to "buy a licence to pollute" — and we are always told pollution is bad. It is true the system allows businesses to buy licences to pollute, but think back to *Fear Factor* and the forsaken ideal of zero pollution. Once we give up on a world with zero pollution because the associated standard of living is unacceptably low, there will be some pollution. The haggling is over the proper prices that balance marginal social benefit and marginal social cost. Pollution can be bought and sold at a price, but only by giving pollution a price that reflects the marginal external cost of the damage done can individuals and businesses make smart choices that are also smart for society as a whole.

Make Polluters (Including You) Pay

The David Suzuki Foundation offers very clear background information about the motivation for a carbon tax or cap-and-trade system. The Foundation's website states that a fundamental problem is that "the atmosphere is treated as a free dumping ground for harmful, heat-trapping emissions," and that Canada is doing poorly at reducing those emissions because it has relied on voluntary measures to do so. According to the Foundation, most of the country's emissions come from burning fossil fuels. It supports pricing emissions using a carbon tax or a cap-and-trade system: "seeing that cost, and making it real, will give us new incentives to change the technologies and habits that created global warming in the first place."

Source: www.davidsuzuki.org

What's the Dif?   Does it make any difference which policy a government uses — a carbon tax or a cap-and-trade system?

There is a difference in who pays *initially*. With a carbon tax, anyone using energy, whether consumers filling up gas tanks or businesses buying energy for their factories, pays the tax up front. With a cap-and-trade system, businesses pay initially for emissions permits. But consumers pay eventually as the additional cost is passed on in higher prices for the products/services.

A carbon tax makes the cost of a negative externality directly obvious to consumers and businesses. The costs of emissions permits in a cap-and-trade system are far less obvious to the final consumer. This hidden quality makes cap-and-trade systems more popular with politicians, who want to be seen to be supporting the environment, but don't want to be blamed for higher prices!

A cap-and-trade system sets a hard limit for emissions, allowing targets to be set and progress toward those targets to be clearly measured. A carbon tax sets an estimated price on the costs of negative externalities, but the outcome in terms of total emissions depends on the interaction of all the choices made by individuals and businesses. More uncertainty of outcome exists with a carbon tax.

Whether government uses a carbon tax or a cap-and-trade system to internalize the externalities of pollution, three benefits are shared:

- As carbon-based energy becomes more expensive, less carbon-based energy will be consumed. The law of demand applies — when something gets more expensive, people economize on its use and look for substitutes.
- Carbon taxes and emissions-permit-auctions raise revenues for government that can be used to remedy environmental damage done, or to further other environmentally friendly initiatives.
- Higher carbon-based energy prices make solar, wind, and hydro power more competitive, and encourage businesses to search for alternative (cheaper) energy sources.

Green Efficiency versus Equity Trade-offs

Smart government policies like a carbon tax or a cap-and-trade system will raise the prices of products/services we use to reflect indirect external costs to the environment on top of direct costs of production. That's a good thing, from the point of view of restoring the power of the invisible hand to coordinate smart private and social choices.

But, as I just noted, the law of demand still applies. As prices rise, the quantity demanded falls because fewer people are willing *and able* to buy at the higher prices. As gasoline and other energy prices are raised by smart government policies, fewer people can afford to buy. This is part of the trade-off between achieving less pollution at the cost of a lower standard of living. As Margaret Wente quips in Economics Out There on page 254, "The trouble with cutting carbon emissions is that doing so usually inflicts economic pain."

Those hurt most by higher energy prices are often those least able to afford them. Once again (as in the Chapter 5 discussion of minimum wage laws), there is a question of balance between efficiency and equity. Policies that are smart in terms of yielding an "efficient" amount of pollution may also be inequitable in hurting lower-income consumers more than higher-income consumers. There is no magic bullet of a policy that can significantly reduce pollution without also reducing living standards, especially of those who are poorest, or those in energy-sensitive industries like trucking, taxis, air travel, or automobile production.

Businesses buy and sell emissions permits. Permit price becomes private cost to business reflecting marginal external cost of pollution — internalizing externality.

By giving pollution a price reflecting marginal external cost of damage done, smart individual and business choices become smart social choices.

ECONOMICS Out There

The Planet or Jobs?

As Margaret Wente wrote in *The Globe and Mail,* the fallout from the doubling of gas prices in 2008 showed that directly feeling the effects of market forces has more influence over people's behaviour than environmentalists' "sermonizing" about the country's addiction to gas-guzzling vehicles. Unfortunately, our decreased interest in giant SUVs, while good for the environment, has not been good for the economy. And, as Wente points out, the "trouble with cutting carbon emissions is that doing so usually inflicts economic pain." As has been demonstrated already in other countries, we tend to be vocal supporters of carbon taxes until we have to pay them — Wente suggests that cap-and-trade systems can be "politically superior because, unlike carbon taxes, hardly anyone can understand them."

Source: Margaret Wente, "A Dilemma: The Planet or Jobs," *The Globe and Mail,* June 5, 2008.

Refresh 10.3

1. What is a carbon tax, and how does it "internalize the externality" for a polluting business?

2. Some environmental groups try to expose businesses that pollute while supporting environmentally friendly businesses by posting information and photos on public websites (for example, www.secrecyistoxic.ca). Explain the strategy and how this may "internalize the externality" for the polluters even without government action.

3. While carbon taxes and cap-and-trade systems have the same objective, governments and political parties differ in which policy they support. What are the positions of the Conservatives, the Liberals, the NDP, and the Green Party? Which position makes the most sense to you?

www.myeconlab.com

10.4 Why Lighthouses Won't Make You Rich: Free-Riding on Positive Externalities

Internet scams offering to make you rich are rampant — emails alert you to forgotten prize winnings, foreign lottery payoffs, oppressed billionaires who direly need your assistance, and cheap stocks about to take off. I hope you ignore them, even though some are temptingly believable. But if you ever get an email promising you riches from a fabulous lighthouse investment opportunity, I can promise you it is a scam. Why am I so sure?

Explain how positive externalities create the free-rider problem and cause markets to fail.

The Free-Rider Problem

Think about the business case for a lighthouse. Lighthouses provide an extremely valuable service. They prevent ships from running aground or sinking, thereby saving millions of dollars every year in lost or damaged cargo (and ships!). Sounds like a service that ship owners would gladly pay for.

But think about the *decision to buy* lighthouse services from the viewpoint of a cost-conscious ship owner. Sure, the service is valuable — but once the lighthouse is operating, the ship owner can get the "service" for free! No one can be excluded from seeing an operating lighthouse beacon. Why be a sucker and pay — let other foolish or naive ship owners pay to start up the lighthouse, and then free-ride on the beacon. All ship owners will figure out this free-riding strategy eventually, so any private lighthouse business will end in bankruptcy.

Lighthouses are a classic example of what economists call a public good. **Public goods** can be consumed simultaneously by everyone; no one can be excluded. National defence is another example. Once a country has a standing army in place, everyone benefits and no one can be excluded. If the United States attacks Canada — say, to take control of oil reserves in Alberta — the Canadian Armed Forces won't protect the citizens who have paid taxes while using those who haven't paid as human shields.

The problem with public goods, even though they provide valuable services, is that markets will not produce them because no business can make a profit. Public goods like lighthouses and national defence are extreme cases of positive externalities. External benefits that do not have to be paid for go to people external to the original activity — others not involved in building the lighthouse or funding the Canadian Forces.

public goods: provide external benefits consumed simultaneously by everyone; no one can be excluded

Positive Externalities   A similar problem of positive externalities applies to education and public transit. While the private benefits of your post-secondary education include higher lifetime earnings for you, there are also external benefits to employers (who do not have to spend as much money and time training you), and to governments and citizens (because you will require less assistance and can be a better participant in democratic activities). When you take public transit instead of driving, others benefit from reduced traffic jams and cleaner air, without having to pay. All these "others" receive positive benefits from your choices, but "free ride" by not having to pay.

Positive externalities are not as "in-your-face" a problem as negative externalities. For products/services with negative externalities, the problem is clear — market coordination of economic activity produces too many "bads," like acid rain, global warming, and traffic jams. For products/services with positive externalities, the more subtle problem is why there aren't *more* such "goods" like education, public transit, and vaccinations. Economists call this the **free-rider problem**.

free-rider problem: markets underproduce products/services with positive externalities

Just as there is a smart social choice of quantities of output associated with an "efficient" level of pollution, there is a smart choice of output of products/services with positive externalities. Market prices do not accurately reflect all costs and benefits, so individuals' smart choices, based on the incentives market prices provide, are not the same as smart choices for society as a whole. Because of the free-rider problem, *markets tend to underproduce products/services that have positive externalities, and the price charged to buyers is too high and to sellers is too low* (because the market price does not incorporate the external benefits). Let me explain.

Efficient Combinations of Output and External Benefits

The rule for finding an efficient combination of output and external benefits is the same as for an efficient combination of output and pollution. For any product/service (output) whose production also generates a positive externality, the rule for smart choices is as follows:

Choose the Quantity of Output Where

Marginal Social Cost = Marginal Social Benefit

$$(MSC) = (MSB)$$

Let's look at an example of *privately* provided post-secondary education (the reason why I use this example of private education will become clear in Section 10.5). The schools produce "educational services" that are sold to students. Recall the definition:

| Marginal Social Cost (MSC) | = | Marginal Private Cost Directly Paid by Producers (MPC) | + | Marginal External Cost Imposed on Others |

Private education has no external costs, so marginal social cost = marginal private cost. All action happens on marginal social benefit side.

To operate their campuses, the schools pay for instructors, buildings, computer systems, energy, and other inputs. These are marginal private costs. We will assume the schools are "green" and, unlike the pulp mills, do *not* produce any pollution or other external costs (marginal external costs = 0). For these schools, marginal social cost (MSC) is equal to marginal private cost (MPC).

When there are positive externalities, social benefits are greater than private benefits:

| Marginal Social Benefit (MSB) | = | Marginal Private Benefit Directly Received by Consumers (MPB) | + | Marginal External Benefit Enjoyed by Others |

Marginal external benefit = price of value or savings to others external to original activity.

The main private benefit to students of post-secondary education is increased lifetime income. But there are also external benefits, like reduced training costs for employers and reduced government expenditures on crime fighting and social assistance. If we could put a price on these external benefits, per student educated per year (equal to reduced average training costs, reduced government expenditures, and value of marginal improvement to democracy), that price would be the marginal external benefit. (See Economics Out There on page 257) for calculations of marginal external benefit of roads that provide positive externalities.)

Figure 10.3 provides some hypothetical numbers for the yearly output of all the private schools producing for the post-secondary education market. Like Figure 10.1, the left three columns show market demand, and the right three columns show market supply. The first column on both the demand and supply sides is *Output*, showing the different quantities of educational services (measured in students educated per year) the schools might choose to produce.

Figure 10.3 Post-Secondary Education Market: Demand, Supply, and Externalities

DEMAND			SUPPLY		
Output (students/ year)	Marginal Private Benefit (*MPB*)	Marginal Social Benefit (*MSB*)	Output (students/ year)	Marginal Private Cost (*MPC*)	Marginal Social Cost (*MSC*)
100	$7 000	$10 000	100	$2 500	$2 500
200	$6 000	$9 000	200	$3 000	$3 000
300	$5 000	$8 000	300	$3 500	$3 500
400	**$4 000**	**$7 000**	400	**$4 000**	**$4 000**
500	$3 000	$6 000	500	$4 500	$4 500
600	$2 000	$5 000	600	$5 000	$5 000
700	$1 000	$4 000	700	$5 500	$5 500

Demand   The second column, *Marginal Private Benefit*, shows the maximum price students or buyers are willing to pay for each quantity. Notice that the private benefit of the first 100 student-years of education (output = 100) is $7000, but that marginal benefit diminishes for successive years: $6000 for the 2nd hundred student-years, $5000 for the 3rd hundred student-years, and so on.

If you think of column 2 as *the price buyers are willing to pay* for the different quantities of education in column 1, then you can see (this time for sure!) the law of demand in the pattern of numbers. Start at the top. When the price is $7000 per student-year, quantity demanded is only from 100 students. As the price falls to $6000, $5000, down to $1000, the quantity demanded increases to 200, 300, up to 700 students. As a product/service becomes cheaper, we buy more of it.

Infrastructure as Public Good

Ever wonder how much certain industries benefit from the infrastructure — like roads, bridges, sewers, water systems — that governments provide as a public good? No, I didn't think so. But the information illustrates well the idea of marginal external benefit. Statistics Canada estimated the "private production cost savings associated with the use of public infrastructure" and found that the biggest "winner" industries were transportation (42-cent payoff for every government dollar spent), retailers (34-cent payoff), and wholesalers (33-cent payoff). And this was on top of "money . . . earned from government purchases to build the infrastructure"! All 37 industries looked at in the study received at least some marginal external benefit.

Source: Bruce Little, "Infrastructure as Public Good," *The Globe and Mail*, Nov. 24, 2003.

Marginal External Benefit/Positive Externality/Marginal Social Benefit

Compared to a market where the invisible hand works well, the difference in the numbers is in the 3rd column, *Marginal Social Benefit*. Let's say each 100 student-years of education generates $3000 in external benefits — cost savings to employers and governments in training and assistance payments from that quantity of education. Employers and government do not have to pay (they get a free ride) students or schools for the benefits, which is why the external benefits do not enter into the demand decisions by students of columns 1 and 2. But these are benefits to society as a whole, and must be added to the marginal private benefits to calculate marginal social benefits. The numbers in the 3rd column are equal to the numbers in the *Marginal Private Benefit* column, plus $3000.

Supply

Column 4 repeats the quantities of output choices from column 1. Column 5, *Marginal Private Cost*, shows the costs the schools actually pay for instructors, buildings, computer systems, energy, and other inputs for each additional 100 students per year. Notice the pattern of increasing marginal cost as output increases, from $2500 for the 1st 100 student-years, to $3000 for the 2nd 100 student-years, up to $6500 for the 7th 100 student-years (increasing marginal costs). Marginal private costs represent the minimum price the schools need to receive to be willing to supply that additional quantity — price must cover all marginal opportunity costs of production. If you think of column 5 this way, as *the minimum price schools are willing to accept*, you can see the law of supply in the pattern of numbers. As the price rises, the quantity supplied increases.

The last column, *Marginal Social Cost*, is the same as *Marginal Private Cost* in column 5 because there are no negative externalities. These last three columns describe the supply side of the private post-secondary education market.

Putting It All Together

What is the market outcome and smart social choice?

Because students (buyers) and schools (suppliers) do *not* get paid for the external benefits their exchange creates, employers and government get a free ride. Together with the fact that there are no external costs, this means externalities do not enter into anyone's private decisions. The only columns that determine the market output are *Marginal Private Benefit* (market demand) and *Marginal Private Cost* (market supply).

Markets coordinate choices of buyers and sellers through prices so that quantity demanded and quantity supplied are equal. Looking only at the three columns in Figure 10.3 of *Output, Marginal Private Benefit*, and *Marginal Private Cost*, you can see (highlighted in red) that the market-clearing price of a student-year of education is $4000, and at that price schools will supply, and students will buy, a quantity of 400 student-years of "educational services." The market-clearing quantity of 400 student-years of educational services occurs where the price buyers are willing to pay and the price sellers need to receive are equal. When those two prices are equal, we have also found the market-clearing price, or the equilibrium price, of $4000 per student-year.

What about the smart choice for society, which should take into account external benefits? The rule says choose the quantity of output where marginal social benefit equals marginal social cost. In Figure 10.4, that means look only at the three columns of *Output, Marginal Social Benefit*, and *Marginal Social Cost*. The smart output (in green) is 600 student-years of post-secondary education, where marginal social benefit equals marginal social cost and each are $5000.

For market-clearing quantity and price in Figure 10.3 (red), look at columns Output, Marginal Private Benefit, Marginal Private Cost.

For smart social choice for quantity and price in Figure 10.3 (green), look at columns Output, Marginal Social Benefit, Marginal Social Cost.

Understanding the Smart Social Choice   To understand why this rule gives us a smart choice of quantity of output (and associated level of external benefits), look at the choice for education, 100 student-years at a time. Reading across the row for Output = 100, the first 100 student-years each has a marginal social benefit of $10 000 (including the external benefit) and a marginal social cost of $2500. Since the additional benefits are greater than the additional costs, it's a smart choice (Key 1). For the 3rd hundred student-years, each has a marginal social benefit of $8000 and a marginal social cost of $3500 — still a smart choice. For output of 600 student-years, the marginal social benefits and costs are both equal to $5000, so society at least breaks even. But to increase output to 700 student-years, marginal social benefit of $4000 is less than marginal social cost of $5500. Not a smart social choice.

Compared to the market outcome, the smart choice for society means producing more of a product with a positive externality (600 student-years of education instead of the market's 400 student-years).

Unfortunately, there is no market-clearing price that can provide incentives for coordinating the demand and supply for 600 student-years of output. Market failure occurs because externalities drive a wedge between individuals' smart choices and the smart choice for society as a whole. To be willing to buy (demand) the smart social quantity of 600 student-years of education, students would pay only $2000 per year (the value of their marginal private benefits only, because students are not compensated for their external benefits to others). But to be willing to supply the smart social quantity of 600 student-years, schools need to receive $5000 per student-year (again because schools are not compensated for their external benefits to others).

These numbers illustrate the general result that markets tend to underproduce products/services that have positive externalities. Furthermore, the market-clearing price is too high for buyers to be willing to buy the quantity of output best for society, and too low for sellers to be willing to supply that socially best quantity, because neither buyers nor sellers are being paid for the external benefits their exchange creates.

For products/services with positive externalities, market-clearing price too high for buyers to be willing to buy socially best quantity output, too low for sellers to be willing to supply socially best quantity. Neither buyers nor sellers are paid for external benefits their exchange creates.

Refresh

10.4

1. What is a free-rider? Why is free-riding a problem?

2. Smart students often don't like group projects. Explain why, using the concept of free-riding.

3. Two physically identical houses can have very different values depending on their neighbourhoods. How do positive (or negative) externalities help explain property values?

www.myeconlab.com

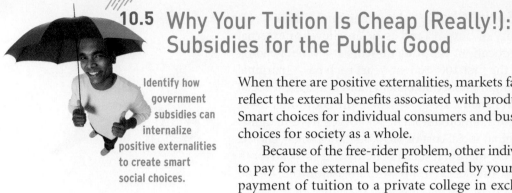

10.5 Why Your Tuition Is Cheap (Really!): Subsidies for the Public Good

Identify how government subsidies can internalize positive externalities to create smart social choices.

When there are positive externalities, markets fail. Market-clearing prices do not reflect the external benefits associated with producing products/services we desire. Smart choices for individual consumers and businesses are not the same as smart choices for society as a whole.

Because of the free-rider problem, other individuals and businesses do not have to pay for the external benefits created by your private market exchanges (your payment of tuition to a private college in exchange for course credits). Smart individual choices by consumers and businesses leave society with too few products/services with positive externalities. If only there were a way to "internalize the (positive) externalities," everyone could end up better off.

Adam Smith's Vote for Government

Government has as much, if not more, of a role to play in remedying market failures from positive externalities as from negative externalities. Adam Smith, the father of the invisible hand, recognized this back in 1776 when he explicitly gave government ("the commonwealth") the responsibility for providing valuable public goods that markets would not supply (see the quote in the margin). There is a reason why all lighthouses are operated by governments.

The key principle for government policy is to set the rules of the game to align smart private choices with smart social choices; the same as for negative externalities. For positive externalities, that means removing the wedge they drive between prices for buyers and sellers, so that self-interested individuals and businesses will choose the outcomes that are also best for society as a whole. That again means implementing policies that get everyone to voluntarily choose the quantity of output where marginal social benefit equals marginal social cost.

The two main policy tools are

- subsidies, and
- public provision.

> *The third . . . duty of the . . . commonwealth is . . . erecting and maintaining those public institutions and those public works, which, though they may be in the highest degree advantageous to a great society, are, however, of such a nature that the profit could never repay the expense to any individual . . .*
>
> *— Adam Smith*
> *Wealth of Nations*

Subsidies

Private individuals and businesses whose choices generate positive externalities somehow need to be compensated for the benefits that go to others outside the original exchange. Governments can do that, and internalize externalities, by granting **subsidies,** or payments, equal to the value of the positive externality. Subsidies are the opposite of taxes. Instead of government imposing a cost on individuals or businesses equal to the damage done by their negative externalities, subsidies reward those whose choices create positive externalities for others.

External benefits are widely spread over many, many others, so government can act on behalf of all ("the commonwealth"), taxing the general public to raise revenues that are then used to pay the subsidies to those whose actual choices generate positive externalities.

Let's look at how a government subsidy would affect the choices of students and schools in the market for private post-secondary educational services. A smart subsidy will be set equal to the marginal external benefit — the savings to others associated with a student-year of education. That marginal external benefit, in our example, is $3000 per student-year, so the subsidy should be $3000 per student-year.

subsidy: payment to those who create positive externalities

Smart subsidy = marginal external benefit of savings to others associated with activity.

The subsidy is being paid to the school by government, for each student-year of education supplied. Figure 10.4 reproduces the numbers in Figure 10.3, with only one change. The last column is now labelled *Marginal Private Cost – Subsidy*. This column lists the costs the school must pay for each additional student-year of education it produces, *after subtracting the subsidy it receives from the government*. For each of the 1st 100 student-years, the schools pay $2500 in marginal private costs for inputs like instructors, buildings, computer systems, and energy, and it now receives a subsidy (the opposite of cost) of $3000. So the net marginal private cost, taking the subsidy into account also, is –$500. That means the school actually makes $500 for each of the first 100 student-years of education it supplies, before collecting any tuition.

Figure 10.4 Post-Secondary Education Market with $3000 Subsidy to Schools

DEMAND			SUPPLY		
Output (students/ year)	Marginal Private Benefit (*MPB*)	Marginal Social Benefit (*MSB*)	Output (students/ year)	Marginal Private Cost (*MPC*)	Marginal Private Cost – Subsidy
100	$7 000	$10 000	100	$2 500	–$500
200	$6 000	$9 000	200	$3 000	$0
300	$5 000	$8 000	300	$3 500	$500
400	$4 000	$7 000	400	$4 000	$1 000
500	$3 000	$6 000	500	$4 500	$2 500
600	$2 000	$5 000	600	$5 000	$2 000
700	$1 000	$4 000	700	$5 500	$2 500

Skipping down to the third row of Figure 10.4, for each of the 3rd 100 student-years, the school pays $3500 in marginal private costs for inputs, and receives a subsidy of $3000, for a net marginal private cost of $500 per student-year. For each of the last 100 student-years (the last row), the school pays $5500 in marginal private costs for inputs, and receives a subsidy of $3000, for a net marginal private cost of $2500 per student-year.

The new subsidy changes the rules of the game by affecting the private costs of the schools. What is now the market-clearing output and price for the post-secondary education industry?

Look only at the three columns in Figure 10.4 that determine smart private choices by students and schools — *Output, Marginal Private Benefit*, and *Marginal Private Cost* − *Subsidy*. You can see (highlighted in green) that the market-clearing price of a school-year is $2000, and at that price schools will supply, and students will buy (demand), 600 student-years of education. If you look back at Figure 10.3, you will see that this is also the smart choice for society, where marginal social benefit equals marginal social cost.

By paying the schools for the marginal external benefits the educational services provide to others beyond the students, government subsidies get students and schools to voluntarily choose the socially best combination of output and price and the associated level of external benefits. The subsidies remove the wedge that positive externalities drive between prices for buyers and sellers, so that self-interested individuals and businesses will choose the outcomes that are also best for society as a whole.

Subsidies remove wedge positive externalities drive between prices for buyers and sellers, inducing individuals and businesses to voluntarily choose quantity of output best for society.

Public Provision

Instead of paying subsidies to private producers, governments may choose to directly provide a product/service with positive externalities. Education from kindergarten to grade 12 falls into this category, as well as most public infrastructure like roads, bridges, streetlights, public transit, and lighthouses. Economists call this **public provision**. Governments provide these services when the positive externalities are widespread and important for citizens, and/or when it is difficult to collect revenues from users. Basic education is the foundation for a literate and socialized workforce and citizenry, so government pays the entire cost. In the Economics Out There on page 257 about public infrastructure, we saw the broad benefits to most industries from having roads and bridges, and industries also provide jobs and tax revenues. And while toll roads are feasible for highways and bridges when there are few entry and exit points, toll booths don't make any sense for city streets (or streetlights, or lighthouses).

With public provision governments *always pay for* these products/services. But governments can choose whether to run the business itself (most primary and secondary schools) or to contract out the actual operations (as in hiring private contractors to build roads and bridges). Public provision is based on the same principle for subsidies — implementing policies that get everyone to voluntarily choose the quantity of output where marginal social benefit equals marginal social cost.

This is where the *private* nature of the earlier post-secondary example is important. As an alternative to paying subsidies to private suppliers, governments instead can directly operate the post-secondary schools. That is what happens in Canada. The smart policy choice is the same. Choose the quantity of output (of educational services), price, and external benefits where marginal social benefit equals marginal social cost. Public colleges and universities still have input costs and choices to make about prices (tuition). A publicly operated college or university should make the same choices as a private post-secondary industry with government subsidies.

Speaking of tuition, how many of you think your tuition is expensive? OK, you can all put down your hands. Well, it depends on what you mean by expensive. If you mean more than you can easily afford, you may be right. But if you evaluate what you pay in tuition relative to the total cost of providing your education, then you are dead wrong. Tuition covers less than 25 percent of the cost of delivering post-secondary education. In that sense, you are getting a bargain, which the government is subsidizing and providing to you below cost because of the massive positive externalities associated with education.

public provision: government provision products/services with positive externalities, financed by tax revenue

Paying for Externalities Governments pay for public provision using tax revenues. If the external benefits are widespread, as they are for education, governments may use general tax revenues or property tax revenues to finance public provision. In the case of roads, governments often use a tax on gasoline to finance construction and upkeep of city streets, on the principle that motorists benefit most from having good roads. (See Economics Out There about whether it is fair to tax motorists to pay for public transit they don't use.)

When there are externalities — negative or positive — markets fail. Smart private choices (using Keys 1 and 2) are different from smart social choices (Keys 1, 2, and 3). Because they don't pay for external costs and don't get paid for external benefits, private individuals or businesses do not have incentives to make choices that are good for society as a whole, and the invisible hand fails to coordinate individual choices to balance social benefits with social costs.

Smart government policies that internalize the externality through taxes, subsidies, emission controls, and public provision are essential for liberating the invisible hand to allow markets to produce more of the "goods" we desire and fewer of the "bads."

Should Drivers Be Taxed to Pay for Public Transit?

When the chairman of the Toronto Transit Commission proposed a tax on drivers to finance more public transit, drivers were outraged. After all, they argued, we don't take the transit, why should we pay for it?

Do you agree?

Before answering, think about externalities, both positive and negative.

Transit riders provide positive externalities to drivers in reducing traffic congestion, commute times, and pollution. So drivers will benefit from more public transit, and the tax is a way of forcing drivers to pay for the positive externality they will receive from transit riders.

Drivers, though they don't intend it, create traffic jams and increased commute times, imposing a negative externality on other drivers. A tax will force drivers to pay for those negative externalities and also encourage some to switch to transit, reducing traffic problems.

Refresh
10.5

1. What should the amount of a smart government subsidy be equal to? Why?

2. What if the government gave the $3000 subsidy from Figure 10.4 directly to students instead of to schools? Construct a table like Figure 10.3 and discover whether the students' private choices would still be the same as the smart choice for society? (*Hint:* The *Marginal Private Benefit* column shows willingness to pay. Create a new column showing willingness to pay *with the subsidy* [*Marginal Private Benefit + Subsidy*].)

3. Some European countries have free tuition for post-secondary education. If you were a member of parliament who wanted to defend this policy (knowing that any money needed to support education had to be raised by new taxes), what arguments would you make? If you wanted to defend the Canadian system, where students must pay some tuition, what arguments would you make?

www.myeconlab.com

Acid Rain on Others' Parades

Externalities, Carbon Taxes, Free Riders, and Public Goods

CHAPTER SUMMARY

10.1 HANDCUFFING THE INVISIBLE HAND: MARKET FAILURE WITH EXTERNALITIES

Negative or positive externalities make smart private choices different from smart social choices.

- Smart choices require that all additional benefits and additional opportunity costs — including *externalities* — are counted.

  - **Negative externalities (external costs)** — costs to society from your private choice that affect others, but that you do not pay.

  - **Positive externalities (external benefits)** — benefits to society from your private choice that affect others, but that others do not pay you for.

- Externalities occur when no clear property rights exist.

- When externalities exist, prices don't accurately reflect all social costs and benefits, preventing markets from coordinating private smart choices with social smart choices. Markets fail:

  - producing too much of things we don't want (second-hand smoke, pollution, traffic jams).

  - producing too little of things we do want (vaccinations, education).

10.2 WHY RADICAL ENVIRONMENTALISTS DISLIKE ECONOMISTS: NEGATIVE EXTERNALITIES AND EFFICIENT POLLUTION

To coordinate smart private choices that generate negative externalities, with smart social choices, choose the quantity of output where marginal social cost equals marginal social benefit.

- As we reduce pollution, "efficient pollution" balances additional environmental benefits with additional opportunity costs of reduced living standards.

- Socially desirable amount of pollution is not zero; at some point additional opportunity costs of reductions in pollution are greater than additional benefits.

- For any product/service that generates an externality, rule for a smart choice is: Choose quantity of output where *marginal social cost equals marginal social benefit.*
  - **Marginal social cost** *(MSC)*
    marginal private cost plus marginal external cost.
  - **Marginal social benefit** *(MSB)*
    marginal private benefit plus marginal external benefit.
- Markets overproduce products/services with negative externalities; price is too low because it does not incorporate external costs.

10.3 LIBERATING THE INVISIBLE HAND: POLICIES TO INTERNALIZE THE EXTERNALITY

Government policies can force polluting businesses and individuals to pay the marginal external costs of their pollution. As a result, polluters internalize their externalities/costs into their private choices, creating smart social choices.

- Without property rights to the environment, businesses have incentives to save money and improve profits by ignoring external costs like pollution and global warming.
- Governments can remedy market failures from externalities by creating social property rights to environment, making polluting illegal, penalizing polluters.
  - **Emissions tax** — tax to pay for external costs of emissions.
  - **Carbon tax** — emissions tax on carbon-based fossil fuels.
  - **Cap-and-trade system** — limits emissions businesses can release into environment.
- **Internalize the externality** — transform external costs into costs producer must pay privately to government.
- By giving pollution a price reflecting marginal external cost of damage done, smart individual and business choices become smart social choices.
- Carbon taxes and cap-and-trade systems are smart policies for efficient pollution, but may also be inequitable in hurting lower-income consumers most.

10.4 WHY LIGHTHOUSES WON'T MAKE YOU RICH: FREE-RIDING ON POSITIVE EXTERNALITIES

Positive externalities create a free-rider problem when neither buyers nor sellers are paid for external benefits their exchange creates. The market-clearing price is too high for buyers to be willing to buy the socially best quantity of output, and too low for sellers to be willing to supply.

- **Public goods** — provide external benefits consumed simultaneously by everyone; no one can be excluded.
  - Public goods like lighthouses and national defence are extreme examples of positive externalities.
  - Free-rider — someone who does not have to pay for external benefits.
- For any product/service that generates an externality, rule for a smart choice is: choose quantity of output where *marginal social cost equals marginal social benefit.*

- Because of **free-rider problem**, markets underproduce products/services with positive externalities.
  - price charged to buyers is too high.
  - price received by sellers is too low.
  - market price does not incorporate external benefits.

10.5 WHY YOUR TUITION IS CHEAP (REALLY!): SUBSIDIES FOR THE PUBLIC GOOD

Government policies can reward businesses and individuals creating positive externalities. As a result, these businesses and individuals internalize the externalities/rewards, turning smart private choices into smart social choices.

- Subsidies and public provision are government policy tools to get everyone to voluntarily choose output where marginal social benefit equals marginal social cost.
  - **Subsidy** — payment to those who create positive externalities.
  - **Public provision** — government provision products/services with positive externalities, financed by tax revenue.
- Subsidies and public provision remove the wedge positive externalities drive between prices for buyers and for sellers, inducing individuals and businesses to voluntarily choose quantity of output best for society.

TRUE/FALSE

Circle the correct answer.

10.1 MARKET FAILURE WITH EXTERNALITIES

1. Social costs are sometimes ignored because decision makers do not have to pay for external costs or benefits.   **True**   **False**

2. Drivers impose a negative externality on non-drivers.   **True**   **False**

3. Smokers impose a positive externality on non-smokers.   **True**   **False**

4. Markets underproduce products/services that have negative externalities.   **True**   **False**

10.2 NEGATIVE EXTERNALITIES AND EFFICIENT POLLUTION

5. Economists believe the ideal or efficient amount of pollution is zero.   **True**   **False**

6. Small reductions in pollution come at a higher opportunity cost than large reductions in pollution.   **True**   **False**

7. The marginal external cost in the pulp market is the cost of preventing or cleaning up the damage from the pollution.   **True**   **False**

8. Marginal social cost is the same as marginal private cost if there are no positive externalities.   **True**   **False**

10.3 POLICIES TO INTERNALIZE THE EXTERNALITY

9. With carbon taxes the government sets the quantity of emissions; with cap-and-trade systems the government sets the price.   **True**   **False**

10. Smart carbon taxes lead individuals and businesses to voluntarily choose the quantity of output where marginal private benefit equals marginal private cost.   **True**   **False**

11. A carbon tax on fossil fuels would raise their relative price and encourage alternatives.   **True**   **False**

10.4 FREE-RIDERS AND POSITIVE EXTERNALITIES

12. Lighthouses are a public good.   **True**   **False**

13. It is not profitable for businesses to provide public goods.   **True**   **False**

10.5 SUBSIDIES AND PUBLIC GOODS

14. A college education is an example of public provision.   **True**   **False**

15. A college education is an example of a subsidy.   **True**   **False**

MULTIPLE CHOICE

Circle the correct answer.

10.1 MARKET FAILURE WITH EXTERNALITIES

1. Which of the following is *not* a negative externality?
   A) Jimbo blasts hip-hop music from his souped-up Honda as he cruises through his neighbourhood late at night
   B) Jericho sings along to hip-hop music on the bus (and everyone on the bus thinks he is horrible)
   C) Jeremiah listens to hip-hop music in his room with his headphones on and his door closed while no one is home
   D) Jerry blasts hip-hop music in the common area while his roommate attempts to study for a test

2. All the following statements are true, *except*:
   A) there is too much pollution in the world.
   B) there are too many cars on the road during rush hour.
   C) there are too many people quitting smoking.
   D) there are too many people getting vaccinations.

3. The opportunity cost of reducing pollution includes the costs associated with
   A) taking shorter showers.
   B) taking public transit rather than your car.
   C) shutting down factories.
   D) all of the above.

4. If there is a negative externality and no positive externality, marginal private cost
   A) *equals* marginal social cost, *and* marginal private benefit
      equals marginal social benefit.
   B) *is less than* marginal social cost, *and* marginal private benefit
      is less than marginal social benefit.
   C) *is less than* marginal social cost, *and* marginal private benefit
      equals marginal social benefit.
   D) *equals* marginal social cost, *and* marginal private benefit
      is less than marginal social benefit.

5. If there is a positive externality and no negative externality, marginal private cost
   A) *equals* marginal social cost, *and* marginal private benefit
      equals marginal social benefit.
   B) *is less than* marginal social cost, *and* marginal private benefit
      is less than marginal social benefit.
   C) *is less than* marginal social cost, *and* marginal private benefit
      equals marginal social benefit.
   D) *equals* marginal social cost, *and* marginal private benefit
      is less than marginal social benefit.

6. If there is a positive externality *and* a negative externality, marginal private cost
   A) *equals* marginal social cost, *and* marginal private benefit
      equals marginal social benefit.
   B) *is less than* marginal social cost, *and* marginal private benefit
      is less than marginal social benefit.
   C) *is less than* marginal social cost, *and* marginal private benefit
      equals marginal social benefit.
   D) *equals* marginal social cost, *and* marginal private benefit
      is less than marginal social benefit.

10.3 POLICIES TO INTERNALIZE THE EXTERNALITY

7. Smart cap-and-trade systems
   A) internalize the fraternity.
   B) internalize the externality.
   C) externalize the majority.
   D) externalize the externality.

8. Smart carbon taxes
   A) are equal to the marginal external cost.
   B) are equal to the damage of the negative externality.
   C) lead to prices and pollution levels that are best for society as a whole.
   D) all of the above.

9. Carbon taxes are inequitable if
   A) lower-income consumers are affected more than higher-income consumers.
   B) higher-income consumers are affected more than lower-income consumers.
   C) lower-income consumers receive a tax break.
   D) energy-sensitive businesses like trucking, taxis, air travel, or automobile production receive a tax break.

10.4 FREE-RIDERS AND POSITIVE EXTERNALITIES

10. Free-riding occurs when there are
    A) negative externalities.
    B) positive externalities.
    C) horses.
    D) unicorns.

11. Public goods are
    A) for the public.
    B) free.
    C) underproduced.
    D) all of the above.

12. Which of the following is *not* a public good?
    A) Parks
    B) National defence
    C) Clothes
    D) Vaccinations

13. Smart subsidies for public goods equal the amount of the

    A) marginal social cost.

    B) marginal social benefit.

    C) marginal external cost.

    D) marginal external benefit.

14. Subsidies are

    A) the opposite of taxes.

    B) paid by the government.

    C) rewards for those creating positive externalities for others.

    D) all of the above.

15. All of the following are examples of public provision by the government, *except*:

    A) education up to grade 12.

    B) post-secondary education.

    C) street lights.

    D) public transit.

SHORT ANSWER

Write a short answer to each question. Your answer may be in point form.

1. In 2008 the Liberal Party of Canada introduced its "Green Shift" plan for reducing carbon emissions. The plan places higher taxes on fossil fuels such as diesel, home heating oil, propane, and coal. These carbon taxes begin at $10 per tonne of greenhouse gas emissions and steadily rise by an additional $10 per tonne each year, reaching $40 per tonne within four years.

    A) Would the carbon tax raise or lower the price of carbon?

    B) If the existing tax on gas at the pump is already at $42 per tonne of carbon, would the tax at the pump rise?

    C) How can consumers adjust or respond to the higher price of carbon?

    D) New Democratic Party environment critic Nathan Cullen questioned how a tax on home-heating fuel would reduce emissions. "It's not as if people have some magical choice about whether they heat their homes," Cullen told reporters. Does Cullen think the demand for home-heating fuel is elastic or inelastic?

    E) The Liberal plan is a graduated tax, rising slowly over several years. Why may a gradual rise in price be better than a sudden rise?

2. The Conservative government warned that the Liberals' "Green Shift" plan will mean Canadians will be "Shift out of luck" and that a better slogan would be "Shift happens." Carbon taxes get priced into products/services because virtually every good and service involves some carbon dioxide emissions, from the transportation of the item, to the electricity used to make it, to the natural gas used to heat the factory.

   A) Name some goods and services that will rise in price as a result of the carbon tax.

   B) What types of individuals would be most likely to argue that a carbon tax is inequitable?

   C) It is estimated that the Liberals' carbon tax would raise $15.4 billion annually by year four. The Liberals say that "Every dollar that is raised from carbon pollution will be returned to Canadians in tax cuts," with individuals in low-income families receiving the largest tax cuts. How would this make the policy more equitable?

3. In 2008, the Green Party of Canada supported the idea of a carbon tax, and introduced its own plan for reducing carbon emissions. The Green Party's carbon tax is slightly higher, at $50 per tonne, and would raise the price of gas, home-heating fuel, and coal-fired electricity by hundreds of dollars a year. Liberal environment critic David McGuinty said the Green Party's proposed $50-a-tonne tax is an "excessive price." What happens to the opportunity cost of reducing carbon emissions as the targeted emissions reduction increases?

4. The New Democratic Party of Canada rejects a carbon tax in favour of a cap-and-trade system that would force big industrial emitters to buy credits from companies that can manage emission reductions. "Our plan is based on our consistent commitment to price carbon through a cap-and-trade system, ensure we reduce pollution, generate revenues for green solutions, and help ensure sustainability for future generations."

   A) How are prices set in a cap-and-trade system?

   B) Why might a cap-and-trade system be difficult to administer?

   C) How do carbon taxes and cap-and-trade systems differ with regard to how price and quantity are determined?

   D) Which policy would be more likely to guarantee that a nation accomplishes its emission targets?

5. The Carbon Tax Center (CTC) was launched in January 2007 to give voice to Americans who believe that taxing emissions of carbon dioxide is the only way to reduce global warming. The CTC estimates that the price elasticity of gasoline demand is 0.4 and the price elasticity of electricity demand is 0.7. Since these figures are less than 1, this means that demand is inelastic — a large increase in price produces a smaller decrease in quantity demanded.

   A) What does this imply about the size of the carbon tax necessary to induce large decreases in emissions?

   B) These estimates are "long-run" elasticities. Are elasticities smaller or larger over the long run?

6. As an alternative to taxing carbon, the government can promote fuel-efficient alternatives by offering tax breaks on these products.

A) In 2007, the federal government introduced tax breaks for purchases of fuel-efficient cars. Which policy tool from this chapter does this initiative resemble best?

B) In a survey conducted in February 2007, more economists favoured "*subsidies* for producers of alternative fuels" versus "*regulations* that require energy companies to use more alternatives." Why might economists prefer subsidies over direct regulation?

C) Bullfrog Power is a tiny swimmer in Ontario's energy pond. Like other providers, Bullfrog buys power in bulk and resells it. But unlike other resellers, all its energy comes from wind-powered or small hydro generating stations. Why would the government need to step in and promote this kind of energy? How could the government promote it?

7. Jeffrey Sachs, Director of the Earth Institute at Columbia University and Special Advisor to the United Nations Secretary, has argued for a global carbon tax, to be designed and administered by the United Nations so as to keep countries on an even footing.

A) Suppose a country sets the price for carbon emissions that forces producers and consumers to fully internalize the cost of carbon emissions in *their own country*. Would the amount of carbon likely be socially desirable from a *global* perspective?

B) A carbon tax can be applied locally, nationally, or globally. Why might a global carbon tax be most preferred if the climate crisis is global ("global warming")?

C) There could be an international agreement that every country would impose a carbon tax at an agreed rate (reflecting the global social cost). If countries have different rates of carbon taxation, how might carbon emitters respond?

8. Beer prices are increasing in Germany, as farmers abandon barley — the raw material for beer — to plant other, subsidized crops for sale as environmentally friendly biofuels.

A) According to one German citizen, "It's absolutely outrageous that beer is getting even more expensive. But there's nothing we can do about it — except drinking less and that's not going to happen." Is the demand for beer for this person elastic or inelastic?

B) Why would the German government currently be subsidizing crops made from environmentally friendly biofuels?

C) Suppose German brewing companies get together and convince the government to stop subsidizing environmentally friendly biofuels. How would this affect the supply and price of barley (a substitute)?

9. In the Economics Out There story, the Chairman of the Toronto Transit Commission (TTC) proposes a tax on drivers (like a gasoline tax) to help pay for public transport.

   A) Does driving result in a positive or negative externality?

   B) How would a tax on driving affect your decision to drive?

   C) If the government gives the revenue from the tax to the TTC, and the TTC then reduces the price of a ticket fare for transit riders, how would this affect the decision to drive?

   D) An alternative for reducing congestion is to build private highways and charge a usage fee to drivers. From the perspective of the price-maker highway owner, would it be more effective to charge a higher price during rush hour or off-peak hours?

10. Carbon taxes can be charged to producers or consumers. **Gilbert Metcalf,** Professor of Economics at Tuft University and the National Bureau of Economic Research, argues for taxing emissions on producers because the number of producers of coal, natural gas, and crude oil is relatively small, making such a program easier to administer. Would taxing *producers* translate into higher prices for *consumers*? Why or why not?

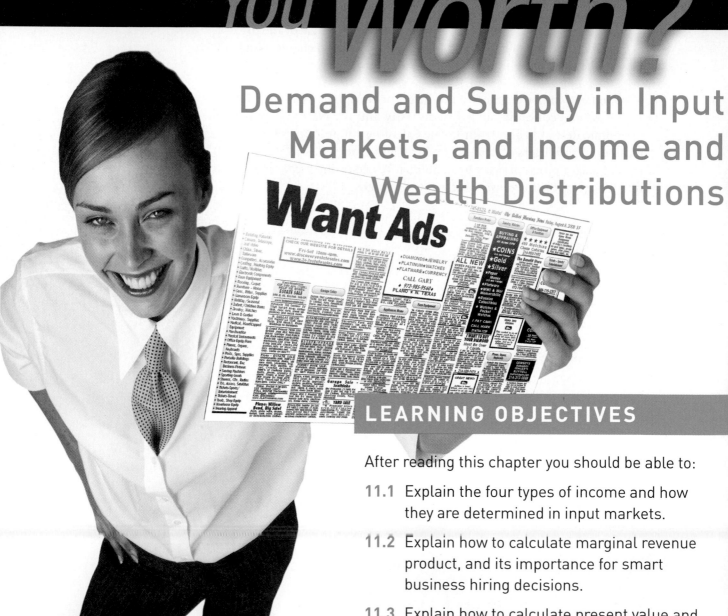

Chapter 11

What Are You Worth?

Demand and Supply in Input Markets, and Income and Wealth Distributions

LEARNING OBJECTIVES

After reading this chapter you should be able to:

11.1 Explain the four types of income and how they are determined in input markets.

11.2 Explain how to calculate marginal revenue product, and its importance for smart business hiring decisions.

11.3 Explain how to calculate present value and how it informs smart investment choices.

11.4 Describe economic rent, and explain its importance for determining income.

11.5 Explain the sources of poverty and describe trade-offs in policies to help the poor.

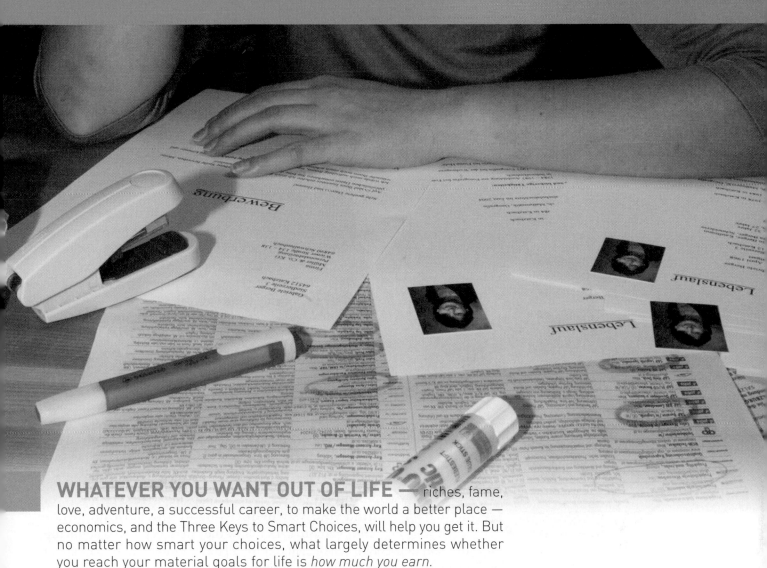

WHATEVER YOU WANT OUT OF LIFE — riches, fame, love, adventure, a successful career, to make the world a better place — economics, and the Three Keys to Smart Choices, will help you get it. But no matter how smart your choices, what largely determines whether you reach your material goals for life is *how much you earn.*

Markets provide the products/services we want to buy, as well as providing jobs and investment opportunities for us to earn money. In *output markets*, consumers are the demanders and businesses are the suppliers. This chapter shifts focus to *input markets*, markets for labour, capital, and other inputs used to produce outputs. In input markets, businesses are the demanders, and consumers (or households) are the suppliers. When you look for a job, you are a supplier in a labour market. If you have money to invest, you are a supplier in a capital market. What you are worth, in a market economy, is what the market is willing to pay for your inputs. Your income depends on your inputs and productivity, and in this chapter you will learn what you can do to improve both.

We have seen how output markets can fail due to economies of scale, monopoly, or externalities. Input markets can also fail in different ways, resulting in poverty and inequality. Input markets for labour and capital can work well to coordinate smart choices of consumers and businesses, ensuring businesses have the inputs they need to produce the products/services consumers want. Adam Smith's invisible hand of competition applies to input markets, too. But even when businesses get the inputs they need, the resulting distributions of income and wealth may not be equitable. Government policies may help remedy inequality and poverty, but even smart policies to help the poor have opportunity costs that should be evaluated.

11.1 Switching Sides: Incomes Are Prices and Quantities in Input Markets

Explain the four types of income and how they are determined in input markets.

We began our economics road trip in Chapter 1 with the road map of the circular flow of economic life (reproduced in Figure 11.1), the simplest "big picture" of how an economist thinks about economic choices.

Finding Your Way Around the Circle

All the complexity of the Canadian economy is reduced to three sets of players — households, businesses, and governments. Households and businesses interact in two sets of markets — *input markets* (where businesses buy from households the inputs they need to produce products/services) and *output markets* (where businesses sell their products/services to households). Governments set the rules of the game and can choose to interact, or not, in almost any aspect of the economy. When markets work well, self-interest and the invisible hand of competition coordinate the smart choices of households and businesses in both sets of markets.

We have now come full circle (pun intended) back to this road map, but we are switching sides to focus more on input markets, where households are the sellers and businesses are the buyers. If you keep that switch clearly in mind, you won't get lost in the stories that follow.

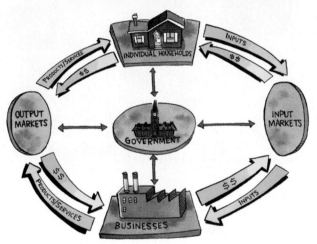

Figure 11.1   Circular Flow of Economic Life

In input markets, households are sellers and businesses are buyers.

In output markets, households are buyers and businesses are sellers.

Input Markets   Good maps like Figure 11.1 help you find your way by focusing on the most important information. Let's follow the circle, beginning at the top. Individuals in households sell or rent out their labour (ability to work), capital, land, and entrepreneurial abilities to businesses. This is the blue flow on the right side of the circle, from top to bottom. In exchange, businesses pay households wages, interest, rent, and other money rewards. This is the green flow on the right side of the circle, from bottom to top. These exchanges, or trades, happen in input markets, where households are the sellers and businesses are the buyers. When Mr. Sub hires you to work at a Mr. Sub store, that interaction happens in an input market — the labour market.

Output Markets   Businesses (at the bottom) use those inputs to produce products/services to sell to households. This is the blue flow on the left side of the circle, from bottom to top. In exchange, households use the money they have earned in input markets to pay businesses for these purchases. This is the green flow on the left side of the circle, from top to bottom. These exchanges, or trades, happen in output markets, where households are the buyers and businesses are the sellers. These are markets where you buy your breakfast from Tim's or Loblaws, or piercings from your neighbourhood piercing parlour.

At the end of the trip around the circle, households have the products/services they need to live, and businesses end up with the money. That sets the stage for the next trip around the circle, where businesses again buy inputs from individuals in households, produce outputs that households buy — and the flow goes on.

Minding the Ps and Qs of Income

What does this circular flow have to do with the income you earn? Everything! Incomes are determined by prices and quantities in input markets. If you earn $10 per hour at Mr. Sub and work 25 hours per week, your income for the week is $250. To calculate income, you normally multiply the price you receive for your input times the quantity of the input that you sell. In the labour market, that price is the wage rate you receive, and the quantity is the number of hours worked ($10 × 25 = $250 per week).

If you loan $5000 for a year to a business (your own or someone else's), at an interest rate of 8 percent (0.08) per year, your income is $400 per year from the input market for capital (0.08 × $5000 = $400 per year). The interest rate is the price of capital (capital here means money for investment purposes) and the quantity is the number of dollars you loan. If instead you put that money in a savings account and earn interest, the total amount of interest earned would likewise be income to you (which Canada Revenue Agency would count at tax time, just as it counts your labour income). If you own 10 hectares of land that you rent out to a farmer for $500 per hectare per month, your income is $5000 per month from the input market for land ($500 × 10 = $5000 per month).

Income Is a Flow, Wealth Is a Stock

When we calculate income as price × quantity for whatever the input — labour, capital, land, or other resources — the resulting number is meaningful *only when there is a time dimension attached*. If someone tells you that her income is $50 000, what does that mean? It makes a big difference if it is $50 000 a year, or $50 000 a month, or $50 000 an hour! When a measurement — like income — makes sense only when there is a time dimension attached, economists call that a **flow**. A flow is measured as an *amount per unit of time*.

On the other hand, your wealth — the total value of all the assets you own — is a **stock**. It is an *amount at a moment in time*. When you read reports about Bill Gates being the third-richest person in the world, the rankings are based on wealth, which is measured as an amount at a moment in time. Bill Gates's wealth in 2008 was estimated to be $58 billion. Your wealth is the total value of all the things you own, including shares of stock in corporations — but that is a different meaning of *stock* (see FYI). While corporate stocks and bonds are a major part of Bill Gates's wealth, for most of us wealth consists of savings, retirement funds, real estate, and even our cars.

Here's another way to think about the difference: *Income is what you earn; wealth is what you own*. We will learn how to calculate wealth using the concept of present value in Section 11.3, and will talk more about income and wealth — and who earns and owns what — in the final section of this chapter.

flow: amount per unit of time

stock: fixed amount at a moment in time

FOR YOUR INFORMATION

The two different economic meanings of *stock* can be confusing. Here, we are defining a stock as a fixed quantity available at a moment in time.

The other meaning is as in "stocks and bonds" or the "stock market." That meaning relates to the capital raised by a business or corporation through the issue of shares. Those shares are also called stocks, and those owning the shares are called shareholders or stockholders.

Entrepreneurs' Income Is Different

The one category of income that does not exactly fit the price × quantity formula is entrepreneurs' income. Individuals in households supply their entrepreneurial talent or services to businesses (often their own). Those services, which involve the entrepreneur's time, are often accompanied by an investment of his or her own money too. Their reward, or "payment," for this entrepreneurial input into production takes the form of *profits*.

Entrepreneurs are smart to offer their services only when they expect to make at least *normal profits*. Recall from Chapter 6 that normal profits represent compensation for an entrepreneur's (or business owner's) time and money. Normal profits are what an entrepreneur could have earned in the best alternative use of his time and money.

But what entrepreneurs are really after are *economic profits*, profits over and above normal profits. Economic profits are the ultimate reward to entrepreneurs, for their innovations and for the risks they take. What sets economic profits apart from all other categories of income is that economic profits are a *residual*. They are what is left over from revenues after all opportunity costs of production (including normal profits) have been paid for other inputs.

Inputs and Incomes

Figure 11.2 summarizes the different kinds of inputs that households supply in input markets, and the corresponding form of income that households receive from businesses for the use of those inputs.

Figure 11.2 Inputs and Incomes	
INPUT	**INCOME**
Labour	Wages
Capital ($)	Interest
Land (and other resources)	Rent
Entrepreneurship	Profits (normal and economic profits)

Refresh 11.1

1. What are the two types of markets in the circular-flow road map? Identify the buyers and sellers in each market.

2. If you have $10 000 in a savings account, and no other assets, what is your income from capital if the interest rate is 8 percent? What is your wealth?

3. When Wahid (Chapter 6) started his own web business using his savings and a small inheritance from his grandfather, he played multiple roles on the circular-flow road map. Identify those roles as he set up his business, and the roles he continues to play as the business begins producing web services. What are his types of income?

www.myeconlab.com

11.2 What Have You Done for Me Lately? Labour and Marginal Revenue Product

So income depends on prices and quantities. And on what do prices and quantities depend? The answer here is the same as it was in Chapter 4 . . . drum roll . . . prices (and quantities) come from the interaction of demand and supply. The only difference is that now we are looking at demand and supply in input markets instead of output markets. Businesses are now the demanders, and households are the suppliers. The resulting prices and quantities determine the income of that input.

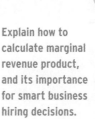

Explain how to calculate marginal revenue product, and its importance for smart business hiring decisions.

Back to (Demand and Supply and) the Future of Wahid's Web Wonders Business

The most important input markets are labour markets. These are the markets where individuals looking for jobs interact with businesses looking for workers. The prices are wage rates, and the quantities tell us how many people will be employed. There is a different labour market for each type of labour — markets for retail sales, construction, accountants, auto mechanics, chefs — each labour market with its own wage rate and quantity of labour employed.

Let's take a look at the labour market for web designers, and go back to our Chapter 6 example of Wahid's Web Wonders. Wahid's business has been booming, and he needs to hire additional web designers to increase his output of web pages. As long as he keeps his web page prices competitive, there seems to be no limit to how much he can expand his output and sales. He needs to figure out how many new designers he should hire. To answer that question, for Wahid or for any business, we need to understand a bit more about demand and supply in input markets. For input markets, the important differences, compared to what you have already learned about output markets, come on the demand side. That's where we will spend the most time. But first, let's quickly get the supply side of input markets out of the way.

Show Me the Money (Again): Supply of Labour

Remember the story in Chapter 3 about your boss calling you in a panic on Sunday night and wanting you to work as many hours as possible in the week ahead? As she increased the wage she was willing to pay you from $10 per hour to double time to triple time, the number of hours you were willing to work increased. In general, a rise in price (the wage rate) causes an increase in quantity supplied. This is the *law of supply*, which applies to input markets as well as output markets.

Paying Increasing Marginal Opportunity Costs   As you shift your time from alternative uses to work, *the marginal cost of your time increases.* You first give up the least valuable time, and continue giving up increasingly valuable time as the price you are offered rises. The market wage is determined when supply decisions of all households are combined with demand decisions of all businesses in a labour market.

To hire any input, including labour, a business must pay a price that matches the best opportunity cost of the input owner. What does that mean for Wahid, hoping to hire labourers in the market for web designers? Wahid is competing with other design businesses to attract workers to his business. So he must pay at least what other businesses are offering to web designers. Suppose the going market wage for web designers is $50 per hour.

Wahid knows what additional workers will cost, but what will they *do* for him?

To hire labour, a business must pay the market wage, which reflects best opportunity cost of person supplying labour.

Why Your Boss Wants You: Derived Demand for Labour

Businesses' demand for workers is not quite the same as consumers' demand for doughnuts. When you buy a tasty doughnut, you own it, you eat (consume) it, it's gone, and you are no longer hungry. When businesses buy labour, they don't own the labourer — that would be slavery. Businesses don't generally hire you because you taste good or look good (well, except for the modelling business). Businesses demand labour, and are willing to pay for the services the labourers can provide, because the labourers help produce outputs that can be sold to earn revenues and (hopefully) profits for the business. Economists call the demand for labour a **derived demand**, because businesses are not interested in the labour for its own sake (like a doughnut), but for the output and profits the business owner (entrepreneur) can derive from hiring labour.

derived demand: demand for output and profits businesses can derive from hiring labour

Wahid has entered the labour market as a demander, or buyer, because he wants to employ web designers to produce web pages that Wahid can sell to customers to earn revenues and profits. How does Wahid make a smart choice about the quantity of web designers to hire?

Smart Business Choices in Hiring Labour

The first two (of the usual three) keys to smart choices are also key to Wahid's decision about how many web designers to hire. (Key 3 about implicit and external costs is not important here.) Although I am sure you know the two keys by heart by now (can you state them without looking?), here they are again:

Key 1: Choose only when additional benefits are greater than additional *opportunity* costs.

Key 2: Count only *additional* benefits and *additional* costs.

For a business, additional opportunity cost of hiring labour is the market wage.

For Wahid's hiring decision, the two keys translate into "Hire only when the *additional* benefits of hiring that worker are greater than the *additional* opportunity costs of hiring that worker." This is yet another cost–benefit comparison at the margin, when only *additional* costs and benefits are relevant. Sunk costs that Wahid has already paid — for office space, printers, insurance, advertising — don't matter.

Additional Costs and Benefits   The cost, or supply-of-labour, side of the comparison is easy. What is the additional opportunity cost of a web designer to Wahid? What must Wahid *give up* to *get* a web designer? It is the $50 per hour he must pay to attract a designer away from the designer's best alternative employment with another business.

The important difference with what you have already learned comes on the benefit, or demand-for-labour, side of the comparison. The *additional benefits* from hiring an additional web designer are derived from the additional output of web pages he can produce, and the revenues and profits from selling those additional web pages. We need more information about additional output and additional revenues to figure out Wahid's smart choice.

Figure 11.3 contains all the additional information Wahid needs to decide how many web designers to hire. Column 1 lists the quantity of designers Wahid is considering hiring, from zero to five. Column 2 contains the first of two new concepts in this figure. **Marginal product** measures the additional *productivity* of this designer (labourer) — how much additional product his or her work adds to output (measured in web pages per hour).

marginal product: additional output from hiring one more unit of labour

Figure 11.3	Labour Hiring Decision for Wahid's Web Wonders Business		
Quantity Labour (designers)	**Marginal Product** (MP) (additional web pages designed per hour)	**Price** (P_{output}) (per web page sold)	**Marginal Revenue Product** $MP \times P_{output}$ (additional revenue generated per designer hour)
0	0	$15	0
1	6	$15	$90
2	5	$15	$75
3	4	$15	$60
4	3	$15	$45
5	2	$15	$30

Notice that while the first designer has a marginal product of six web pages per hour, subsequent designers each have lower marginal products. Economists call the pattern of numbers in column 2 **diminishing marginal productivity**, and it occurs in most businesses that have some fixed inputs. Wahid has limited office space, only one printer, and a part-time technical support person. Plus, there is only one Wahid to supervise all the designers he hires. As Wahid hires more designers, the office starts to get more crowded, there are problems sharing the printer, designers have to wait longer for technical support when their computers malfunction, and each receives less supervision. Each additional designer hired stresses the sharing of these fixed inputs a bit more, causing the drop in marginal productivity.

Column 3 is simple and familiar. It lists the price (always $15) that Wahid can sell each additional web page for in the output market for web design services. Wahid's output market, using the categories of market structure from Chapter 7, is pretty close to extreme competition. He has little pricing power. If he tries to charge more than the going market price of $15 per web page, his customers will desert him and switch to one of his many competitors. That's the bad news.

diminishing marginal productivity: each additional labourer has lower marginal product than previous labourer

Wahid runs a small business in a competitive industry, so he is a price taker; but can increase output/sales without lowering price.

The good news about being a small competitor relative to the size of the entire market for web design services is that Wahid can increase his output and sales without having to lower his price from $15 per web page. If, instead, Wahid were one of only a few big producers in an oligopolistic industry, or a monopoly, he would have to lower his price in order to sell more output.

Column 4 contains the second new concept, which is the key concept for Wahid's smart choice about how many designers to hire. **Marginal revenue product** is calculated by multiplying marginal product (column 2) times price of output (column 3). Look at the first designer hired. She produces six additional web pages per hour, each of which can be sold for $15. So, hiring that first designer would add $90 of revenue per hour (6 web pages per hour × $15 per page = $90). Hiring the second designer would add $75 of revenue per hour (5 web pages per hour × $15 per page = $75). Marginal revenue product is the additional revenue the business will receive from hiring an additional designer. Just like marginal products, *marginal revenue products* diminish in value as Wahid's business adds more designers.

Now that we have information about additional costs of hiring a web designer ($50 per hour), and additional benefits in the form of marginal revenue products ($90 per hour for the first designer, $75 per hour for the second designer, down to $30 per hour for the fifth designer), what is Wahid's smart choice?

Let me state the rule for a smart choice in hiring inputs to production, and then show you why it works. The rule that yields maximum profits for a business is:

> Hire additional hours of labour (or any input) as long as
> marginal revenue product is greater than the wage (or price of the input).

Figure 11.4 shows the data from Figure 11.3 in a graph. The graph clearly shows why the rule works. The marginal revenue product per hour for each designer is represented by a green (for revenue) bar, and the wage rate Wahid must pay for each hour of designer labour is the red (for cost) line at $50 per hour.

marginal revenue product: additional revenue from selling output produced by additional labourer

To calculate labourer's marginal revenue product, multiply marginal product × price of output. Marginal revenue product diminishes as business hires additional labourers.

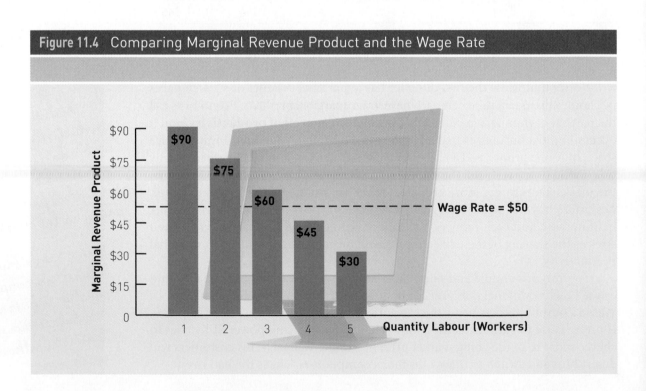

Figure 11.4 Comparing Marginal Revenue Product and the Wage Rate

Comparing Additional Costs and Benefits   Using Figure 11.4, let's evaluate Wahid's choices, designer by designer. If he hires the first web designer, Wahid's revenues go up by $90 per hour, while his costs go up by only $50 per hour (the pay of the new designer). This is clearly a smart choice that adds to profits, since additional revenues are greater than additional costs. Hiring the second web designer adds $75 per hour to revenues and only $50 per hour to costs. Again, this is a smart choice. Even though the additions to profits aren't as great as for the first designer, there is still a net increase of $25 per hour in profits. Hiring the third designer adds $60 per hour to revenues and $50 per hour to costs, again a smart choice. But look at what happens if Wahid hires a fourth designer. Revenues still go up, by $45 per hour, but costs go up even more, by $50 per hour. If Wahid hires a fourth designer, he will be losing $5 per hour for every hour the designer works. Not a smart choice. It's even worse for a fifth designer, with additional revenues of $30 per hour, and additional costs of $50 per hour. So Wahid should hire three designers. For each of the first three designers hired, marginal revenue product is greater than the wage rate, just as the rule suggests.

Marginal Productivity and Income

As a labourer, your boss wants you for your productivity, and there is a close connection between how much you are paid in wages and what you contribute to the productivity, revenues, and profits of your employer. Your marginal productivity is what you have done for your boss lately.

When input markets work well, the market-clearing, or equilibrium, wage is equal to the best alternative use of the time of individuals in households who are supplying labour to the market. Individuals are making smart choices, in earning as much as the best alternative use of their time. That same market-clearing wage is also roughly equal to the marginal revenue product that the last labourer hired contributes to the businesses that are demanding labour in the input market. The hiring businesses are making smart choices in hiring the quantity of labour that yields the greatest profits.

1. What is marginal revenue product?

2. In the example from Chapter 3, your boss is willing to pay you triple-time wages for working extra time. Explain the calculation she must have made in offering you that much money if she was making a smart hiring decision.

3. In the example in Figure 11.3, what would happen to Wahid's hiring decision if the price he could sell web pages for rose from $15 per page to $20 per page? Does that fit with your general impression of business hiring when sales and revenues are strong? Explain your answer.

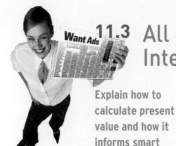

11.3 All Present and Accounted For: Interest on Capital and Present Value

Explain how to calculate present value and how it informs smart investment choices.

While your income is likely to depend mostly on the wage or salary you earn for your labour, I hope you will be able to accumulate some savings, which you can invest to also earn input income in the form of interest. If you invest your "capital" of $5000 in a savings account that pays 8 percent interest per year, the calculation of your interest income uses the simple *price × quantity* formula, where the price of capital is the interest rate and the quantity is the number of dollars. At the end of the year, you earn $0.08 \times \$5000 - \$400$ in interest income.

Comparing the Present and Future

Most investment calculations are not so simple because the payoffs from today's investment extend far into the future. When businesses build new factories that will last decades, or invest in expensive machine tools that will improve productivity, output, and revenues for years to come, how do they decide whether those are smart choices for investing their capital? If someone offers to sell you a small apartment building with six tenants who pay a total of $9000 in rent per month, how much should you pay today for that building? These long-lived investments produce a stream of revenues over many years, yet the business or investor is faced with a single purchase price in the present. How do we apply Key 1 for smart choices, "Choose only when additional benefits are greater than additional opportunity costs," when the benefits are spread out over the future and the cost is in the present? It feels like comparing apples and oranges. How do you simplify today that future stream of revenues to a single number you can compare with cost to make a smart choice?

The key concept for that simplification is called **present value**. If you are like me, when you first see the definition of present value you won't understand it. But I am going to give it to you anyway, and then work through some examples to help you to make sense of it.

> The **present value** of a future amount of money is the amount that, if invested today, will grow as large as the future amount, taking account of earned interest.

What did I tell you? Does your brain hurt? Read on for the cure.

Key 3 to the Rescue: Implicit Costs and Interest Rates

Even if you don't understand the definition of present value, you can see that interest rates play an important role. Let's start with a super-simple example to illustrate.

Suppose Wahid is thinking about buying a laminating machine for producing sharper-looking printed reports for clients. The machine costs $1000 and wears out entirely after one year. During that time, Wahid estimates that, because of the beautiful-looking reports, clients will pay him an additional $1100 in revenues. This sounds like a good investment according to Key 1, since $1100 in additional revenues is greater than $1000 in additional costs.

Concept of present value — what money earned in the future is worth today — necessary for smart investment choices.

present value: amount that, if invested today, will grow as large as future amount, taking account of earned interest

But that comparison of revenues and costs is not taking into account the role of time and interest. If Wahid's bank is offering a special 12 percent interest rate on a guaranteed investment certificate (GIC), then the laminating machine investment decision does not look so good. If Wahid invested the $1000 in the GIC instead of the machine, at the end of the year he would have $1200 guaranteed instead of his expected $1100 in additional revenues the machine would bring in.

Key 3 comes back into play here, "Be sure to count *all* additional benefits and additional costs, including implicit costs and externalities," especially the *implicit costs of forgone interest* from Chapter 6. The $1100 value for future income does not take into account implicit costs — the interest he could have earned if he had invested that $1000 in the present and then collected the interest after a year.

The concept of present value takes that interest into account, and allows us to reduce, or discount, Wahid's (simple) stream of future income into a number he can compare with the $1000 cost to see if buying the new machine is a smart choice.

Even though I haven't finished explaining the definition of present value, I am going to give you the formula for making the calculation that Wahid — and any investor — needs to make:

$$\text{Present Value} = \frac{\text{Amount of Money Available in } n \text{ Years}}{(1 + \text{Interest Rate})^n}$$

In the formula, n stands for the number of years the investment pays revenues. If a machine was expected to last 10 years, $n = 10$. This formula is scary looking (I never liked exponents, and even worse are exponents in the denominators of fractions), but for our simple example, where $n = 1$, it is not so scary.

For Wahid's example, where $n = 1$ year and an interest rate of 12 percent (0.12), the formula becomes

$$\text{Present Value} = \frac{\$1100}{(1 + 0.12)} = \frac{\$1100}{1.12}$$
$$\text{Present Value} = \$982.14$$

Going back to the definition of present value, $982.14 is the amount of money that, if invested today, will grow to be as large as $1100, taking account of earned interest.

So how does this tell us whether Wahid is making a smart investment choice? The modification of Keys 1, 2, and 3 for investment decisions comes down to this:

> Choose as long as the present value of the stream of future earnings is greater than the price of the investment.

For Wahid, the present value of $982.14 is *less than* the price of the investment ($1000), so it is not a smart choice. Wahid would make more money if he put his money in the bank.

Look at what happens to the choice when the interest rate changes. If the interest rate were to fall to 5 percent (0.05), while everything else about the investment stays the same, the present value calculation becomes

$$\text{Present Value} = \frac{\$1100}{(1 + 0.05)} = \frac{\$1100}{1.05}$$
$$\text{Present Value} = \$1047.62$$

To check the present value calculation — amount that, if invested today, will grow to $1100, taking account of earned interest — start with $982.14 today, and add 12 percent interest for the year ($982.14 × 0.12), which is $117.86. Total = $1100.

Now the present value of $1047.62 is *greater than* the price of the investment ($1000), so it becomes a smart choice. You can check the wisdom of this choice by calculating what Wahid would earn in the bank if he invested his $1000 at 5 percent interest. At the end of the year he would have $1050 from the bank, which is *less than* the $1100 he would have from investing in the laminating machine. (To keep things simple, I am assuming Wahid believes there is a 100 percent probability he will get the $1100, so there is no need to add the complication of risk compensation.)

Don't be concerned about other complications of the formula for investments with longer payoffs (when *n* is greater than 1), or uneven amounts of money available in different years. That's what accountants are for (and calculators and accounting software) — you don't need to master those calculation details. But it is important to understand the *principle* of present value, which underlies all those calculations. Understanding present value calculations is essential for any business owner or investor. Besides business machinery investments, present value calculations are behind the valuation of financial investments like corporate stocks and bonds. Those assets promise a stream of future payments in the form of dividends on stocks, or fixed coupon payments on bonds. How much is that future stream worth? Is a stock overvalued or undervalued? All those questions depend on present value calculations.

The intuition behind the definition of present value is that $1 in the future is not worth as much as $1 today because if you had the dollar invested today you could be earning interest on it. That's why, to calculate the *value today* of a stream of future revenues, you can't simply add up those future revenues. They are not worth as much as the same sum today because they don't take into account the interest that you could have earned if you had invested that sum today.

Accountants (and economists) would say you have to **discount** the future revenues to adjust for forgone interest. In the original example, Wahid's revenues of $1100 next year from the laminating machine are discounted to be worth only $982.14 in the present, taking into account forgone interest. Now try the definition again (and hopefully this time it should make sense):

The **present value** of a future amount of money is the amount that, if invested today, will grow as large as the future amount, taking account of earned interest.

The concept of present value gives you, and any investor, a method to simplify the future stream of revenues from an investment to a single number today. Present value converts a *flow* of future revenues into a *stock* concept, into a value at a moment in time — today — that you can compare with cost today to make a smart choice. And, to repeat, the rule for a smart investment choice is this:

Choose as long as the present value of the stream of future earnings is greater than the price of the investment.

Revenues available in future not worth as much as revenues today, because today's revenues earn interest.

discount: reduction of future revenues for forgone interest

Refresh 11.3

1. In your own words, explain present value. What is its formula?

2. What is the comparison problem that the concept of present value helps solve?

3. Suppose someone offers you a bond that will pay you $2000 at the end of a year. If the interest rate is 7 percent (0.07), what is the most you would be willing to pay for the bond today? Why?

11.4 Why Sidney Crosby Plays By Different Rules: Land, Economic Rent, and Superstar Salaries

What does the rent you pay your landlord have in common with Sidney Crosby's income? More than you think.

Describe economic rent, and explain its importance for determining income.

Economic Rent

Economists have a concept called **economic rent**, which is a form of income that is paid to any input in relatively inelastic supply. Elasticity is about responsiveness, and inelastic supply means, as I'm sure you remember, that the quantity supplied is *un*responsive to a rise in price. As the price rises, the quantity supplied hardly increases at all.

Land is a classic example of an input in inelastic supply. Consider the block of land at the corner of Burrard and Alberni streets in downtown Vancouver. No matter how high rents go for that piece of land, it won't cause more land to grow at the corner of Burrard and Alberni. The retail shops on this block pay very high rents to the landowners, and the shops also charge very high prices for the luxury products/services they sell to the wealthy consumers who shop in this neighbourhood.

How do we explain these high prices — both the high rents paid to landlords and the high prices of products/services sold in the shops? The usual answer for an economist is that . . . drum roll . . . prices (and quantities) come from the interaction of demand and supply. But it turns out that for inputs like land in inelastic supply, the answer is different — prices are effectively determined by demand only.

For most outputs and inputs, the law of supply applies. A rise in price causes an increase in quantity supplied. If the price is high enough to generate economic profits, more businesses enter the industry (an increase in supply), and the price falls until businesses are just earning normal profits. The invisible hand of the market adjusts quantities so that once again demand and supply are in balance, and the market provides the products/services we value most along with the inputs necessary to produce those outputs.

With land and other inputs in inelastic supply, there is no supply response. If demand increases, the price of the input rises but there is no increase in quantity supplied. If demand for the input decreases, the price of the input falls but there is no decrease in quantity supplied. This part of the story shouldn't sound that strange. The strange part is what this does to the relationship between high rents and high prices for products/services sold in the high-rent shops.

economic rent: income paid to any input in relatively inelastic supply

For inputs like land and superstars in inelastic supply, prices are effectively determined by demand only.

▼

Superstars and expensive condominiums located on prime real estate are good examples of inelastic supply. What other examples of inelastic supply do you see every day?

High Input Prices Cause High Output Prices   For most products/services, high input prices cause high output prices. If businesses have to pay higher prices for inputs like energy or labour or raw materials, they usually pass on those higher costs to consumers in the form of higher output prices. If I asked you to explain the high prices of products/services in the shops in downtown Vancouver, you, and most people, would probably say, "The high prices for products/services are caused by the high rents the shopkeepers have to pay to landlords." But you would be dead wrong.

High Output Prices Cause High Input Prices   When an input like land is in inelastic supply, it goes to the highest bidder (demander). Why would shopkeepers be willing to pay such high rents, when they know cheaper rents are available elsewhere in the city? They know that in real estate, the three most important factors are location, location, and location. A good location generates high customer traffic, and this location brings in many high-income, free-spending customers. Smart shopkeepers know they can charge these customers high prices for products/services, so the shopkeepers bid up the rents.

For inputs in inelastic supply like land, high output prices cause high input prices (economic rents). The shopkeepers have to earn normal profits, or they wouldn't continue at that location. But it is the landlords, the owners of the input in inelastic supply, who really do well. The price, or rent, paid for the land is not proportional to the productivity of land as an input, as is the case for labour. Rents are demand driven, determined by "what the market will bear." Owners of inelastically supplied inputs are like mini-monopolists with barriers to entry. Their economic rents, like economic profits, stay high because no new competitors can enter. You can't build two buildings on one spot.

Is Sidney Crosby a Landlord?

What does this have to do with Sidney Crosby, and the income he and other superstars earn? Sidney Crosby, Tiger Woods, Angelina Jolie, Madonna, and landlords actually have much in common — they all own inputs that are in relatively inelastic supply.

When salaries go up for all professional athletes and entertainers, there is a large, elastic response in the quantity supplied of people with average talent. But superstars have rare talent that is not easily reproduced. And fans will pay plenty to see superstars, but very little for average talent. That means much of superstars' income takes the form of economic rent, rather than wages paid for their marginal productivity. Superstars, like landlords, are like mini-monopolists with barriers to entry. Their talents go to the highest bidders, and their incomes are largely demand-determined, just like the rent on land.

Are Superstar Salaries to Blame for High Ticket Prices?

In July 2007, Sidney Crosby signed a five-year, US$43.5-million contract with the Pittsburgh Penguins. He also has tens of millions of dollars in product endorsement income from Gatorade, Nike, and other companies. Fans have long loved to complain about astronomical superstar incomes. Economics Out There describes fan anger during the National Hockey League lockout of players that cancelled the 2004/2005 season. Fans blamed the players for being too greedy, and continue to believe that high player salaries are to blame for the high ticket prices that make NHL games unaffordable for your average fan.

But fans are making the same mistake you made if you explained high retail prices in trendy Vancouver shops as being caused by the high rents the shopkeepers have to pay landlords.

For most products/services, high input prices cause high output prices.
For inputs in inelastic supply, high output prices cause high input prices — high economic rents.

Superstars, like landlords, are mini-monopolists whose income comes from economic rent. Talents go to highest bidders, and incomes are demand-determined like rent on land.

Why are NHL owners willing to bid against each other to sign Sidney Crosby and other superstars to high-priced contracts? The owners know that fans will pay a lot of money to see real talent on the ice, and those fans who can't afford to go to the games in person will flock to TV sets to watch. That means owners can sell the TV rights to the games for even more money. Fan willingness to pay so much to watch superstar hockey players causes high ticket prices; tickets are priced to "what the market will bear." In turn, high ticket prices (and TV revenues) are the reason why owners bid against each other and drive up superstar salaries. *The Globe and Mail* sportswriter in Economics Out There knows his economics!

The salary cap implemented after the lockout was designed not to prevent players from being too greedy but to limit the bids owners could make for players, to ensure some of the economic rents earned by scarce superstars would end up with the owners instead of the players. Since incomes of inputs in inelastic supply are entirely demand determined, the salary cap limited the demand by owners and thereby limited (believe it or not) superstar salaries, leaving more of the ticket and TV revenues for the owners.

Economic rent is an important concept for understanding not only incomes from land and real estate, but also incomes of superstars and the economics of industries like professional sports, music, and entertainment.

ECONOMICS Out There

Fans Stick It to NHL Players

The 2004/2005 hockey season lives in infamy for its lockout of players. During the dispute, fans were vocal with their opinions. When player rep Bob Goodenow went on *The National* to field fans' questions, he heard variations on one theme: the players are paid too much, causing ticket prices to be too high, and should accept a salary cap. Polls showed that fans blame the lockout on the players. Goodenow explained that ticket prices are dictated not by the players' salaries, but by the team owners' assessment of what fans are willing to pay — what the market will bear. Goodenow was correct to point out that in the World Cup of Hockey, owners priced top tickets in Toronto at $650 even though the players were paid only expenses and a contribution to their pension fund. According to *The Globe and Mail* writer David Shoalts, Goodenow is right, and fans have to realize that "owners charge $200 a ticket and $12 a beer in some cities because you will pay it," not because of player salaries.

Source: David Shoalts, "Fans Stick It to NHL Players," *The Globe and Mail*, September 23, 2004.

Refresh
11.4

1. Define economic rent.

2. For most products/services, what is the relationship between input prices and output prices? For inputs in inelastic supply, what is the relationship between input prices and output prices?

3. Music groups usually go on tour to promote a new album. Given the availability of digital album downloads, what is the difference in the elasticity of supply of albums versus the elasticity of supply of concert performances? Where are (talented) musicians more likely to earn economic rents?

www.myeconlab.com

Explain the sources of poverty and describe trade-offs in policies to help the poor.

In all your hopes and dreams about what you want out of life, do you ever dream of being poor? So why do 3.4 million Canadians (more than 1 in 10 individuals) live in poverty in the midst of a market economy that supposedly does such a good job of efficiently providing the products/services we desire?

Connected through the circular flow, we all depend on markets for producing outputs that support our standard of living, and for providing jobs and investment opportunities so we can earn money to afford to buy those outputs. The income you earn depends on the quantities of inputs you own — labour, capital, land, and entrepreneurship — and the prices you can sell them for on input markets. Poverty results from those same quantities and prices — but from *not* owning enough of a labour skill or asset that the market values, or from *not* getting a high enough price for what you do own.

In this last section, we will look at data on who is rich, who is poor, and how equally or unequally incomes and wealth are distributed among the population. We will briefly explain why incomes vary, what might be done to help the poor, and trade-offs in so doing.

The interconnectedness of the circular flow is important in thinking about these questions. What you *are* worth depends on the prices the market places on what you own, which are derived from the prices the market places on the outputs that can be produced using your inputs. What you, or any human being, *should be* worth, and whether governments should help those who are poor, are normative questions that economics does not answer but that you must answer as a citizen evaluating policy choices or charitable commitments.

"What are you worth?" is a positive question; depends on quantities of inputs you own and prices markets place on those inputs. "What should you, or any person, be worth?" is a normative question you must answer as a citizen.

What Do We Earn and Own?
Measuring (In) Equality of Income and Wealth

Statistics Canada (www.statcan.gc.ca) collects data on all aspects of the Canadian economy, including income and wealth. The most recent comprehensive data were collected for 2006. These numbers, which are organized by family, not individuals, give an idea of how your family's income and wealth compare to that of other Canadian families.

Income   Figure 11.5 displays data for average market income in 2006. Market income consists of income (*before* taxes and government transfer payments) from selling on markets the inputs we have been discussing — wages from labour, investment income from capital and other resources, and entrepreneurial income from self-employment. For families as a whole, the majority of income comes from labour earnings. Of every $100 earned, $78 comes from employment and $10.10 comes from investment income. The remainder comes from self-employment and other income sources.

Statistics Canada arranges all families in order, from lowest to highest earning, and then divides the population into five equal groups called quintiles. The lowest quintile is the 20 percent of all families earning the lowest incomes. The highest quintile is the 20 percent of all families earning the highest incomes.

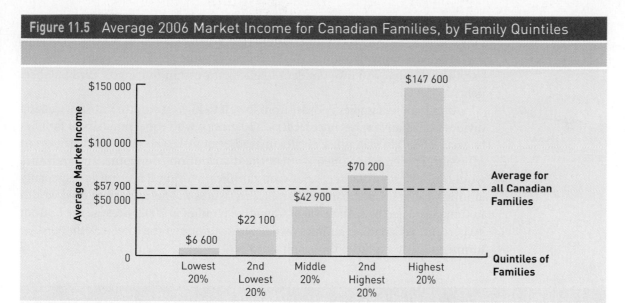

Figure 11.5 Average 2006 Market Income for Canadian Families, by Family Quintiles

Source: Adapted from Statistics Canada, "Income in Canada 2006," Catalogue No. 75-202-X, Table 8-1, May 2008, p. 76.

The average market income for all Canadian families was $57 900. But that average comes from combining very different incomes. As you can see, the average market income was only $6600 for the poorest 20 percent of families, $42 900 for the middle 20 percent, and $147 600 for the richest 20 percent of families.

One way statisticians measure inequality is by calculating what *percentage of total income earned in Canada* is earned by each quintile. When you add the percentages for all five quintiles, it sums to 100 percent. If income were distributed perfectly equally, each 20 percent of families would earn 20 percent of total income. Figure 11.6 shows what those calculations look like for 2006.

If income were distributed perfectly equally, each 20 percent of families would earn 20 percent of total income.

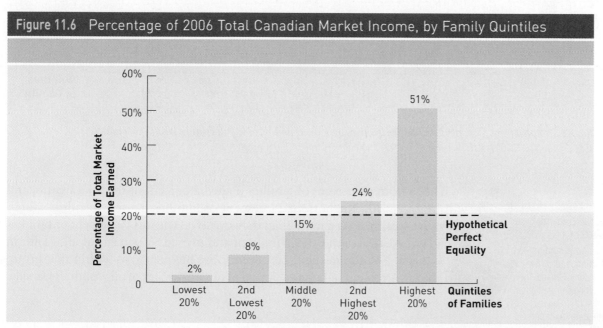

Figure 11.6 Percentage of 2006 Total Canadian Market Income, by Family Quintiles

Source: Adapted from Statistics Canada, "Income in Canada 2006," Catalogue No. 75-202-X, Table 8-1, May 2008, p. 76.

The poorest 20 percent of families earned 2 percent of total income in Canada, the middle 20 percent earned 15 percent of total income, and the richest 20 percent earned 51 percent of total income.

Wealth   Income is what you *earn*, while wealth is what you *own*. Income is a flow concept, measured per unit of time (per year), and wealth is a stock concept measured at a moment in time. Wealth is the net value of all your assets, minus any liabilities of what you owe (student loans, that outstanding credit card balance, debts to anyone else).

After ranking families in order from lowest to highest wealth, Statistics Canada divides Canadian families into deciles — 10 groups with equal numbers of families in each. The statisticians use deciles instead of quintiles because the distribution of wealth is even more unequal than the distribution of income, and quintiles would hide large differences between families *within* each quintile, especially among wealthier Canadians. Figure 11.7 measures the percentage of total wealth in Canada owned by each decile of Canadian families in 2006. Because the bottom 40 percent of Canadian families owned almost none of the total wealth, they are lumped together to keep the graph simpler.

A "decile" is 10 percent (one-tenth) of a population.

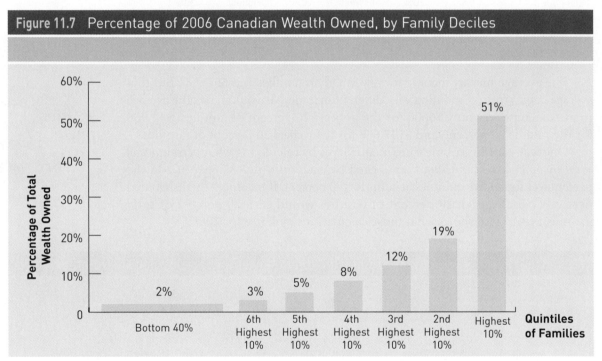

Figure 11.7   Percentage of 2006 Canadian Wealth Owned, by Family Deciles

Source: Adapted from Statistics Canada, Perspectives on Labour and Income, "Revisiting Wealth Inequality," Catalogue No. 75-001-XIE, volume 7, no. 12, Table 8, December 2006, p. 14.

The bottom 40 percent of families owned 2 percent of the total wealth, and within that group the bottom 24 percent of families had no wealth at all (or negative wealth, owing more than they owned). The top 10 percent of families had a median wealth of $1.2 million, and owned 51 percent of all wealth in Canada. The top decile masks even more inequality, as within that group the top 1 percent of families owned about 24 percent of all wealth in Canada.

Other Wealth Issues   Besides these dramatic differences in quantities of wealth, there are also differences in the kinds of assets owned. Wealth owned by the bottom half of families consists largely of the value of their automobiles, and some savings. For the wealthy, assets consist largely of equities, bonds, real estate, life insurance, and pension plans.

There is also a connection between wealth and income. The capital and land assets you own as wealth also produce a flow of income in the form of interest, dividend, and rent payments. For families in the higher range of the income distribution of Figures 11.5 and 11.6, more of their income consists of investment income. For families in the lower ranges, most of their income consists of labour income. Income is what you earn, but it is also increased by the flows from what you own.

Why Are You (Not) Rich?

Besides wealth, what accounts for inequalities in income — what factors are connected with being poor and being rich? Let's start by defining what it means to be poor in terms of income.

Poverty   The income and wealth data show dramatic differences between families but do not clearly identify who is poor. There are many different definitions of poverty, and poverty is a relative concept. Families considered poor in Canada would be considered extremely wealthy in many African or Asian countries, where millions survive on less than $1000 per year. Statistics Canada defines low-income families as those who spend at least one-fifth *more* of their income than the average family on the basic necessities of food, shelter, and clothing. For a family of three in Toronto, that makes the "poverty line" $26 624.

In 2006, 633 000 families in Canada lived below the poverty line, about 7 percent of all families. In those families were 760 000 children (under 18), meaning about 1 out of 10 children lived below the poverty line. Of those low-income families, over 28 percent were headed by a single, female parent.

There are many possible explanations for poverty that go far beyond the scope of this book — discrimination, cultural factors, immigration adjustments, health and disability difficulties, to list just a few. We will focus only on the key *economic* factor that helps explain both lower and higher incomes — human capital.

Human Capital Most Canadians' incomes come from employment, and we have seen that the price you receive in the labour market depends on your productivity. Your productivity, your value to your boss, and your income all increase with your experience, your training, and your education. Economists use the term **human capital** to capture the increased earning potential individuals acquire through work experience, on-the-job training, and education.

Figure 11.8 shows the impact on income of the education component of human capital.

human capital: increased earning potential from work experience, on-the-job training, education

Figure 11.8 Education and Income in Canada, 2005	
Education	**Median Income**
Less Than High School	$32 029
High School	$37 403
Trades or Apprentices	$39 996
College	$42 937
University below Bachelor Degree	$47 253
University Bachelor Degree	$56 048
Post-Bachelor Study	$66 535

Remember that you receive these education-based differences in income not just for one year, but for every year of your working life. In addition, wealth is correlated with education. For 2005, the average wealth of a Canadian without a university education was $214 700. The average wealth of university graduates was $364 800.

Of the choices under your control, your choice to pursue an education is a smart one when it comes to increasing your income, wealth, and ability to reach your material goals for life.

What Can Be Done to Help the Poor?

What can be done to address inequality and poverty? Let's look at this *positive* question before confronting the *normative* question of whether governments *should* use tax revenues to help the poor and change the market distribution of income. If, as a society, we want to reduce inequality and poverty, two of the most powerful policy options are 1) education and training, and 2) a progressive system of taxes and transfers. Let's look at each.

Policy options to reduce inequality and poverty: education, training, progressive tax and transfer system.

Education and Training Poverty means not having enough income. But lack of income is only a symptom of the underlying problem — a lack of inputs that the market values. Enhancing a person's human capital addresses this underlying problem. Government support for programs that increase human capital, whether through apprenticeships, training, or education, will increase a person's ability to earn income and rise above poverty lines.

In addition, as we saw in Chapter 10, education and training have positive externalities, with benefits that extend to employers, governments, and citizens who are not directly involved in the programs that improve human capital. Education and training are win–win policies for the poor and for society as a whole.

Improving human capital through education and training treats underlying cause of poverty, lack of inputs the market values.

Progressive Taxes and Transfers Governments can also directly reduce poverty and inequality by using the tax system to implement Robin Hood's motto — take from the rich and give to the poor.

In principle, a tax system may be progressive, regressive, or proportional. Both the federal and provincial tax systems use **progressive taxes**, meaning that as your income increases, you pay a higher percentage in tax. With **regressive taxes**, as your income increases you pay a lower percentage in tax. **Proportional taxes** — often called flat-rate taxes — charge the same percentage regardless of your level of income.

progressive taxes: tax rate increases as income increases

regressive taxes: tax rate decreases as income increases

proportional (flat-rate) taxes: tax rate same regardless of income

Both the federal and provincial governments have progressive tax systems that take more from the rich than from the poor. While tax rates vary from province to province, the combined federal and provincial income tax rates look something like this. The poorest Canadians pay no income tax at all. The tax rate on *additional* dollars earned (the **marginal tax rate**; see the word *additional*?) is roughly 25 percent up to $35 000, 35 percent up to $75 000, and 45 percent over $125 000. That means, for example, for every dollar you earn between $35 000 and $75 000, the government takes 35 cents and you keep 65 cents.

marginal tax rate: rate on additional dollar of income

The progressive income tax is combined with a system of **transfer payments** that redistribute the tax revenues to those toward the bottom of the income distribution. Transfers are like negative income taxes. The main types of transfers occur through welfare programs (Canada Child Tax Benefit, Canada Assistance Plan), social security programs for seniors (Old Age Security), and Employment Insurance (for the unemployed).

transfer payments: payments by government to households

As a direct result of the progressive tax and transfer systems, the distribution of income *after transfers and taxes* is more equal than the market distribution of Figures 11.5 and 11.6. Figures 11.9 and 11.10 on the next page show the income distribution data for 2006 *after transfers and taxes*.

Source: Adapted from Statistics Canada, "Income in Canada 2006," Catalogue No. 75-202-X, Table 8-5, May 2008, p. 80.

In Figure 11.9 the average income of the lowest 20 percent of families rises from $6600 (in Figure 11.5) to $13 100 after taxes and transfers are applied. The second-lowest 20 percent of families' average incomes rise from $22 100 to $29 100. And the average income of the highest 20 percent of families *falls* from $147 600 to $119 300 after taxes and transfers. The result is that income shares, compared to Figure 11.6, move slightly closer toward the hypothetical equality where each quintile of families earns 20 percent of the total income in Canada. In Figure 11.10, after taxes and transfers, the share of total income for the lowest quintile of families rises from 2 to 5 percent, the share for the second-lowest quintile of families rises from 8 to 11 percent, and the share for the highest quintile of families *falls* from 51 to 44 percent.

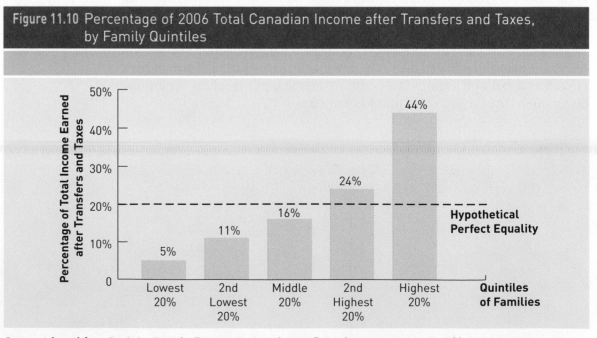

Figure 11.10 Percentage of 2006 Total Canadian Income after Transfers and Taxes, by Family Quintiles

Source: Adapted from Statistics Canada, "Income in Canada 2006," Catalogue No. 75-202-X, Table 8-5, May 2008, p. 80.

Incentive Effects of Redistribution   This redistribution of income from the rich to the poor is not as straightforward as it appears because of incentive effects and the interconnectedness of input and output markets through the circular flow. When governments take some of your income in taxes, leaving you less, it reduces the incentives you have to provide inputs and produce outputs. A market economy is based on the coordination of self-interest — and from a self-interest point of view, taking home 65 cents on the dollar is not as good as taking home all 100 cents. Because of incentive effects, taxes do not simply redistribute an unchanged quantity of products/services and income. If taxes cause some individuals to supply less to the market, because the rewards aren't as high (that's the law of supply), then input owners will earn less and output markets will produce fewer products/services. To sum up the incentive effect in a phrase, "A more equally shared pie may be a smaller pie."

Economists disagree about just how significant is the incentive effect, but unlike the largely win–win nature of education and training policies, this is a trade-off that must be considered for tax and transfer policies.

Due to incentive effects, "A more equally shared pie may be a smaller pie."

What Should Be Done to Help the Poor? Equity and Efficiency One More Time

Clearly, policies exist that can be used to reduce poverty and inequality. But *should* governments use tax revenues for that purpose? This normative question is not as coldhearted as it might sound. True, most religions throughout history have treated helping the poor as a moral obligation. Basic human compassion inclines us to help others in need, and the Golden Rule — do unto others as you would have them do unto you — even suggests an element of self-interest in charity. But if I have taught you anything, it's that every choice involves trade-offs. To know whether government policies to reduce poverty and inequality are smart choices, we must once again apply Key 1. Are additional benefits greater than additional costs?

Comparing costs and benefits is relatively easy for personal choices, where you both pay the costs and reap the benefits. But policies to help the poor are different, as the costs and benefits apply to different people. How you feel about Robin Hood's motto depends considerably on whether you are being taken from or given to. And a personal choice to be charitable is different from a social choice by a government (even a democratically elected government) to implement a progressive tax and transfer system that takes from some to give to others.

One of the policy trade-offs that arises from the analogy "a more equally shared pie may be a smaller pie" is the classic efficiency versus equity trade-off from Chapter 5. Let me remind you that when we say markets are efficient in producing the products/services we value the most, with the least waste, we mean outputs go to those most *willing and able to pay*. An efficient market outcome may include (poor) people who are unable to pay for basic necessities like shelter or food or medical care. An efficient market outcome is not necessarily fair or equitable.

Costs and benefits of policies to help the poor apply to different people. How you feel about Robin Hood's motto depends on whether you are being taken from, or given to.

Efficient market outcome not necessarily fair or equitable. May include (poor) people unable to pay for basic necessities like shelter, food, medical care.

Suppose the incentive effect of a progressive tax and transfer policy is large, and a more equal income distribution and reduced poverty come at the expense of slightly lower standards of living for everyone else in Canada. What is the smart policy choice? Economics alone does not provide the answer. The answer, which will be different for everyone, depends on the *value* you place personally on efficiency versus equity. If you value efficiency far more than equity, you may not be willing to sacrifice lower standards of living for all to benefit those who are poorest. If you value equity more than efficiency, the policies will seem desirable and the trade-offs acceptable.

What Is Equity? These differing valuations of efficiency and equity are also combined with differing views about equity. You are not likely to hear abstract philosophical debates about the meaning of equity, but you will hear politicians opposing or supporting tax and transfer policies — and you have to decide whom to vote for.

A conservative politician on the right end of the political spectrum might oppose progressive taxes and transfers because she believes the efficiency of markets is most important for generating the economic prosperity that will ultimately help the poor. She might also believe that markets are already equitable because they provide everyone with *equal opportunities* (and fully expects that each person's accomplishments in life and income will differ with differences in talents, initiative, and luck). From her perspective, inequality and poverty are the result of either personal choices, failures, or misfortunes. They are not systemic "market failures" that require government intervention to correct. Personal charity is a more appropriate response for personal misfortune.

A left-leaning politician might favour progressive taxes and transfers because he believes equity is more important than efficiency. He is concerned with improving the equality of incomes, and does not believe poor children have the same opportunities as rich children. Inherited wealth stacks the rules of the game in favour of children who are born into wealth, and he believes the misfortune (only from an income perspective) of being born into a family with a single, female parent should not consign such children to a lifetime of poverty. He thinks all individuals are worthy of having the basic necessities, and takes issue with the market principle that what you are worth is simply what the market is willing to pay for the inputs you provide. From his perspective, poverty and inequality are market failures, failures of a market system that responsible, democratic governments are obligated to remedy.

You cannot decide that one politician is right and the other is wrong just on the basis of facts, or by using the Three Keys to Smart Choices. What you can — and, as a citizen, *must* decide — is which politician's *values* best match your own.

Refresh 11.5

1. Explain the differences between income and wealth.

2. What are the two main policy options for reducing poverty and inequality? What other policies can you think of that would address other causes of poverty?

3. Where does your family fit into the Canadian distribution of income? Of wealth? Are you surprised?

www.myeconlab.com

What *Are You* Worth?

Demand and Supply in Input Markets, and Income and Wealth Distributions

CHAPTER SUMMARY

11.1 SWITCHING SIDES: INCOMES ARE PRICES AND QUANTITIES IN INPUT MARKETS

Incomes are determined by prices and quantities in input markets. In the input markets of the circular flow of economic life, households supply to businesses labour, capital, land, and entrepreneurship in exchange for wages, interest, rent, and profits.

- In input markets, households are sellers and businesses are buyers.
- Income — what you earn — is a flow.
  - **Flow** — amount per unit of time.
  - Income for labour, capital, and land = price of input × quantity of input
- Wealth — total value of assets you own — is a stock.
  - **Stock** — fixed amount at a moment in time.
- Entrepreneurs' incomes are not determined by price × quantity. Entrepreneurs earn profits. Economic profits are a residual — what is left over from revenues after all opportunity costs of production (including normal profits) have been paid for other inputs.

11.2 WHAT HAVE YOU DONE FOR ME LATELY? LABOUR AND MARGINAL REVENUE PRODUCT

For maximum profits, businesses should hire additional labour as long as labour's marginal revenue product (additional benefit) is greater than the wage paid for labour (additional cost).

- To hire labour, business must pay market wage, which reflects best opportunity cost of person supplying labour.
- Business demand for labour is **derived demand** — demand for output and profits businesses can derive from hiring labour.

- **Marginal product** — *additional* output from hiring one more unit of labour.
  - When businesses hire additional labourers to work with fixed inputs, there is **diminishing marginal productivity** — each additional labourer has lower marginal product than previous labourer.
- **Marginal revenue product** — additional revenue from selling output produced by additional labourer.
  - To calculate labourer's *marginal revenue product* multiply *marginal product × price of output*.
  - *Marginal revenue product* diminishes for additional labourers.
- Rule for maximum profits for business:
  Hire additional hours of labour (or any input) as long as marginal revenue product is greater than the wage (or price of the input).

11.3 ALL PRESENT AND ACCOUNTED FOR: INTEREST ON CAPITAL AND PRESENT VALUE

Present value tells you what money earned in the future is worth today. Present value compares the price you pay for today's investment against the investment's future earnings. For a smart choice, the present value of the investment's future earnings should be greater than the investment's price today.

- The **present value** of a future amount of money is the amount that, if invested today, will grow as large as the future amount, taking account of earned interest.

$$\text{Present Value} = \frac{\text{Amount of Money Available in } n \text{ Years}}{(1 + \text{Interest Rate})^n}$$

- Revenues available in future not worth as much as revenues today because today's revenues earn interest.
  - **Discount** — reduction of future revenues for forgone interest.
- Present value gives you a method to simplify future stream of revenues from an investment to a single number today. Converts flow of future revenues into stock concept, a value at a moment in time — today — you can compare with cost today to make a smart choice.
- For a smart choice, the present value of investment's stream of future revenues should be greater than the price of the investment today.

11.4 WHY SIDNEY CROSBY PLAYS BY DIFFERENT RULES: LAND, ECONOMIC RENT, AND SUPERSTAR SALARIES

Income for any input in inelastic supply, for example land or superstar talent, is economic rent, which is determined by demand alone.

- **Economic rent** — income paid to any input in relatively inelastic supply.
  - Land is a classical example of an input in inelastic supply.
- For inputs like land in inelastic supply, prices effectively determined by demand alone.
- For most products/services, high input prices cause high output prices.
- For inputs in inelastic supply, high output prices cause high input prices — high economic rents.

11.5 WHAT *SHOULD* YOU BE WORTH?
INEQUALITY AND POVERTY

Government policies to address the market's unequal distributions of income and wealth involve trade-offs between efficiency and equality.

- "What are you worth?" is a positive question; depends on quantities of inputs you own and prices markets place on those inputs.

- "What should you, or any person, be worth?" is a normative question you must answer as a citizen.

- Poverty results from not owning labour skills or assets the market values, or from not getting high enough price for what you do own.

- Policy options to reduce inequality and poverty: education, training, progressive tax and transfer system.

- Improving human capital through education and training addresses underlying cause of poverty: lack of inputs the market values.

  - **Human capital** — increased earning potential from work experience, on-the-job training, education.

- Federal and provincial tax systems use **progressive taxes** — tax rate increases as income increases.

  - **Regressive taxes** — tax rate decreases as income increases.

  - **Proportional (flat-rate) taxes** — tax rate same regardless of income.

  - **Marginal tax rate** — rate on additional dollar of income.

  - **Transfer payments** — payments by government to households.

- Due to incentive effects, "A more equally shared pie may be a smaller pie."

- Efficient market outcome not necessarily fair or equitable. May include (poor) people unable to pay for basic necessities like shelter, food, medical care.

- Governments can directly reduce poverty and inequality using tax and transfer system to take from rich and give to poor (like Robin Hood).

  - Costs and benefits of policies to help the poor apply to different people. How you feel about Robin Hood's motto depends on whether you are being taken from or given to.

TRUE/FALSE

Circle the correct answer.

11.1 PRICES AND QUANTITIES IN INPUT MARKETS

1. What you are worth, in a market economy, is what the market is willing to pay you for the inputs you provide.   **True   False**

2. If you earn $10 per hour and work 50 hours per week, your weekly income is $500.   **True   False**

3. Income is a stock of earnings received by an individual.   **True   False**

11.2 MARGINAL REVENUE PRODUCT

4. Businesses' demand for labour is derived from the input market.   **True**   **False**

5. For maximum profits, a business should hire labour only when the marginal revenue product is greater than the wage.   **True**   **False**

6. An employer will be more likely to hire more workers if the price of output rises.   **True**   **False**

11.3 INTEREST ON CAPITAL AND PRESENT VALUE

7. If someone offers you $1 today or $1 tomorrow, you should prefer $1 tomorrow.   **True**   **False**

8. When interest rates increase, present value increases.   **True**   **False**

9. If interest rates decrease, an investment that was smart before the decrease may no longer be smart.   **True**   **False**

11.4 LAND AND ECONOMIC RENT

10. For most products/services, high input prices cause high output prices.   **True**   **False**

11. Superstar salaries are to blame for high ticket prices.   **True**   **False**

11.5 INEQUALITY AND POVERTY

12. In Canada, income is more unequally distributed than wealth.   **True**   **False**

13. A regressive income tax redistributes income from the rich to the poor.   **True**   **False**

14. Compared with the market distribution of income, government transfers and taxes reduce the inequality of income distribution.   **True**   **False**

15. Earnings from work account for the majority of income in Canada.   **True**   **False**

MULTIPLE CHOICE

Circle the correct answer.

11.1 PRICES AND QUANTITIES IN INPUT MARKETS

1. Wealth differs from income because
   A) income is a stock, wealth is a flow.
   B) wealth is derived from income.
   C) income is what you earn, wealth is what you own.
   D) income is what you own, wealth is what you earn.

2. Which of the following statements is *false*?
   A) Wealth is income received from supplying labour.
   B) Rent is income received from supplying land.
   C) Normal profits are income received from supplying entrepreneurial abilities.
   D) Interest is income received from supplying capital.

11.2 MARGINAL REVENUE PRODUCT

3. The additional benefits from hiring an additional web designer are derived from the additional
   A) output of web pages he/she can produce.
   B) revenues from selling those additional web pages.
   C) profits from selling those additional web pages.
   D) all of the above.

4. Consider Figure 11.3 on page 281. How many designers (which cost $50 per hour) should Wahid hire if he can charge $20 per web page sold, rather than $15 per wage page sold?
   A) 2
   B) 3
   C) 4
   D) 5

5. Economic rent is
   A) paid only for the use of land.
   B) paid only for the use of capital.
   C) determined only by supply.
   D) income paid to any input in relatively inelastic supply.

11.3 INTEREST ON CAPITAL AND PRESENT VALUE

6. An investment choice is smart when the
    A) future stream of revenues is greater than the price of the investment.
    B) future stream of revenues is less than the price of the investment.
    C) present value of the future stream of revenues is greater than the price of the investment.
    D) present value of the future stream of revenues is less than the price of the investment.

7. The present value of a future amount of money is
    A) a stock concept.
    B) less than the future amount because future revenues are discounted to adjust for forgone interest.
    C) the amount that, if invested today, will grow as large as the future amount, taking account of earned interest.
    D) all of the above.

11.4 LAND AND ECONOMIC RENT

8. Rents are determined by
    A) demand.
    B) input prices.
    C) the price of capital.
    D) all of the above.

9. For inputs in inelastic supply, such as land or superstar talent,
    A) there is no supply response to higher prices.
    B) the price paid for the input is not proportional to its productivity.
    C) input prices are explained by output prices.
    D) all of the above.

10. During the lockout that cancelled the 2004/2005 hockey season, fans blamed
    A) the players.
    B) the owners.
    C) the CBC.
    D) themselves.

11. During the lockout that cancelled the 2004/2005 hockey season, fans *should* have blamed
    A) the players.
    B) the owners.
    C) the CBC.
    D) themselves.

12. Which of the following statements about the distribution of market income in Canada is *true*?

    A) The poorest 20 percent of families earn 2 percent of total income.

    B) The middle 20 percent of families earn 10 percent of total income.

    C) The poorest 40 percent of families earn 15 percent of total income.

    D) The richest 20 percent of families earn less than half of total income.

13. Which of the following statements about the distribution of wealth in Canada is *false*?

    A) The bottom 24 percent of families have no wealth or negative wealth.

    B) The bottom 40 percent of families own 20 percent of the total wealth.

    C) The wealthiest 10 percent of Canadian families own 51 percent of total wealth.

    D) The wealthiest 1 percent of Canadian families own 24 percent of total wealth.

14. If the marginal tax rate increases as income increases, the income tax is defined as

    A) progressive.

    B) proportional.

    C) negative.

    D) regressive.

15. Which of the following statements is *false*?

    A) A family of three in Toronto that makes less than $26 624 per year is considered to be in poverty.

    B) More than 50 percent of families in poverty are headed by a single, female parent.

    C) More than 600 000 families in Canada lived below the poverty line in 2006.

    D) One out of 10 children lived below the poverty line in 2006.

SHORT ANSWER

Write a short answer to each question. Your answer may be in point form.

1. Households and businesses interact in two sets of markets: input markets and output markets.

   A) Explain the difference in how households and businesses interact in the two markets.

   B) Provide an example of each type of market interaction.

2. Suppose Gordon Ramsay, world-renowned chef and star of the hit TV series *Hell's Kitchen,* is trying to determine how many cooks to hire for a new restaurant.

   A) Use the cliché "too many cooks in the kitchen" to describe the concept of diminishing marginal revenue product.

   B) The table below describes the marginal product of chefs Gordon is considering hiring. Assume the cost of a chef is $50 per hour and that the price for a buffet at his gourmet restaurant is $20. Because of his fame, Gordon can sell as many $20 lunches as he chooses to produce. Calculate the marginal revenue products for each quantity of labour and determine how many chefs he should hire.

Quantity Labour (workers)	Marginal Product (MP) (additional meals prepared per hour	Price P_{output} (per buffet sold)	Marginal Revenue Product $MP \times P_{output}$ (additional revenue generated per worker hour)
0	0	$20	0
1	10	$20	$200
2	8	$20	$160
3	6	$20	$120
4	4	$20	$80
5	2	$20	$40

   C) The table below shows Gordon Ramsay's choices if he considers a more productive set of chefs. Assume the wage rate for these workers is higher, at $70 an hour, but the price charged for a buffet remains the same. Calculate the marginal revenue products and determine how many chefs he should hire.

Quantity Labour (workers)	Marginal Product (MP) (additional meals prepared per hour	Price P_{output} (per buffet sold)	Marginal Revenue Product $MP \times P_{output}$ (additional revenue generated per worker hour)
0	0	$20	0
1	12	$20	$240
2	10	$20	$200
3	8	$20	$160
4	6	$20	$120
5	4	$20	$80

3. Suppose that Wahid is offered two different business investments:

   A) A man named Alberto, dressed in a pin-striped suit and wearing Dolce & Gabbana sunglasses, shows up at Wahid's office and makes the following business proposition:

      "*I've got the best web page development software on the market. It's guaranteed to boost your revenues by $3000 by the end of the year. I'll lease it to you for the year for $2800, cash up front.*"

      What is the present value of the investment if the interest rate is 10 percent? Is it a smart investment? Why or why not?

   B) A man named Arthur, wearing suspenders and thick-rimmed glasses, shows up at Wahid's office and makes the following business proposition:

      "*For the low-low price of $700 (cash up front) for a one-year lease, I can offer you web page development software that will increase your revenues at the end of the year by $800.*"

      What is the present value of the investment if the interest rate is 10 percent? Is it a smart investment? Why or why not?

4. Hockey is a favourite sport among many Canadians, so it deserves at least one short-answer problem.

   A) Who are the demanders and the suppliers in the NHL output market?

   B) Who are the demanders and the suppliers in the NHL input market?

   C) Explain why a high percentage of a hockey superstar's income takes the form of an economic rent rather than wages paid for their marginal productivity.

   D) Why might the public think a salary cap would lead to lower ticket prices?

5. What is human capital and why do those with higher amounts of human capital have higher income?

6. Reducing income inequality by redistributing income from the rich to the poor has disadvantages. Explain why there is a trade-off between equality and efficiency.

7. When a family receives social assistance benefits without working, an unintended consequence of this government policy is to reduce incentives to work. There may be a trade-off between greater equality and reduced output and efficiency. To encourage work, an alternative government policy can provide *additional* income to low-income individuals *if* they work. Explain why this alternative policy can reduce the trade-off between equality and efficiency.

8. Have federal and provincial governments adopted the Robin Hood motto?

9. What type of politician is more likely to favour progressive taxes and large social transfers? Do you favour progressive taxes and large social transfers? Why or why not?

10. Suppose you have finished your college degree and are considering whether it is a smart choice to invest in a university degree (bachelor level). Remember when I said "don't be concerned about other complications of the formula for investments with longer payoffs (when *n* is greater than 1)"? Well, because this is our last Study Guide question — and because I want you to use economics for making the most of life — this time I'm going to ask you, anyway. To help out, I will walk you through some of the present value calculations.

A) If the cost of tuition is $10 000 per year for 4 years, what is the opportunity cost of investing in a university bachelor degree? (*Note:* Assume the full $40 000 tuition is paid up front and that the opportunity cost of your time is zero.)

B) Many financial analysts compare the present value of an investment with the financial cost (or with what economists call the "opportunity cost of money"). However, economists compare present value with all relevant opportunity costs. Recalculate the present value of the opportunity cost in question A) using *all* opportunity costs and assuming your earnings would have been $20 000 per year (for 4 years) without the university bachelor degree. Assume the interest rate is 5 percent (or 0.05) and that you are paid at the end of each year.

C) Suppose your parents offer to give you $45 000 once you obtain your university bachelor degree (4 years from today), and this is the only additional stream of income you will receive from doing your degree.

    i) What is the present value today of investing in a university bachelor degree? (*Hint:* Use the formula with *n* = 4 years and an interest rate = 0.05.)

    ii) Is this a smart investment?

D) As Figure 11.8 on page 294 shows, individuals with a university bachelor degree have average incomes that are $13 000 per year higher than individuals with a college degree. Suppose your parents find out about this fact and no longer provide you with the $45 000 completion gift because they expect the $13 000 per year in additional income will apply to you for the next 20 years.

    i) What is the present value of the university investment if the interest rate is 5 percent during the 4 years of university and 0 percent during the 20 years of working?

    (*Hint:* Key 1 is to figure out what the present value of $13 000 per year for 20 years adds up to at the end of university; key 2 is to bring this amount to the present.)

    ii) What is the present value of this investment if the interest rate is 5 percent (or 0.05) during the 4 years of university and 5 percent (or 0.05) during the 20 years of working? (*Hint:* Key 1 is to figure out what the $13 000 per year for 20 years adds up to at the end of university; key 2 is to bring this amount to the present.)

E) Determine whether any scenario in question D is a smart investment.

Summing Up

In a very real way, you and I took an economics road trip in this book, leading you to better understand how to make smart choices in life. Together, we toured around the circular flow of economic life:

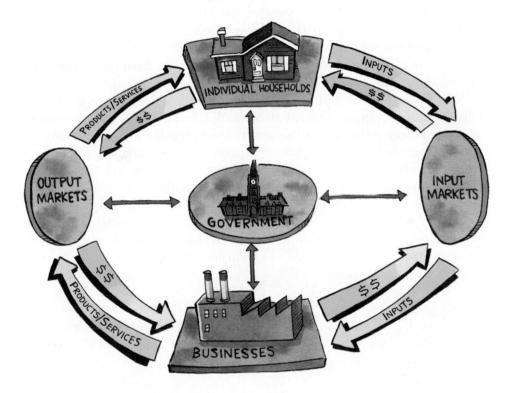

We visited individuals, businesses, and governments as they made choices to get what they wanted, and we looked at how those choices interact in markets — output markets and input markets.

Most importantly, you saw how to use the Three Keys to Smart Choices as directional signposts to guide your decision making. Those Three Keys are the key to smart choices for you personally and for society as a whole.

The Three Keys are like a map, helping you choose a direction to take at key decision points — forks in the road. When you face a decision, the Three Keys help you focus on the information that is most useful for you to make a smart choice.

We constantly make choices in life — as individuals, businesspeople, and citizens (say, for example, by voting). By following the Three Keys, you are more likely to achieve personal success in life — as a consumer, as a businessperson, and as an investor. You are also more likely to achieve success as a citizen by having a better understanding of the social consequences of your decisions, and by being able to intelligently and systematically evaluate the benefits and costs of policies that governments offer. You may yourself become a politician or policymaker, and will be able to use the Three Keys to make smart decisions.

Simply understanding the Three Keys to Smart Choices does not guarantee you will get the most out of your life. Setting goals based on your personal values is just as important. Do you value efficiency more than equity? Which system of health care is best for Canada? Are you willing to change your standard of living for a greener planet? Should governments redistribute income to help those who are poor? These decisions grow from your personal values. But, once you decide on a political position or social goal based on your values, economic thinking guides you in identifying the smart policy or personal action that will most efficiently achieve your goal. The Three Keys will help you get the most out of the goals your values lead you toward.

While our microeconomics road trip together is done, your life trip is continuing. By learning to think like an economist (using the Three Keys to Smart Choices), the key "roads" to making smart choices become clearer, and difficult decisions become simpler and more manageable. The economic way of thinking presented in this book will help you choose paths in life that lead to more satisfying and successful destinations — economics for making the most of life.

The only way for me to know how close I've come to achieving the goal of helping you make smart choices is to hear from you. Let me know what works for you in this book — and, more importantly, what doesn't. You can write to me at **avicohen@yorku.ca.** In future editions I will acknowledge by name all students who help improve *Economics for Life*.

Professor Avi J. Cohen
Department of Economics
York University

Glossary

A

absolute advantage: ability to produce a product/service at lower absolute cost than another producer (p. 8)

accounting profits: revenues minus obvious costs (including depreciation) (p. 138)

B

barriers to entry: legal or economic barriers preventing new competitors from entering a market (p. 165)

breakeven point: business just earning normal profits (no economic profits, no economic losses) (p. 146)

business cycles: ups and downs of overall economic activity (p. 176)

C

cap-and-trade system: limits emissions businesses can release into environment (p. 251)

capture view: government regulation benefits regulated businesses, not public interest (p. 224)

carbon tax: emissions tax on carbon-based fossil fuels (p. 250)

cartel: association of suppliers formed to maintain high prices and restrict competition (p. 218)

***caveat emptor* ("let the buyer beware"):** buyer alone responsible for checking quality of products before purchasing (p. 222)

collusion: conspiracy to cheat or deceive others (p. 218)

comparative advantage: ability to produce a product/service at lower opportunity cost than another producer (p. 9)

competition: active attempt to increase profits and gain market power of monopoly (p. 171)

complements: products/services used together to satisfy the same want (p. 39)

copyrights and **patents:** exclusive property rights to sell or license creations, protecting against competition (p. 165)

creative destruction: competitive business innovations generate economic profits for winners, improve living standards for all, but destroy less productive or less desirable products and production methods (p. 175)

Crown corporations: publicly owned businesses in Canada (p. 213)

D

decrease in demand: decrease in consumers' willingness and ability to pay (p. 38)

demand: consumers' willingness and ability to pay for a particular product/service (p. 29)

depreciation: tax rule for spreading cost over lifetime of long-lasting equipment; decrease in value because of wear and tear and because equipment becomes obsolete (p. 138)

derived demand: demand for output and profits businesses can derive from hiring labour (p. 280)

diminishing marginal productivity: each additional labourer has lower marginal product than previous labourer (p. 281)

discount: reduction of future revenues for forgone interest (p. 286)

E

economic losses: negative economic profits (p. 143)

economic profits: revenues minus all opportunity costs (obvious costs plus hidden opportunity costs) (p. 143)

economic rent: income paid to any input in relatively inelastic supply (p. 287)

economics: how individuals, businesses, and governments make the best possible choices to get what they want, and how those choices interact in markets (p. 3)

economies of scale: average cost of producing falls as quantity (scale) of production increases (pp. 166, 213)

efficient market outcome: coordinates smart choices of businesses and consumers so outputs produced at lowest cost (prices just cover all opportunity costs of production) and consumers buy products/services providing most bang per buck (marginal benefit greater than price) (p. 118)

elastic demand: large response in quantity demanded when price rises (p. 44)

elastic supply: large response in quantity supplied when price rises (p. 74)

elasticity (or **price elasticity of demand**): measures by how much quantity demanded responds to a change in price (p. 43)

elasticity of supply: measures by how much quantity supplied responds to a change in price (p.74)

emissions tax: tax to pay for external costs of emissions (p. 250)

equilibrium price: the price that balances forces of competition and cooperation, so that there is no tendency for change (p. 95)

excess demand (or **shortage**): quantity demanded exceeds quantity supplied (p. 91)

excess supply (or **surplus**): quantity supplied exceeds quantity demanded (p. 92)

explicit costs (or **obvious costs**): costs a business pays directly (p. 138)

external benefits (or **positive externalities**): benefits to society from your private choice that affect others, but that others do not pay you for (p. 242)

external costs (or **negative externalities**): costs to society from your private choice that affect others, but that you do not pay (p. 240)

externalities: costs or benefits that affect others external to a choice or a trade (p. 17)

extreme competition: many sellers producing identical products/services (p. 161)

F

fixed costs (or **sunk costs**): do not change with changes in quantity of output (p. 186)

flat-rate (proportional) taxes: tax rate same regardless of income (p. 295)

flow: amount per unit of time (p. 277)

free-rider problem: markets underproduce products/services with positive externalities (p. 255)

G

game theory: mathematical tool for understanding how players make decisions, taking into account what they expect rivals to do (p. 216)

government failure: regulation fails to serve public interest, instead benefits industry being regulated (p. 227)

H

human capital: increased earning potential from work experience, on-the-job training, education (p. 294)

I

implicit costs: opportunity costs of investing your own time and money (pp. 16, 139)

incentives: rewards and penalties for choices (p. 6)

increase in demand: increase in consumers' willingness and ability to pay (p. 38)

increase in supply: increase in businesses' willingness to produce (p. 69)

inelastic demand: small response in quantity demanded when price rises (p. 44)

inelastic supply: small response in quantity supplied when price rises (p. 74)

inferior goods: products/services you buy less of when your income increases (p. 39)

internalize the externality: transform external costs into costs producer must pay privately to government (p. 251)

L

law of demand: if the price of a product/service rises, quantity demanded decreases (p. 34)

law of supply: if the price of a product/service rises, quantity supplied increases (p. 67)

living wage: estimated at $10 per hour, defined to be enough to allow an individual in a Canadian city to live above the poverty line (p. 115)

M

macroeconomics: analyzes performance of the whole Canadian economy and global economy, the combined outcomes of all individual microeconomic choices (p. 14)

marginal benefits: additional benefits from the next choice, and changes with circumstances (pp. 16, 30)

marginal cost: additional opportunity cost of increasing quantity supplied, and changes with circumstances (p. 58)

marginal opportunity costs: additional opportunity costs from the next choice (pp. 16, 64)

marginal product: additional output from hiring one more unit of labour (p. 281)

marginal revenue: additional revenue from selling one more unit or from extension of sales (p. 186)

marginal revenue product: additional revenue from selling output produced by additional labourer (p. 282)

marginal social benefit (*MSB*): marginal private benefit plus marginal external benefit (p. 246)

marginal social cost (*MSC*): marginal private cost plus marginal external cost (p. 246)

marginal tax rate: rate on additional dollar of income (p. 295)

market: the interactions of buyers and sellers (p. 88)

market demand: sum of demands of all individuals willing and able to buy a particular product/service (p. 34)

market equilibrium: quantity demanded equals quantity supplied, economic profits zero, no tendency for change (p. 146)

market power: business's ability to set prices (p. 160)

market structure: characteristics that affect competition and pricing power—availability of substitutes, number of competitors, barriers to entry of new competitors (p. 162)

market supply: sum of supplies of all businesses willing to produce a particular product/service (p. 66)

market-clearing price: the price when quantity demanded equals quantity supplied (p. 95)

microeconomics: analyzes choices that individuals in households, individual businesses, and governments make, and how those choices interact in markets (p. 14)

minimum wage laws: example of price floor — minimum price set by government, making it illegal to pay a lower price (p. 115)

monopolistic competition: many small businesses make similar but slightly differentiated products/services (p. 169)

monopoly: only seller of product/service; no close substitutes available (p. 160)

N

Nash equilibrium: outcome of game where each player makes own best choice given the choice of the other player (p. 217)

natural monopolies: one business can supply entire market at lower cost than can two or more businesses (p. 167)

natural monopoly: technology allows only single seller to achieve lowest average total cost (p. 213)

negative externalities (external costs): costs to society from your private choice that affect others, but that you do not pay (p. 240)

normal goods: products/services you buy more of when your income increases (p. 39)

normal profits: compensation for business owner's time and money; sum of hidden opportunity costs (implicit costs); what business owner must earn to do as well as best alternative use of time and money (p. 142)

normative statements: about what you believe *should* be; involve value judgments (p. 121)

O

obvious costs (explicit costs): costs a business pays directly (p. 138)

oligopoly: few big sellers control most of market (p. 169)

opportunity cost: cost of best alternative given up (p. 5)

P

patents and **copyrights:** exclusive property rights to sell or license creations, protecting against competition (p. 165)

positive externalities (external benefits): benefits to society from your private choice that affect others, but that others do not pay you for (p. 242)

positive statements: about what is; can be evaluated as true or false by checking the facts (p. 121)

preferences: your wants and their intensities (p. 28)

present value: amount that, if invested today, will grow as large as future amount, taking account of earned interest (p. 284)

price ceiling (or rent controls): maximum price set by government, making it illegal to charge higher price (p. 112)

price discrimination: charging different customers different prices for same product/service (p. 196)

price elasticity of demand (or elasticity): measures by how much quantity demanded responds to a change in price (p. 43)

price floor: minimum price set by government, making it illegal to pay a lower price (p. 115)

price maker: pure monopoly with maximum power to set prices (p. 160)

price taker: business with zero power to set price different from the market price (p. 161)

prisoner's dilemma: game with two players who must each make a strategic choice, where results depend on other player's choice (p. 216)

product differentiation: attempt to distinguish product/service from competitors' products/services (p. 163)

progressive taxes: tax rate increases as income increases (p. 295)

property rights: legally enforceable guarantees of ownership of physical, financial, and intellectual property (p. 89)

proportional (flat-rate) taxes: tax rate same regardless of income (p. 295)

public goods: provide external benefits consumed simultaneously by everyone; no one can be excluded (p. 255)

public provision: government provision products/services with positive externalities, financed by tax revenue (p. 262)

public-interest view: government regulation eliminates waste, achieves efficiency, promotes public interest (p. 224)

Q

quantity demanded: amount you actually plan to buy at a given price (p. 33)

quantity supplied: quantity you actually plan to supply at a given price (p. 61)

R

rate of return regulation: set price allowing regulated monopoly to just cover average total costs and normal profits (p. 214)

regressive taxes: tax rate decreases as income increases (p. 295)

rent controls: example of price ceiling — maximum price set by government, making it illegal to charge higher price (p. 112)

S

scarcity: the problem that arises because we all have limited money, time, and energy (p. 4)

shortage (or excess demand): quantity demanded exceeds quantity supplied (p. 91)

stock: fixed amount at a moment in time (p. 277)

subsidy: payment to those who create positive externalities (p. 260)

substitutes: products/services used in place of each other to satisfy the same want (p. 38)

sunk costs: past expenses that cannot be recovered (p. 60)

supply: businesses' willingness to produce a particular product/service because price covers all opportunity costs (p. 61)

surplus (or excess supply): quantity supplied exceeds quantity demanded (p. 92)

T

total revenue: all money a business receives from sales, equal to price per unit (*P*) multiplied by quantity sold (*Q*) (p. 46)

transfer payments: payments by government to households (p. 295)

Answers to the Study Guide Questions

CHAPTER 1
TRUE/FALSE

1. True
2. False. Even people who win the lottery can never satisfy all of their wants; they also face trade-offs and have to make smart choices.
3. False. The opportunity cost is the value of what you give up to take that path, action, or activity.
4. False. The grant covers the money cost of getting an apprenticeship but does not cover the opportunity cost — the total value of what the individual gives up by taking an apprenticeship, which includes the money that the individual could have earned in a job that year.
5. False. Women have a larger incentive because the return on post-secondary education — the gap between the incomes of post-secondary graduates and high-school graduates — is higher for women than it is for men.
6. False. If men held a comparative advantage in performing housework then traditional gender roles would be reversed (that is, men would have been the ones doing the housework) because individuals are supposed to specialize in the activity where they hold a comparative advantage.
7. True
8. False. Darrel should stay home because the hourly wage he gives up to stay at home ($26) is less than the wage Sheryl gives up ($30).
9. True
10. True
11. False. The labour market is an input market.
12. True
13. False. They are microeconomic choices.
14. True
15. False. They are the costs that affect others.

MULTIPLE CHOICE

1. d) all of the above.
2. d) a challenge for everyone.
3. b) animals.
4. d) all of the above.
5. a) how much tuition you paid.
6. d) all of the above.
7. d) women with high-school diplomas earn more than men with high-school diplomas.
8. b) opportunity costs of upgrading to a college diploma will decrease.
9. b) comparative advantage.
10. a) give up/ get.
11. a) what interest rates to set.
12. c) Increasing the exchange rate of the Canadian dollar
13. d) all of the above.
14. b) past costs and benefits.
15. c) external costs will result in too much of that activity.

SHORT ANSWER

1. Weather, cost of trip (gas), if your partner tells you the relationship is over if you go, if your partner offers to cook for you or take you out to dinner if you stay.
2. Freedom, some privacy, parties at the residence, readily available study partners.
3. Decreasing tuition costs or guaranteeing minimum pay levels for people with degrees.
4. Include all money costs (gas, parking) and opportunity costs (earnings given up).
5. a) The increased penalty represents a rise in the price (or cost) of not wearing a seat belt, which will likely motivate more individuals to wear their seat belt.
   b) Drivers adjust their behaviour and drive more dangerously because they think they are now safe wearing a seat belt.
6. a) The opportunity cost of Jack spending all his time making bread (expressed per unit of what he gets) is $\frac{105}{70} = \frac{3}{2}$ cords of wood.

   The opportunity cost of Jack spending all his time cutting wood (expressed per unit of what he gets) is $\frac{70}{105} = \frac{2}{3}$ loaf of bread.

   The opportunity cost of Jacqueline spending all her time making bread (expressed per unit of what she gets) is $\frac{100}{50} = 2$ cords of wood.

   The opportunity cost of Jacqueline spending all her time cutting wood (expressed per unit of what she gets) is $\frac{50}{100} = \frac{1}{2}$ loaf of bread.

Opportunity Costs for Jack and Jacqueline

	Opportunity Cost of 1 Additional . . .	
	Loaf of Bread	**Cord of Wood**
Jack	Give up $\frac{105}{70} = \frac{3}{2}$ wood (cords)	Give up $\frac{70}{105} = \frac{2}{3}$ bread (loaves)
Jacqueline	Give up $\frac{100}{50} = 2$ wood (cords)	Give up $\frac{50}{100} = \frac{1}{2}$ bread (loaves)

Therefore, Jack has a comparative advantage in making bread and Jacqueline has a comparative advantage in chopping wood.

b) The opportunity cost of Jack spending all his time making bread (expressed per unit of what he gets) is $\frac{105}{70} = \frac{3}{2}$ cords of wood.

The opportunity cost of Jack spending all his time cutting wood (expressed per unit of what he gets) is $\frac{70}{105} = \frac{2}{3}$ loaf of bread.

The opportunity cost of Samantha spending all her time making bread (expressed per unit of what she gets) is $\frac{20}{40} = \frac{1}{2}$ cord of wood.

The opportunity cost of Samantha spending all her time cutting wood (expressed per unit of what she gets) is $\frac{40}{20} = 2$ loaves of bread.

Opportunity Costs for Jack and Samantha

	Opportunity Cost of 1 Additional . . .	
	Loaf of Bread	**Cord of Wood**
Jack	Give up $\frac{105}{70} = \frac{3}{2}$ wood (cords)	Give up $\frac{70}{105} = \frac{2}{3}$ bread (loaves)
Samantha	Give up $\frac{20}{40} = \frac{1}{2}$ wood (cords)	Give up $\frac{40}{20} = 2$ bread (loaves)

Therefore, Jack has a comparative advantage in chopping wood and Samantha has a comparative advantage in making bread.

7. Before trade, Jack gets 20 loaves of bread and 75 cords of wood. If Jack trades with Jacqueline, he specializes in making bread because this is the activity he has a comparative advantage in. After trading with Jacqueline, Jack ends up with 50 loaves of bread (the 70 he produced minus the 20 he traded away) and 20 cords of wood (the 0 he produced plus the 20 he traded for). This is worse than his allocation when being self-sufficient, which could have been 50 loaves of bread and 30 cords of wood (that is, he produces the same number of loaves of bread but 10 fewer cords of wood by trading with Jacqueline, compared to being self-sufficient).

If Jack trades with Samantha he specializes in cutting wood because this is the activity he has a comparative advantage in. After trading with Samantha, Jack ends up with 20 loaves of bread (the 0 he produced plus the 20 he traded for) and 85 cords of wood (the 105 he produced minus the 20 he traded away). This is better than his allocation when being self-sufficient, which is 20 loaves of bread and 75 cords of wood (that is, he produces the same amount of loaves of bread but gets 10 additional cords of wood by trading with Samantha, compared to being self-sufficient).

To summarize:

Jack's Consumption Possibilities

	Before Trade (2 possibilities shown)		After Trading with Jacqueline	After Trading with Samantha
Loaves of bread	20	50	50	20
Cords of wood	75	30	20	85

Therefore, Jack will prefer to go into partnership with Samantha.

8. **a)** Smokers often ignore the cost that non-smokers incur from inhaling their cigarettes. If they considered this cost in their decision-making process, then they may have found that the cost exceeded the benefit.

   b) No — if they did, they wouldn't have smoked indoors because the external cost would likely have been high enough to offset personal gains.

   c) Since a tax represents a rise in price to the end user, an increase in the tax on cigarettes should cause smokers to reduce the number of cigarette packs they buy, assuming they are sensitive to changes in the price. However, it is possible that some smokers may be addicted to the point where they cannot reduce their consumption.

9. The parents should be more willing to allow the daughter to pursue post-secondary school instead of work as the difference between college and without-college earnings is greater for women.

10. **a)** Too much pollution; carbon taxes, fines for cars that don't pass emission tests

    b) Too high; cigarette taxes, banning smoking indoors

    c) Too little education; tuition subsidies, loans

CHAPTER 2
TRUE/FALSE

1. False. Demand is a stronger word, meaning willing and able to pay.
2. True
3. True
4. True
5. False. Marginal benefit will equal average benefit only in special circumstances. For example, if a basketball player with a shooting percentage of 50 percent successfully makes one out of her next two shots, then the additional points she adds are equal to the amount of points she usually (on average) adds.
6. False. Quantity demanded is a much more limited term than demand. Only a change in price changes quantity demanded. A change in any other influence on consumer choice changes demand.
7. True
8. True
9. False, for normal goods. A decrease in income causes a decrease in demand. But True, for inferior goods.
10. False. As the holidays get nearer, people's willingness and ability to pay for certain products/services increases, for any given price. Therefore, an increase in demand drives the rising prices.
11. True
12. True
13. False. The fewer substitutes there are, the harder it is to switch away from a product whose price rises, and the less responsive and elastic is demand.

14. True
15. True

MULTIPLE CHOICE

1. d) preferences.
2. b) whatever we are willing to give up.
3. c) decreasing marginal benefits to eating.
4. d) additional costs of dating are greater than the additional benefits of dating.
5. a) 1.
6. c) consumers look for cheaper substitutes.
7. d) decrease in quantity demanded.
8. a) fast food
9. c) changes with income.
10. b) decrease.
11. d) all of the above
12. d) decrease in the quantity demanded of Kraft Dinner.
13. b) greater than 1.
14. a) demand for butter more elastic.
15. c) quantity demanded will decrease; total revenue will rise.

SHORT ANSWER

1. For a smart choice when making a decision, consider only additional (marginal) costs and additional (marginal) benefits of the decision. Ignore all sunk costs.
2. No. Demand is a willingness and ability to pay, so when you can't pay, your ability does not exist.
3. Water is scarce in the desert, so its marginal benefit is very high, while having pockets full of diamonds makes their marginal benefit low. In this situation, the price of water may exceed the price of diamonds.
4. Answers will vary but may include such responses as; "There's always Coca-Cola" (you should keep on having colas); "You've always got time for Tim Hortons" (go out of your way but come to the doughnut shop); "Harveys: Have it your way" (have a customized burger every time).
5. **a)** Quantity demanded will increase because price of consuming additional water has fallen to zero.

   b) Demand will decrease because water, a substitute product, is now cheaper.

   c) Demand will increase because water, a complement product, is now cheaper, allowing longer showers.

   d) Demand will increase because these are a complement product.

6. **a)** Number of consumers

   b) Prices of related products/services

   c) Expected future prices

7. (a) and (c) decrease demand. (b) causes a decrease in quantity demanded.

8. **a)** Elastic
   b) Elastic
   c) Inelastic
   d) Elastic
   e) Elastic
   f) Inelastic
9. Lower income earners respond to increases in income by having more children. Higher income earners respond to increases in income by having fewer children.
10. Demand for the latest fashions is more inelastic than demand for clothing in general. Shoppers are willing to pay higher prices for the latest fashions, but will snatch up older fashions if the price is right.

CHAPTER 3
TRUE/FALSE

1. False. When workers have fewer alternatives, they may be willing to accept lower wages.
2. True
3. True
4. True
5. False. Monthly rent payments are sunk costs that are not relevant to the decision of how much to produce.
6. False. Sunk costs are not part of opportunity costs.
7. True
8. False. Opportunity cost equals what you give up divided by what you get.
9. False. As you spend more time in any activity (for example, working instead of relaxing), the marginal opportunity cost of doing that activity increases.
10. True
11. True
12. False. Rise in price decreases market supply of the other product/service.
13. False. Supply is elastic when quantity supplied is very responsive to price.
14. True
15. True

MULTIPLE CHOICE

1. c) you have an exam the next day.
2. b) has to give up a job paying $15 an hour.
3. c) sunk costs are marginal costs
4. b) sunk cost.
5. c) sunk cost.
6. c) the same.
7. d) all of the above.
8. c) price of the supplied product/service
9. a) improvement in technology producing it.
10. a) the price of oil — a major input used to produce tires — rises.
11. a) increases supply.

12. c) inelastic supply.
13. a) snow shovels.
14. b) in a large town with many available workers.
15. d) inelastic.

SHORT ANSWER

1. **a)** No — you would receive only $10/hour × 20 hours = $200 for the weekend, which is lower than the value you place on spending time with your significant other on a weekend ($300).
   b) Perhaps — you would receive $15/hour × 20 hours = $300 for the weekend, which is equal to the value you place on spending time with your significant other. You may want to say no if you place additional value on other things that you may have to miss out on by working (for example, watching television, talking on MSN, going on Facebook, and so on). On the other hand, you may want to say yes if these other additional benefits from saying no are lower than some other additional benefits from saying yes (for example, getting on your boss's good side).

2. Employees who spend up to one-third of their life at work — 8 hours out of 24 in a day — value their free time. As employers want workers to put in more hours of work, the workers' free time becomes more scarce and valuable, so the marginal opportunity cost of an additional hour of work is greater.

3. Since women's decision to work is more elastic/sensitive to wage rates, higher income taxes (lower wage rates) will lead to women reducing their hours worked more than it would for men.

4. Some workers (particularly those with high income) will respond to wage increases by working fewer hours because they value additional hours of leisure over additional hours of work at this wage rate (possibly because they are earning so much money). This would violate the law of supply because as the price of labour (the wage) rises the quantity of labour supplied decreases.

5. **a)** True
   b) False. Higher wages — higher input prices — decrease supply.
   c) True
   d) True
   e) False. It will increase quantity supplied, not supply.

6. The money invested in the factory is a sunk cost because it cannot be undone. This cost, however, should not be considered in the decision to abandon the project. The project should be abandoned only if the additional costs of operating the business exceed the additional benefits.

7. Oil is a major input in the production of these products, so higher prices of inputs will cause their supply to decrease.

8. To produce air conditioners and bring them to the market is not easy; it involves long supply chains and the cooperation of many companies on wholesale and retail levels. Therefore, the price elasticity of supply of air conditioners is low (inelastic).

9. a) $33
   b) $152
   c) Fines have been set so that the marginal cost of raising your speed an additional 10 km/hour when you are already going at 130 km/hour is higher than when you are going at 120 km/hour ($152 versus $33). This is done to deter drivers from speeding at really high rates.

10. Open ended

CHAPTER 4
TRUE/FALSE

1. False. Transactions would not be voluntary and there would be no incentive to supply the product to consumers.
2. False. Price should cover all opportunity costs.
3. False. Price and quantity adjustments do not require the consumer or business to know anything about anyone's personal wants or production capabilities.
4. True
5. True
6. True
7. False. The surplus would put pressure on the price to fall because if prices increased Apu would sell even less and his surplus would grow larger.
8. False. An increase in supply will cause a surplus rather than a shortage.
9. True
10. True
11. False. The increased supply lowers the price of grey seals, which reduces the cost of producing seal coat fur, which results in a lower price charged to the consumer.
12. True
13. False. More Americans coming to Canada with a bachelor's degree will increase the supply of these workers and create downward pressure on the wages of educated workers.
14. True
15. True

MULTIPLE CHOICE

1. d) a market.
2. d) all of the above.
3. c) Leon's Furniture Ltd eliminating sales tax on all patio furniture items.
4. d) market-clearing price.
5. a) the price consumers are willing to pay equals the price suppliers are willing to accept.

6. a) higher prices.
7. d) demand decreases and supply increases.
8. c) allowing the price to fall.
9. c) demand is greater than supply for restaurant workers.
10. d) all of the above.
11. d) all of the above.
12. d) the demand for food service is greater than the supply of food service.
13. b) demand for *Harry Potter* novels may decrease.
14. c) the demand for nutrition-promoting foods will increase.
15. a) increase in demand.

SHORT ANSWER

1. The market price performs a communication function between buyers and sellers. A rise in price will communicate to suppliers that more must be produced and brought to the market, while a fall in price will communicate to the suppliers that they should produce less. The market-clearing price is the price at which no shortages or surpluses occur and no signals are sent to firms and consumers to change their smart choices.

2. a) $2, since this is the price for which there is no shortage or surplus.
   b) Quantity supplied is greater than quantity demanded, so there will be a surplus.
   c) Apu will end up with excess inventory, which will create pressure for the price to fall.

3. The demand for houses in Saskatchewan have increased because more Albertans are moving to Saskatchewan. This puts an upward pressure on housing prices in Saskatchewan if the supply of housing available remains the same over this time.

4. a) In a shortage, workers are in scarce supply and have a bargaining advantage.
   b) The use of temporary foreign workers reduces the size of the shortage in Canada, which lowers the price (wage) offered to workers.

5. The panic buying of flashlights will raise the price, signaling a profit opportunity of increasing the production of flashlights. The increased production (increased quantity supplied) will need more flashlight parts and equipment, generating additional demand for those inputs. Inputs prices will rise, and the quantity supplied of inputs will increase, and the need for flashlights will be satisfied.

6. Consumers in this case would be parents and children, while the supplier would be the government and its school boards. However, the school system is free and so no price signals are communicated from consumers to suppliers. The needs of consumers and the resources of school boards are not coordinated, which causes shortages and surpluses. The centralized system of communication doesn't work as efficiently and effectively as the market system.

7. The effect on wages is uncertain. Job placement agencies make markets function better, bringing together workers (suppliers) and employers (demanders). As a result, we would expect more workers hired, but there isn't enough information about shortages or surpluses to predict what would happen to wages.

8. It would reduce the available supply of these workers and put an upward pressure on the price (wage) offered to Canadian workers.

9. a) Given that the cost of producing or selling clothes is now very high, the supply of clothes to the market will decrease and cause an increase in clothing prices. Although clothing prices will fall slightly because of the comparatively smaller fall in demand for clothes, the overall effect will be to raise prices.

   b) If the cost of supplying clothes is no different than before the election, the slight fall in demand is the only impact on market prices. Therefore, prices of clothes will decrease in this situation.

10. Denying work permits to foreign strippers would increase the shortage of adult entertainment workers. This would put an upward pressure on the price (wage) offered to adult entertainment workers, which increases the cost and raises the price of supplying adult entertainment services.

CHAPTER 5
TRUE/FALSE

1. True
2. True
3. True
4. True
5. False. The unsatisfied demand from the controlled market spills over to the uncontrolled market, pushing rent levels even higher in the uncontrolled market.
6. False. Statement cannot be evaluated as true/false because there is a value judgment involved in defining what is a problem.
7. False. Statement cannot be evaluated as true/false because it is a value judgment.
8. True
9. False. Elasticity of demand for labour for teen employment is highest because businesses reduce teen employment the most in reaction to a government-imposed wage increases.
10. True
11. True
12. False. Longer waiting times are a trade-off Canadians make in order to have a more *equitable* health care system that does not discriminate on the basis of ability to pay.

13. True
14. False. Statement cannot be evaluated as true/false because it is a value judgment.
15. True

MULTIPLE CHOICE

1. **b)** price ceiling, set below the market-clearing price.
2. **a)** this would be a price floor.
3. **d)** search for cheaper input substitutes.
4. **a)** keep rental prices below the market-clearing price.
5. **d)** all of the above.
6. **d)** all of the above.
7. **c)** supply would increase.
8. **d)** all of the above.
9. **d)** all of the above.
10. **c)** a minimum wage below $7.00 would be irrelevant.
11. **d)** all of the above.
12. **c)** most willing and able to pay.
13. **c)** minimum wage increases can significantly improve the lives of low-income workers and their families, without the adverse effects that critics claim.
14. **b)** rent ceilings would reduce the number of homeless people.
15. **b)** the United States.

SHORT ANSWER

1. **a)** Many minimum wage workers are in low-income families. Raising the minimum wage can reduce wage inequality by moving low-wage workers up the wage distribution.
   b) Businesses would feel pressured to increase wage for the others too, which could result in no improvement in income inequality or equity.
   c) Some minimum wage workers do not live in poor families — think of the typical student living at home.

2. **a)** Minimum wages are aimed at assisting low-paid workers, which aren't all low-income workers, because minimum wages are received by workers with low earnings, independent of their family income situation.
   b) It supports helping workers with low earnings independent of their family economic situation, because many working students, for example, live with their parents and are not living in poverty.
   c) Yes. Poverty rates may actually increase if many workers lose their jobs and are unable to get jobs once the minimum wage is raised. This is an unintended consequence.

3. **a)** Unlike wage floors where the higher wage is paid for by businesses (and consumers), an income tax refund would have to be paid for by the government through taxes (and taxpayers).

b) The opportunity costs are the benefits from other social policy programs that could have been funded with the same cost, or the reduction in taxes if no money were spent on such social policies.

4. **a)** Pass cost increases to consumers through higher prices.

b) The business could adjust by substituting away from workers altogether (by using automated machinery or automated checkout), or by substituting away from low-skilled (and toward higher-skilled) labour, reducing output, shutting down, moving their business to a different location, or cutting back on non-wage benefits (for example, extra health and dental benefits).

5. **a)** Open ended. I would say OK because my time is scarce!

b) You should be more likely to reduce hours in exchange for an hourly wage increase during exam time. This suggests that your labour supply is more elastic (more responsive) to a change in the wage during exam time because for the same changes in wage you would be willing to reduce your hours more.

c) Yes. A worker with a higher wage is a happier worker, which could turn into increased productivity and less employee turnover (which would lower business costs).

6. If the price of rental housing in Canada was determined only by willingness and ability to pay, anyone who could not afford the market-clearing price would not be able to afford a place to live. Although the market functions very well for those above a certain income level, if you are poor, the housing market does little to address your needs. It has been argued that shelter is a human right that is necessary for survival and should be provided if individuals don't have the ability to pay.

a) Rent ceilings limit how high prices for rental housing can rise, which prevents landlords from increasing rents to market values. Rent ceilings are intended to (i) increase the amount of money poor households have available for other necessities and luxuries; and (ii) reduce the likelihood that poor households will become homeless.

b) Inefficiencies (uncoordinated demand and supply) such as shortages occur because (i) with rent prices less than their market value landlords don't have as much incentive to increase the quantity of apartments; and (ii) tenants who are willing and able to pay more do not because of the maximum price.

c) Since the quantity of housing supplied is less than it would be at the market-clearing rent, there will be fewer apartments available, and those who cannot find rental housing as a result of the rent ceiling — many of whom are those the policy was intended to help — will be worse off.

7. **a)** Poor individuals or households will likely be worse off because rent controls restrict the supply of affordable housing.

b) These are the individuals who truly benefit from rent controls because their rental prices won't increase with rent ceilings. However, the quality of these units will likely deteriorate because landlords have no incentive to improve or update them.

c) These individuals will likely suffer because tenants lack the incentive to move to new housing or home ownership and landlords lack the incentive to request repairs or build new apartment buildings — business will be slow!

8. **a)** Government housing is a supply-side initiative; housing vouchers is a demand-side initiative.

b) A housing voucher would increase the incentive of builders to supply new units because demand would increase after the policy from increasing ability to pay.

c) Open ended.

9. **a)** No. We would have to consider the opportunity costs because there may be alternative uses that represent even greater cost savings (for example, actions to reduce child poverty). Otherwise, the benefits would outweigh the costs (assuming the report is accurate) and it would be a smart choice.

b) i) The overall economic cost of child poverty in Canada would be one-tenth of the U.S. figure, which is about $50 billion a year.

ii) Lower. Since health care costs are already being paid in Canada, there would be no savings from reduced health care costs.

10. **a)** Those able to pay for health care services would receive them, but those unable to pay the market-clearing price — despite how willing or how much in need of care — would not receive medical care.

b) The number of visits to the doctor and hospital would be higher than the efficient number because patients face a price of zero in Canada, so they would be more likely to visit the doctor or hospital than they would if doing so had a financial cost.

c) With shortages, prices would rise, quantities demanded would decrease while quantities supplied would increase, and waiting lists would disappear.

d) The Canadian-style outcome is more equitable, but at the cost of being less efficient.

CHAPTER 6
TRUE/FALSE

1. True
2. False. Cost is value of best alternative use of his or her time in that year.
3. False. You could have invested the borrowed money in a bank and earned interest instead.

4. False. The reverse is true.
5. True
6. True
7. False. It is the best alterative use of the owner's time.
8. True
9. False. Economic profits = Accounting profits − Hidden opportunity costs = $20 000 − ($50 000 × 10%) = $15 000
10. False. It is a smart choice to remain in business if accounting profits are greater than normal profits (or hidden opportunity costs). Someone can be making accounting profits of $15 000, but if the person could be earning $20 000 in a different job then owning the business is not the smart choice.
11. True
12. False. Lower prices lead to lower revenues, which makes leaving the industry a smarter decision.
13. False. Accountants miss hidden opportunity costs, which can be very important for making smart decisions.
14. False. Businesses are at the breakeven point when revenues equal the total of all opportunity costs (including obvious costs and hidden opportunity costs).
15. False. Businesses making economic profits of zero will remain in the industry since they are earning normal profits — covering all opportunity costs of production.

MULTIPLE CHOICE

1. c) hidden opportunity costs.
2. d) economic profits.
3. c) $30 000.
4. d) all of the above.
5. b) risk-loving.
6. d) all of the above.
7. a) explicit costs.
8. c) subtract hidden opportunity costs when calculating profits.
9. d) all of the above.
10. b) $30 000.
11. d) $70 000.
12. d) all of above.
13. c) economic profits
14. d) all of the above.
15. b) rising prices.

SHORT ANSWER

1. a) Yes. Accountants and economists agree on the size of obvious costs.
   b) Yes. Accountants and economists agree on the size of accounting profits.
   c) Obvious costs = $10 000 + $3000 + $5000 + $2000 = $20 000

d) Accounting profits = Revenue − Obvious costs = $50 000 − $20 000 = $30 000

2. a) The opportunity cost of time equals the value of the alternative opportunity for that year, which is $25 000.
   b) This would not affect the accounting profits, but it would affect the economic profits, which are now = Revenue − (Obvious Opportunity Costs + Hidden Opportunity Costs) = $50 000 − ($20 000 + $25 000) = $5000.
   c) Yes. You should go ahead with this business opportunity because you are making positive economic profits of $5000.

3. a) The opportunity cost of money equals the value of the interest she could have earned in that year, which is $20 000 × 10% = $2000.
   b) This would not affect the accounting profits, but it would affect the economic profits, which are now = Revenues − (Obvious Opportunity Costs + Hidden Opportunity Costs) = $50 000 − ($25 000 + $2000) = $3000.
   c) Yes. You should choose this business opportunity because you are making positive economic profits of $3000.

4. a) Yes — You are right.
   b) While it is true that economic profits will be zero, it is not true that you should leave the industry. You can remain in an industry as long as you are covering all your opportunity costs (which you are, because you are breaking even).

5. a) The increase in demand will cause prices to rise.
   b) The rise in prices will increase revenues and economic profits, which will make staying in the industry a smarter decision.

6. a) Prices will fall since supply increases.
   b) Since her price would be higher than the market price offered elsewhere, fewer customers will demand her product/service, so quantity sold and revenues decrease.
   c) Revenues would be less than they were at the peak because the price received has fallen.

7. a) No. Lex should not offer his time for free, because he likely could be making money doing something else during that time (that is, there is an opportunity cost of time to helping Angelina).
   b) Paying the costs of labour will increase her obvious costs by $40 000 and decrease accounting profits by $40 000.
   c) Adding these two workers may increase revenues if they are able to generate new sales. Adding these workers may also free up some of Angelina's time and allow her to work part time, which would reduce her opportunity cost of time. By pursing this business opportunity she would be giving up only *some* of the money she could have earned at the marketing company.

8. **a)** Yes. Interest payments will become an out-of-pocket expense.
   b) No. Whether the loan is from the bank or from her parents, the cost of what else she could have done with it (for example, put it in the bank) is the same.
9. **a)** A rise in the minimum wage would increase obvious costs and decrease economic profits.
   b) The removal of rent ceilings will increase rent costs, which will increase obvious costs and decrease economic profits.
   c) No. With rent costs increasing by $1200, adding the minimum wage worker will result in negative economic profits = +$5000 − $1200 − $4000 = −$200. Therefore, staying in business would not be a smart choice.
10. **a)** This reduces obvious opportunity costs, thus increasing economic profits.
   b) This causes prices to fall, thus reducing revenues and economic profits.
   c) This causes prices to rise, thus increasing revenue and economic profits.

CHAPTER 7
TRUE/FALSE

1. False. Monopolist's market power is limited by what buyers are willing and able to pay.
2. True
3. True
4. False. A seller may earn more revenues by cutting prices instead of raising them if demand is elastic
5. True
6. True
7. False. This would increase their economies of scale because the acquisition would result in a higher amount of burger production, which would reduce average costs per burger.
8. True
9. False. There are differentiated substitutes.
10. True
11. False. Consumers are more sensitive to price changes in a monopolistic competition because there are more businesses selling similar substitutes
12. False. The gaming industry is an oligopoly because only a few companies — Nintendo, Microsoft, and Sony — control the market.
13. True
14. False. Competition is about figuring out new ways to *beat* your rivals, not just match them.
15. True

MULTIPLE CHOICE

1. **d)** is all of the above.
2. **b)** lower sales.
3. **c)** reduce the number of substitutes available.
4. **d)** all of the above.
5. **c)** preventing other businesses from competing.
6. **c)** an iPhone.
7. **c)** competitopoly.
8. **d)** extreme competition.
9. **d)** extreme competition.
10. **d)** extreme competition.
11. **d)** extreme competition.
12. **a)** monopoly.
13. **d)** all of the above.
14. **b)** makes demand more inelastic.
15. **c)** creative destruction.

SHORT ANSWER

1. If we shift from a narrow definition of the market for iPhones to a broader definition of the market for handheld combined cell/music/web devices, then Apple is no longer the single seller, and buyers have a wider variety of choices. There are always substitutes, and the more broadly we define a market, the more substitutes there are — and the more competitors.
2. **a)** To create perceived differences
   b) Since beer companies could no longer compete on the basis of creating perceived differences, they would be forced to compete on the basis of price or cost or taste.
   c) Economic barriers to entry — economies of scale
3. **a)** Open ended
   b) Brand loyalty
   c) Open ended
4. Without patents/copyrights, other businesses would be able to copy inventions or great ideas for free and sell them for substantial profits — without ever having to invest the time, money, or effort required to come up with an invention. Therefore, patents/copyrights are essential for ensuring that businesses have the incentive to invest in the research and innovation required to come up with an invention.
5. The entrance of a new competitor would reduce the pricing power of the existing companies.
6. Workers can differentiate themselves from the competition (other workers) in a number of ways, including taking extra years of education; taking fields of study that are high in demand and not widely attended; obtaining work experience the competition lacks.
7. **a)** Location, location, location. They are at every corner.

b) Starbucks has less pricing power in Canada because Tim Hortons, Second Cup, and other national brands have been able to prevent Starbucks from setting up coffee shops at every corner.

c) Elasticity of demand is probably higher in Canada — that is, Canadian consumers are more responsive to a change in price than American consumers — because Canadian streets already have coffee businesses at or near most busy intersections.

d) Starbucks could acquire a Canadian company, such as Tim Hortons or Second Cup, and set up a Starbucks at that location.

8. a) Reduces power to price
  b) Increases power to price
  c) Increases power to price

9. He should hand them out to individuals who wouldn't have otherwise bought an iPod, not to those already planning to buy an iPod. Therefore, he should hand them out to people who say, "I want to buy an electronic device today" — because they may have purchased a different item if they didn't have the coupon — that is, they are responsive to a change in price.

10. Open ended. Destruction improved living standards and product choices for customers.

CHAPTER 8
TRUE/FALSE

1. False. Profits increase only if marginal revenue is greater than marginal cost.
2. False. Price equals marginal revenue for businesses in extreme competition, but marginal revenue is less than price for all price makers, including oligopolies.
3. True
4. False. To sell more, monopolists must lower the price on *all* units because of the one-price rule.
5. False. Fixed costs don't affect a smart decision, only marginal costs do.
6. True
7. True
8. False. Although the marginal cost of adding passengers is above zero — since additional snacks are served and fuel consumption increases — when each additional ticket is sold, marginal cost is constant as long as the airplane is below 100-percent capacity.
9. False. It means total costs always increase by the same amount when quantity increases.
10. True
11. False. A change in fixed costs does not change smart decisions about price or quantity.
12. False. Prices should be chosen to sell all quantities for which marginal revenue is greater than marginal cost. If a business has increasing marginal costs, marginal

costs change depending on the quantity of output chosen.
13. True
14. False. Products are more likely than services to be resold. Things that can easily be resold tend to have a single price.
15. False. Discounts, which lower prices, should be given to the elastic-demand group, which is sensitive to prices.

MULTIPLE CHOICE

1. **a)** sales revenues from staying open later.
2. **b)** coffee.
3. **d)** all of the above.
4. **b)** total revenue between one and two textbooks.
5. **b)** marginal revenue equals price for businesses in extreme competition.
6. **d)** all of the above.
7. **d)** do all of the above.
8. **a)** workers are sending text messages and checking Facebook instead of working.
9. **d)** marginal revenue falls by more than price.
10. **a)** 1.
11. **c)** 3.
12. **b)** 2.
13. **d)** do all of the above.
14. **c)** lower prices for customers with elastic demand.
15. **c)** travelling for business.

SHORT ANSWER

1. **a)** Determine whether the additional sales revenues from advertising exceed the amount you have to pay in labour costs and any associated advertising fees.
   b) Determine whether the additional sales revenues exceed the amount you have to pay in labour costs.
   c) Determine whether the additional sales revenues exceed the additional amount you have to pay in labour costs, electricity, and so on in order to stay open during that period.

2. Although the additional person adds to the meal cost, this should be weighed against monetary benefits like the financial gift he/she will bring, plus the non-monetary additional benefits such as the added emotional or social value they provide.

3. If his price is $3, total revenue is $150 (50 × $3). If price is $2, total revenue is $160 (80 × $2). Therefore, the marginal revenue is $10 ($160 − $150).

4. In the market structure of extreme competition, businesses can't raise their price because consumers will react by buying from one of the thousands of other businesses selling identical products at the lower (market) price. There is no incentive to lower prices since they can sell as much as they can produce at the market price.

5. **a)** Producing three units is the highest output for which marginal revenues exceed marginal costs.

   b) $14 is the highest possible price that allows her to sell her profit-maximizing quantity.

   c) Paola should keep increasing output as long as it leads to *any* increase in total profits. Her goal is maximum *total* profits, not the quantity with the largest additional profits.

   d) If Paola increases quantity from 3 units to 4 units it costs her an additional $8. Since the additional costs are higher than the additional revenues, it is not a smart, profit-maximizing choice.

6. If marginal costs are rising, the marginal cost of producing 3 units would be higher than it currently is ($8). If the marginal cost of producing 3 units becomes *higher than $10,* producing 3 units will no longer be profit-maximizing since marginal costs would exceed marginal revenues ($10) when 3 units are produced. Therefore, the profit-maximizing quantity of piercings would likely decrease if Paola had increasing marginal costs.

7. We do not need information about fixed costs or total profits to determine profit-maximizing choices of output and price, because fixed costs are irrelevant for smart decision making.

8. **a)** An additional hour of studying becomes increasingly burdensome as the number of hours increases. For example, studying an extra hour after you've studied for only one hour isn't a huge deal. However, after studying for four hours, studying for that extra hour requires much more concentration and is taking away from increasingly valuable alternative uses of your time.

   b) The numbers in the columns for Marginal Cost and Impact on Studying depend on the figures you chose.

Hours of Study	Marginal Revenue from Studying	Marginal Cost of Studying	Impact on Studying on Total Profits
1	5% × $6 = $30	$10	+ $20
2	4% × $6 = $24		
3	3% × $6 = $18		
4	2% × $6 = $12		
5	1% × $6 = $6		

   c) Answer depends on the figures chosen for column three.

   d) Answer depends on the answer chosen for part c. The answer is 5 minus your answer in part c.

9. **a)** Since movie tickets cannot easily be resold, Tifo can discriminate by giving the age group with the most elastic demand (for example, teenage students) a discount. This can be enforced by requiring valid student ID.

   b) Since students are more likely than non-students to be available to watch movies during the daytime (in the summer), Infamous Players could offer reduced movie ticket prices for movies playing in the afternoon (in the summer).

10. **a)** Business travellers are willing to pay full price. They are less sensitive to changes in price because: 1) their company usually pays; 2) their tickets are booked at the last minute; and 3) they wish to take a return flight as soon as possible.

   b) Frequent-flyer programs are a form of price discrimination because they divide customers into elastic and inelastic consumer groups, with lower prices (quantity discounts) being offered to the most loyal customers.

CHAPTER 9
TRUE/FALSE

1. True
2. False. Crown corporations also exist in industries deemed to be publicly important for political or social reasons (for example alcohol control, lotteries).
3. False. The payoffs do depend on the other prisoner's choice.
4. True
5. False. Each player is better off confessing only if they cannot trust the other player to deny the murder.
6. False. OPEC is not an illegal agreement because there is no international law on cartels that cross national borders.)
7. True
8. False. They will prevent a merger if the costs of decreased competition exceed the benefits of increased efficiencies.
9. False. Penalties for *criminal* offences include prison sentences. Penalties for civil offences are limited to fines and legal prohibitions.
10. False. It means consumers, not government, are responsible for monitoring quality ("let the buyer beware").

11. True
12. False. While for many products/services the costs exceed the benefits of regulation, for products like nuclear power and medicine the benefits exceed the costs.
13. True
14. False. This supports the capture view, because the regulated industries were operating like a cartel, restricting output and raising prices.
15. False. Higher profits in regulated industries would support the capture view of government regulation.

MULTIPLE CHOICE

1. **a)** diamonds.
2. **c)** high fixed cost and low marginal cost.
3. **b)** taxi service.
4. **b)** how to gain the low-cost efficiencies of economies of scale, but avoid the inefficiencies of monopoly's restricted output and rise in price.
5. **c)** *A Beautiful Mind.*
6. **b)** both prisoners deny.
7. **c)** the cycle of trust and non-trust among gasoline station owners.
8. **d)** all of the above are true.
9. **c)** prevent monopoly practices.
10. **d)** all of the above.
11. **c)** Petro-Canada.
12. **c)** government-appointed agencies.
13. **b)** previous regulations in the airline industry led airlines to provide more luxuries than consumers would choose to pay for.
14. **d)** all of the above.
15. **d)** all of the above.

SHORT ANSWER

1. **a)** Size matters because the efficient number of businesses in an industry depends on whether there are economies of scale.
   b) It is efficient to have one large business supplying the entire market when it results in lower average costs for businesses and lower prices for consumers.
2. **a)** By implicitly agreeing to keep prices high they can get more from consumers without fearing that they will lose their consumers to a nearby gas station.
   b) Cooperation or collusion keeps prices high.
   c) If owners don't trust one another, they have an incentive to cheat on the cartel agreement.
   d) Gas stations charge high prices when cooperating or colluding with competitors through cartels but should cheat on the cartel if they cannot trust competitors or be trusted. (Answers vary; there is no single right answer).
3. **a)** It's in both characters best interest to co-operate and deny the murder because they trust each other.
   b) It's in both characters' best interests to cheat and confess to the murder because they don't trust each other.

   c) It's in both characters' best interests to cheat and confess to the murder because they cannot trust the other character.
4. **a)**

		Jill	
		Cheat	Faithful
	Cheat	(2, 2)	(4, 1)
Jack			
	Faithful	(1, 4)	(3, 3)

   b) If Jill suspects that Jack will cheat, then Jill should cheat because cheating would give her 2 units of happiness and being faithful would give her only 1 unit.
   c) If Jill suspects that Jack will be faithful, then Jill should cheat because cheating would give her 4 units of happiness and being faithful would give her only 3 units.
   d) The Nash equilibrium occurs where Jill and Jack both cheat.
   e) If businesses cannot trust one another, then both will end up cheating on the collusive agreement, which gives lower profits (or happiness) than the outcome where both trust one another and cooperate.
5. **a)** More competitors might mean more stores and therefore easier access.
   b) The profit motive is likely to encourage businesses to: employ low-skilled and low-paid staff; serve minors and intoxicated customers; and stay open late at night.
6. This evidence supports the public-interest view because government actions (regulating tuition fees) resulted in market outcomes favourable to the public (lower price of education).
7. **a)** Suppliers would not need to invest in cost-saving innovations because consumers would be required to pay higher prices when costs increase.
   b) If prices were allowed to rise, then firms would make higher profits, and higher profits would attract new firms and make the industry more competitive.
8. **a)** Fixed costs in the cable TV industry are high, so if there were competition in the industry every new entrant would have to make a complete network, resulting in high average total costs and therefore higher prices for consumers. To achieve lowest average total cost, the technology of production allows only a single seller.
   b) The amount of advertising would decrease since television viewers tend to dislike commercials.
9. **a)** If the market for electricity is not a natural monopoly, then privatizing the generation of electricity will result in lower prices as competitors try to attract customers through lower prices.
   b) The capture view would support this position, all else being equal. The capture view of government

regulation supports the position that prices and profits under regulation were higher than they should be, so deregulation would result in lower prices. The public-interest view would not support this position because it believes government regulation is efficient.

    c) If prices were below marginal opportunity costs, producers would not produce electricity because additional costs exceed additional benefits.

10. a) Canadians who live in rural communities would likely pay higher prices to cover higher delivery costs.

    b) This would support the public-interest view of government regulation, since prices were lower under public ownership, possibly due to economies of scale.

CHAPTER 10
TRUE/FALSE

1. True
2. True
3. False. Smokers impose a negative externality on non-smokers.
4. False. Markets overproduce products/services that have negative externalities and underproduce products/services that have positive externalities.
5. False. Achieving zero pollution would mean eliminating all cars and airplanes, outlawing all power except solar and hydroelectric power, shutting down most factories, and so on. Therefore, some level of pollution is desirable.
6. False. It becomes increasingly difficult and costly to reduce pollution levels.
7. True
8. False. Marginal social cost equals marginal private cost only if there are no negative externalities; if there are no positive externalities this means marginal social benefit equal marginal private benefit.
9. False. With carbon taxes the governments sets price, and with cap-and-trade systems the government sets quantity.
10. False. Smart taxes lead individuals and businesses to choose the outcomes that are best for society as a whole, where marginal *social* benefit equals marginal *social* cost).
11. True
12. True
13. True
14. False. Colleges are not directly provided by the government (but they are subsidized by the government).
15. True

MULTIPLE CHOICE

1. c) Jeremiah listens to hip-hop music in his room with his headphones on and his door closed while no one is home.
2. c) there are too many people quitting smoking.
3. d) all of the above.
4. c) *is less than* marginal social cost, *and* marginal private benefit *equals* marginal social benefit.
5. d) *equals* marginal social cost, *and* marginal private benefit *is less than* marginal social benefit.
6. b) *is less than* marginal social cost, *and* marginal private benefit *is less than* marginal social benefit.
7. b) internalize the externality.
8. d) all of the above.
9. a) lower-income consumers are affected more than higher-income consumers.
10. b) positive externalities.
11. d) all of the above.
12. c) clothes.
13. d) marginal external benefit.
14. d) all of the above.
15. b) post-secondary education.

SHORT ANSWER

1. a) The tax raises the price of carbon.
    b) No.
    c) Consumers can reduce gasoline consumption, carpool, sell their cars, re-insulate their homes, buy new types of furnaces, and so on.
    d) Inelastic. He claims people aren't able to adjust to the higher prices.
    e) Provides individuals with time to adjust.
2. a) Home-heating fuel, coal-fired electricity.
    b) Individuals in colder climates, because they are more reliant on fossil fuels for home heating, and individuals from rural areas who have fewer choices for "going green."
    c) Carbon taxes have a bigger hit on the income of the poorest families. The money raised by the tax would be used to offset other taxes in ways that could compensate lower-income households for higher prices of home-heating fuel, coal-fired electricity, and other carbon sources.
3. The opportunity cost of reducing carbon emissions increases as the targeted emissions reduction increases because it becomes increasingly difficult to adjust to the higher carbon prices through further carbon emissions reductions.
4. a) The trading market would set a price for carbon emissions based on the supply and demand of permits.
    b) Thousands of companies would be involved in the buying and trading of permits, and "haggling" over price.

c) With a cap-and-trade system, the government has direct control over quantity, and price adjusts. With a carbon tax, the government has direct control over price, and quantity adjusts.

d) The cap-and-trade model guarantees the chosen emissions reduction goals will be met because the government would set an overall limit on the amount of carbon dioxide that can be pumped into the atmosphere.

5. a) Since demand is inelastic, a very large tax (increase in price) is required to reduce emissions.

b) Price-responsiveness grows over longer periods, as households have opportunities to buy more fuel-efficient vehicles and appliances.

6. a) A subsidy, since it reduces the relative price of these products.

b) As long as the amount of the subsidy is set equal to the marginal external benefit, society will *voluntarily* choose where marginal social benefit equals marginal social cost.

c) Since there is a positive externality associated with making greener choices, too few people will be purchasing Bullfrog Power. Therefore, the government could subsidize the price of energy coming from wind power or small hydro generating stations to promote it.

7. a) No. National governments have inadequate incentives to take account of global impacts; they would not be internalizing the externality they impose on other countries.

b) It would force countries to internalize the full externality.

c) Carbon emitters would move their combustion of carbon from countries that tax carbon to those that do not or that have lower rates of taxation.

8. a) The demand for beer is inelastic, according to this German citizen.

b) To encourage production of environmentally friendly biofuels, which are underproduced due to the positive externality they create.

c) The elimination of subsidies on other crops would make them less profitable, leading to an increase in the supply of barley and a reduction of its price.

9. a) Driving results in a negative externality because one's decision to drive adds to pollution and to delays to other motorists from traffic congestion.

b) It reduces the incentive to drive because it raises the cost of driving.

c) The subsidy for public transit would increase the relative cost of driving, and encourage less driving and more transit.

d) Rush hours. Revenues increase more when consumers don't respond to higher prices by reducing their quantity demanded. Demand is less responsive (or more inelastic) during rush hour, so drivers would be less sensitive to higher prices.

10. Yes. Taxes on petroleum products, for example, cause a decrease in supply and increase in price, which will be passed on to oil wholesalers and eventually to retail customers.

CHAPTER 11
TRUE/FALSE

1. True
2. True
3. False. Income is a flow.
4. False. Businesses' demand for labour is derived from the output market — that is, businesses' interest in profits from selling output.
5. True
6. True
7. False. $1 today is more valuable because if you had the dollar invested today you could be earning interest on it (even if you didn't want to spend it).
8. False. If interest rates increase, you have to further discount future revenues to adjust for more forgone interest.
9. False. When interest rates decrease, present value increases. Therefore, an investment that was smart before the decrease would become even more profitable.
10. True
11. False. What price sports team owners can get for output (ticket prices) determines what owners are willing to pay for inputs (player salaries).
12. False. Wealth is more unequally distributed.
13. False. Regressive taxes take more from the poor.
14. True
15. True

MULTIPLE CHOICE

1. c) income is what you earn, wealth is what you own.
2. a) wealth is income received from supplying labour.
3. d) all of the above.
4. c) 4.
5. d) income paid to any input in relatively inelastic supply.
6. c) present value of the future stream of revenues is greater than the price of the investment.
7. d) all of the above.
8. a) demand.
9. d) all of the above.
10. a) the players.
11. d) themselves.
12. a) the poorest 20 percent of families earn 2 percent of total income.
13. b) the bottom 40 percent of families own 20 percent of the total wealth.
14. a) progressive.
15. b) more than 50 percent of families in poverty are headed by a single, female parent.

SHORT ANSWER

1. **a)** In output markets, businesses sell their products/services to households. In input markets, businesses buy from households the inputs they need to produce products/services.
    b) Gasoline station owners sell gasoline to households in exchange for money in the output market, and gasoline station owners pay workers in exchange for work in the input market.

2. **a)** As more cooks are hired the kitchen gets more crowded, and fewer additional meals can be prepared because there is a fixed amount of cooking space and materials.
    b) He should hire 4 chefs since the marginal revenue product is greater than the wage rate for the first 4 chefs but not for the fifth.
    c) He should hire 5 chefs since the marginal revenue product is greater than the wage rate for all 5 chefs.

3. **a)** The present value is approximately $2727 ($3000/1.1), which is less than the cost of $2800. It is not a smart investment because Wahid could have invested the $2800 in the bank and earned more than $3000 in interest ($2800 × 1.1 = $3080).
    b) The present value is approximately $727 ($800/1.1), which is greater than the cost of $700. It is a smart investment because Wahid could not have earned more than $800 by investing the money in the bank at that interest rate ($700 × 1.1 = $770).

4. **a)** Demanders = ticket purchasers. Suppliers = owners of the hockey teams.
    b) Demanders = owners of the hockey teams. Suppliers = players on the hockey teams.
    c) Superstars, like landlords, are like monopolists with barriers to entry. Their talent goes to the highest bidders and their salaries are largely demand-determined.
    d) For most products and services, high input prices cause high output prices, so a salary cap that limits input prices was thought to lead to lower ticket prices.

5. Human capital is the increased earning potential individuals acquire through work experience, on-the-job training, and education. Productivity and income increase with experience, training, and education.

6. Higher income taxes on the rich allow the government to redistribute income and reduce inequalities. However, if taxes cause some individuals to supply less to the market because the rewards aren't as high, then workers will earn less and output markets will produce fewer products/services..

7. Increasing the income of low-income working families reduces income inequality while at the same time increasing work incentives and output.

8. Yes, they have progressive tax systems, which take more from the rich than from the poor, and they give to the poor through transfer payments. Examples of transfer payments include the Canada Child Tax Benefit, social security programs for seniors (Old Age Security), and Employment Insurance (for the unemployed).

9. A left-leaning politician might favour progressive taxes and large social transfers because he believes equity is more important than efficiency.

10. **a)** Opportunity Cost of the Investment = Tuition Cost + Opportunity Cost of Time = $10 000 per year × 4 years + $0 = $40 000
    b) Here is the worked-out answer: Opportunity Cost of Investment = Tuition Cost + Present Value of Earnings Forgone. The tuition cost, as calculated in part a, is $40 000. The present value of earnings forgone requires that we apply the present value formula:

$$\text{Present Value} = \frac{\text{Amount of Money Available in } n \text{ Years}}{(1 + \text{Interest Rate})^n}$$

In this example, you would receive an amount of money ($20 000) in 1 year ($n = 1$), and an amount of money in 2 years ($n = 2$), and an amount of money in 3 years ($n = 3$), and an amount of money in 4 years ($n = 4$). Therefore, you need 4 calculations and then add them to calculate the present value of the future stream of earnings from working instead of going to university:

$20 000 received 1 year from today is worth $20 000 / $(1 + 0.05)^1$ today.

$20 000 received 2 years from today is worth $20 000 / $(1 + 0.05)^2$ today.

$20 000 received 3 years from today is worth $20 000 / $(1 + 0.05)^3$ today.

$20 000 received 4 years from today is worth $20 000 / $(1 + 0.05)^4$ today.

If you add up each of these present values you get $19 047.62 + $18 140.59 + $17 276.75 + $16 454.05 = $70 919.01. In present value terms, $20 000 in earnings over each of the next 4 years is worth, in total, roughly $71 000 today. Therefore, the opportunity cost of the investment, which is the tuition cost in part a plus the present value of earnings forgone, is $40 000 + $71 000 = $111 000.

c) i) Present value = $45 000 / $(1 + 0.05)^4$ = $37 021.61

   ii) No. The present value is less than the tuition cost, even if we ignore the opportunity cost of time.

d) i) *Step 1*: Since the interest rate during the 20 years of working is 0, finding the value, at the end of university, of $13 000 per year over 20 years is relatively easy because the denominator in the present value formula is equal to 1 when the interest rate is 0 (try it!). Therefore, the present value, at the end of university, of the future stream of additional income is the sum of $13 000 + $13 000 + $13 000 ... + $13 000. In other words, the sum is equal to $13 000 × 20 years = $260 000. However, we need step 2 because this stream of additional income occurs only *after* the 4 years of university.

Step 2: To determine whether enrolling in a university bachelor degree is a smart decision today, we need to know what the value of the future stream of additional income is *today*. Since the value of the income stream is $260 000 4 years from now, we can bring it to the present by discounting $260 000 at an interest rate of 5 percent (or 0.05).

Therefore, the present value = $260 000 / $(1 + 0.05)^4$ = $213 902.64.

ii) *Step 1:* Since the interest rate during the 20 years of working is 5 percent, summing up the value is complicated because the value in the denominator of the formula is different each year.

$13 000 received 1 year from the end of university is worth $13 000 / $(1 + 0.05)^1$ at the end of university.

$13 000 received 2 years from the end of university is worth $13 000 / $(1 + 0.05)^2$ at the end of university.

$13 000 received 3 years from the end of university is worth $13 000 / $(1 + 0.05)^3$ at the end of university.

... (and so on) ...

$13 000 received 20 years from the end of university is worth $13 000 / $(1 + 0.05)^{20}$ at the end of university.

If you sum up the values when *n* is equal to 1 through 20, you get $162 008.73. This is the value of the additional income at the end of university (which is four years from today).

Step 2: To determine whether enrolling in a university bachelor degree is a smart decision today, we need to know what the value of the future stream of additional income is *today*. Since the value of the income stream is $162 008.73 4 years from now, we can bring it to the present by discounting $162 008.73 at an interest rate of 5 percent.

Therefore, the present value = $162 008.73 / $(1 + 0.05)^4$ = $133 284.99

e) In the scenario where the interest rate is 5 percent during the 4 years of university and 0 percent during the 20 years of working, the present value ($213 902.64) exceeds the true opportunity cost ($111 000) and is therefore a smart investment.

In the scenario where the interest rate is 5 percent during the 4 years of university and 5 percent during the 20 years of working, the present value ($133 284.99) is greater than the true opportunity cost ($111 000) and is therefore still a smart investment.

Index

Credits